S0-ELZ-731

Penguin modern
psychology Readings

Cross-cultural
studies
edited by D. R. Price-Williams

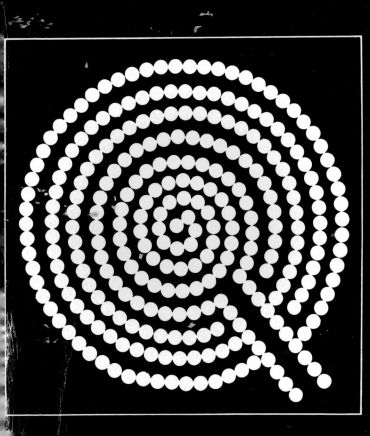

Penguin Modern Psychology

Cross-Cultural Studies

Penguin Modern Psychology Readings

General Editor
B. M. Foss

Advisory Board
P. C. Dodwell
Marie Jahoda
S. G. Lee
W. M. O'Neil
R. L. Reid
Roger Russell
P. E. Vernon
George Westby

Cross-Cultural Studies

Studies

Selected Readings

Edited by D. R. Price-Williams

Penguin Books

Penguin Books Ltd, Harmondsworth,
Middlesex, England
Penguin Books Inc., 7110 Ambassador Road,
Baltimore, Maryland 21207, U.S.A.
Penguin Books Australia Ltd, Ringwood,
Victoria, Australia

First published by Penguin Books Ltd. 1969
First published by Penguin Books Inc 1970
This selection copyright © D. R. Price-Williams, 1969
Introduction and notes copyright © D. R. Price-Williams, 1969

Printed in the United States of America by
Kingsport Press, Inc.
Set in Monotype Times

Contents

Contents

Editor's Acknowledgements

The editor is indebted to Miss Nancye Fleming and Miss Bess Repana for secretarial assistance. Funding was assisted by the Dean of Humanities, Rice University, and by the Advanced Research Projects Agency under A R P A Order No. 738, monitored by the Office of Naval Research, Group Psychology Branch, under contract Number N00014–67–A–0145–0001, NR 177–909.

Introduction

Interest in and speculation upon peoples other than the group one happens to have been born in, has been practised from the days of the historian Hecateus of Miletos, who lived four or five centuries before Christ, up to the philosopher Voltaire in the eighteenth century. It was not until the nineteenth century, however, that systematic studies of national character appeared and in that century field studies of customs and beliefs by anthropologists also began. At the turn of the twentieth century a team from Cambridge University started the first experimental psychology project among what would now be called under-developed peoples. Curiously perhaps, this early lead was not followed up until some years after the Second World War when experimental psychologists became interested in groups quite outside the urbanized and literate samples of Europe and North America. In the meantime interest in the psychology of under-developed peoples was kept up by psychologically minded anthropologists and psychologists working at the level of personality and child behaviour. In recent years, due partly to the growth of academic and research institutions in such regions of the world as Africa and Latin America, and partly to an interest in international concerns among psychologists themselves, there has been a prolific increase in studies which for want of a better term have been labelled 'cross-cultural'.

The progress of cross-cultural studies has been right across the gamut of psychology, from relatively 'molecular' aspects of behaviour such as those involved in perceptual processes for example, to relatively 'molar' concepts of personality or attitudes. It has embraced the theoretical concerns of experimental psychologists interested in the basic processes of perception, learning and thinking, along with child psychologists, clinical psychologists and of course social psychologists. It has also meant at all levels a meeting point with the discipline of anthropology. Psychologists interested in probing the intelligence and aptitudes of either completely illiterate people or partially educated people,

11

have been pre-occupied with the relevance of tests with such populations; the advice of anthropologists has been sought in order to make such tests meaningful. At the other end of the scale certain hypotheses have been taken from theories of cultural evolution and theories concerning the integration of cultures, which belong to the domain of anthropology, but which have obvious relevance to the discipline of psychology.

The relationship with anthropology raises the question of definition of the field. Recently F. L. K. Hsu (*Psychological Anthropology*, Dorsey Press, 1961) has coined the term 'psychological anthropology' to replace the older term of 'culture and personality'. A clear division could be made between cultural studies which are aimed at finding out information concerning theories in experimental psychology, and those studies which are concerned with the relationship of the individual to his culture. The first group raises clearly *psychological* questions (of minimal interest to the anthropologist); the second group raises clearly *anthropological* questions (which have minimal interest for the psychologist). While this is a valid distinction for the two ends of a fairly long pole, it does not do at all for points in the middle region. Some of the contributions in this volume fall squarely within this middle region, and while some may have stemmed from the interest of psychology and others from the interest of anthropology, the ensuing data are of interest and importance for the student of human nature whatever his discipline.

The relevant point concerns the nature of the variable being tested. It is the nature of the cultural context, whether of the subjects themselves or the circumstances in which they live, that gives cross-cultural psychology its place in the sun. Exploration of such contexts has revealed a wide assortment, which include: the nature of the physical environment (whether, for example, people live in open steppes or are immersed in rain forests); type of living quarters (whether they live in round huts or what Campbell has called the 'carpentered environment' of modern urban life); methods of production, degrees of literacy, exposure to the world of print and pictorial productions, family types, child-training techniques, varieties of organization in social, economic and religious spheres. The list could be expanded, but it is clear that whatever the field is called, a vast array of factors that influence psychological processes, is being explored.

Focus on the factors or variables tends to undermine also the divisions of cross-cultural, intra-cultural and cross-national which are sometimes made. 'Cross-cultural' refers to studies which employ two or more cultures or societies, while 'intra-cultural' refers to investigations made in the one culture. It is clear, though, that both types are put together when searching for factors that pertain to culture, and the distinction of *cross*-cultural research is, as Frijda and Jahoda have pointed out in Reading 2, merely an extension of intra-cultural group comparison. Similarly the term 'cross-national' as referring to studies within Western nations, is also somewhat artificial, and here again Frijda and Jahoda deal with this in their article.

Various types of methodologies, however, can be noted in the full range of cross-cultural studies. We have laboratory-type researches, whose only difference from traditional laboratory experimentation lies in the fact that it is conducted in a different cultural context. We have observational studies; we use a variety of paper-and-pencil kind of tests. Often some cross-cultural studies are made without the investigator stepping out of his country, indeed out of his library. Some of the articles printed here adopt as their method the analysis of documents of many cultures, the basic data of which have been collected previously by other people. Sometimes, also, collaborators in many countries combine to attack the same problem. In short, cross-cultural psychology includes a variety of methods. The problems and the difficulties of conducting research outside the traditional confines of one's own laboratory and one's own culture has attracted much attention, and an important part of the present book of readings is the one on methodology, but it will be seen that many other readings often refer to and are sensitive about points of method. A note needs to be added about the policy of choice of selections for these readings. Certain branches of study have had to be omitted, mainly because of the fact that they constitute a separate field in their own right and have been given copious treatment in the literature. The first branch is 'personality and culture' of which we have already spoken. There are many books – which for convenience are listed in the Further Readings chapter at the end of this book – on this subject and much of the material appears in books on personality. We have contained in this book some material which might be thought to have been included under the traditional personality and culture rubric – Part Eight dealing with Freudian hypotheses, for example – but the direct data on personality traits in relation to the culture analysed by the Rorschach Technique and other projective techniques have been omitted.

A second branch is what has been called 'trans-cultural psychiatry'. Although this contains much of direct psychological interest, again it constitutes a major field, and moreover can be interpreted as being further away from the main concerns of cross-cultural psychology than the discipline of personality and culture.

A third branch is 'ethno-linguistics'. The study of the relationship between language and psychology should really underpin all investigations in those areas in which the investigator is working with or through a language other than his own. But here again systematic attention has been given to this theme and, moreover, it leads into issues which concern linguistics proper (in the same way as the study of personality and culture leads into issues which concern anthropology proper), and thus have less psychological concern.

The readings with which we are left nevertheless have still had to be taken from a wide set of possibilities. The policy has been twofold. First, those articles have been taken which are directly relevant to psychological theory or questions – as distinct from anthropological or sociological theory or questions. Second, we have attempted to group the material in a sequence, wherein a germinal finding or idea has been directly followed up by other research so that a body of knowledge is represented. This results in some inevitable repetition, but the reader is given a measure of continuity and the sense in which cross-cultural research merges into the corporate body of basic psychological research. This has not always been possible to follow in this volume, but the more experimental type of investigations on the processes of perception and cognition certainly show this plan.

A last word needs to be said. The mere fact that a research is done in Mexico, Zambia, Thailand or wherever, does not of itself make the investigation amenable to cross-cultural analysis.

With the advent of psychology departments in new developing countries it is to be expected that the laboratory output from these countries will be huge. Unless, though, a cultural variable is clearly put to the test in researches, the resulting experiment or observation does not qualify for cross-cultural (or intra-cultural) inclusion. In the selections which follow it will be seen that the distinguishing feature is a salient cultural factor which is thought to influence some psychological mechanism.

Part One Theory and Method

As was pointed out in the Introduction, cross-cultural psychology as a possible field is in need of definition. Part One deals explicitly with this very issue. It should be remembered that the cross-cultural method stems from the discipline of anthropology. The nineteenth-century anthropologist, Tylor, applied the comparative approach to the study of kinship and marriage systems. The modern renewal of interest in this sphere, as Whiting (1954) has pointed out, lies in testing hypotheses which have been derived from theories of cultural evolution, theories of the integration of culture and theories of individual and social psychology. Whiting and his school in particular have applied the cross-cultural comparative approach to the investigation of human behaviour commonly recognized as customs. Such subject areas as weaning, toilet training, aggression and the rules pertaining to interpersonal relationships, come under this rubric. In Reading 1, Strodtbeck moves towards the psychological, as distinct from sociological or anthropological, issues. He works out the logic and strategies operating in the various methodologies used. While Strodtbeck is nevertheless still partly concerned with anthropological matters (the paper was primarily published in an anthropological journal), the Frijda and Jahoda paper (Reading 2) is more exclusively related to direct psychological problems.

In particular they deal with such thorny methodological problems as adequate sampling, equivalence of tasks and tests across cultures and the comparability of descriptive categories.

Taken as a unit, these two Readings underpin all of the empirical investigations which are reported in this volume. Indeed, most of the selections in this volume are already noted in their references.

It can be safely anticipated that the extent of cross-cultural studies is likely to increase. In order to ensure that some discipline and methodological care is introduced into what is already a somewhat diffuse domain, the various points raised in these two papers should be thoughtfully entertained.

Reference

WHITING, J. W. M. (1954), 'The cross-cultural method', in G. Lindzey (ed.) *Handbook of Social Psychology*, vol. 1, Addison-Wesley, pp. 523–31. Reprinted (1968) as 'Methods and problems in cross-cultural research', in G. Lindzey and E. Aronson (eds.), *Handbook of Social Psychology*, vol. 2, second edition, Addison-Wesley.

1 F. Strodtbeck

Considerations of Meta-Method in Cross-Cultural Studies

F. Strodtbeck, 'Considerations of meta-method in cross-cultural studies', *American Anthropologist*, vol. 66 (1964), pp. 223–9.

In this paper I should like to examine some of the (profitable) reasons which might lead a scientific investigator of human behavior to work in more than one culture. I will be especially interested in the logic or strategy behind using a given technique or method in different cultures. Such reasons or strategies will be defined as considerations of *meta-method*. Finally, in the latter part of the paper, I will discuss discovery processes in the social sciences more generally, contrasting *hypothetico-deductive* with *retroductive* strategies of inference.

Studies involving cognition have been selected to illustrate the kinds of meta-method considerations which underlie cross-cultural research. However, it is assumed that, at the level of meta-method, the problems and advantages of cross-cultural study as they arise in linguistics, child socialization, social psychology, social organization, etc., will have similar features. Also, it is assumed that some of the inference strategies used in one of these fields may not yet have been used in another and that, if the characteristics of these operations were described as propositions of meta-method, then new designs would be popularized and inquiry would be facilitated.

Type I. The Culture as an Experimental Treatment for Individual Subjects

The most easily conceptualized form of transcultural study equates cultural experience with the laboratory treatment administered to an individual subject. Perhaps the investigator has reason to believe that some kind of experience may affect individuals in a particular way; he may then search for a culture which can serve as a natural experiment to test this idea. Often this type of inference strategy will be selected when the investigator wishes to question the universality of some phenomena, such as adolescent trauma or visual acuity. The classic work of this type was undertaken by W. H. R. Rivers in his Torres Straits expedition (1901). Recently, Segall, Campbell and Herskovits have more fully documented some of Rivers' early findings concerning optical illusions (Rivers, 1905, p. 321; Segall, Campbell and Herskovits, 1963, pp. 769–71). They have collected responses to four optical illusions from 1878 subjects in fifteen different societies. The results indicate that Europeans experience the Müller–Lyer and Sander Parallelogram more sharply than non-Europeans, i.e. they are more disposed to interpret an acute or obtuse angle on a 2-dimensional surface as representative of rectangular objects in 3-dimensional space. This error-producing habit is interpreted as a product of residence in a highly carpentered, urban, European environment. Also, it was found that some non-European groups experience horizontal–vertical illusions more sharply than Europeans. It is suggested that this is related to inference habits built by interpreting vertical lines as extensions away from the horizontal plane – a perceptual disposition which would be more likely to develop if one lived on a flat plain.

The experimental treatment in these studies is considered to be the culture in which the adult subjects had spent their lifetime. However, notice that if the test which is administered is considered to be culture-free, the results would be interpreted differently. Stanley D. Porteus, for example, whose maze test has proven to have such remarkable diagnostic power in brain injury cases, has consistently interpreted cultural differences in performance on his tests (by the Tamil, the Ainu, the Karadjeri, the Senoi, the Bajou, the Negritos of Zambali, the Sakai-Jeram and Bushmen) as representing genetically transmitted racial differences under the assumption that his test was 'culture-free' (Porteus, 1961, pp. 187–200). These assertions go against the weight of the evidence from other investigations. While there may be moot points relating to how the differences he observed did arise, the present commentary will proceed on the assumption that cross-cultural research must proceed without culture-free instruments if it is to proceed at all.

The issue of the degree to which tests can or should be culture-free ought not to be confused with the issue of whether or not a test is culturally appropriate. For example, Price-Williams (1961b, p. 304) has carefully worked through a series of Piaget's tests with Tiv children. He finds age norms which are not sharply at variance with Swiss norms *if* familiar materials like native acorns are substituted for the materials used by Piaget with European children. Mission school and illiterate Tiv children were found to reach the various stages of performance with respect to concrete operations at the same ages (Price-Williams, 1962, p. 59), though slightly later than Europeans. An attractive part of these papers is the special pains which the author takes to tell how he communicated with his subjects. For example, to communicate the concept of squares and triangles, in the absence of these configurations as abstract shapes in the Tiv language, he used the analogy of house floor plans. Price-Williams' care and ingenuity result in his demonstrating both that cultural differences can be reduced with the substitution of culturally appropriate materials and that even when this is done, some differences remain – and these are in the direction we would expect.

To demonstrate that a cognitive process is similar in children as different as Swiss and central Nigerian children is quite valuable, but where does one go from there? It is easy to be illegitimately drawn to the conclusion that if such results are obtained, then some universal process is involved. While such a deduction is logically false, this exercise leads to recognition that with Type I approaches, one may wish either to demonstrate the effect of culture or to demonstrate that culture does not matter. The first task is easier than the latter. For example, in the Triandis survey, there are at least a dozen instances in which a test operation was taken to a second culture, given with only the most rudimentary concessions to the second culture, and then interpreted so one must conclude that a common process was involved (Triandis, 1964, vol. 1). But as Segall, Campbell and Herskovits have pointed out with regard to visual illusions, ' ... If groups perceived in radically different ways one could not distinguish between total failure in communication and total difference in perception. It is just because we perceive and respond essentially alike that we can note the small difference which results' (1962, p. 25). If such limits are inherent in the nature of the problem, one should take particular pains not to accept a near miss, in either direction, as a positive score for the investigator.

Type II. The Differential Incidence Survey

The method pioneered in Durkheim's *Suicide* has found its greatest relevance in the study of disease but may be extended to any phenomena for which rates can be collected. 'The basic method is to locate populations with high rates of illness and those with low rates, and then to search the factors which may be responsible for these differences' (Kennedy, 1961, pp. 405–26). In the health field this technique has assisted in the understanding and control of such diseases as yellow fever, typhus, tuberculosis, beri beri and sickle cell anemia. Once actual prevalence is determined and plotted, a scientific game begins. The investigator becomes responsible for suggesting an explanation for a real difference. This suggestion may be viewed as a hypothesis which, if proven, completes a cycle of discovery originated ordinarily *without* the benefit of theory.

As Kennedy has shown, this approach is not as cut and dried as the above description implies. There are always problems of definition and classification. The solution in each case is less a discovery process than a pragmatic strategy for getting the enumeration under way, adopted by investigators who choose to work back from instances of differential incidence toward explanation of greater precision.

It will surprise some to find that opinion survey, by this classification, would ordinarily be considered a differential incidence technique. There are some interesting variations in survey methods which permit the use of the respondent as a stable point of reference, despite cultural differences between individuals. Hadley Cantril, for example, presents respondents in different (Western) cultures with a picture of a ladder. The top of the ladder is designated as 'the best possible life' and the bottom, 'the worst possible life'. The respondent is than asked to point, on the ladder, to where he stands now, to where he was five years ago, and to where he expects to be five years from now. Thus, the self-anchoring scale allows 'an individual's expression of his concerns, values, and perceptions to establish the top and bottom points of a self-defined measurement continuum' (Cantril, 1963, p. 41). This approach is explicitly not one which assumes cross-cultural comparability in the first instance. Cantril reports that 'there is ample testimony in the record of the interviews that the anchor points of respondents in various countries are very different.'

From the data Cantril has presented, one can conclude that citizens of many countries think they are somewhat better off today than they were five years ago and that they will be somewhat better off in five more years. However, there are wide variations in the size of the perceived improvements. Cubans perceived their country as jumping from 2·2 five years ago to 7·0 now and expect to reach 8·8 within the next five years. Americans perceived the U.S.A. as declining from 7·2 five years ago to 6·5 now but anticipate a recovery to 7·6 within five years. Thus the optimism and expectations for rapid economic advance in the under-developed countries as contrasted with the expectation of greater stability in the U.S.A. are readily captured by the scale.

A second example of a technique which uses the individual as a stable point of reference is the perceived consensus technique. In the appendix to *Variations in Value Orientations*, Strodtbeck analyses the response of subjects to the question, 'how do most of the people (in subject's community) feel about X?' where the respondent has just answered the question, 'how do you feel about X?' Using responses from a set of subjects, it is possible to measure how accurately the subjects perceive others' attitudes (consensus) and to what degree the subject departs from actual or perceived consensus. Differences in the amount of consensus and in the perception of that consensus have been clearly demonstrated (Kluckhohn and Strodtbeck, 1961, pp. 401–15).

Type III. The Culture as a Locus for the Development of a New Category of Experience

One exciting aspect of cross-cultural research is the potentiality it provides for the revision of the investigator's culturally given taxonomy of human experience. Anthropologists' interest in discovering and describing patterns in language and culture is well illustrated in the classic studies of kinship terminology. The model for the process by which the new conceptualizations in folk classification are discovered is now formalized in componential analysis.

However, componential analysis, as Triandis (1964, p. 13) has noted, '. . . is a very elaborate process, and is unlikely to be adopted for any except the most important lexical fields.' Even if the method were less unwieldy, it would be ill-advised if the potentialities for the discovery of new concepts were restricted to this mode of approach. One can argue that it is the tension between the need to describe the observed social data (according to inherent contrasts) and still communicate with others which motivates the search for new modes of conceptualization. Since all new conceptualizations do not by any means appear to have arisen from a systematically detailed approach such as componential analysis, other methods of formalization will doubtless be discovered.

Perhaps it can be said that much of the contribution of anthropology arises out of the attempt to generalize, to all or many cultures, categories that were discovered in one culture. While this strategy is not always successful – as the fate of such categories as 'totemism' attests – it has served well to help create a more adequate vocabulary for the social sciences. Such categories as the phoneme, status and role, values, etc., as well as the very concept of culture itself, have been gradually refined out of cross-cultural experience.

Type IV. The Comparative Content Analysis of Ethnographies

The tactic of taking the ethnographies of world cultures and placing them on separate cards in the Human Relations Area Files deserves special attention because of its implications for meta-method. It is apparent that the quality of the ethnographies will not be improved by this process. Indeed, the need for a standard set of culture traits and customs involves some loss, at least temporarily, of precision in the primary information. Missing information and the lack of independence between cultures which have participated in the same streams of diffusion harass the investigator. The process is expensive. Yet despite this negative consideration, the weight of the evidence is still in favor of the files, and it arises from the degree to which they facilitate data retrieval.

With modern computers and with use of averaged judges' ratings to quantify measures, the content of the files can be compressed, searched by multi-variate methods, and the significant relationships published for inspection by an analyst competent to review the assumptions made in the process and, if necessary, submit new instructions. While this mechanization is a far cry from Hobhouse, Wheeler and Ginsberg (1915), the content of the files is not. It is understandable that the requirements for maximal technical efficiency of the retrieval and analysis systems can emerge to dictate the need and, to a degree, the direction of new ethnographies. The Whiting six cultures study is an impressive first report on studies which arose as a conscious response to recognized shortcomings of available data. But the process will be insatiable, for the more we know, the more we will want to know. New observations embedded in new categories will, in all probability, be periodically required even though the revisions will probably not greatly increase our ability to differentiate grossly between cultures.

From a methodological standpoint, an ethnography is an abstraction from a culture just as a trait entry in a file is an abstraction from an ethnography. The scientific game involves the correlational assessment of the traits in differing combinations and with different associated traits factored out. It is assumed that 'the customs of a society are truly comparable to the habits of an individual' (Whiting, 1954, p. 525), or alternatively, a custom is the habit of a typical member of a society. Thus the psychological principles which apply to habits are assumed by definition to apply to customs; and secondly, 'that customs can be compared from one society to another.' When a sample is selected, variables chosen, scales defined, judges trained, and reliability established, one can determine over a much greater range in variation of variables the distribution of customs. Once these results are in hand, the analyst's task is to give an explanation which, if true, will remove the surprise which arose from the original juxtaposition of data. At the stage of formal analysis, there is an equivalence between the search of ethnographies and the epidemiological method previously discussed. There may be both hypothetico-deductive hypotheses which are checked and surprising associations which initiate new theory construction as well. It is generally agreed that hypothetico-deductive inference proceeds by four steps: (a) the statement of a hypothesis; (b) logical deductions from this hypothesis; (c) a check to determine that the deductions square with what is observed; and (d) a conclusion that the hypothesis is, in this instance, confirmed (Hanson, 1958a, p. 1085). It has at various times been thought that, in some nonsocial sciences, this is *de rigueur* and a pathway to greatness. Recent books like Hanson's *Patterns of Discovery* (1958b) cast doubt upon the possibility that either classical mechanics or particle physics developed in this way. But, if one had no information other than that printed in the article, one might well conclude, because of their silence as to how they originated, that perhaps six out of ten of the articles in the *Journal of Abnormal and Social Psychology* were the result of research operations which parallel those of classical hypothetico-deductive inference studies.

Whiting (1954, pp. 523–31) has defined cross-cultural methods as 'the utilization of data, collected by anthropologists, describing the culture of various peoples throughout the world, to test hypotheses concerning human behavior, drawn from the theory of general behavior science.' This formulation errs in equating the scope of science with the logic of testing hypothetico-deductive hypotheses. It has been argued here that the proper scope of the cross-cultural method is not simply the testing of hypotheses. From the viewpoint of the logic of discovery, it is expressly in the generation of new hypotheses that the cross-cultural method has its particular strength.

The hypothetico-deductive inference paradigm should be challenged not only because it is an inaccurate view of the scientific process, but also because the hypothetico-deductive myth interacts with other characteristics of the present development in social science (such as the failure to inspect alternative hypotheses, the reporting of positive findings only, and the human weakness of unwillingness to relinquish one's 'own hypotheses') so as to be particularly inhibiting of research productivity.

The Alternative of Retroductive Reasoning

To make this argument clearer, let me draw upon the distinction of Aristotle, re-emphasized by Peirce, as to the three types of inference. They argue that, in addition to deduction and induction, there is another process, abduction or retroduction, and that these three processes are not reducible to one another. Schematically, in terms parallel to our prior analysis of hypothetico-deductive inference, retroduction, or R-inference, would go as follows (Hanson, 1958a, p. 1087):

(a) Surprising phenomena p_1, p_2, p_3, ... are encountered.
(b) The p_1, p_2, p_3, ... would not be surprising or astonishing if the hypothesis were true – they would follow as a matter of course from the hypothesis.
(c) Therefore, there is good reason for elaborating the hypothesis and proposing it as a possible hypothesis from whose assumptions p_1, p_2, and p_3 might be explained.

This third mode of inference deals with the rational context of discovery. It may or may not be congenial to the psychology of the scientist or the sociology of science as we know it; but, whether or not a social science of knowledge is involved, this distinction deals with the structure of the *logic* of the inference – not the source. It deals with 'the *rational* context within which the hypothesis might come to be "caught" in the first place' (Hanson, 1958a, p. 1087). Thus, in the first instance, the cross-cultural method increases the probability that surprising phenomena will be encountered. But, in the continuing process, it is the responsibility of the investigator to elaborate the alternative hypothesis which, if true, will explain the observed relations and so insure the continuing growth of the discipline.

References

CANTRIL, H. (1963), 'A study of aspirations', *Scientific American*, vol. 208, pp. 41–5.
HANSON, N. R. (1958a), 'The logic of discovery', *Journal of Philosophy*, vol. 55, pp. 1073–89.

HANSON, N. R. (1958b), *Patterns of Discovery*, Cambridge University Press.

HOBHOUSE, L. T., WHEELER, G. C., and GINSBERG, M. (1915), *The Material Culture and Social Institutions of the Simpler Peoples: An Essay in Correlation*, Chapman and Hall.

KENNEDY, D. (1961), 'Key issues in the cross-cultural study of mental disorders', in B. Kaplan (ed.), *Studying Personality Cross-Culturally*, Row, Peterson.

KLUCKHOHN, F. R., and STRODTBECK, F. L. (1961), *Variations in Value Orientations*, Row, Peterson.

NAGEL, E. (1961), *The Structure of Science*, Harcourt, Brace and World.

PORTEUS, S. D. (1961), 'Ethnic group differences', *The Mankind Quarterly*, vol. 1, pp. 187–200.

PRICE-WILLIAMS, D. R. (1961a), 'Analysis of an intelligence test used in rural areas of Central Nigeria', *Overseas Education*, vol. 33, pp. 124–33.

PRICE-WILLIAMS, D. R. (1961b), 'A study concerning concepts of conservation of quantities among primitive children', *Acta Psychologica*, vol. 18, pp. 297–305.

PRICE-WILLIAMS, D. R. (1962), 'Abstract and concrete modes of classification in a primitive society', *British Journal of Educational Psychology*, vol. 32, pp. 50–61 (part I).

RIVERS, W. H. R. (1901), 'Vision', in A. C. Hadden (ed.), *Reports of the Cambridge Anthropological Expedition to the Torres Straits 2: (Part 1)*, Cambridge University Press.

RIVERS, W. H. R. (1905), 'Vision', *British Journal of Psychology*, vol. 1, p. 321.

SEGALL, M. H., CAMPBELL, D. T., and HERSKOVITS, M. J. (1962), *The Influence of Culture on Perception*. Monograph in preparation.

SEGALL, M. H., CAMPBELL, D. T., and HERSKOVITS, M. J. (1963), 'Cultural difference in the perception of geometric illusions', *Science*, vol. 139, pp. 769–71.

STRODTBECK, F. L. (1955), 'Husband–wife interaction over revealed differences', in P. Hare, E. Borgatta and R. F. Bales (eds.), *Small Groups*, Knopf.

TRIANDIS, H. C. (1964), 'Cultural influence upon cognitive processes', in L. Berkowitz (ed.), *Advances in Experimental Social Psychology*, vol. 1, Academic Press.

WHITING, J. W. M. (1954), 'The cross-cultural method', in G. Lindzey, (ed.), *Handbook of Social Psychology, vol. 1, Theory and Measurement*, Addison-Wesley.

2 N. Frijda and G. Jahoda

On the Scope and Methods of Cross-Cultural Research

N. Frijda and G. Jahoda, 'On the scope and methods of cross-cultural research', *International Journal of Psychology*, vol. 1 (1966), pp. 110–27.

What is 'Cross-Cultural'?

With the increasing interest in this sphere over the past decade, a great variety of different studies have been somewhat loosely labelled 'cross-cultural'. It is thus somewhat easier to indicate what is usually excluded from this title, namely research concerned with sub-cultural groups such as social classes, regional differences as between England and Scotland, or cross-ethnic work within the same culture, e.g. comparisons between American whites and Negroes. A distinction is sometimes drawn between 'cross-national' and 'cross-cultural', the former term being mainly confined to studies within Western nations; thus U.S. *v.* Germany would be cross-national, and U.S. *v.* Japan cross-cultural, although all three are highly industrialized modern countries. Underlying the distinction there appears to be a notion of degrees of cultural contrasts, though this is not fully consistent with the general usage; for instance, as regards Western nations it is quite possible that sub-groups of similar social status such as the professions are more similar in terms of cultural background to their peers in other nations than they are to unskilled labourers in their own, the one conspicuous exception being as a rule language.

Traditionally the cross-cultural study is one in which Western industrial cultures are compared with pre-literate tribal ones. As regards the latter, however, it must be pointed out that psychologists have arrived too late on the scene: hardly any cultures have remained unaffected by Western ideas and technologies. One of the most important aspects of this, as Bruner (1965) rightly emphasized, has been the rapidly increasing introduction of formal education at school. Since they involve no fundamental contrasts in methodology, cross-national studies will here be included under the general heading of 'cross-cultural'. One task we intend to shirk is the definition of 'culture' in the present context. Like most other psychologists, we are not anxious to dispel the illusion (which could be readily shattered by, say, Kroeber, 1952) that we know what we mean by this concept; as employed here, it is wide enough to include ecological factors.

Types and Goals of Cross-Cultural Research

It is conventional to divide cross-cultural research into taxonomic *v*. nomothetic, or descriptive *v*. explanatory. Such a simple dichotomy is misleading, since most descriptive studies are made to yield some generalizations, be it only from sample to population within a given culture; moreover, description is rarely free from causal-type interpretation, however speculative. This is not necessarily a short-coming for, as Strodtbeck rightly emphasized in opposition to Whiting (1954), the hypothetico-deductive method is by no means the only fruitful one, especially when it comes to generating new hypotheses. Many descriptive investigations, of course, are merely concerned to demonstrate the range and kind of cross-cultural variability of some psychological attribute (e.g. Blum, 1956, preference for defence mechanisms; Aubert *et al.*, 1954, teachers' attitudes to some international problems).

The moment more complex interrelationships are made the object of description, distinction between nomothetic and taxonomic becomes somewhat arbitrary. This can be seen in those studies in which clusters of relationships among variables are compared within two or more cultures, rather than the variables as such. An example is the study of parent behaviour in the U.S. and Germany by Devereux, Bronfenbrenner and Suci (1962), who are among the few to comment explicitly on their reasons for cross-cultural comparisons; they say that these provide the chance of 'shaking hypotheses free from particular sets of cultural entanglements and for catching strategic variables in new ranges'. In so far as the comparison was restricted to two Western countries, the extent to which the hypotheses can be said to have been freed from 'cultural entanglements' is naturally limited; but this kind of research strategy is clearly appropriate for such complex spheres as family relationships.

At any rate, the majority of cross-cultural studies aim at uncovering causal relationships. Unfortunately, even the attempt to demonstrate relatively narrow and specific connections requires consideration of a large array of variables. This emerges, for example, from the work of McClelland (1961), designed to show the influence of certain aspects of child-rearing on the formation of *n Ach*. In trying to establish this, a systematic exploration of a multitude of clusters of relationships in a wide variety of cultures had to be undertaken, and still the result is less clear-cut than would be desirable. Whatever reservations one might have about this *tour de force*, it does indicate the scale of operations needed if subtle and complex causal nexus is to be satisfactorily unravelled cross-culturally.

Where the main purpose of cross-cultural research is causal interpretation, it is in principle merely an extension of intracultural groups comparisons. The ultimate goal, in both cases, is the elaboration of general behaviour laws. Culturally different groups may be chosen because more extreme values of the independent variables can be obtained (cf. Whiting, 1954) or influences of much longer duration and pervasiveness than would otherwise be possible. Sometimes cross-cultural replications are performed merely to make sure that particular generalizations are not restricted to one specific culture. An example is the study by Schachter *et al.* (1954), on threat and rejection in small groups; it should be noted, however, that only western cultures were involved.

Much of the work on group behaviour would be difficult, if not impossible to replicate in a tribal non-literate culture. This is because such studies usually entail the bringing together of persons unknown to each other, followed by suitable treatments designed to produce particular types of interaction relevant to the hypothesis being tested. The difficulty, rather briefly and crudely, would be that pre-existing social relationship would determine the nature of the interaction; if the people involved did not know each other, they would either seek to find some such basis in terms of remote kinship, or they would have insufficient common ground for effective interaction. It therefore cannot be taken for granted that all experiments do lend themselves to direct cross-cultural replication.

Another important goal of cross-cultural work, historically prior to most of those hitherto mentioned, is the investigation of the generality or variability of some psychological characteristics; as Strodtbeck (1964, p. 224) put it 'one may wish either to demonstrate the effect of culture or to demonstrate that culture does not matter.' This concerns such fundamental questions as the extent of biological dispositions of mankind, and of susceptibility to learning influences. Since such research has in the past been predominantly in the area of personality, it has tended to emphasize the profound formative influence of cultural environment upon the human disposition; it has only been more recently, with mounting interest in basic processes such as cognition, that the importance of a common biological disposition has returned to the foreground (cf. Singer, 1961; Triandis, 1964). In this way, new problems have emerged in addition to old ones in a fresh guise. Suppose that a given characteristic, e.g. the ability to identify certain emotions from the tone of voice (cf. Davitz, 1964) were found to be cross-culturally universal: one could probably infer from this a biological disposition to express certain emotions in particular sound patterns. In other fields no such conclusion might be readily warranted, as for example cognitive development. It was at one time assumed that this represented the mere unfolding of innate potential, culminating in a certain 'racial intelligence'. Wide covariations of measured I.Q. with environmental variables among people drawing from the same genetic pool led first to search for a 'culture-free' test and later to the recognition that the category was cross-culturally inappropriate. Now the problem reappears in a more subtle form, following Piaget's claim that the stages of cognitive development are biologically determined (cf. Tanner and Inhelder, 1960, p. 119). The use of culturally appropriate test materials by Price-Williams (1961, 1962) has narrowed the gap between European and African performance at given ages, though certain methodological shortcomings that will be elaborated later remain. If these were overcome, and stages were found to be essentially identical at least in sequence in a variety of different cultures, could one be certain that a universal biological process is involved? Or does this merely indicate that the environmental conditions of child growth in human cultures are sufficiently similar to produce these results? If one wishes to answer this kind of question, it is necessary to combine cross-cultural studies with intra-cultural ones seeking out specially unusual conditions of child development.

Critique of the Older Conceptual Framework

Until recently, the major activity in the field have been the so-called culture–personality studies. In proportion to the immense amount of effort invested, the yield has been rather disappointing. Among the numerous reasons for this only one will be singled out for discussion, namely the conceptual framework employed. Lest it be thought that this would merely be of historical interest, the Cornell–Harvard–Yale project will be examined, which dates back only a few years. Moreover, it represents in many ways a distinct advance on traditional modes of approach, since it involved a concerted plan of fieldwork in six widely separated cultures. So far only the descriptive results have been published (Whiting, 1963), but these are prefaced by an account of the overall conceptual framework. This turns out to be basically similar to that elaborated by Kardiner (1945). It therefore seems to be open not only to the objections raised against his theoretical framework at the time, but also fails to take any account of the rapid acceleration of social change over the past three decades. The schematic diagram given by Whiting (1963, p. 5) envisages basically the sequence indicated by solid lines in Figure 1. Whatever allowance one might make for necessary simplification, this just will not do; it is too remote from reality, for reasons that will be briefly summarized.

1. Even in a relatively stable traditional society child-rearing practices merely need to be such as to produce a range of personality types which is not inconsistent with major cultural demands; and considering the complexity of the processes involved, this leaves far more room for variations in personality than a simple moulding-into-shape model would imply. It is likely that such

33

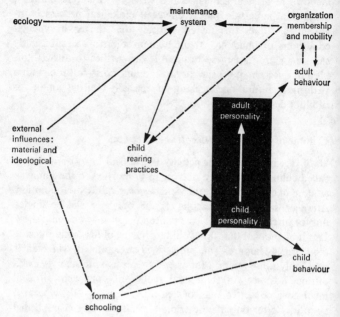

Figure 1

variations are adaptive, in the biological sense, since 'adaptation is the enemy of adaptability.'

2. Given the element of variability, the linear deterministic system implied in the scheme becomes inappropriate, since it ignores the feedback from changes in adult personality that may directly affect both the nature of the maintenance system and child rearing patterns.

3. More recently, external elements have become so obtrusive that a conception of the system as self-contained is now highly unrealistic. The external elements, mainly technical add ideological, exert a kind of multiplier effect. They produce changes in the maintenance system and thereby also in child rearing practices; the changes in the maintenance system also insert situational factors between childhood and maturity, substantially modifying adult behaviour away from the patterns laid down in

the family setting; for instance, migration to urban areas leaves dependency needs unsatisfied, which leads to the joining of voluntary organizations; these in turn are learning situations, in which the person acquires facility in new adult roles (cf. Little, 1965). New adult roles then affect child rearing patterns, and so forth. The other important aspect of external influences, already pointed out, is the introduction of formal schooling, which changes child and adolescent behaviour.

It is contended that an intricate system of interlocking variables such as presented in Figure 1 defies causal analysis by the methods at present at our disposal; it also invalidates the assumption of linear causal sequences. On the basis of these considerations one is tempted to conclude that investigations of this global type are not likely to be profitable until satisfactory methods of objectively assessing personality have been established; at present these are not even available for our own culture (cf. Vernon, 1964). It may well be a more effective strategy to concentrate on more limited associations between particular aspects of mode of child rearing found in Western cultures, and seek to discover which of them appear to be universal. Apart from *n Ach*, already mentioned, one might refer to Witkin's work on 'field-dependence' and 'field-independence' as a function of severity of socialization practices. This was taken up by Dawson (1963) in Sierra Leone, who studied tribes differing on this dimension and obtained the corresponding differences in perceptual abilities. More recently, Berry (1965) carried this a step further by juxtaposing the Temne, who are exceedingly harsh with their children, to the Eskimos who allow them extreme freedom, and the results were according to expectation.

These studies are of course only a beginning, but they probably show a promising avenue for advance. Their conceptual framework is appropriate to the problem, referring to variables that have a reasonable chance of being adequately assessed in the field. The conceptual framework of culture-personality studies tried to encompass everything, irrespective of the extent to which it was amenable to empirical investigation. This whole sphere has been examined from a fresh standpoint by Wallace (1961), whose work also contains references to the most important critical surveys.

Methodological Problem Areas

Methods used in cross-cultural research can be grouped into three classes (Duijker and Rokkan, 1954, p. 9):

1. 'documentary' studies: comparative analysis of characteristics and relationships in already existing records and materials; 2. 'current statistics' studies: comparative analysis made possible through increased standardization of data-collection and classification procedures in regularly operating statistical agencies and other organizations for the registration of social facts; 3. 'field and laboratory' studies: analysis of data specifically collected and classified for the comparative purposes in mind, whether through direct observation, interviewing, test administration, field experiments or laboratory experiments.

Methods from each of the three classes can be, and have been, applied in connexion with the different research goals. For surveys of methods used, see Anastasi and Foley (1958), Duijker and Frijda (1960), Lindzey (1961) and Triandis (1964). Use of methods from each class presents its particular difficulties and requirements. Most methodological considerations which are characteristic for cross-cultural research are relevant to all of them, however. The difficulties of cross-cultural research have two sources: the pitfalls of fair group comparisons, and the baffling complexity of conditions and variables surrounding the variables under study. The different areas of methodological concern will now be discussed in more detail.

Adequacy and comparability of descriptive categories

Comparison requires dimensional identity (Duijker and Frijda, 1960, p. 138). In order to compare two cultures, or individuals from two cultures, they have to be described within identical category systems. This at least is the case if comparison is to reach beyond the mere assessment of the fact of differences, and if it is to serve in the search for causal relationships. It is the assumption of cross-cultural research that such a dimensional identity exists. This in turn rests upon, on the one hand, the assumption of the 'psychic unity of mankind' (Kroeber, 1948, p. 527); and, on the other, upon the possibility of describing cultural universals (Kluckhohn, 1953).

However, the specific psychological and cultural realities built upon those fundamental identities may differ to such an extent that different conceptual systems are needed to describe them fully and adequately. Different cultures use different category systems to describe similar phenomena, and it may well be that such systems are more appropriate for description of that given culture, do more justice to its functions and meanings, than one imposed from without. The discussions on the contrast between 'emic' and 'etic' approaches attest to the reality of this problem (see the reports of the Conference on Transcultural Studies in Cognition – Romney and D'Andrade, 1964). Although the discussion has arisen in the area of ethnolinguistics, its point is of relevance for psychology. Suppose one desires to compare the 'connotative meanings' of certain concepts for Japanese and other subjects. Since the factorial structure of Japanese 'meaning space' is, according to at least one study, different from the one generally found by Osgood (Sagara *et al.*, 1961), comparison is not entirely meaningful. Of course, the difference in conceptual system as such can be evaluated in terms of higher-order concepts; but phenomena described within the system become elusive.

While this problem certainly is real, it does not seem unduly severe. So far, no examples of basic conceptual differences in really important areas have been mentioned in the literature. Also, the movement from emic descriptions to successively more refined etic approximations seems to work rather satisfactorily. Of more immediate concern is the fact that, in any case, concepts and dimensions developed within the context of Western culture need by no means be the most appropriate to describe human behaviour in general. Strodtbeck (1964, p. 226) points out that one of the functions of cross-cultural research resides precisely in the possibility for 'revision of the investigators culturally given taxonomy of human experience'. One of the ways to do this is by means of 'componential analysis'; another by means of procedures derived from Kelly's personal construct approach (Triandis, 1964); or by factorization of semantic differential type data. The outstanding example of efforts in this direction is Osgood's (1964) research, although it did produce results which did largely correspond to those already found in Western culture.

Whatever the dimensions of comparison used, it is evident that the general conceptual system must be explicit and unambiguous. This is not a particular requirement of cross-cultural research. However, in cross-cultural research, maybe more than in some other areas of psychology, this quite often leaves much to be desired. Particularly in culture-and-personality studies, the basic concepts tend to be ill-defined, shifting in meaning and employed inconsistently (cf. Duijker and Frijda, 1960). Dependent and independent variables are not kept separate, as when Mead (1949, p. 665) calls 'emphasis upon moral choice' a 'peculiarity of American character structure' rather than of the value system.

Functional equivalence of the phenomena under study

Obviously, if similar activities have different functions in different societies, their parameters cannot be used for comparative purposes. It is a problem which constantly plagues comparative research, and which emerges at all levels of investigation.

Functional non-equivalence may play a part in sampling problems; comparative study with, for instance, teachers from different countries as exponents of their culture may be invalidated if teachers have different social prestige, social background or general functions in those societies (teachers in western Europe being a quite incomparable group from teachers some 100 years ago, when teaching was the first step upward for the socially underprivileged). Non-equivalence of certain social relationships may strongly disturb testing procedures, and will be discussed in the next section. The problem is most serious with regard to customs and institutions. Obviously, institutions such as the church may have a variety of functions. Data on church attendance can therefore be used as indicators of religiousness, or whatever other trend, only with caution. This means, they can only be used after preparatory research has established functional similarity. Non-equivalence may also be encountered at much more subtle levels. Hymes (in the discussion in Romney and D'Andrade, 1964, p. 235) mentions the varying functions of conversation and, therefore, of language data. Fantasy products such as folk tales, art products or free fantasies, may serve either soothing or expressive functions; they may reflect superficial, socially approved wishes or, rather, culturally repressed desires. Comparison of themes may be misleading, and inferences as to achievement needs, infantile frustrations or cultural values, should be made with extreme caution. Naturally, functional non-equivalence belongs as such to the most enlightening results of research. Yet, it will usually be extremely difficult to disentangle non-equivalence and performance-differences-under-equivalence.

The reverse side of this problem will also present the investigator with difficult choices. In search of measures for some variables, say 'aggression', there is not one single operationalization which would work in every culture. Some method would have to be found to select behaviours of similar meaning. It is clear that such an approach necessitates a number of controls to render the quantitative measures of these behaviours comparable. This problem of 'conceptual equivalence' has been discussed in detail by Sears (1961).

Comparability of investigation procedures

The problem of comparability of investigation procedures is manifest at a number of different levels.

1. Equivalence of verbal materials, instructions and tasks. Translation problems are notorious. It has, at least in the larger research projects, become general practice to translate back into the source language, in order to check translation fidelity. However, quite often even the most careful translation does not necessarily dispose of all difficulties. In a study of attitude change, the Japanese consultants were unable to agree on whether a 'harsh' or 'soft' style of written Japanese was the most appropriate (McGinnies, 1963). An investigation of child animism among the Ga in West Africa came up against the problem that certain common objects, such as a stone, may have different names according to the context in which they occur; one would refer to its every-day form as people know it, the other when it is part of a traditional story or myth, when it may be endowed with properties characteristic of a living being (Jahoda, 1958). Even as between European languages, literal equivalence may result in differing connotations, sometimes to the extent of rendering test items meaningless (Duijker and Rokkan, 1954, p. 20).

If literal equivalence is not the answer, the utilization of different items of similar intent cannot be avoided, which in turn entails complications when it comes to interpretation.

Methods are available for developing comparable items for each culture separately, as shown by Osgood's (1964) project. Where this is not feasible, it is at least highly advisable to develop the investigation procedures with explicit consideration of the range of cultures in which they are to be applied. Carry-over of procedures developed for study in some Western culture may involve needless complications or limitations. In several studies (e.g. the O.C.S.R. study, Duijker and Rokkan, 1954; Jacobsen, 1954) the strong desirability has been emphasized of planning research, right from the start, with a team consisting of investigators from each of the cultures concerned. The violent discussions in such planning meetings attested to their necessity.

2. Equivalence of test materials. Nowadays every raw undergraduate knows that there can be no such thing as a 'culture-free' test or task. Instead, the aim is said to be so-called 'culture-fair' tests, which give no undue advantage to some groups. This could, theoretically, be achieved in at least two contrasting ways: one is to construct tests equally unfamiliar to all; but since tests are devised within particular cultures, we shall have to await the arrival of a space-ship before this can be fully realized. Some suggestions for an approximation to this aim in certain limited spheres will be offered later. The second alternative is to devise culturally 'appropriate' tests or tasks, whereby a particular psychological dimension is assessed by means of a medium familiar to the members of each culture; in other words, the aim is to create optimal conditions at the cost of literally identical procedures.

The need for such culturally appropriate variants is now widely accepted. For instance, T.A.T.-modifications adapting the ethnic characteristics of the persons represented against suitable backgrounds are employed by many investigators. The ingenious devices used by Price-Williams (1961, 1962) have already been mentioned. Even in questionnaire-type studies some investigators have felt compelled to assess attitudes in certain areas by sets of questions varying in different countries (Aubert *et al.*, 1954, p. 37).

There are two main problems in this approach. In the first place, the devising of culturally appropriate materials and procedures presupposes a very intimate knowledge of the cultures concerned, which many outside investigators lack. Subtle differences in perceptual habits or symbolic processes ought, ideally, to be studied prior to the devising of more complex tests or tasks. For example, Abel and Hsu (1949) suggest that white space in the Rorschach may mean white to the Chinese, whilst many other cultures seem to perceive it as space. There is thus an element of circularity, if not infinite regress, involved, unless one is prepared to make assumptions about 'appropriateness' that may not always be justified. The second, related, problem is that comparability becomes a matter of intuitive judgement instead of objective standardization. Comparability in the strictest sense is probably unattainable, and all one can do with the approaches outlined is to arrive at a reasonable compromise.

In the discussion so far the aim of 'fairness' to all cultures has been tacitly accepted, but it may itself be questioned and viewed as a problem of the sociology of knowledge. Following an era when Western superiority was unthinkingly taken for granted, have we as social scientists perhaps fallen into a different trap by our declared purpose that we must be 'fair' to everybody? The notion of 'fairness' looks suspiciously as though there were an underlying feeling that, given appropriate measures, cultural differences ought to disappear. This of course is a deliberate overstatement, designed to raise the question whether there is not perhaps an unduly exclusive emphasis on the so-called 'culture-fair' or 'culture-appropriate' tests. A good deal can be said in favour of the alternative strategy of using the same test in various cultures and attempting to tease out the causes of such differences as are found, or even of looking for tests which maximize cultural differences, as was done in a recent study by Berry (1965). The optimal strategy will depend on one's goals.

Apart from such fundamental issues, it is also worth noting a series of differences in response tendencies pertaining to questionnaires and other verbal procedures. The proportion of 'don't know' answers, or number of checks in check lists (Triandis, 1964, p. 10) shows significant differences. Tendency to respond in terms of cultural stereotypes may vary, as does, to some extent, social desirability of traits. Triandis (1964), who discusses this topic, describes some ways of escape from these problems, such as forced sorting or utilization of self-judgements as anchors (Cantril, 1963). Still, even these methods do not offer full solutions. If someone has to indicate the position of something, relative to his own, as in Cantril's method, the range he is willing to consider is still left uncontrolled.

3. Equivalence of test situations. The testing situation involves two main elements: the experimenter–subject relationship, and the expectations, attitudes and response-sets aroused in the subject by the situation. Since both are closely connected, they will be dealt with under the same heading.

In Western cultures the tester, and to a lesser extent even the psychological investigator, is crystallizing as a social role. This means that both parties to the interaction have mutually compatible expectations about each other's behaviour. In certain sub-cultures, notoriously college students, the testing situation has sometimes acquired an almost ritual character; below the surface there may be a battle of wits, engendered by the realization on the part of the subjects that deception may be practised by the experimenter. When testing takes place in the context of selection for employment, there is strong motivation to perform optimally on tests of ability, which is in line with the aims of the tester, but also to 'project the right kind of image', as the jargon has it, on personality measures; so the tester is forced to use various stratagems in an attempt to defeat the subject's purpose. Thus even within Western culture, the testing situation presents far from negligible problems; across cultures, especially widely divergent ones, these are multiplied.

In order to highlight main issues, a caricature (in the sense of 'overemphasis on characteristic traits' – *Oxford English Dictionary*) will be presented; although fortunately exceptional, it is actually based on fact. A peripatetic psychological researcher landed for the first time in an African country for a study lasting a week. He obtained his subjects by enlisting the help of a literate foreman who ordered the illiterate labourers in his charge to appear before the distinguished visitor. The latter thrust a pencil into hands that had never before wielded one and, with the foreman translating the instructions, asked them to perform a task. Whilst this may sound ridiculous, it exhibits in extreme form certain features common to more adequately conducted work. First, there is a gulf between investigator and subject that is hard to bridge. The role of the researcher is out with the conceptual categories of the subjects; since the interaction is not part of a role system, it is necessary to establish some kind of personal link with the subjects, on the basis of which one can then make some claim for co-operation; alternatively, one can use one's status and power to enforce the subject's participation, in either case with or without a reward. Whatever the means for ensuring compliance, the situation will evoke certain expectations, guesses or hypotheses on the part of the subject. Unless some attempt is made to control these, they may diverge widely in different subjects; some may show by an indulgent smile, or even say, that this is just another example of the white man's senseless and obviously crazy ways; others may see some potential advantage for themselves and scan the investigator's expression anxiously for a sign that he is doing the right thing, or he may ask the interpreter, where there is one; and unless he is very well trained he is likely to give his opinion. It is therefore highly desirable to make some attempt to communicate one's aims, assimilating them to two spheres now commonly known in practically every population, namely medicine and education. Otherwise quite apart from divergent expectations, suspicions may be aroused that one works for the tax collector or is a political snooper.

However sustained the effort to control the testing situations, in most researches to date two disturbing factors have probably persisted. One of these is the variation in attitudes and expectations aroused; these are likely to affect in some degree even studies on sensory discrimination and thresholds, as the experiments suggested by statistical detection theory have demonstrated. They are also likely to have a considerable effect on responses to projective techniques; yet group differences in Rorschach productivity or constriction tend to be interpreted at the personality level without much consideration for these simple and relatively accidental factors.

The other feature of nearly all this kind of work is that the investigator is a stranger from a different culture. However friendly the relationships he has established, however culturally appropriate his materials and procedures, the fact remains that he cannot escape his position as an alien authority figure; and this may well inhibit performance at least to some extent. One way to avoid this is to train indigenous assistants to a level where they can operate independently (Jahoda, 1958, 1961); but this is no real substitute for fully fledged researchers within the various cultures, able to conduct a complete project from the planning stage onwards.

Adequacy, representativeness and comparability of samples

The importance of sampling, and the intricacy of its problems, differ rather strongly from one type of research to another. For descriptive studies, whether of the modal personality, behaviour trend or value system type, representativeness is essential. In many causal studies, e.g. for the demonstration of cross-cultural variability as such, it is much less important, comparability being the prime consideration. For testing descriptive hypotheses derived from impressionistic studies, randomness of the samples is more relevant than representativeness. Incidentally, deficiency of sampling is the rule in impressionistic studies, but need not detract from their value as sources of hypotheses. They often contain quite 'representative' samples not of subjects but of culturally relevant situations. Representative sampling is extremely difficult to achieve. Anthropologically oriented studies usually focus upon one small community and the extent to which their findings can be generalized is hard to assess. The problems of representative sampling are such that modal personality study of any larger cultural group, and particularly of modern nations, must remain for all practical purposes an unattainable goal.

Comparability of samples is the nearest substitute for representative sampling; in case the composition of the two populations is quite different it may actually be preferable. Of course, all problems of equivalence mentioned in earlier sections recur in this connection. Differences between sentence-completions by salesmen in England and America, for instance (Farber, 1953), may reflect little more than the different social backgrounds or functions of this profession in the two countries. The same applies to value patterns of students (Morris, 1956), teachers' attitudes and the like.

It may be added that, in view of the importance of sampling

for the conclusions to be drawn from any study, the least a reader of reports may expect is awareness of sampling problems by the investigator, and consequent explicitness with regard to procedures and sample–population relationships. Too often these data are absent or vague. Sampling problems not only arise in connection with sampling of subjects, but also with regard to situations, behaviour items, institutions, or documents selected for observation or analysis. Problems and procedures, particularly with a view to obtaining comparability, are discussed and illustrated by Barker and Barker (1961). Selection of relevant observation occasions must result in unequal, but hopefully equivalent, collections. Particularly relevant for nomothetic research is the sampling of cultures. All too often chance plays a large role, and culture comparisons result frequently from the coincidence of research interests and Fulbright scholarships. There is nothing wrong with this, but results can hardly be final. Also, comparison of just two groups permits only of dichotomous analysis. Very often in personality study graded comparisons give quite different results from comparison of extremes or dichotomies, with attendant consequences for causal interpretation.

One important research possibility consists of the use of subcultural groups, such as city-dwelling Zulus in addition to Zulus from the bush and city-dwelling whites (Allport and Pettigrew, 1957) or Africans with different amounts of school education (Maistriaux, 1955; Jahoda, 1961; Kellaghan, 1965). Another is of course the extension of study over a large number of cultures, selected on the basis of expected relevance rather than convenience. The number of multi-comparative studies has increased during recent years (Gillespie and Allport, 1955; McClelland, 1961; Osgood, 1964; Schachter et al., 1954; Segall, Campbell and Herskovits, 1963). They are, of course, costly. Perhaps more than hitherto, use could be made of available cross-cultural data collections; apart from the Human Relations Area Files, there are public opinion survey archives at Williamstown, Berkeley, Cologne, Amsterdam and elsewhere. Although final comparison results have still to be published, the research strategy of testing hypotheses by means of such materials, and going into the field for additional data (Whiting, 1963) is probably a very good one.

Problems of interpretation

The complexity of the culture-variate situation renders interpretation hazardous. Alternative interpretations are hard to exclude, particularly such as may render results trivial. Many studies leave one wondering as to the necessity or compellingness of the conclusions.

This holds even for the purely descriptive studies. Attribution of some specific personality trait to some cultural group usually carries three connotations: supposed transsituational generality of the trait (Rorschach anxiety is taken to reflect anxiety in dealings with an unspecified range of realities); relative immutability of the behaviour concerned when in new situations, e.g. after cultural dislocation; and early origin during the life-cycle. Too readily, behaviours are taken to be parts of a pattern, elements of some 'cultural orientation', instead of specifically learned, isolated reaction tendencies. There is, it seems to us, quite some romanticism in culture-and-personality theorizing, and although learning theory is not the last word in personality study, neither is psychoanalysis, particularly in its ethnopsychological applications. In principle, every implication of the kind mentioned has to be investigated, as demonstrated by the Lanhan (1956) criticism of Gorer (1943) and La Barre (1945); Japanese personality traits appear not to be results of early toilet training, but rather of explicit later indoctrinations. Many of the alternatives indeed can be investigated, considering for instance the amount of transcultural movement of persons. Migration study may help to answer some of these questions, although it has hardly been used for this purpose. Acculturation studies (e.g. Hallowell, 1955) tend more in this direction. In many other cases additional intra-cultural materials may clarify the situation, as has been argued even in studies concerning rather superficial attitudes (Aubert *et al.*, 1954, p. 38). In any case, the unity of culture and cultural training should not be overrated and taken as an axiom in interpretative efforts.

The need for additional comparisons, and for the testing of consequences of interpretations, is greatest in explanatory studies. Partialling-out of covarying factors by more involved experimental designs, and extension of lines of reasoning to intra-cultural differences is often indispensable. For instance, supposed cross-cultural influences of ecological variables should also hold within one and the same culture; white American inhabitants of the Great Plains should show as much horizontal–vertical illusion, in comparison to New Yorkers, as plains-versus-city dwellers separated by cultural boundaries (cf. Gregor and McPherson, 1965; Jahoda, 1966). Age trends should correspond to theory if cultural differences reflect learning, as indeed they sometimes turn out not to do (e.g. Spitz, 1963).

Conclusion

Cross-cultural research is like virtue – everybody is in favour of it, but there are widely differing views as to what it is and ought to be. There is such a welter of divergent approaches that it would be presumptuous to claim for this paper any more than an attempt to clarify what we consider to be some major issues. Since it is already highly condensed, a summary would be inappropriate. Instead, some proposals will be put forward which, it is hoped, may indicate some lines of further development.

1. Research techniques

One major difficulty has been shown to lie in ensuring equivalence of verbal instructions across different cultures. There are a number of possibilities for trying to circumvent this problem, which have so far not been adequately exploited. One such approach has been clearly described by Reuning (in Reader, 1963, p. 3):

(1) The test situation must be such as to be understandable without any verbal explanation. (2) It must have the character of inviting action; it must present a challenge to the testee such that, looking at the test problem, he knows without further instruction what he must do. (3) It must be such that the testee's whole response is in terms of this action, and not in terms of verbalization which has to be back-interpreted. This sounds hard to achieve, but Reuning did in fact devise a series-completion test consisting of pieces of rubber of varying shapes and colours; and he administered this without the aid of an interpreter to Kalahari Bushmen (Reuning, 1959).

Along similar lines a learning technique of test administration might be considered, that would be specially suitable for children.

This is most easily explained with reference to a particular application, say the Witkin Embedded Figures Test. The subject would have in front of him a set of boxes, each with one symbol on the lid. In a few preliminary trials the subject could learn that a reward is found in a box with a particular symbol, e.g. 'X'; then another series is presented, all with more complex symbols, one of which contains the embedded 'X'. This procedure is so simple that it may well have been employed before in cross-cultural studies, though we could find no trace of it.

Another learning procedure was devised by Hammond *et al.* (1965) in an effort to reduce the effect of the past history of a subject as a source of variance in experimental research. A preliminary training session ensures that the subject is 'programmed' with regard to the issue being investigated. Although unsuitable for cross-cultural work in its present form, it seems likely that this method would lend itself to adaptation.

Lastly, on the response side, it may be promising to extend the use of those behavioural and physiological methods which are obtaining prominence in individual research also: pupil-size measurement of attitudes (Hess, 1965), physiological modification of moods (Schachter, 1964), eye-movement or perception-time indices of interest (Berlyne, 1963), binocular rivalry assessment of familiarity or salience (Bagby, 1957) and the like. A few of these methods have already been put to cross-cultural use and they may, with the development of observational methods and factual interviews (Barker and Wright, 1955; Barker and Barker, 1961) put comparative study on a somewhat more solid footing.

2. Research strategies

Consideration of the various problem-areas of cross-cultural research all point to one and the same conclusion: the number of variables and the equivalence problems make it inevitable to employ complicated and elaborate research designs, some of which will be outlined.

Cross-cultural comparisons may have to be supplemented by intra-cultural comparisons, in order to ascertain the intra-cultural variability due to variables which could not be controlled cross-culturally.

Cross-cultural comparisons may have to be supplemented by

cross-cultural comparisons on other dimensions to rule out obvious alternative interpretations of results.

Cross-cultural comparisons may have to be supplemented by intra-cultural comparisons along the same, or similar dimensions as are supposed to operate cross-culturally; examples would be developmental trends, ecological variations not necessarily coinciding with cultural differences, or pathological subgroups. A closer integration of cross-cultural and general experimental findings seems required.

Cross-cultural comparisons may have to be made in a graded, and not only a dichotomous way, either by including intra-cultural subgroups falling along the same continuum as the cross-cultural difference, or by producing a larger and more appropriate sample of cultures.

The potentially sizeable investigator effect may be controlled by a kind of cross-over design, which will be briefly explained by reference to hypothetical cultures A and B: culturally appropriate procedures are elaborated for A and B respectively; the investigator indigenous to A administers both procedures in each of the two cultures, and the one from B does the same.

As regards general research planning, the need is stressed for setting up experiments in close cross-cultural co-operation, instead of merely carrying over designs originating in one culture.

3. Thoughts about future development

The cross-cultural field was, until the fairly recent past, dominated by the theme of relationships between child rearing and adult personality; and in proportion to the amount of effort devoted, the findings have been rather meagre. Again in proportion to the effort, studies on the cultural aspects of cognition have perhaps tended to be somewhat more fruitful; yet the specific factors responsible for such differences as have been found are by no means well understood. One might venture the suggestion that a line of research that could hold promise for the advancement of both these areas is the study of behaviour in early infancy. Unlike the lengthy stretch all the way to maturity, subject to a vast multitude of diverse influences, child care practices during the first year of life are rather readily open to systematic observation. At the same time, increasingly reliable methods of study of infant behaviour have been developed (Foss, 1961, 1963). Very little cross-cultural work has been done in this field, but the few studies that have been undertaken (Geber, 1958, 1960; Ainsworth, 1963) indicate the existence of pronounced cross-cultural differences in the behaviour of infants. More intensive and systematic exploration in this area might greatly enhance our understanding at the crucial stage where developmental divergences first manifest themselves.

At the beginning of this paper, reference was made to the growing pace of social and cultural change all over the world. In much cross-cultural research this aspect is treated peripherally, or even viewed as a disturbing element. It is surely time that the psychological implications of this process, one of the salient ones of modern times, should become a primary focus of our endeavours. Moreover, many of us may feel that psychology might not only contribute to an understanding of this process, but also to do something for the people caught up in it. Some psychologists, notably Vernon (1965a and b) have expressed some impatience with those who are still grubbing around for ethnic differences; he emphasizes the need 'to study the effects of controllable environmental factors on the development of various types of ability, either within a particular culture or between contrasted cultures' (1965a, p. 9). The operative phrase here is 'controllable environmental factors', which points to the possibility of action for removing obstacles in the way of individual development. Vernon goes so far as to say 'I would urge that this is the major responsibility of applied psychology in the second half of the twentieth century' (1965b, p. 728).

A further consequence flows from this argument, if it be accepted. It is not enough for us to establish the existence of differences in performance, and the factors responsible for it. Part and parcel of our work should be a further step of attempting to find out to what extent various forms of training can reduce or eliminate such differences. There have been a few minor cross-cultural exercises of this kind in the past (Ombredane *et al.*, 1956; Jahoda, 1956), and a more substantial one recently (Dawson, 1963); but a really concerted attack on the problem still remains to be done.

Lastly, as Tajfel (1966) has stressed, another major task is to encourage and assist the training of social scientists in the emerging countries. Until this is under way, several of the schemes proposed in this paper cannot properly get off the ground.

Reference

ABEL, T. M., and HSU, F. L. K. (1949), 'Some aspects of personality of Chinese as revealed by the Rorschach test', *Rorschach Research Exchanges*, vol. 13, pp. 285–301.

AINSWORTH, M. D. (1963), 'The development of mother–infant interaction among the Ganda', in B. M. Foss (ed.), *Determinants of Infant Behaviour*, vol. 2, Methuen.

ALLPORT, G. W., and PETTIGREW, T. F. (1957), 'Cultural influence on the perception of movement: the trapezoidal illusion among Zulus', *Journal of Abnormal and Social Psychology*, vol. 55, pp. 104–13.

ANASTASI, A., and FOLEY, J. P. (1958), *Differential Psychology: Individual and Group Differences in Behavior*, Macmillan, 3rd edn.

AUBERT, V., FISCHER, B. R., and ROKKAN, S. (1954), 'A comparative study of teachers' attitudes to international problems and policies', *Journal of Social Issues*, vol. 10, pp. 25–39.

BAGBY, J. W. (1957), 'A cross-cultural study of perceptual predominance in binocular rivalry', *Journal of Abnormal and Social Psychology*, vol. 54, pp. 331–4.

BARKER, R. G., and BARKER, L. S. (1961), 'Behavior units for the comparative study of cultures', in B. Kaplan (ed.), *Studying Personality Cross-Culturally*, Row, Peterson.

BARKER, R. G., and WRIGHT, H. F. (1955), *Midwest and its Children*, Row, Peterson.

BEIER, H., and HANFMANN, E. (1956), 'Emotional attitudes of former Soviet citizens as studied by the technique of projective questions', *Journal of Abnormal and Social Psychology*, vol. 53, pp. 143–53.

BERLYNE, D. E. (1963), 'Motivational problems raised by exploratory and epistemic behavior', in S. Koch (ed.) *Psychology, A Study of a Science*, vol. 5, McGraw-Hill.

BERRY, J. W. (1965), A study of Temne and Eskimo visual perception. *Report from the Psychological Laboratory, University of Edinburgh*.

BLUM, G. S. (1956), 'Defense preferences in four countries', *Journal of Projective Techniques and Personality Assessment*, vol. 20, pp. 33–41.

BRUNER, J. S. (1965), 'The growth of the mind', *American Psychologist*, vol. 20, pp. 1007–17.

CANTRIL, H. (1963), 'A study of aspirations', *Scientific American*, vol. 208, pp. 41–5.

DAVITZ, J. R. (1964), *The Communication of Emotional Meaning*, McGraw-Hill.

DAWSON, J. L. M. (1963), Psychological effects of social change in a West African community. *Unpublished doctoral dissertation, University of Oxford*.

DEVEREUX, E. C., BRONFENBRENNER, U., and SUCI, G. H. (1962), 'Patterns of parent behaviour in the United States of America and the

Federal Republic of Germany: A cross-national comparison', *International Social Science Journal*, vol. 14, pp. 488–506.

DUIJKER, H. C. J., and FRIJDA, N. H. (1960), *National Character and National Stereotypes*, Noord-Hollandse.

DUIJKER, H. C. J., and ROKKAN, S. (1954), 'Organizational aspects of cross-national research', *Journal of Social Issues*, vol. 10, pp. 8–24.

FARBER, M. I. (1953), 'English and Americans: Values in the socialization process', *Journal of Psychology*, vol. 34, pp. 243–50.

FOSS, B. M. (1961), *Determinants of Infant Behaviour*, vol. 1, Methuen.

FOSS, B. M. (1963), *Determinants of Infant Behaviour*, vol. 2, Methuen.

GEBER, M. (1958), 'The psycho-motor development of African children in the first year, and the influence of maternal behavior', *Journal of Social Psychology*, vol. 47, pp. 185–95.

GEBER, M. (1960), 'Problèmes posés par le développement du jeune enfant Africain en fonction de son milieu social', *Le Travail Humain*' vol. 23, pp. 97–111.

GILLESPIE, J. M., and ALLPORT, G. W. (1955), *Youth's Outlook on the Future: A Cross-National Study*, Doubleday.

GORER, G. (1943), 'Themes in Japanese culture', *New York Academy of Sciences, Transactions*, vol. 2, pp. 106–24.

GREGOR, A. J., and MCPHERSON, D. A. (1965), 'A study of susceptibility to geometric illusion among cultural subgroups of Australian aborigines', *Psychologia Africana*, vol. 11, pp. 1–13.

HALLOWELL, A. I. (1955), *Culture and Experience*, University of Pennsylvania Press.

HAMMOND, K. R., TODD, F. J., WILKINS, M., and MITCHELL, T. O., (1965), A research paradigm for the study of cognitive conflict between two persons, *Report of the Institute of Behavioral Science, University of Colorado*, no. 71.

HESS, E. H. (1965), 'Attitude and pupil size', *Scientific American*, vol. 212, pp. 46–54.

JACOBSEN, E. (1954), 'Methods used for producing comparable data in the O.C.S.R. seven-nation study', *Journal of Social Issues*, vol. 10, pp. 40–51.

JAHODA, G. (1956), 'Assessment of abstract behavior in a non-Western culture', *Journal of Abnormal and Social Psychology*, vol. 53, pp. 237–43.

JAHODA, G. (1958), 'Child animism. II. A study in West Africa', *Journal of Social Psychology*, vol. 47, pp. 213–22.

JAHODA, G. (1961), 'Traditional healers and other institutions concerned with mental illness in Ghana', *International Journal of Social Psychiatry*, vol. 7, pp. 245–68.

JAHODA, G. (1961–2), 'Aspects of westernization', *British Journal of Sociology*, vol. 12, pp. 375–86 and vol. 13, pp. 43–56.

JAHODA, G. (1966), 'Geometric illusions and environment: A study in Ghana', *British Journal of Psychology*, vol. 57, pp. 193–9.

KARDINER, A. (1945), *Psychological Frontiers of Society*, Columbia University Press.

KELLAGHAN, T. P. (1965), The study of cognition in a non-western culture, with special reference to the Yoruba of south-western Nigeria, *Unpublished doctoral dissertation, University of Belfast*.

KLUCKHOHN, C. (1953), 'Universal categories of culture', in A. L. Kroeber (ed.), *Anthropology Today*, Chicago University Press.

KROEBER, A. L. (1948), *Anthropology*, Harcourt, Brace.

KROEBER, A. L. (1952), *The Nature of Culture*, Chicago University Press.

LA BARRE, W. (1945), 'Some observations on character structure in the orient. I. The Japanese', *Psychiatry*, vol. 8, pp. 319–42.

LANHAN, B. B. (1956), 'Aspects of child care in Japan: A preliminary report', in D. G. Haring (ed.), *Personal Character and Cultural Milieu*, Syracuse University Press.

LI AN CHE, ZUNI (1937), 'Some observations and queries', *American Anthropologist*, vol. 39, pp. 67–76.

LINDZEY, G. (1961), *Projective Techniques and Cross-Cultural Research*, Appleton-Century-Crofts.

LITTLE, K. (1965), *West African Urbanization*, Cambridge University Press.

MAISTRIAUX, R. (1955), 'La sous-evolution des noirs d'Afrique. Sa nature, ses causes, ses remèdes', *Revue de Psychologie des Peuples*, vol. 10, pp. 397–456.

MCCLELLAND, D. C. (1961), *The Achieving Society*, Van Nostrand.

MCGINNIES, E. (1963), 'Cross-cultural investigation of some factors in persuasion and attitude change', *Technical Report, Institute of Behavioral Research, University of Maryland*, no. 1.

MEAD, M. (1949), 'Administrative contributions to democratic character formation at the adolescent level', in C. Kluckhohn and H. A. Murray (eds.), *Personality in Nature, Society and Culture*, Knopf.

MEAD, M. (1949), *Cultural Patterns and Technological Change*, Mentor.

MORRIS, C. (1956), *Varieties of Human Value*, Chicago University Press.

OMBREDANE, A., ROBAYE, F., and PLUMAIL, H. (1956), 'Résultats d'une application répétée du matrix-couleur à une population de Noirs Congolais', *Bulletin C.E.R.P.*, vol. 6, pp. 129–47.

OSGOOD, C. E. (1964), 'Semantic differential technique in the comparative study of cultures', *American Anthropologist*, Special Publication, vol. 66, no. 3, part 2, pp. 171–200.

PRICE-WILLIAMS, D. R. (1961), 'A study concerning concepts of conservation of quantities among primitive children', *Acta Psychologica*, vol. 18. pp. 297–305.

PRICE-WILLIAMS, D. R. (1962), 'Abstract and concrete modes of classification in a primitive society', *British Journal of Educational Psychology*, vol. 32, pp. 50–62.

READER, D. H. (1963), 'African and Afro-European Research', *Psychologia Africana*, vol. 10, pp. 1–18.

REUNING, H. (1959), 'Psychologische versuche mit buschleuten der Kalahari', *Umschau*, vol. 59, pp. 520–3.

ROMNEY, A. K., and D'ANDRADE, R. G. (1964), 'Transcultural studies in cognition', *American Anthropologist*, Special Publication, vol. 66, no. 3, part 2.

SAGARA, M., YAMAMOTO, K., NISHIMURA, H., and AKUTO, H. (1961),

Japanese Psychological Research, vol. 3, pp. 146–56, (quoted from Triandis, 1964).

SCHACHTER, S. (1964), 'The interaction of cognitive and physiological determinants of emotional state', in L. Berkowitz (ed.), *Advances in Experimental Social Psychology*, vol. 1, Academic Press.

SCHACHTER, S., NUTTIN, J., DE MONCHAUX, C., MAUCORPS, P. H., OSMER, D., DUIJKER H., ROMMETVEIT, R., and ISRAEL, J. (1954), 'Cross-cultural experiments on threat and rejection', *Human Relations*, vol. 7, pp. 403–39.

SEARS, R. R. (1961), 'Transcultural variables and conceptual equivalence', in B. Kaplan (ed.), *Studying Personality Cross-Culturally*, Row. Peterson.

SEGALL, M. H., CAMPBELL, D. T., and HERSKOVITS, M. J. (1963), 'Cultural differences in the perception of geometrical illusions', *Science*, vol. 139, pp. 769–71.

SINGER, M. (1961), 'A survey of culture and personality theory and research', in B. Kaplan (ed.), *Studying Personality Cross-Culturally*, Row, Peterson.

SPITZ, H. H. (1963), 'Cross-cultural differences', letter in *Science*, vol. 140, pp. 422.

STRODTBECK, F. L. (1964), 'Considerations of meta-method in cross-cultural studies', *American Anthropologist*, Special Publication, vol. 66, no. 3, part 2, pp. 223–9.

TAJFEL, H. (1966), 'Social and cultural factors in perception', in G. Lindzey and E. Aronson (eds.), *Handbook of Social Psychology*, Addison Wesley, 2nd edn.

TAJFEL, H. (1966), 'International co-operation in social psychology: Some problems and possibilities', *Bulletin of the British Psychological Society*, vol. 19, pp. 29–36.

TANNER, J. M., and INHELDER, B. (1960), *Discussions on Child Development*, Tavistock.

TRIANDIS, H. (1964), 'Cultural influences upon cognitive processes', in L. Berkowitz (ed.), *Advances in Experimental Social Psychology*, vol. 1, Academic press.

VERNON, P. E. (1964), *Personality Assessment*, Methuen.

VERNON, P. E. (1965a), 'Environmental handicaps and intellectual development. Part I', *British Journal of Educational Psychology*, vol. 35, pp. 9–20.

VERNON, P. E. (1965b), 'Ability factors and environmental influences', *American Psychologist*, vol. 20, pp. 723–33.

WALLACE, A. F. C. (1961), *Culture and Personality*, Random House.

WHITING, B. B. (1963), *Six Cultures: Studies in Child Rearing*, Wiley.

WHITING, J. W. M. (1954), 'The cross-cultural method', in G. Lindzey (ed.), *Handbook of Social Psychology*, vol. 1, Addison Wesley.

WHITING, J. W. M., and CHILD, I. L. (1953), *Child Training and Personality: A Cross-Cultural Study*, Yale University Press.

Part Two **Tests**

It has to be admitted that many psychologists in the past have rushed into testing populations all over the world with more zeal than care. Intelligence, ability, attitude and personality tests, all constructed and standardized in Europe and the United States, have been fostered on groups in Africa, Asia, Latin America and Oceania. Generalizations from the results of these tests have often given rise to criticism from those authorities more intimately knowledgeable about the populations in question. Specifically, the criticism has been levelled that psychologists have been guilty of a certain ethnocentrism in their unconsidered use of tests, which may be fine for residents of London, Paris or New York, but are completely inappropriate for inhabitants of the African bush, Arabian desert and even Negro ghetto areas. Since the early criticisms of this nature, far more sophistication has crept into the psychologist's use of tests. Already in this volume, both Strodtbeck and Frijda and Jahoda (Readings 1 and 2) have dwelt on this issue. The present pair of selections are introduced both on account of their empirical content and their sensitivity towards the usual methodological errors.

Reading 3 is by Biesheuvel, a pioneer of psychological tests in their application to non-European peoples. Although this was originally published twenty years ago, the issues he focuses upon are very much alive today. Biesheuvel displays the range of questions which the would-be tester has to face. The Reading is almost exclusively methodological and covers everything from the kind of test that should be used with non-European groups (in his case, African) to the kind of factors which would influence test scores with these groups, such as nutrition and parental care.

The second paper by Vernon (Reading 4) takes as its starting-point the thesis that we stand to gain in cross-cultural testing more by probing a wide range of abilities than by detecting the over-all level of intelligence. His paper gives information not only on Uganda, but also on Jamaicans and the Canadian Indians. Vernon's contribution makes the important point that it is thoroughly misleading to think merely in terms of lowered I.Q. in less technologically advanced cultures. If a wide range of abilities in any cultural group is tested, it can be noted which kind of abilities this group does well on and which it does poorly. Cultural influences can then be properly abstracted so as to account for the differentials found. This approach seems more promising than the early cultural intelligence testing with its extreme theoretical framework of nature versus nurture.

3 S. Biesheuvel

Psychological Tests and their Application to Non-European Peoples

Excerpt from S. Biesheuvel, 'Psychological tests and their application to non-European peoples', in G. B. Jeffrey, ed., *The Yearbook of Education*, Evans, 1949, pp. 90–104.

[...]

The Study of the Educational Potentialities of Non-European Peoples by Means of Psychological Tests

The study of the educational potentialities of non-Europeans has been virtually confined to comparisons of European and non-European intelligence quotients as measured by a variety of pencil-and-paper and performance tests. These studies uniformly reveal an inferiority on the part of non-Europeans, which grows less the more closely the group approximates in its way of life to European culture, but which never vanishes altogether. Claims that inferiority also diminishes according to the degree of admixture with white blood (1) have been disproved by the work of Herskovits (2), Petersen and Lanier (3), Klineberg (4), Witty and Jenkins (5).

A survey of a large number of investigations carried out on American Negroes reveals that on the average 83 per cent of the whites exceed the Negro mean and only 15 per cent to 18 per cent Negroes reach the white mean (6). In South Africa, Fick found school-going African children to be inferior to a European control group by 4 to 5 years of mental age (7). Needless to say, these findings were challenged in scores of investigations, which attempted to prove that environmental, rather than genetic, factors were responsible for the apparent intellectual inferiority of the non-European racial groups. The discussions became closely linked with the dispute about the relative importance of heredity and environment in determining individual differences in intelligence among Europeans, a psychological battle-ground which is more noteworthy for the vehemence with which the issues are contended than for the finality of the results produced (8, 9). A critical summary of the most significant results in this field is given by Woodworth (10), who also restates the essentials of the problem and indicates the lines along which conclusive research might be conducted.

As the study of inter-racial differences in intelligence is a complex variant of the more general nature–nurture problem, we are not likely to obtain conclusive facts about the intellectual potentialities of non-European races from it at this stage.

There is no doubt that the measurement of inter-racial differences has side-tracked the study of the intellectual potentialities of races from its primary purpose, which should have been to survey the manifestations of non-European abilities in a general way; to follow up this exploration with both qualitative and quantitative studies of individual differences *within* racial and cultural groups; and to study the nature of their determinants. Comparisons with European groups should in the first instance have been qualitative only, in order to reveal significant features in the ability patterns obtained from inter-racial studies, and to throw further light on the influence of certain cultural factors. Only then will we know subject to what controls and in what areas we can legitimately make quantitative comparisons. In the last resort, some quantitative evaluation of racial differences is inevitable, and it is equally inevitable that Western culture should provide the yard-stick. Western culture is still dominant, and its most typical achievement, technology, is likely to remain a feature of whatever civilization may take its place. Consequently the ultimate capacity, given time and opportunity, to adapt to the Western way of life, to meet the many requirements which a technological society imposes on the individual, to contribute to its technical advancement, and most important of all, to maintain and further its democratic creed, will be the criterion whereby the educability and equivalence of other races will be judged. That this is a relative judgement cannot be denied; but the fixation of an absolute criterion would involve us in a discussion about values which is outside the scope of science and which in any case could not yield an answer to the question which prompted the inquiry into inter-racial differences.

Comparative studies are therefore legitimate, provided that no comparisons are made until a scientifically valid basis for making them has been established, and provided also that value judgements are made relative only to our Western criteria of success and ability.

In order to demonstrate that the type of inter-racial control-group investigation, by means of which the genetic intellectual capacities of races have generally been studied, does not provide such a basis, and to indicate which determinants of test performance need special investigation, the factors known to contribute to inter-racial differences in test performance will be briefly discussed.

What kind of ability should be tested?

Educability has been almost universally assessed in terms of g, a general factor of mental ability which was believed to determine the level of intellectual capacity regardless of minor individual differences in the ability to handle such symbols as words, numbers, or forms.

This factor g was measurable by means of a wide variety of tests, individual and group, verbal or perceptual, concrete or conceptual. A number of quite differently constituted batteries could therefore give equally good estimates of g.

This hypothesis lent itself remarkably well to the study of inter-racial differences in educability. No scientifically valid objection could be raised against expressing these differences in terms of g, defined as a universal factor in terms of Spearman's three neogenetic laws (11, 12). As the measurement of g was not limited to a specific battery, tests could be chosen of which the contents were equally familiar to the two cultures being compared.

Throughout the period during which the concept of a general factor dominated the theory of intelligence, dissenting voices were heard which have now gained a definite hearing on the strength both of accumulated experimental evidence and of the mathematical theory developed in support of their views.

The most thorough-going restatement of the Spearman hypothesis has come from Thurstone, who holds that intellectual capacity can be adequately stated only in terms of a number of primary mental abilities, represented by factors whose combination ratio varies from individual to individual (13, 14). In his later work (15) Thurstone recognizes that these factors are correlated, and that Spearman's g may exist as a secondary factor, though it is by no means clear which primary mental abilities should be combined, and in what ratio, to give the best estimate of g.

The difference of opinion between the general- and multiple-factor schools of thought is not purely theoretical, but materially affects the practice of intelligence testing and the validity of the I.Q. as a single index of educability. The implication of the Thurstone theory is that until such time as g can be restated in terms of a particular combination of primary mental abilities, the concept of general educability must give way to specific educability for particular trades or professions in terms of the patterns of abilities known to be relevant in each particular case.

For inter-racial intelligence testing this means that instead of comparing two groups in respect of one index, as many comparisons will have to be made as there are factors. It will also be necessary to determine differences between the correlations of the factors, and between their ratios.

A serious difficulty at once presents itself. Whereas a reasonably good estimate of g could be obtained from batteries which differed greatly in their test composition, the primary mental abilities discovered so far require tests of a far more specific type for their definition. It will therefore not be easy to find batteries which, whilst differing in content to suit the cultural requirements of particular racial groups, yet remain equally diagnostic of a given primary mental ability. Nor will it be easy, as we shall see, to construct tests for each primary mental ability which are culturally neutral. Acceptance of the Thurstone theory therefore virtually rules out the possibility of valid inter-racial comparisons of a quantitative kind, at least in the present stage of our knowledge.

The trend in the evolution of the concept of intelligence therefore favours a qualitative rather than a quantitative approach to the study of the intellectual capacities of different racial and cultural groups. The patterns of primary mental abilities and their determinants, rather than differences in hypothetical levels, emerge as the proper objectives of investigation. Quantitative *techniques*, such as multiple-factor analysis, are of course appropriate to this study. By means of this powerful weapon it should be possible to discover not only the basic constituents of intelligence in any given case, but also its cultural and genetic determinants. It should reveal where the current racial strengths and weaknesses lie, and in what direction control-group investigations might ultimately be undertaken.

The research worker need not be deterred by the fact that the Thurstone theory is not yet generally accepted, and may have to be modified in the light of further research data. Quite apart from its theoretical merits or demerits, it favours the formulation of a research programme which commends itself to common sense, in that it proposes the intensive study of the thing to be compared, before comparisons are undertaken.

What kind of tests should be used?

Even if we assume that educability is best assessed in terms of g, it does not follow that tests which are valid measures of this factor in a European group are equally valid in groups with a different cultural background.

As each test performance is, in Spearman's view, the product of both g and of one or more special factors, a poor scope might be due either to a low level of g, or to weakness in respect of the special factors, or to both these causes.

As cultural conditioning was held to occur in relation to the s factors and not to g, tests were therefore chosen in such a way as to eliminate specific cultural associations. The following were considered to be the most important of these associations:

(a) complete familiarity with a given language;

(b) knowledge and habits acquired by a specific type of scholastic education;

(c) knowledge and habits acquired by living within a given socio-economic context.

Of these three, the language factor proved the easiest to control, by the elimination of all verbal material from the tests. The full implications of educational and socio-economic conditioning were not as readily appreciated. Testers were usually satisfied when they had excluded scholastic skills (such as writing, calculating, reading) which the two groups had not had an equal opportunity to acquire, and when representations of objects in common use in one culture (such as dimes, apartment houses, cabs) had been replaced by their appropriate equivalents in another. Consequently, tests involving the use of blocks or formboards, perceptual tests using diagrammatic material, tests which set problems through the medium of pictorial representations of objects familiar to a particular culture, were considered to be valid for inter-racial comparisons. Cultural associations go far deeper than content, however, and far deeper than the mental habits established by school education. They affect manipulative habits, symbolic reactions, possibly the entire approach to and interpretation of the perceptual world. Current research work on the aptitude testing of African mineworkers and non-European operatives in the clothing industry presents ample evidence in support of this contention.

1. Use of pencil and paper. Tests which exclude written responses or verbal material nevertheless frequently make use of paper for the presentation of problems (pictorial, diagrammatic, mazes). They may require candidates to answer by underlining, placing a cross between brackets, tracing a path, or dividing an area. The use of pencil and paper for any purpose whatever is not permissible unless the groups to be compared have had an equal amount of schooling. Unfamiliarity with pencil and paper as a medium of expression is very obvious in most non-European groups in South Africa, even those who have had a little school education in the Grades or Standards 1 and 2. African schooling in these standards is at a low level, and the necessary basic materials are often lacking. Children often use slates, and where pencil and paper are available, the opportunities of becoming fully conversant with their use are still limited. Some evidence will be presented in Section III [not included in this excerpt] to show that pencil-and-paper test performance tends to be inferior in non-European groups, even when intelligence is not greatly involved in the test performance.

2. Use of pictorial material. Many testers have resorted to pictorial material, not only because it could set a problem without the use of language, but also because the appropriate cultural note could be introduced. Thus the Directorate for the Selection of

Personnel of the War Office made a 'cultural translation' of the Bennet Mechanical Comprehension Test, in which men operating pulleys are replaced by women drawing water from a deep well, and loads suspended from a beam resting on the shoulders of two men are replaced by pots, or sheafs of grass or bundles of faggots, carried on the heads of native women. Classification tests are also frequently used in which native dwellings, utensils, or musical instruments, domestic animals, plants, etc., are the items between which meaningful relations are to be established. An absurdities test can be given by making a foal follow a cow, or by making water in an irrigation furrow flow uphill. All these tests overlook the fact that the picture, particularly one printed on paper, is a highly conventional symbol, which the child reared in Western culture has learned to interpret because he is confronted with pictures from his earliest days, gets much of his pre-school education from picture-books and toys with pictures on them, and is encouraged to draw pictures for himself. To make the object pictured culturally meaningful is of little avail, if pictorial representation itself is unfamiliar, and if it does not evoke the attitude of interpretation which a European group automatically assumes. In our battery of tests for African mineworkers, we used the Kohs' Blocks test technique to make the candidates reproduce some typical native cultural patterns and familiar objects, such as a native hut and an earthenware pot with conventional pattern. Before a candidate attempted to reproduce a pattern, he was asked to say what the pictures represented. Very few could identify the hut, and a large number also failed to recognize the pot. Had these two objects been presented pictorially in a complete setting (say a kraal scene) recognition might have been easier. But as pictures by themselves, cut out of cardboard, they were apprehended as pieces of coloured cardboard, and no more. In the same battery, a mechanical-aptitude test was included which required the candidates to assemble a model of a cocopan with which they were familiar, as it is in common use in the mines, though there are a number of different types. To guide them in this task they were provided with a photograph of the model, in which the relationship of the various parts was distinctly shown. Virtually none of the candidates was able to guide his assembly by means of the photographic details. Attempts were made which to the onlooker bore little or no resemblance to the model in the photograph. In many instances it was clear that the photograph was not being used at all, and that construction was guided by images of the particular type with which the candidate was familiar on the job. Those who did attempt to use the photograph as a guide were apparently unable to break it down imaginatively into its constituent elements or to note the rather obvious relatedness of the parts.

3. Use of non-representational drawings. Non-representational drawings are used in the form of line drawings, geometric figures, coloured patterns, in such tests as Progressive Matrices, Kohs' Block Designs, Gottschaldt Figures, Porteus Maze Test, paper formboards, form relations tests, etc. The non-European with a limited scholastic background has some difficulty in appreciating the purport of the figures and designs presented in these tests, despite the fact that he uses abstract design in decorating the walls of dwellings or objects in daily use, and in making beadwork or other ornaments. Part of this difficulty may be due to mode of presentation on paper; but one suspects that more fundamental factors are involved. In daily use such designs are part of the objects decorated, and are never seen as entities by themselves. Though obviously they are constructed piece by piece and step by step, the pattern as a whole and in relation to the object decorated is no doubt present in the mind of the decorator all the time; it is unlikely ever to be studied analytically, or to be built up into an aggregate or mosaic of separate units. That, however, is the task which is set in virtually all the tests using diagrammatic or pattern material. Meaningful wholes, in terms of background-foreground articulation, 'good continuation', 'good shape', etc. (16), are ignored, and the closure principle may have only limited application. Most of the patterns in the Matrix Test, for instance, have a logical, rather than an organismic, unity. The use of patterns and colours drawn from native culture had no noticeable effect on test performance, presumably because the test situation demanded an attitude, or perceptual habits, not naturally associated with these patterns in their proper context.

4. Appreciation of spatial relations. The appreciation of spatial relations, divorced from culturally meaningful wholes, is closely related to the use of abstract designs or diagrammatic material in tests. In reproducing a given pattern by arranging blocks on the card presenting the pattern, African mineworkers frequently inverted or arranged the blocks at a different angle. In an adaptation of the Matrix Test in which we used patterns on the wall of a model hut, the correct piece to complete a pattern was sometimes chosen but placed upside down or on its side in the appropriate space on the wall. An extraordinary feature of these solutions was that the candidates, on being asked whether they were sure that they had correctly completed their assignment, appeared to be quite satisfied with their effort. It is likely, therefore, that the task which they set themselves was different from that which they were set by the tester; that they dealt with certain features of the situation and ignored others; that spatial position in a test which was abstract anyway did not appear to matter. In our European culture, orientation with reference to the four main points of the compass, or to the vertical–horizontal axes of the body, is an accepted feature of daily life. We take rectangularity in our buildings, in the positioning of windows, in our books and writing-paper, very much for granted. The African domestic servant however, after dusting the pictures on the walls, tends to leave them at any odd angle without noting anything wrong. Position within space as a separate entity is not, as a rule, abstracted from his holistic perception of reality. Hence tests which assume this habit of mind, or which require facility in this mode of thinking, place the non-European, who through lack of early contact with European culture has not acquired this analytic approach, at a distinct disadvantage. Even if he does not completely misapprehend what is required of him in the test, he is slow in the mental manipulation of the unfamiliar material. It is instructive to watch the adult tribal African's approach to a form-board test. Shapes are tried out in holes where they could not possibly fit. He appears to be unable to visualize the possible spatial positions of the blocks and proceeds by a process of trial and error. If he has a triangular block in his hands, with apex pointing away from him, and the appropriate space in the board has the apex towards him, he may not appreciate at once that the difference is only one of spatial orientation and not one of shape. In fact the correct triangle, held with the apex pointing away from the body, may appear as inappropriate to him for that particular hole as, say, a diamond-shaped piece. Hence his performance in form-boards, more particularly in the paper variety, in form-relations tests, or even in the Kohs' Block Design Test, tends to be low.

5. *Manipulation*. Many of the performance tests used for intelligence testing involve some degree of manipulative skill which, though not of a high order, may nevertheless account for some of the test variance. An element of clumsiness is often apparent in African children who have not had much opportunity to play with blocks or jig-saw puzzles. In adults used to heavy manual labour, this is even more apparent. A good deal of fumbling may occur when picking up pieces or placing them in their appropriate spaces. When two or more pieces go into one space, African candidates are sometimes inclined to force a piece home when any 'feel' for what constitutes a good fit would have told them that they were trying the wrong piece.

It might be argued that the handicaps experienced by non-Europeans in attempting to cope with non-verbal and performance tests of intelligence derive less from culturally determined associations and habits, than from a basic inability to manipulate symbols, to think conceptually, and to handle abstract relations. This is unlikely, as there is ample evidence that within their own cultural context they are able to do all these things.

Spoken and written language involves symbolic activity of a much higher order than pictorial representation, and Africans are great linguists, even though their languages had, until recently, no written form. Since orthographies have been developed, they have had no difficulty in assimilating them, nor have they been backward in acquiring knowledge of European languages. Many an African school child will know English and Afrikaans in addition to two Bantu languages, and will master some Latin on top of that as well.

There are African tribal games which resemble 'noughts and crosses', draughts, and chess, and one game, involving the movement of stones along rows of holes, which is quite incomprehensible to the European.

It is possible, however, that their thought is holistic, rather than analytic; that their mental processes tend towards the 'minimum simplicity of complete uniformity' rather than the 'maximum simplicity of perfect articulation', two concepts discussed by Koffka (17) in his analysis of perceptual organization; or that their mental function is integrated rather than unintegrated, a distinction defined by Jaensch (18) and applied by him to individual, cultural, and racial differences. Only impressionistic evidence is available on this non-analytic element in the thought processes of Africans, and no evidence at all to indicate whether its origins are genetic or cultural.

It is obvious that research work into the perceptual, manipulative, and problem-solving habits of various racial groups, with special emphasis on cultural determination, is badly needed.

Until more facts are available from studies of this kind, it will not be possible adequately to control the cultural factor in tests to be used for inter-racial comparisons of educability.

Test administration

Though verbal material can be excluded from test performance, it is difficult to dispense with the use of language in test administration. The use of English or other European language is justified only if both groups are equally familiar with it. The exclusion of verbal material from the test itself suggests that this is generally not the case. If the test instructions are translated into the vernacular, it may be difficult to equate the amount and equivalence of the information which the two groups are given, more particularly if circumlocutions are required for the one to express concepts which are more appropriate to the other. The use of interpreters to give the vernacular instructions is inadvisable. Experience has shown that they do not stick to their brief. The European tester should himself be perfectly fluent in the native tongue, or else a properly trained non-European tester should be used. There remains mime as a medium for test administration. That it can be successfully used for inter-racial testing will be shown in Section III [not included here]. Difficulties arise only when the tests are of a more advanced kind, involving higher mental processes. Thus it was found extraordinarily difficult in an associative learning test to indicate to African mineworkers by means of gestures that they had to memorize the connexion between certain shapes and symbols or to make them switch from repetitive to progressive series on a counting frame. When mime is used, it is as well to explain briefly to the candidates the reason for this unusual mode of communication. Without such explanation they tend to adopt an unfavourable attitude, believing the testers to be unfriendly, or wondering why they are not being treated as ordinary people. Such an explanation can be given by any means which are practicable. If group comparisons are to be made, it is of course essential that test instructions should be given through the medium of mime to *both* groups. Mime is not easily standardized. Variations are likely to occur, not only from tester to tester but also in the same tester from day to day. The mimed instructions must therefore be very carefully worked out, and in the case of control-group studies should be given by the same person. An attempt at more perfect standardization of mime by means of cine films and lantern slides will be referred to in Section III [not included here].

Attitude towards the test situation

Attitudinal factors are serious disturbers of test performance and very difficult to control. First and foremost we should be sure that motivation is constant. For a number of reasons it is virtually impossible to equate motivation in different cultural groups. The competitive spirit is not as strong in non-European as in European groups, where it is one of the chief cultural manifestations. The non-European will therefore not be greatly concerned about doing well in order to beat his fellows, unless of course he has acquired the European outlook. Doing well in the test for its own sake is likely to occur only when the purpose of testing and its full implications are appreciated. The uneducated non-European has very little notion of what it is all about, and those who are educated know only too well from past experience that conclusions unfavourable to their racial or cultural group are likely to be drawn from the findings. This produces attitudes varying from outright hostility and refusal to do the tests, to going through the motions without making much effort, or to an uneasiness which by its inhibiting effect impairs the efficiency of thought. The use of a tester belonging to their own race does not materially alter the attitude of this test-conscious group. As part of the test situation he is equally suspect. In groups where hostility is absent, an inhibitory effect on performance may nevertheless be operative as a result of the awe which the novel test situation or the strange tester inspires in the minds of people who have never gone through anything of the kind before, not even a school examination, to which everyone in a European group tends to get inured. An important aspect of the mental set required for examination writing is the need to maintain attention at a high pitch of concentration, whilst working at high speed. This does not come easily to the African, in whose culture speed plays no part, who likes to take his time over things, who is seldom called upon to concentrate his thoughts on one problem to the exclusion of everything else and never required to combine speed with concentration for a prolonged period without some relaxation of effort. That the non-European does not respond well to tests in which the speed factor plays a part is demonstrated by research data quoted in Section III [not included here]. Whether this is due to cultural conditioning, to a temperamental difference, or to a genetic limitation in intellectual efficiency cannot be stated with certainty; but it is a reasonable assumption that cultural factors play some part. Until research data are available on this point, the control of this mental-set factor compels the use of tests in which the score can be stated in terms of quality of performance rather than of speed. As this is often not practicable, tests in which the score is based on performance put up within given time-limits may be used as a compromise.

Temperamental factors

It is possible that the inability of many non-European groups to work continuously at high speed may be derived from temperamental differences which have a constitutional basis. Such a constitutional factor may also play a part (19) in determining capacity for sustained effort, although physical condition, incentives and motivation generally account for the major differences in drive. Virtually nothing is known of inter-racial differences in temperament, partly because the concepts of temperament and personality have not yet been properly defined by general psychology; but chiefly because of the extreme difficulty of unravelling the genetic components from a form of human behaviour which more than any other is socially conditioned. Here, then, is another psychological field which eagerly awaits development. Research could usefully be undertaken *pari-passu* with the study of genetic intellectual potentialities.

School education

Allowance is generally made for the effects of schooling on test performance by eliminating tests for which such scholastic skills as reading, writing, and arithmetic are required. As schooling also improves familiarity with pictorial representation, the use of pencil and paper, the perception of abstract spatial relations, manipulative skills and habits of work and attention, the control of the educational factor cannot be achieved merely by choosing tests without an obvious scholastic content. Regardless of test medium, the groups to be compared should have had an equivalent amount of schooling from equally well-trained teachers. The need for comprehensive control is well demonstrated by Dent's (20) study of the test performance of three groups of 12- to 14-year-old Zulu school children. These groups, equated for age and tested through the medium of the Zulu language, differed chiefly in the amount of schooling which they had received, though also in the amount of contact with urban European culture. Group I was a rural group which had received no school education at all and was tested in the kraals. Group II had attended only rural African schools where the opportunities for contact with European culture are limited. The children in group III were all in town schools and lived in town locations. The test results are given in Table 1.

The superiority of the school-going groups over the non-school-going groups is marked and consistent, and cannot be due to general environmental factors only, as these would not be greatly different for the school-going and non-school-going country children. Nor is it likely that only parents with superior native endowment are sufficiently progressive to send their children to school. Only 38 per cent of African children of school-going age in the Union go to school, and of this group only 16 per cent proceed beyond Standard II, limitation of opportunity, the persistence of tribal customs and economic considerations being the determining factors.

The extensive control of the educational factor which appears to

S. Biesheuvel

be desirable cannot, however, be achieved, unless the two races to be compared share a common culture or one has thoroughly assimilated the culture of the other and enjoys equality of opportunity within it. As these conditions cannot be satisfied in the majority of inter-racial intelligence studies, the use of the control-group technique is once again found to be impracticable.

Table 1
Comparison of the Performance of Zulu Children (a) Without School Education, (b) With Country-School Education and (c) With Town-School Education – in a Number of Performance Tests of Intelligence

Test	Group I (N = 40)		Group II (N = 40)		Group III (N = 40)	
	Mean	S.D.	Mean	S.D.	Mean	S.D.
Mare and Foal Test	35·4	10·6	46	7·2	45·3	7·9
Healy Picture Completion, I	58·5	51·3	145·3	92·3	161·5	91·2
Mannikin Test	2·5	1·3	2·7	1·1	3·4	2·4
Profile Test	3·1	1·4	3·1	1·1	3·7	·9
Goddard Formboard	29	6·7	16·2	10·5	14·5	7·6
Five Figure Formboard	18·4	12·9	28·6	14·8	33·1	12·9
Dearborn Formboard	6·1	3·6	11·3	3·1	11·4	3·8
Cube Construction Test	5·2	2·5	8·6	3·4	9·9	4·3
Kohs' Blocks Test	9	6·5	12·1	6·2	20·6	11·1

A high score indicates a superior performance, except in the case of the Goddard Formboard.

Factors which influence the development of genetic capacity

Intelligence-test performances can be affected both extrinsically and intrinsically by environmental influences. Extrinsic factors are those which affect performance only, leaving intelligence itself unaltered. Intrinsic factors are those which influence the development of intelligence itself, either qualitatively or quantitatively. Qualitative modifications to be taken care of in the measurement of inter-racial differences have already been discussed in relation to the cultural conditioning of modes of perception, thought, and action. Factors exercising intrinsic quantitative effects remain to be dealt with. Their discussion is hampered by the fact that no finality has been reached in the nature-nurture controversy.

71

Though we can state with certainty that genetic capacity can be completely realised only under optimum environmental conditions, we do not know which aspects of the environment have the most potent effect, at which point in the life-cycle these effects are most crucial, and to what extent effective intelligence can be reduced by successive degrees of shortfall from the environmental optimum. The following factors are, however, known to have some significance:

1. Nutrition. Little is known about the effects of malnutrition on the growth of intelligence; but certain physiological and clinical facts suggest that it is a factor which cannot be ignored. In a general way there is a relationship between degree of intelligence and development of the central nervous system. Anything which impairs this development should therefore adversely affect intellectual growth. The central nervous system has been shown to be remarkably resistant to underfeeding during the development stage. It grows at the expense of other organs. For qualitative malnutrition, more particularly deficiency of the vitamin B complex in the diet, there can be no such compensation. The body does not synthesise these substances for itself, and any lack of them will immediately affect nervous growth, which is particularly dependent on an adequate supply of nicotinic acid. Severe shortage of this substance in the diet causes pellagra, a deficiency disease which may be accompanied by marked mental disturbances. It is probable that lesser degrees of deficiency produce sub-clinical conditions in which impairment of the same type occurs. Shortage of the B complex in the diet of the mother during gestation and again during the lactation period is virtually certain to have a permanent effect on nervous growth in the foetus and neonate. The genetic intellectual potentialities in such a case may never be fully realized, even if considerable improvement in the nutritional condition occurs at a later stage. Corroborative evidence is provided by experiments on rats, which showed that nursing rats, suckled by vitamin B-depleted mothers, had a much lower maze-learning ability than a normal control group (21, 22).

Non-European groups who live in close association with Europeans are on the whole the poorer section of the community. Even those communities whose way of life has been little affected by Western civilization have often a precarious existence, as is indicated by the high incidence of deficiency disease found among them. One would therefore expect to find a lower level of intelligence – irrespective of test medium and condition – in any group which has been unable to maintain normal nutritional conditions.

As the germ plasm itself is not affected by malnutrition, such inferiority is not genetic. Though irreversible in the individual, it would gradually disappear in the group with improvement in its nutritional status.

2. Parental care. That man does not live by bread alone applies as much to the infant as to the adult. Just as the body needs certain foods for adequate growth, so the mind needs its sustenance. It has been shown that children on whom care and affection are bestowed develop more rapidly intellectually than those to whom proper parental solicitude is denied (23). If this deprivation is prolonged beyond the second year of life, it is probable that retardation will be permanent (24). Parental attitude towards children varies greatly from culture to culture. In non-European groups whose cultural life has been disrupted, who have not yet acquired European ways, and whose socio-economic position is too precarious to enable them to devote time to their children, impairment of intellectual growth as a result of lack of parental care is inevitable.

3. Parental intelligence and home environment. Optimum intellectual growth can be ensured only if, in addition to the proper bodily and emotional care, the child receives adequate stimulation from its environment. Among the most important of these stimuli are the personalities of the parents, whose intelligence, education, interests, and attitudes have been shown to exercise an intrinsic environmental effect. The diversity of objects in the home, the variety of experiences to which the child is subjected, the frequency and quality of its contacts with other children and people, are also significant influences.

It is only rarely that the non-European child can enjoy opportunities in respect of this type of environmental stimulation which is normal for the average European child. [. . .]

References

1. FERGUSON, G. O., 'The psychology of the Negro', *Archives of Psychology*, vol. 5 (1916) no. 36.

2. HERSKOVITS, M. J., 'On the relation between Negro–White mixture and standing in intelligence tests', *Pedagogical Seminary*, vol. 33 (1926), pp. 30–42.

3. PETERSEN, J., and LANIER, L. H., 'Studies in the Comparative Abilities of Whites and Negroes', *Mental Measurement Monograph*, no. 5 (1929).

4. KLINEBERG, O., *Negro Intelligence and Selective Migration*, Columbia University Press, 1935.

5. WITTY, P. A., and JENKINS, M. A., 'Intrarace testing and Negro intelligence', *Journal of Psychology*, vol. 1 (1936), pp. 179–92.

6. GRAHAM, J. L., 'A quantitive comparison of national responses of Negro and White college students', *Journal of Social Psychology*, vol. 1 (1930), p. 97.

7. FISCK, M. L., The Educability of the South African Native, *Research Series, S.A. Council for Educational and Social Research*, no. 8 (1939), Pretoria.

8. BURKS, B. S., 'A summary of literature on the determiners of the I.Q. and the E.Q.' *Twenty-seventh Yearbook of the National Society for the Study of Education*, part 2, 1928, 248.

9. BURKS, B. S., 'Intelligence: Its nature and nurture', *Thirty-ninth Yearbook of the National Society for the Study of Education*, part I, 1940, pp. 257–69.

10. WOODWORTH, R. S., *Heredity and Environment*, Social Science Research Council, New York, 1941.

11. SPEARMAN, C., *The Nature of Intelligence and the Principles of Cognition*, Macmillan, 1923.

12. SPEARMAN, C., *The Abilities of Man*, Macmillan, 1927.

13. THURSTONE, L. L., *The Vectors of Mind*, University of Chicago Press, 1935.

14. THURSTONE, L. L., Primary Mental Abilities, *Psychometric Monographs*, no. 1 (1938).

15. THURSTONE, L. L., *Multiple Factor Analysis*, University of Chicago Press, 1947.

16. KOFFKA, K., *Principles of Gestalt Psychology*, Kegan Paul, 1936.

17. Op. cit., pp. 171–4.

18. JAENSCH, E., *Eidetic Imagery*, Kegan Paul, 1930.

19. BIESHEUVEL, S., 'The nature of temperament', *Transactions of the Royal Society of South Africa*, vol. 23 (1936), p. 311.

20. DENT, G. R., 'An investigation into the applicability of certain performance and other mental tests to Zulu children: Educational adaptations in a changing society', in E. G. Malherbe, (ed.), *Report of New Education Fellowship Conference*, Cape Town, 1937, p. 456.

21. MAURER, S., and TSAI, L. S., 'Vitamin B deficiency in nursing young rats and learning ability', *Science*, no. 701 (1929); 'Vitamin B de-

ficiency and learning ability', *Journal of Comparative Psychology*, vol. 14 (1930), pp. 51–62; 'The effect of partial depletion of vitamin B complex upon learning ability in rats', *Journal of Nutrition*, no. 4 (1931), pp. 507–16.

22. BERNHARDT, K. S., 'The effect of vitamin B deficiency during nursing on subsequent learning in the rat', *Journal of Comparative Psychology*, vol. 17 (1934), pp. 123–48.

23. BUHLER, C., *From Birth to Maturity*, Kegan Paul, 1936.

24. MURCHISON, C., *Handbook of Child Psychology*, Clark University Press, 1931, p. 422.

4 P. E. Vernon

Abilities and Educational Attainments in an East African
Environment

P. E. Vernon, 'Abilities and educational attainments in an East African
environment', *Journal of Special Education*, vol. 1 (1967), pp. 335–45.

It is generally believed by psychologists and anthropologists that
inferences regarding racial or national differences in intelligence
cannot be drawn from the application of American and British
tests to members of other ethnic groups. However, as the writer
has argued elsewhere (Vernon, 1965b), there is more justification
for using such tests to study the effects of extreme environmental
differences on intellectual and educational development. Hence
he has undertaken a series of cross-cultural researches in which
the same battery of individual and group tests has been applied to
samples of boys aged 11 years in England, in the Hebrides, in
Jamaica (Vernon, 1965a), to Canadian Indians and Eskimos
(Vernon, 1966) and now in East Africa. The tests, which last four
to five hours in all, were chosen to cover as wide a range of
abilities as possible, since it is the pattern of scores on different
abilities rather than the overall level or general intelligence which
is of interest. In all the non-English groups, English was the main
medium of school instruction, though not the mother tongue.
Hence by the age of 11 the boys had acquired sufficient fluency to
understand instructions and give verbal responses without the
use of an interpreter.

The results are considered to be meaningful for yet another
reason, namely that the developing countries of Africa, the
West Indies and elsewhere, together with incompletely acculturated minorities such as Indians and Eskimos, are aiming at
economic viability and self-sufficiency. In other words, they wish
to achieve civilizations comparable to those of the Western
technological nations, but are severely handicapped at present
by lack of intelligent, well-educated man-power to provide the
necessary professionals, teachers, administrators and technicians.

Under these circumstances it becomes reasonable to study their performance on Western-type tests, which are known to be relevant to educational and vocational success, in an attempt to determine their present strengths and weaknesses and to point to the environmental handicaps that must be remedied if they are to make more rapid progress.

In the East African countries of Uganda, Kenya and Tanzania, as in many other ex-British territories that have recently achieved independence, the educational system which provides access to most skilled and high-grade jobs is largely inherited from the British pattern. Primary schooling is available to 50 per cent or so of children aged 6 and up (more in the towns, less in agricultural and desert areas). It lasts for seven years; but many enter late or withdraw for, or repeat, a year or two. Hence the range of ages in the top class may be from 12 to 17 and over. Owing to the large drop-out, and to restricted entry to higher classes, roughly one half complete the primary courses and are eligible to take a selection examination for entry to secondary school, to teacher training and certain other options. Despite tremendous expansion of education and particularly of secondary schooling in recent years, there are secondary places only for some 10 per cent of school-leavers, i.e. about $2\frac{1}{2}$ per cent of the child population. The examination consists of one or more tests in English and arithmetic, constructed by the Ministry of Education (sometimes also a General Knowledge and, in Tanzania, a Swahili test).

The secondary curriculum is entirely geared to passing the General Certificate of Education – a series of examinations set and marked by an Examining Board in England, which are parallel to the examinations taken by pupils in English secondary schools. Success in the G.C.E. provides entry to the university, to higher-grade teaching, the civil service and other jobs which may pay more in a month than the average, educationally unqualified, citizen is likely to make in a year. Hence there is tremendous pressure throughout the educational system, and extremely high motivation among the pupils, to pass examinations, in particular the secondary school selection and the G.C.E. Partly for this reason, partly because primary teachers themselves mostly possess a low standard of education and partly because most teaching and almost all examinations have to be conducted in a foreign language – English – there is an extreme emphasis on formal learning and memory work. There is much talk among politicians of the need for an education which will be of more benefit to the $97\frac{1}{2}$ per cent who will never reach secondary school, or the 20 per cent or so who complete primary schooling but then have little or no opportunity to go further. But it is difficult to see how the system can be reformed when there is such urgent need for the $2\frac{1}{2}$ per cent to achieve an English-type academic secondary qualification and the financial rewards for this achievement are so attractive.

The Sample

Uganda itself is an almost wholly agricultural country, inhabited by numerous tribes, each with its own dialect. Because there is no common language, English is generally introduced as early as possible in the primary school, though practices vary and in many country schools the local vernacular is used in the lower classes. In the towns, however, where there are also many people of Asian descent, Africans are engaged in the whole range of occupations normal to an urban community. Particularly is this true of Kampala, the capital city, which also adjoins the capital of the Buganda, the largest and most advanced of the tribes. Here too is established the oldest university of East Africa, Makerere College, with a mixed expatriate, African and Asian staff.

With the assistance of the Faculty of Education of the university and the kind permission of the Ministry of Education, a sample of fifty African boys aged 12 years was tested in two primary schools, during September and October, 1966, by the writer and his wife and two senior university student assistants. (It should be noted that exact records of ages are not usually available; all one can do is to take the school's estimates.) One of the schools was in a poor central area, but it has a high reputation and can afford to select its intake; eleven out of nineteen fathers were in clerical or higher-grade jobs. The other school was on the outskirts of the city and accepted all-comers whose parents could afford the fees of up to £2 a year. They came mostly from nearby housing estates and from the surrounding countryside. The overall parental occupational distribution was:

	per cent
Professional – lawyer, university lecturer, teacher	6
Clerical, supervisory – police inspector, probation officer, bank clerk, small business owner	28
Skilled trades – laboratory assistant, painter, tailor	20
Police, driver, small shopkeeper	32
Peasant, night watchman	14

Clearly such a sample is considerably superior to the East African population in general. But it would have been impossible to secure anything like a representative sample of boys in any one African country, both because of tribal and linguistic heterogeneity and because of the fact that scarcely 30 per cent of this age group even attend school. However the sample would be fairly typical of the whole range of urbanized Africans. Also it should be noted that, according to researches by Irvine (1966) in Rhodesia, and others, lower correlations exist between socioeconomic class and abilities or attainments among Africans than in Western countries. This may be because the children of well-off parents know that they are comfortably situated and are therefore less strongly motivated to learn than children of poorer families, for whom education is valued pre-eminently as a means to greater security and prosperity.

Among 56 per cent of the boys the mother tongue was Luganda; among the remainder 15 other tribal languages were represented. Only in 26 per cent of homes was any English spoken, and in none was it the dominant medium. An attempt was made by the interviewer to elicit household compositions, though the intricacies of African family relationships are notorious. However, it appeared that in this sample 52 per cent of households approximated to the Western nuclear family, consisting of father, mother and siblings, with sometimes a few additional blood relatives or servants. The boys' teachers were generally aware of, and disapproved of, polygamous households. In a few cases one or both parents were dead, or the boy was living with an uncle or grandparent. Length of schooling could not be elicited reliably, but the majority had started at 6 or 7 years. They were mostly now in the 5th or 6th Standards, though four of the brightest had reached Standard 7 and seven of the most retarded were in Standard 4.

Tests and Results: Educational and Verbal Tests

On the basis of the results of a representative sample of boys in
S.E. England, the scores on every test were converted to Deviation
Quotients with a mean for Whites of 100 and standard deviation
15. The 90th, 50th and 10th percentile Ugandan 'quotients' are
shown in Table 1. For comparison are included the medians of:

Table 1
Deviation Quotients for Three Groups of Boys

	Ugandan 90th 50th 10th Percentiles			Canadian Indian Medians	Urban Jamaican Medians
Arithmetic	96	86	77	76	86
English reading, usage	89	80	74	78	88
Spelling	104	90	78	85	95
Word learning	115	94	66	75	97
Information learning	94	78	66	72	83
Terman vocabulary	68	57	—	70	74
Concept formation	100	88	77	91	94
Piaget total score	96	73	64	73	97
Shipley abstraction	95	84	72	82	—
Matrices	93	81	68	81	83
Porteus mazes	111	99	80	98	97
Picture recognition	95	79	66	91	—
Gottschaldt figures	108	94	82	86	97
Reproduction of designs	113	93	76	91	102
Kohs' blocks	91	78	70	88	84
Formboard	97	80	54	85	80
Draw-a-Man (Witkin)	124	97	80	101	104
Rorschach N	128	115	93	125	—
If I Could Fly N	119	100	84	91	—
Tin Can N	110	98	86	112	—
Rorschach U%	97	69	50	74	—
If I Could Fly U%	114	94	84	75	—
Tin Can U%	108	94	71	83	—
Incomplete drawings	118	97	82	91	—

1. Forty Canadian Indian boys who live on reservations in
Alberta prairie land but may be regarded as almost equally
handicapped linguistically.
2. Twenty of a sample of fifty West Indian boys who had taken

most, though not all, of the same tests. They were chosen because they lived in Kingston, Jamaica, and were quite similar in socio-economic distribution to the Ugandans. They too had language difficulties, though less severe, since Jamaican vernacular is a kind of 'pidgin' or 'Creole' very different from standard English.

All groups are very low on Terman–Merrill Vocabulary, the Ugandans being right off the scale with a median raw score of three to four words. On straightforward group tests of English reading comprehension, usage and vocabulary they are much better, and better still in spelling. Similarly Ugandans and Jamaicans are fairly good at Arithmetic (a group test of mechanical sums and elementary processes) with scores of 86. Indians are much lower (76), probably because they are taught by the 'New Maths' approach, which is much too verbose for them.

It will be seen that Ugandan schools do a good job of teaching children the more mechanical aspects of the 3 Rs, but that there is a basic difficulty of understanding and thinking in a second language; and this helps to explain why so few are capable of secondary school work and then only of a very formal nature. The contrast is further emphasized by two classroom learning tests. Word Learning involves studying and reproducing in writing a list of twenty simple verbs. Ugandans and Jamaicans score 94 and 97 – little below English boys. However the test also involves willingness to concentrate and the Indians, being more suspicious of White testers, drop to 75. In Information Learning, a series of fifteen simple statements is read out twice, slowly, and after each reading, questions on each statement are given in a different order. For example, 'the first three letters on the bottom row of a typewriter are Z, X and C'; this involves understanding of sentences, as well as memorization, and all three groups do worse than on other educational tests.

Conceptual Tests

The Concept Formation test required sorting and resorting twenty toy objects into groups of things alike, and labelling the groups. Scores were based on number of objects per group and the abstractness of the label. Both the categories and associations were much the same as those of English boys. Though poor vocabulary was evidenced, the average score of 88 did not suggest any special difficulty in 'abstracting', which is sometimes attributed to African peoples. This confirms Price-William's (1962) investigation in Nigeria of classifications of familiar objects. Similarly Bruner and Olver (1966) report well-developed equivalence grouping of pictures of common objects among Senegalese children who are attending school, though not among unschooled or bush children.

Conceptual Development was tested by thirteen sets of items derived from Piaget's writings (cf. Vernon, 1965a), including conservation of liquids, plasticene, lengths and areas, number and time concepts, logical inclusion, knowledge of left and right and other orientation tasks. This was one of the weakest performances (73), far lower than that of Jamaicans (97), and it was equally poor among the Indians. The worst deficiencies were in all the conservation tasks, over 50 per cent being non-conservers in every item. To some extent the failure may be attributed to verbal inability, though the tester made every effort to get the tasks across simply and to accept any formulation of the correct response, however halting. Actually the main contrast between Ugandans and Jamaicans lies not so much in linguistic facility as in sophistication. Jamaicans have had far more contact with British and North American cultures and have long outgrown tribalism and multilingualism. Though magical beliefs and superstitions persist, particularly in rural areas of Jamaica, they would certainly play a smaller part than in African thinking. If we follow Piaget's views, we would expect magical beliefs to be linked with non-conservation as aspects of the preoperational stage.

Creativity Tests

Four tests were given individually: (1) three of the Rorschach inkblots; (2) six of Torrance's Incomplete Drawings; (3) verbal responses to: 'What would you do if you had wings and could fly' and (4) 'What could you do with this empty tin can?' The Drawings were scored both for Unusual choice of subject and for Elaboration (combined in Table 1). The other three tests were scored for ideational fluency or number of responses, and for per cent of unusual or clever responses (given by less than 10 per cent of subjects), minus the percentage of perseverative responses.

Both Ugandans and Indians gave numerous Rorschach responses of low quality, almost all Animal or Human Details, with many perseverations and small details. No attempt was made to interpret the responses projectively. The other tests all yield scores within the normal range for Whites, though this was partly because there was no time limit, and considerable pressure was exerted by the tester to elicit responses. Generally it seemed more difficult to get these tests across to Ugandan boys than any others, or to create the desired set. Most of them were unwilling to 'suppose' and notably failed to exploit the possibilities of wings, e.g. for helping others. Likewise, while they found many uses for tin cans they scarcely ever suggested making toys or models, as did English boys. Drawing Test responses, however, were very similar to those of the English.

Inductive Reasoning, Planfulness and Drawing

A version of the Shipley Abstractions test was given, consisting of number, letter and other series items where the subject has to grasp the principle and write the number, letter or word that comes next. The Non-Verbal Matrices test is similar: the subject draws the figure needed to fill the empty space. Both of these are highly g-saturated (in Spearman's sense), or good measures of Thurstone's I- (Induction) factor. The poor performance of Jamaican boys on these, despite their non-verbal nature, led to the hypothesis that such tests measure independent, resourceful thinking. Jamaican upbringing at home and at school appears to reinforce passivity rather than initiative, and the same might be said of East Africans. By contrast, a group of Eskimo boys, whose life in the Arctic must involve far more resourcefulness, scored 93 on these same tests (Vernon, 1966).

Porteus Mazes proved disappointing as a measure of planfulness in the writer's researches, yielding no significant group differences. The Ugandan boys succeeded partly by extreme slowness and caution, partly by frequent breaking of the instruction not to lift the pencil or trace ahead. Draw-a-Man also gave scores within the normal White range in all groups, whether scored by Goodenough's schedule, or by a scale based on Witkin's (1962) work which emphasizes articulation and activity (field independence). The Ugandan drawings showed much the same range as those of English boys from extreme primitiveness to considerable skill and sophistication.

Perceptual and Spatial Abilities

Expatriate teachers in many African countries have commented on the great difficulties of their pupils in interpreting pictures three-dimensionally, whether photographs or line drawings; and research by Hudson (1960), Dawson (1963) and others with perspective drawings and the Kohs' Block test have yielded very low scores. Is this a general deficit in the S- (spatial) or Vz- (visualization) factor? Apparently not, since the Ugandan boys scored well (93 and 94) on two paper-and-pencil tests which normally load highly with this factor. One consisted of several of the Bender–Gestalt designs, plus the two Memory for Designs items from Terman–Merrill, and here the performance was characterized by meticulous attention to detail. More surprising was a version of the Gottschaldt Embedded Figures where a simple figure has to be discriminated within an adjacent complex figure and marked out with colored pencil. Many who failed abysmally on Kohs were quite quick in breaking the complex Gestalt, even when it was presented upside-down.

The writer's Picture Recognition test involved perception of the third dimension in ten drawings (including several of Hudson's). The Ugandan score of 79 was lower than that of any other group. The same was true of Kohs' Blocks (78), although the W.I.S.C. designs were given according to Goldstein's and McConnell's (McConnell, 1954) method, with demonstration after each failure. The majority could copy the block models, but were incapable of breaking down the printed designs and transferring them to the blocks, and many were satisfied with false solutions such as that shown in Figure 1.

Characteristic also were reversals of color or direction, and rotations. One other test was very difficult both for Ugandans and Jamaicans – a speeded formboard which required fitting a set of triangular pieces together to make a number of shapes.

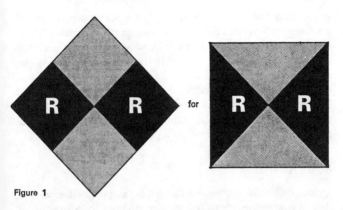

Figure 1

Explanations of this peculiar difficulty have been offered at many levels, one being simply that, unlike Western children, African children up to 6 years would scarcely ever see a picture book or play with blocks and bricks. But this would also be true of Eskimos, who score 92 and 95 on Kohs' and Picture Recognition. Segal, Campbell and Herskovits (1963) stress the effect of an 'uncarpentered' environment on visual illusions. Many Africans live in rounded houses and see curved trees and hills, but little furniture or rectangles. However, the present writer's sample were mostly reared in town houses with rectangular rooms, windows and doors, and some furnishings. More plausible, perhaps, is the suggestion that most African babies are bound to and carried on their mothers' backs for the first year or two; hence not only is their vision restricted (largely to a rounded object), but also they obtain very little manipulative or kinesthetic experience. To this the writer would add the inadequacies of psychomotor experience throughout childhood (cf. Biesheuvel, 1966) and the absence of interest in constructive play or of cultural pressures to practical achievements. Few homes would provide knives and forks, door-knobs, scissors, buttons, pencils or toy objects to manipulate, and African parents seem more apt to frustrate than to encourage curiosity and exploratory activities or to reward the acquisition of skills. Thus to a remarkable extent preschool children are content just to sit doing nothing, and they are notably passive and submissive when school attendance starts. This apparent apathy may also derive in part from poor health conditions and malnutrition – protein deficiency is widespread in Uganda. However, the deficit in practical spatial ability may not be irremediable. In an experiment by McFie (1961), also in Uganda, a group of youths took several of the W.I.S.C. and other tests before and after trade training in a technical school. They greatly improved their scores on Kohs' Blocks and Memory for Designs. In our own group it was noteworthy that almost all boys had achieved complete competence in drawing with a pencil.

Factor Analysis

Irvine (1966) has pointed out that we are not entitled to assume that Western tests measure the same abilities in African as in Western cultures. We can, however, use factor analysis to explore the organization or structure of abilities. Though the correlations from fifty cases are, of course, apt to be unreliable, they should show whether various tests cluster in a manner similar to that observed in their country of origin. Correlations were run between eighteen main tests scores, thirteen Piaget tasks, sixteen creativity measures and assessments of ten environmental variables. Table 2 shows four rotated centroid factors extracted from the main tests, together with economic level and a rating of the boys' initiative in leisure pursuits and vocational aspirations. The loadings of the other variables on these factors were calculated, and those reaching 0·30 or over are listed below. Though there are differences from the analyses made among English boys (Vernon, 1965a), they are quite logical and generally support our interpretations of what the tests measure.

The main difference is that instead of a strong g-factor and subsidiary verbal-educational and spatial-practical abilities, verbal ability is much more distinctive among Ugandans, having no relation at all to Kohs' Blocks and little to Mazes or Formboard. Clearly, non-verbal tests such as Matrices, Draw-a-Man etc. would have even less predictive value for school work than in Western cultures, since this depends so largely on the highly specialized factor of acquiring the English Language. This V-factor shows significant loadings for School Class, Stable Home

Table 2
Rotated Centroid Factors in Main Tests

	Verbal	Induction	Practical	Drawing
Arithmetic	0·573	0·359	0·000	—0·105
English reading, usage	0·839	0·191	—0·024	0·073
Spelling	0·850	0·114	—0·223	0·283
Word learning	0·571	—0·068	0·201	—0·152
Information learning	0·734	—0·116	0·332	—0·120
Terman vocabulary	0·774	0·029	0·074	—0·002
Concept formation	0·334	0·096	0·352	—0·196
Piaget total score	0·490	0·389	0·310	—0·138
Shipley abstraction	0·295	0·675	0·114	0·180
Matrices	0·399	0·682	0·229	—0·026
Porteus Mazes	0·162	0·281	0·552	0·272
Picture recognition	0·266	0·213	0·390	0·093
Gottschaldt figures	0·298	0·125	0·358	0·526
Reproduction of designs	0·446	0·119	0·193	0·506
Kohs' blocks	—0·087	0·382	0·499	0·324
Formboard	0·168	0·163	0·401	0·630
Draw-a-Man (Witkin)	0·373	0·353	—0·098	0·497
Socio-economic level	0·225	0·257	0·550	0·089
Initiative rating	0·220	0·359	0·401	—0·166

Background, Cultural Stimulus in the Home, English Spoken at Home, Purposefulness of Home; also for most of the Piaget items, for fluency and originality in the 'Wings' and 'Tin Can' verbal creativity tests, for Elaboration (but not originality) of incomplete drawings, and not for any Rorschach score.

The nearest to a general intelligence factor has been labelled Induction, since it most strongly loads Abstraction and Matrices. It affects Arithmetic and the Piaget number items, but not other scholastic measures. The only significantly loaded environmental ratings are Buganda versus other tribal affiliations, and boys' Initiative. In the creativity battery, the factor loads Rorschach Animal responses positively, Human responses negatively. Responses to 'Wings' which refer to helping others or to studying things are positive, while responses involving self-enjoyment or profit are negative.

Perceptual, spatial and practical tests fall into two overlapping but distinctive types. Kohs' Blocks, Picture Recognition and Mazes demarcate the 3-dimensional and practical factor discussed above, which also enters into Arithmetic, Information, Concept Formation, Gottschaldt, and all the conservation items but not the other tasks in the Piaget battery. It gives no significant creativity test loadings. On the environmental side, it is strongly loaded with Social class, also with Initiative, Cultural Stimulus and English in the Home. One other large loading is of interest, namely Mischel's (1958) Delayed Gratification test. At the first session each boy was offered a small bar of candy now, or a bar twice the size if he waited till the end of the testing. Only 32 per cent agreed to delay, but they were superior on almost all the practical tests just mentioned, though not on most verbal or inductive tests.

The last major factor involves paper-and-pencil spatial and drawing tests and the Formboard test of perceiving shape combinations, also both Incomplete Drawings scores. It correlates negatively with percent of small Details in Rorschach, but has no considerable loadings with other creativity, nor with any Piaget or any environmental variables.

In England (Vernon, 1965a) the Piaget battery appeared to measure three main components identified as numerical-orientational, conservation and visuospatial. Here the picture is rather different since, as already mentioned, almost all items involve a good deal of Verbal ability, the numerical ones Inductive ability, and the conservation ones Practical ability.There is still something common to most items after these factors are removed, which might be identified as a Concept Development factor. But the residual correlations are small and irregular, suggesting that environmental influences specific to Ugandan upbringing largely affect particular items.

The correlations among the creativity scores are even more discrepant, and though there are some positive residuals among the fluency, or the originality, measures, it would be rash to claim that the tests are valid measuring factors which are really comparable to those underlying the responses of English boys. This is not surprising in view of the writer's suspicions, at the time of testing, that the tests were not working well.

Discussion and Conclusions

For the most part the results confirm those reached with other ethnic groups. They show first that it is misleading to think merely in terms of lowered I.Q. in less advanced cultures. This group is certainly above average for East Africa generally, but the fact that the deviation quotients range around 90 is much less striking than their spread from 57 to 115. Secondly the pattern of high and low performances is quite similar to that of the Jamaicans (with the one exception of Piaget Concept Development) and largely different from that of the Indians. This was unexpected if only because Jamaicans are descended from West, not East, Africans. The rank orders of scores on fourteen tests taken by all three groups (excluding Piaget) give the correlations: East African–Jamaican 0·90, East African–Indian 0·62, Jamaican–Indian 0·65.

Third, it is usually possible to discern cultural influences which plausibly account for the high and low scores, though admittedly impossible to prove which of many complex factors are primarily responsible without much more intensive research. (It must be remembered also that with small samples of boys the median quotients listed in Table 1 are imperfectly reliable. With fifty cases the 5 per cent confidence limit of any median is approximately 4 points.) In this research there are strong indications that poor understanding of English (which depends very little on home environment) is the major educational difficulty and that the methods of teaching develop a remarkable capacity for rote learning. Non-verbal and mathematical thinking are to some extent stimulated by a home that encourages resourcefulness, and the Buganda tribe show some superiority in this respect. The severe deficit among Africans in 3-dimensional perception extends to a variety of tests such as Kohs' Blocks, Mazes, Concept Formation, Piaget conservation and willingness to delay gratification. This is considerably affected by socio-economic and cultural level of the home and can plausibly be attributed to traditional versus more progressive methods of child rearing.

The following implications may be drawn for the educationist. There will be very general learning difficulties among East African pupils, and it will hardly be possible to push up educational standards, or to increase the potential numbers of highgrade personnel, until there are vast improvements in methods of teaching and changes in child-rearing practices which tend to inhibit intellectual development. Improvements in material conditions, health and nutrition would doubtless contribute, but would not be sufficient in themselves. If education must be given in a second language,[1] a very different approach is needed to get pupils to understand and think in English – more active and less mechanical. Interesting and hopeful experiments are being conducted in several Ugandan and Kenyan schools, but they have not yet been adequately followed up. At least as important would seem to be the introduction of more concrete activities to compensate for the inadequacy of psychomotor stimulation at home. Only a few schools seem to be making rudimentary attempts to develop handwork and the visual and constructive arts. No doubt costs are an inhibiting factor, but much could be done with inexpensive materials if the teachers – themselves handicapped in this respect and brought up in the rote learning tradition – could be converted.

References

BIESHEUVEL, S. (1966), 'Some African acculturation problems, with special reference to perceptual and psychomotor skills', Symposium: *The Inter-Relation of Biological and Cultural Adaptation*, Wenner–Gren Foundation.

BRUNER, J. S., and OLVER, R. (1966), *Studies in Cognitive Growth*, Wiley.

DAWSON, J. L. (1963), Psychological effects of social change in a West African community. *Ph.D. thesis, University of Edinburgh*.

HUDSON, W. (1960), 'Pictorial depth perception in sub-cultural groups in Africa', *Journal of Social Psychology*, vol. 52, pp. 209–19.

IRVINE, S. H. (1966), 'Towards a rationale for testing attainments and abilities in Africa', *British Journal of Educational Psychology*, vol. 36, pp. 24–32.

MCCONNELL, J. (1954), 'Abstract behavior among the Tepehuan', *Journal of Abnormal and Social Psychology*, vol. 49, pp. 109–10.

MCFIE, J. (1961), 'The effect of education on African performance on a group of intellectual tests', *British Journal of Educational Psychology*, vol. 31, pp. 232–40.

MISCHEL, W. (1958), 'Father-absence and delay of gratification: cross-cultural comparisons', *Journal of Abnormal and Social Psychology*, vol. 56, pp. 57–61.

1. In Tanzania the situation is worse, since a large proportion of children have first to learn Swahili, and English is their third language.

PRICE-WILLIAMS, D. R. (1962), 'Abstract and concrete modes of classification in a primitive society', *British Journal of Educational Psychology*, vol. 32, pp. 50–61.

SEGALL, M. H., CAMPBELL, D. T., and HERSKOVITS, M. J. (1963), 'Cultural differences in the perception of geometric illusions', *Science*, vol. 139, pp. 769–71.

VERNON, P. E. (1965a), 'Environmental handicaps and intellectual development', *British Journal of Educational Psychology*, vol. 35, pp. 1–12 and 117–26.

VERNON, P. E. (1965b), 'Ability factors and environmental influences', *American Psychologist*, vol. 20, pp. 723–33.

VERNON, P. E. (1966), 'Educational and intellectual development among Canadian Indians and Eskimos', *Educational Review*, pp. 79–91 and 186–95.

WITKIN, H. A., *et al.* (1962), *Psychological Differentiation: Studies of Development*, Wiley.

Part Three Visual Illusions

The issue of nativism versus empiricism, which we met with in the study of intelligence, is focused more sharply in the investigation of visual illusions across the world. The set of articles now introduced are a selection from a sequence of studies brought to bear on the question of visual inference. The sequence dates back to a classic study by Rivers (1905) who had worked with the Todas of Southern India, and before that with inhabitants from the Torres Straits (1901). Rivers' interpretation of his findings favoured the role of experience in the reaction to these visual illusions. A more ambitious project was carried out by Segall, Campbell and Herskovits, which was first reported in an article in *Science* and included here as Reading 5, and later in a book (1966), in which more than a dozen groups in Africa, the Philippines and the United States, were given variations of four basic visual illusions (pictured in the article). The actual hypotheses upon which this study was based are expressed in the opening passages of Reading 6 by Gustav Jahoda. It will be noticed that certain kinds of illusions are predicted as being noticed more by Europeans, and other kinds more by people living in non-urbanized, open environments. In a word, the ecological and cultural environments in which people live are seen as influencing their visual habits. The findings of Segall, Campbell and Herskovits followed more or less the course of their prediction, but, as Reading 6 shows, complications arise. Again, the precise method of instruction shows itself as a variable always to be carefully watched in cross-cultural work. Bonte (1962), working with forest-living Pygmies and agricultural Bashi, in the Congo, found differences, when both groups were compared with Europeans, according to whether the Müller–Lyer illusion was presented in a formboard apparatus as Rivers had employed, or whether he used drawings. Jahoda (Reading 6) records the criticisms of Segall *et al.* of the Bonte article; these criticisms are from their 1966 monograph. Jahoda's line of inquiry centres on the difficulty of illiterates in interpreting 2-dimensional representation from the daily world of 3-dimensional objects. Jahoda's failure with Ghanaian tribes to validate completely the ecological hypothesis is interpreted in the light of this difficulty.

References

BONTE, M. (1962), 'The reaction of two African societies to the Müller–Lyer illusion,' *Journal of Social Psychology*, vol. 58, pp. 265–8.

RIVERS, W. H. R. (1901), 'Vision', in A. C. Haddon, (ed.), *Reports of the Cambridge Anthropological Expedition to the Torres Straits*, vol. 2, part 1, Cambridge University Press.

RIVERS, W. H. R. (1905), 'Observations on the senses of the Todas', *British Journal of Psychology*, vol. 1, pp. 321–96.

SEGALL, M. H., CAMPBELL, D. T., and HERSKOVITS, M. J. (1966), *The Influence of Culture on Visual Perception*, Bobbs-Merrill.

5 M. H. Segall, D .T. Campbell and M. J. Herskovits

Cultural Differences in the Perception of Geometric Illusions

M. H. Segall, D. T. Campbell and M. J. Herskovits, 'Cultural differences in the perception of geometric illusions', *Science*, vol. 139 (1963), pp. 769–71.

Abstract. Data from fifteen societies are presented showing substantial intersocietal differences of two types in susceptibility to geometric optical illusions. The pattern of response differences suggests the existence of different habits of perceptual inference which relate to cultural and ecological factors in the visual environment.

Stimulus materials based upon geometric illusions were prepared in 1956 for standardized administration under varying field conditions in an effort to encourage the collection of cross-cultural data that might bear on the nativist–empiricist controversy concerning space perception (1). Over a 6-year period anthropologists and psychologists administered these tests to fourteen non-European samples of children and adults, ranging in size from forty-six to 344 in twelve locations in Africa and one in the Philippines, to a sample ($N = 44$) of South Africans of European descent in Johannesburg, to an American undergraduate sample ($N = 30$), and to a house-to-house sample ($N = 208$) in Evanston, Ill. In all, data were collected from 1878 persons. Analysis of these protocols provides evidence of substantial cross-cultural differences in response to these materials. The nature of these differences constitutes strong support for the empiricistic hypothesis that the perception of space involves, to an important extent, the acquisition of habits of perceptual inference.

The stimulus materials to be considered here consisted of thirty-nine items, each one a variation of one of four figures constructed of straight lines, generally referred to in the psychological literature as perceptual, or geometric illusions. These were the Müller–Lyer figure (twelve items), the Sander Parallelogram (seven), and two forms of the horizontal–vertical figure (nine and eleven). For each illusion the discrepancy in length of the segments to be compared varied from item to item so as to permit the employment of a version of the psychophysical method of constant stimuli. As each stimulus was shown to a respondent, his task was simply to indicate the longer of two linear segments. To minimize difficulties of communication, the materials were designed so that the linear segments to be compared were not connected to the other lines, and were printed in different colors. Respondents could indicate choice by selecting one of two colors (saying *red* or *black*) in response to the horizontal–vertical items, and by indicating *right* or *left* for the other illusions. Other steps taken to enhance the validity of response protocols included the administration of a short comprehension test requiring judgements similar to, but more obvious than, those demanded by the stimulus figures. Nonetheless, since no amount of precautionary measures could insure the elimination of all sources of error (for example, communication difficulties, response sets, and so forth) which could result in artifactually produced cross-cultural differences, an internal consistency check was made and all protocols containing gross departures from orderliness were withheld from analysis. (Another analysis was performed with all 1878 cases included, and the results were substantially the same as those obtained in the analysis of consistent cases only.)

The analysis proceeded as follows: Each respondent's four protocols were first examined for evidence of internal consistency. To be considered consistent, a protocol had to contain no more than one Guttman error (2). Each consistent protocol was then assigned a score which was simply the total number of times in that stimulus set, that the respondent chose the typically over-estimated segment. The mean of these scores was computed for each sample, and differences between pairs of means were evaluated by *t*-tests with significance levels modified by the Scheffé procedure (3) to compensate for the increase in error rate that accompanies non-independent, multiple comparisons.

On both the Müller–Lyer and Sander Parallelogram illusions the three 'European' samples made significantly more illusion-produced responses than did the non-European samples. (The innumerable *t*-ratios resulting can only be sampled here. For example, on the Müller–Lyer illusion, comparisons of the Evanston sample with the non-European samples resulted in *t*-ratios ranging from 7·96 to 15·39. A value of 3·57 is significant at the $p = 0.05$ level by the Scheffé test.) On the latter two illusions, the European samples had relatively low scores, with many, but not all, of the non-European samples having significantly larger mean scores. (For these illusions, the largest *t*-ratios, up to 17·41, were found between pairs of non-European groups. Comparisons involving the Evanston sample and five non-European groups resulted in *t*s ranging from 11·04 to 4·69.) When the samples were ranked according to mean number of illusion responses on each illusion, and the rank order correlations among the five illusions factor-analysed, two orthogonal factors emerged; the Müller–Lyer and Sander Parallelogram illusions loaded highly on one, and the horizontal–vertical illusions loaded highly on the other. Thus, the over-all pattern of intersample differences indicates not only cross-cultural differences in illusion susceptibility, but in addition a systematic variation in those cross-cultural differences over two classes of illusion figures.

Both to illustrate and substantiate the findings which emerged from the analysis just described, proportions of individuals in each sample choosing the typically overestimated segment were computed for each item, separately for each illusion set. Psycho-physical ogives were then constructed from these proportions and points of subjective equality (P.S.E.) determined graphically. Table 1 contains P.S.E. scores and mean number of illusion-responses for all samples on each of the illusions. (The scores shown in Table 1 were computed for internally consistent cases only, and, except where otherwise noted, the groups consisted of children and adults combined. In samples containing both children and adults, children typically had higher means and P.S.E.s. Combining children and adults as in Table 1 tends to attenuate some intersample differences.) Figure 1 contains four sets of ogives which illustrate (i) the lesser susceptibility of the combined non-European samples as compared with the combined European samples to the Müller–Lyer and Sander Parallelogram illusions, and (ii) the greater susceptibility to the two horizontal–vertical illusions shown by one non-European sample group as

Table 1. Points of Subjective Equality and Mean Number of Illusion Responses

Müller-Lyer illusion

Group	N	P.S.E. %	Mean
Evanstonians	188	20·3	5·36
N.U. students*	27	16·2	5·00
S.A. Europeans*	36	13·5	4·33
Dahomeans†	40	11·9	4·23
Senegalese	125	12·2	4·18
Ijaw School†	54	6·6	3·67
Zulu	35	11·2	3·66
Toro	86	10·3	3·56
Banyankole	224	9·3	3·45
Fang	85	6·2	3·28
Ijaw	84	6·5	3·16
Songe	89	6·2	3·07
Hanunoo	49	7·7	3·00
Bete	75	3·2	2·72
Suku	61	2·8	2·69
Bushmen*	36	1·7	2·28
S.A. Mineboys*	60	1·4	2·23

Sander Parallelogram illusion

Group	N	P.S.E. %	Mean
N.U. Students*	28	19·9	3·54
Evanstonians	196	19·1	3·27
Ijaw School†	53	18·3	3·15
S.A. Europeans*	42	17·4	2·98
Zulu	67	18·5	2·97
Senegalese	198	15·7	2·90
Fang	96	17·3	2·86
Ijaw	98	16·9	2·74
Banyankole	262	17·3	2·69
Dahomeans†	58	16·0	2·55
Hanunoo	52	13·5	2·52
Toro	105	14·3	2·49
Songe	97	14·7	2·41
Bete	86	12·8	2·37
Suku	91	9·7	2·14
S.A. mineboys*	71	8·7	2·06
(Bushmen not administered this set)			

Horizontal-vertical illusion (⊥)

Group	N	P.S.E. %	Mean
Suku	69	21·0	6·55
Banyankole	260	22·5	6·54
Dahomeans†	57	22·3	6·49
Toro	105	20·0	6·44
Ijaw School†	46	20·7	6·28
S.A. mineboys*	69	19·3	6·27
Fang	98	19·3	6·18
Senegalese	130	22·7	6·11
Ijaw	86	19·5	6·06
Bushmen*	41	19·5	5·93
Evanstonians	198	18·4	5·81
Songe	91	18·2	5·80
N.U. students*	29	18·7	5·72
Hanunoo	52	15·3	5·46
S.A. Europeans*	42	15·0	5·33
Zulu	35	9·5	4·80
Bete	79	9·8	4·62

Horizontal-vertical illusion (⌐)

Group	N	P.S.E. %	Mean
Dahomeans†	63	19·2	6·52
Toro	98	19·5	6·38
Banyankole	291	17·0	6·15
Ijaw School†	57	18·4	6·02
Suku	69	9·0	5·74
S.A. mineboys*	69	11·5	5·71
Songe	95	8·9	5·60
Ijaw	97	8·9	5·55
Fang	105	9·1	5·49
Bushmen*	39	8·6	5·15
Zulu	74	7·8	5·03
Evanstonians	203	7·2	4·90
N.U. Students*	30	7·2	4·83
Hanunoo	53	6·3	4·70
S.A. Europeans*	42	5·0	4·67
Senegalese	168	6·0	4·45
Bete	88	2·0	3·81

compared to one European sample, and the lesser susceptibility of another non-European sample. Examples of the four illusions are also presented in Figure 1.

Cross-cultural comparisons made over a half-century ago by Rivers (4) also indicated that two non-Western peoples were simultaneously less susceptible to the Müller–Lyer illusion and more susceptible to the horizontal–vertical illusion than were a group of English respondents. Since the non-European samples uniformly perform better than Europeans on one type of illusion and generally worse on the others, any explanation based on presumed contrasting characteristics of 'primitive' and 'civilized' peoples is difficult to maintain. Rather, evidence seems to point to cross-cultural differences in visual inference systems learned in response to different ecological and cultural factors in the visual environment. In a monograph now in preparation which reports the present study in detail (5), Rivers' findings as well as our own are shown to be in accord with an empiricistic, functionalistic interpretation which relates visual response habits to cultural and ecological factors in the visual environment.

An example of a cultural factor which seems relevant is the prevalence of rectangularity in the visual environment, a factor which seems to be related to the tendency to interpret acute and obtuse angles on a two-dimensional surface as representative of rectangular objects in three-dimensional space. This inference habit is much more valid in highly carpentered, urban, European environments, and could enhance, or even produce, the Müller–Lyer and Sander Parallelogram illusions. This interpretation is consistent with traditional explanation of these illusions. Less clearly, the horizontal–vertical illusion can perhaps be understood as the result of an inference habit of interpreting vertical lines as extensions away from one in the horizontal plane. Such an inference habit would have more validity for those living in open, flat terrain than in rain forests or canyons. An examination of such factors, and thorough examination of alternate explanations of our findings, are contained in the forthcoming monograph. Whether or not the correct environmental features have been isolated, the cross-cultural differences in susceptibility to geometric illusions seem best understood as symptomatic of functional differences in learned visual inference habits.

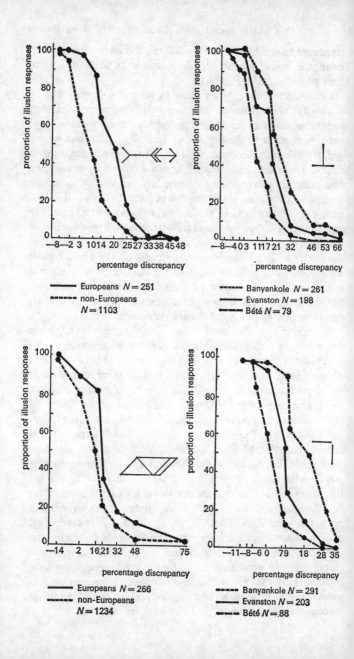

proportion of illusion responses

percentage discrepancy

——— Europeans N = 251
- - - - non-Europeans
N = 1103

proportion of illusion responses

percentage discrepancy

- - - - Banyankole N = 261
——— Evanston N = 198
– – – Bété N = 79

proportion of illusion responses

percentage discrepancy

——— Europeans N = 266
- - - - non-Europeans
N = 1234

proportion of illusion responses

percentage discrepancy

- - - - Banyankole N = 291
——— Evanston N = 203
– – – Bété N = 88

References and notes

1. HERSKOVITS, M. J., CAMPBELL, D. T., and SEGALL, M. H., *Materials for a Cross-Cultural Study of Perception*, Program of African Studies North-western University, 1956.

2. GUTTMAN, L., 'The Cornell technique for scale and intensity analysis', *Educational and Psychological Measurement*, vol. 7 (1947), p. 247. In the present study a Guttman error was defined as an illusion-produced response to one item combined with a non-illusion response to an item of lesser percentage discrepancy. Percentage discrepancy refers to the percentage by which the segment that is usually underestimated is actually longer than the other comparison segment in a particular illusion drawing. A choice of the usually overestimated segment is termed an illusion-produced response. Thus, a perfectly internally consistent protocol would consist of illusion-produced responses to one or more items, followed by non-illusion responses to all items of greater percentage discrepancy within a figure set.

3. SCHEFFE, H., 'A method for judging all contrasts in the analysis of variance', *Biometrika*, vol. 40 (1953), p. 87. It is generally agreed that the Scheffe procedure is the most conservative of several available techniques for making postmortem, non-independent comparisons. If our use of this procedure has led to any errors in conclusions other than the usual *a*-level type 1 error, such errors can only be failures to reject the null hypothesis when it should have been rejected (type 2 errors). We assume the heightened risk of type 2 errors in order that confidence in the obtained significant differences may be enhanced.

4. RIVERS, W. H. R., 'Vision', in A. C. Haddon, ed., *Reports of the Cambridge Anthropological Expedition to the Torres Straits*, vol. 2, part 1. Cambridge University Press; *British Journal of Psychology* vol. 1 (1905), p. 321.

5. SEGALL, M. H., CAMPBELL, D. T., and HERSKOVITS, M. J., 'The influence of culture on perception'. *The Influence of Culture on Visual Perception*, Bobbs–Merrill, 1966. This report includes an examination of age differences as well as total sample differences. Included also is a development of the theoretical arguments suggested here, presented in the context of a review of the literature bearing on the nativist–empiricist controversy, and a discussion of the significance of these data for the anthropological concept of cultural relativism.

Figure 1 Psychophysical ogives based on proportions of illusion responses to item of varying percentage discrepancy. (Upper left) Müller–Lyer illusion responses plotted for Europeans (three samples combined) and non-Europeans (all other samples combined). (Lower left) Sander Parallelogram illusion responses plotted for same two combined groups. (Upper right) Horizontal–vertical (⊥) illusion responses by one European and two non-European samples. (Lower right) Horizontal–vertical (⌐) illusion responses by same three samples. These graphs are all based on internally consistent cases only

6 G. Jahoda

Geometric Illusions and Environment: A Study in Ghana

G. Jahoda, 'Geometric illusions and environment: A study in Ghana', *British Journal of Psychology*, vol. 57 (1966) pp. 193–9.

Segall, Campbell and Herskovits (1963, 1966) put forward the view that the Müller–Lyer illusion is a function of rectangularity in the environment, and that the horizontal–vertical one depends on openness of terrain. Existing contrasts in these two variables in Ghana were used in an attempt to investigate the hypotheses. A total of 213 illiterate subjects were tested, and forty-one subjects in Britain. A significant over-all difference in the expected direction between Ghanaian and British subjects was obtained with the Müller–Lyer, but no differences corresponding to environmental variations emerged on either of the illusions within the subgroups of Ghanaian subjects. The reasons for this partial failure to replicate are examined in the light of other studies, and some theoretical implications discussed.

Half a century after Rivers (1901, 1905), interest in the cross-cultural study of visual illusions has revived as a result of the initiative by Segall *et al.* (1963, 1966). By means of carefully devised stimulus material they obtained responses to illusions from samples of Europeans, Africans and some other cultures. Their findings were, in brief, that European samples were more susceptible to the Müller–Lyer (M–L) and Sander parallelogram illusions than non-European samples; on two forms of the horizontal–vertical (H–V) illusions, by contrast, most non-European samples proved more susceptible. Their explanation of these results is in terms of 'learned habits of inference' based on variations in physical and cultural environments. More specifically, the following processes were postulated by Segall *et al.* (1966).

    1 'For figures constructed of lines meeting in non-rectangular junctions, there will be a learned tendency among persons dwelling in carpentered environments to rectangularize these

junctions, to perceive the figures in perspective, to interpret them as 2-dimensional representations of 3-dimensional objects'.

2. 'The horizontal–vertical illusion results from a tendency to counteract the foreshortening of lines extended into space away from a viewer, so that the vertical in the drawing which is the stimulus for the illusion is interpreted as representing a longer line. Since the tendency has more ecological validity for peoples living mostly outdoors in open, spacious environments, it is predicted that such peoples will be *more* susceptible than Western peoples in urban environments. On the other hand, some non-Western persons should be *less* susceptible to the illusions, e.g. rain forest or canyon dwellers.'

The general trend of their findings is of course broadly consistent with these interpretations, but the fit is not very close, especially as regards the H–V illusions. The authors were well aware of this, and in connexion with the latter Campbell (1964, p. 316) has written: 'If this ecology is a factor, as I do believe it is, it is obviously only one of many factors.' In their extensive exploratory survey, Segall *et al.* (1966) perforce left many of the factors uncontrolled, one of the major ones being literacy. Its potential importance may be indicated with reference to their first hypothesis, concerning the M–L illusion, which contains two elements: the 'carpentered environment', and the interpretation of 2-dimensional drawings. Although closely associated in western cultures, these are in fact distinct, and ought to be treated as such. There is thus a need for some cross-validations of these hypotheses, and the present study is an attempt to make use of the geographical as well as cultural variations in Ghana for this purpose.

Method

Subjects

In Northern Ghana, the Lobi and Dagomba are tribes closely similar in cultural characteristics and physical environment. They live in open parkland in rolling country. The huts of both are round, the main difference being that those of the Dagomba tend to be considerably larger; both kinds are usually devoid of rectangular furnishings.

The Ashanti in central Ghana are geographically and culturally quite distinct. They live in a dense forest belt, and remote villages enclosed in high tropical rain forest were specially singled out. Their houses are rectangular, though the edges are not always sharply defined; they contain a good deal of 'carpentered' furniture, tables and chairs being well-nigh universal.

From the point of view of design, it would have been desirable to test both literates and illiterates; but in northern Ghana the bulk of the adult population is illiterate, and the same is true of Ashanti outside the urban areas. Hence testing was confined to illiterates. Subjects were obtained by getting the chiefs or elders to assemble the people in the homestead or village, and from among these a roughly equal proportion of men and women within the approximate age-range 16–50 years were selected.

In addition to the Ghanaian sample, forty-one subjects were also given the illusions in Britain. They were undergraduates not taking psychology, and university administrative staff.

Materials

Since the aim of the work was to test the hypotheses put forward by Segall *et al.* (1966), it would have been best if their own materials could have been used. Unfortunately circumstances precluded any possibility of these being obtained in time. The conventional forms of the Müller–Lyer and horizontal–vertical (⊥) illusions, incorporating movable slides, were therefore employed. These were constructed in white plastic with black lines, according to the dimensions specified by Fraisse (1963). In view of the objections raised by Segall *et al.* (1966) to the work of Bonte (1962) it should be mentioned that, apart from the fact that there is no grain as in the wooden device, the illusions were wholly enclosed in a plastic frame, so that there was little apparent discontinuity between the stationary and moving parts. Nonetheless, careful precautions were taken to ensure that the comparisons to be made were correctly understood. The procedures were tried out on illiterate subjects in the southern coastal region, with the assistance of the interpreter who subsequently took part in the actual experiment.

The pilot exercise clearly showed the need to keep the number of trials demanded of any one subject to an absolute minimum.

The tolerance of illiterates for a strange task, whose purpose is obscure, is limited; unless one has some special claim on their co-operation, fatigue and boredom set in fairly soon and the performance then becomes perfunctory. In the course of the pilot study a slight mishap also occurred when one end of the black line of the H–V illusion was damaged; hence it was only possible to start from the shorter position. This means that the absolute amount of the illusion effect could not be validly determined, but the group comparisons for testing the hypotheses are of course not affected. The number of trials for each subject was as follows: six for the Müller–Lyer illusion (three in and three out) and five for the horizontal–vertical illusion (out only). Sequence of presentation was randomized throughout.

Procedure

Subjects were told at the outset that we wanted to find out 'how well they could see'. The subject was seated and given the apparatus to hold flat on his lap, at a viewing distance of some 14–18 in. He was allowed to familiarize himself with it by moving the slide in and out. The interpreter then told him that he should make 'the two things like twigs the same', simultaneously demonstrating: for the M–L illusion, two straight twigs were held first end to end, and then in parallel to show their identical length. For the H–V illusion, one twig was first held up horizontally or vertically and turned 90°. The writer, sitting next to the subject, then ran his index from one end of the standard to the other; in the case of the M–L illusion, he also indicated (either in the 'in' or 'out' position, as appropriate) the line from the end of the arrow on the left to the point where the line joined the Y, being careful to stop just short of the junction. Next, subjects were asked to do what they had just been shown; if they went to the end of the total Y part of the M–L illusion, or confined themselves to half the base line with the H–V one, their results were discarded. In order to avoid causing offence, such subjects were actually allowed to make some responses, and rewarded like all others with a small packet of biscuits. This was the only stage at which subjects were eliminated; the loss amounted to about one in twenty, rates being similar in the different tribes.

The use of the method of average error has the drawback that one obtains responses influenced in part by movement, and not purely perceptual ones as those of Segall *et al.* (1963, 1966); furthermore, their stimulus material was presented in a different spatial orientation, namely vertically at eye level. Accordingly, direct comparisons of the extent of illusion effects would be unwarranted. The aim was thus confined to undertaking group comparisons designed to test the two hypotheses below.

Hypotheses

I. Lobi and Dagomba, living in open country, will be *more* susceptible to the H–V illusion than Ashanti, whose surroundings consist of dense tropical forest.

II. Ashanti, living in relatively more 'carpentered' surroundings, will be *more* susceptible to the M–L illusion.

Results

In analysing the data, the median was used as measure of central tendency so as not to give undue weight to occasional extreme responses. The medians were transformed into percentage discrepancies from the standard, and the arithmetic means of these discrepancies computed. When Bartlett's test was applied to the H–V illusion data, a significant heterogeneity of variance ($p < 0.02$) was found; hence all data were analysed by the median test, using a two-tailed χ^2 test of significance. No significant sex differences emerged for either of the illusions with any of the tribes, and responses from men and women were therefore pooled.

Horizontal–vertical illusion

On examining the responses to this illusion it became immediately evident that Lobi and Dagomba could not, as originally intended, be treated as a single population. Accordingly they are shown separately in Table 1. The performance of Europeans is near the midpoint of the total range, differing significantly from that of both Lobi and Ashanti ($p < 0.01$ and $p < 0.02$ respectively). The fact that Europeans do not fall outside the range of the African samples is consistent with the global aspects of the findings by Segall *et al.* (1966), but the pattern within the African samples does not fit their ecological interpretation. The value for Ashanti

G. Jahoda

(tropical forest) falls between those of the two others (both open parkland). At one extreme the Dagomba gave the largest illusion

Table 1
Mean Percentage Discrepancies in the Horizontal–Vertical Illusion

Sample	N	Mean percentage	S.D.
Lobi	34	1·65	13·95
Europeans	41	11·16	8·63
Ashanti	127	16·22	9·74
Dagomba	52	22·71	10·34

Median test: $\chi^2 = 39 \cdot 59$; d.f. = 3; $p < 0 \cdot 001$.

responses; at the other, the Lobi had a mean percentage discrepancy close to zero; over half of them in fact either gave no illusion response or even a negative one, whereby the vertical segment is made longer than the horizontal one. These results thus provide no support for hypothesis I.

Müller–Lyer illusion

The picture presented by Table 2 is totally different. All the mean percentage discrepancies are closely similar, so that hypothesis II also fails to find support. On the other hand, it appears from the comparison between the combined African versus the European group that the latter exhibits a significantly greater illusion effect, which is in accordance with the postulates of Segall *et al.* (1966).

Table 2
Mean Percentage Discrepancies in the Müller–Lyer Illusion

Tribe	N	Mean percentage	S.D.
Lobi	34	15·18	8·46
Dagomba	52	17·44	8·15
Ashanti	127	17·61	7·93
Europeans	41	23·22	6·94

Median test: between the three tribes – $x^2 = 3 \cdot 91$; d.f. 2; $0 \cdot 20 > p > 0 \cdot 10$; combined tribes versus Europeans—$x^2 = 7 \cdot 48$; d.f. 1; $p < 0 \cdot 01$.

Discussion

Since the findings were not in conformity with the hypotheses put forward by Segall *et al.* (1966), the question of how the negative outcome is to be interpreted arises. The first and most obvious possibility would be to attribute it merely to the differences in the methods employed. Some of these have already been mentioned, and it should be added that Segall *et al.* (1966) had an elaborate scheme for eliminating non-scale and inconsistent sets of responses; this was of course essential, since the bulk of their testing was done indirectly. Owing to the limited number of trials per individual subject in the present study, elimination of subjects was confined to the initial stage of the testing session, supervised throughout by the same experimenter; thereby external control of the uniformity of administration in all three tribal areas was ensured.

However, in the case of the M–L illusion such external control would not constitute a fully reliable safeguard against one gross source of error which Segall *et al.* (1966) have regarded as invalidating the work of Bonte (1962). They suggest that Bonte's subjects were led both by the nature of her apparatus (similar to the one used in the present study) and by the instructions to misinterpret their task as a matching of the *total figure* on the left ←→ with the *total figure* ≺ on the right; this would of course have resulted in a crass over-estimation of the illusion effect. The precautions taken in the present study to obviate this have been indicated previously; but since the illusion effects in the present study were substantially higher than most of those found by Segall *et al.* (1966) in their African samples, it might be objected that the same spurious factor may have been operative; it is therefore necessary to consider this argument.

For this purpose, let us suppose that this factor *was* operative, so that the two total figures were mistakenly matched. If one assumed, for the sake of simplicity, that this matching was on the average free of error, a spurious illusion effect amounting to 25 per cent would result in each case. Given this base line, one can go on to try out various ways in which the results of the present study, namely a mean value of some 17 per cent for the M–L illusion, could have come about. Clearly, not every subject could have matched total figures, or the mean would be in the region of 25 per cent; if half the subjects had matched total figures, and the other half had matched in the correct manner but with a nil illusion effect, the net resultant would be an overall mean illusion effect of some 12 per cent, which is too low; a more realistic assumption would be that the other half showed a moderate genuine illusion effect of some 9 per cent; this would yield an overall mean of about 17 per cent, close to the value actually obtained. If something like this had in fact happened one would predict *bimodality* of the distribution of responses, with two major clusters around 25 per cent and 9 per cent respectively. The actual distribution is shown in Table 3 to be grouped around the mean; there is no indication whatsoever of bimodality, and it is therefore highly unlikely that the results of the present study can be accounted for by assuming mistaken matching.

Table 3
Distribution of Percentage Discrepancies for the Müller–Lyer Illusion for the Three Tribes Combined

			Mean value				
% illusion	—7	8—12	13—17	18—22	23—27	28—	Total
N	21	35	50	51	37	19	213

Apart from this, the difference in magnitude in the M–L illusion effects may well be in part a function of the different methods employed; Segall *et al.* (1966) themselves have admitted that their method tends to weaken the effect somewhat. In any case, it has already been stated that the concern of the present study was to test predicted group differences, not to establish absolute amounts of illusion effects.

In the case of the H–V illusion, however, it must be pointed out that the spatial orientation of the apparatus may have had some bearing on the outcome. As the illusion was presented horizontally, the 'vertical' line was in fact only symbolically vertical, whereas with Segall *et al.* (1966) it was actually so. There seems to be no definite evidence concerning such a position effect, which calls for further investigation.

Could any other elements have contributed to the findings?

One possibility that suggests itself is that the overall range of the variables, namely rectangularity and openness of terrain, may have been too restricted. This no doubt may have reduced the effect, but one would still have anticipated some trend in the expected direction.

At this point it is perhaps desirable to view the problem in a wider perspective, beginning with the M–L illusion. In the introduction it was noted that Segall *et al.* (1966) failed to distinguish between a 'carpentered environment' and 'the interpretation of two dimensional drawings', both of which form part of their hypothesis. There is considerable evidence for the inability of illiterates to interpret two-dimensional representations of 3-dimensional objects. Biesheuvel (1952) has reported on this; Hudson (1960) carried out a detailed study, which is referred to by Segall *et al.* (1966), though they apparently remained unaware of its full implications. They certainly do not seem to have obtained any details of the cultural and especially the educational background of their individual subjects, relying instead on global information about culture and ecology.

On the basis of the distinction, one might venture to propose that illusion effects of the M–L type may be a combined function of two distinct variables: (1) the degree of rectangularity in the environment, which is the primary one; (2) the extent of the ability to interpret 2-dimensional representations. It may well be that in the absence of (2), or with a deficiency in it, relatively moderate variations in (1) produce such limited changes in habits of perceptual inference that the difference cannot be detected by the relatively crude methods employed in the present study. It is even possible that, as far as test responses are concerned, radical differences in (1) may not manifest themselves at all if there is a marked deficiency in (2). At any rate, there is some evidence for this from a study by Mundy-Castle and Nelson (1962) of a backward community of white forest workers in South Africa. The environment of these forest workers is far more 'rectangular' than that of the bushmen; yet they resemble the bushmen in (2), since none of them was able to give consistent 3-dimensional responses on the Hudson pictorial perception test. Their responses on the M–L illusion did not differ significantly from those of two samples of bushmen, but were very significantly smaller than those of ordinary white adults. In view of Gregory's (1963) theory, it is also of interest to note that the forest workers showed a significant tendency to underconstancy.

In his article Gregory refers to the findings that for people living in houses without corners the geometrical illusions are reduced; however, this does not apply to the H–V illusion. A variety of at least partial explanations of this type of illusions have been suggested by various workers such as Künnapas (1955, 1957, 1958). None of the theories familiar to the present writer help to throw any light on the totally unexpected contrast found in the present study, with one possible exception: Kohler and Pissarek (1960) put forward, it seems independently, a hypothesis identical with that of Segall *et al.* (1966). They arrived at this in the course of experiments in which subjects wore glasses producing artificial astigmatism. This suggests what is admittedly not more than a speculation: since there is rather rigid endogamy within the tribes studied, there might be a difference in genetically determined astigmatism which could outweigh ecological variations. This would be consistent with the exceptionally high standard deviation of H–V illusion responses among the Lobi, although any other factor tending to dichotomize the population would of course have a similar effect. Moreover, it has been suggested to the writer that permanent astigmatism would probably become compensated, thus not leading to any distortion. Again, this problem appears to be open to specific test.

Whatever the causes of the contrasts encountered, it is worth pointing out that the present findings concerning the H–V illusion are not the only ones inconsistent with a simple ecological interpretation; this is evident from the comment by Campbell (1964) quoted earlier, but a more directly comparable instance may be cited; two successive expeditions to the Kalahari by the same team used the tests of Segall *et al.* (1966) with two groups of bushmen; on one version of the H–V illusion results were substantially the same, with the other version they differed very significantly ($p < 0.01$); here again both tribe and ecology were constant (based on data contained in Morgan, 1959; Reuning, 1959; Mundy-Castle and Nelson, 1962).

One final aspect of the present findings may be briefly noted; it

111

relates to the possible effects of later experience. All subjects in Ghana were asked if they had travelled elsewhere in the country; it emerged that nearly all the men had occasionally visited urban areas; some had worked as seasonal labourers for varying periods, others were employed for spells in the mines. By contrast, nearly all the women had spent their lives in the village or settlement, rarely going beyond a radius of a few miles. In spite of this, there were no significant sex differences in the responses to either of the illusions. Thus such environmental factors as were operative must have been confirmed to childhood or adolescence.

In conclusion, the present findings highlight the complexity of the problem, which is apt to be obscured by the tendency of investigators to view the issue in terms of Europeans versus non-Europeans. More specific hypotheses are needed, that can stand the test of accounting for differences within, as well between, these categories.

References

BIESHEUVEL, S. (1952), 'The study of African ability. Part II. A survey of some research problems', *African Studies*, vol. 11, pp. 105–17.

BONTE, M. (1962), 'The reaction of two African societies to the Müller–Lyer illusion', *Journal of Social Psychology*, vol. 58, pp. 265–8.

CAMPBELL, D. T. (1964), 'Distinguishing differences of perception from failures of communication in cross-cultural studies', in F. C. S. Northrop and H. H. Livingston, eds., *Cross-Cultural Understanding: Epistemology in Anthropology*, Harper and Row.

FRAISSE, P. (1963), *Manuel pratique de Psychologie expérimentale*, Presses Universitaires.

GREGORY, R. L. (1963), 'Distortion of visual space as inappropriate constancy scaling', *Nature, London*, vol. 199, pp. 678–80.

HUDSON, W. (1960), 'Pictorial depth perception in sub-cultural groups in Africa', *Journal of Social Psychology*, vol. 52, pp. 183–208.

KOHLER, I., and PISSAREK, T. (1960), 'Brillenversuche sur Vertikalentäuschung', *Psychologische Beitraege*, vol. 5, pp. 117–40.

KÜNNAPAS, T. M. (1955), 'Influence of frame size on apparent length of a line', *Journal of Experimental Psychology*, vol. 50, pp. 168–70.

KÜNNAPAS, T. M. (1957) 'The vertical–horizontal illusion and the visual field', *Journal of Experimental Psychology*, vol. 53, pp. 405–7.

KÜNNAPAS, T. M. (1958), 'Influence of head inclination on the vertical–horizontal illusion', *Journal of Psychology*, vol. 46, pp. 179–85.

MORGAN, P. (1959), 'A study in perceptual differences among cultural groups in southern Africa using tests of geometric illusions', *Journal of the National Institute of Personnel Research*, vol. 8, pp. 39–43.

MUNDY-CASTLE, A. C., and NELSON, G. K. (1962), 'A neuropsychological study of the Knysna forest workers', *Psychologia Africana*, vol. 9, 240–72.

REUNING, H. (1959), 'Psychologische Versuche mit Buschleuten der Kalahari', *Die Umschau in Wissenschaft und Technik*, no. 17, 520–23.

RIVERS, W. H. R. (1901), 'Vision', in A. C. Haddon, ed., *Reports of the Cambridge Anthropological Expedition to the Torres Straits*, vol. 2, part 1, Cambridge University Press.

RIVERS, W. H. R. (1905), 'Observations on the senses of the Todas', *British Journal of Psychology*, vol. 1, pp. 321–96.

SEGALL, M. H., CAMPBELL, D. T., and HERSKOVITS, M. J. (1963), 'Cultural differences in the perception of geometric illusions', *Science*, vol. 139, pp. 769–71.

SEGALL, M. H., CAMPBELL, D. T., and HERSKOVITS, M. J. (1966), *The Influence of Culture on Visual Perception*, Bobbs-Merrill.

Part Four   Pictorial Depth Perception

In Reading 6 Jahoda had raised the difficulty of perceiving 3 dimensions from the 2-dimensional representation of a drawing or a photograph, for those people unaccustomed to such things. With his article 'Pictorial depth perception in sub-cultural groups in Africa', (*Journal of Social Psychology*, vol. 52, 1960, pp. 183–208), W. Hudson became the first person to examine this problem in detail, and this in turn has given rise to subsequent studies, so that we can present a sequence of studies as we did for visual illusions. In that article Hudson presented the issue clearly:

Pictorial representation of a 3-dimensional scene requires the observance and acceptance of certain artistic or graphic conventions. Pictorial depth perception depends upon response to these conventional cues in the 2-dimensional representation. There are three such cues concerned with form only, viz. object size, object superimposition or overlap, perspective. In the visual world, of two objects of equal size, that object nearer the observer is larger. When one object overlaps another the superimposed object is nearer to the observer. Parallel lines tend to converge with distance from the observer. In the 2-dimensional representation of the 3-dimensional scene, foreground objects are depicted larger than background items. Superimposed objects are perceived as near. Pictorial structuring by perspective techniques is accepted as a convention for depicting distance (p. 185).

Mundy-Castle (Reading 7) takes up the subject again among Ghanaian children. He accepts the view that familiarity with pictorial material is essential for 3-dimensional interpretation. He pursues the issue into the realm of perceived causality, with which it is linked. A later (1967) paper of Hudson is also included, which gives a survey of the state of our knowledge on this subject, and indicates its importance to education and communication (Reading 8).

7 A. C. Mundy-Castle

Pictorial Depth Perception in Ghanaian Children

Excerpt from A. C. Mundy-Castle, 'Pictorial depth perception in Ghanaian children', *International Journal of Psychology*, vol. 1 (1966), pp. 290-300.

[...] Following the lead of Hudson (1960, 1962) in South Africa, cross-cultural studies of pictorial depth perception suggest that cognizance of depth cues in pictures is a function of culturally-determined familiarity with pictorial material [Mundy-Castle, and Nelson (South Africa), 1962; Dawson (Sierra Leone), 1963; Vernon (England and West Indies), 1965]. At least three factors are operative in the attainment of this familiarity: cultural stimulus, schooling, and intelligence as measured by psychological tests. The first appears to be the most critical, deriving from the exploitation of such cultural products as pictures, posters, photographs, movies, television, and activities such as drawing, painting and the playing of games with a pictorial content. Absence of this cultural stimulus may prevent or retard the development of 3-dimensional pictorial perception, even in subjects with an advanced level of education (Hudson, 1960). If however pictorial depth perception is achieved, the rate of its development has been found to depend both on amount of previous schooling and on size of score on intelligence tests (Hudson, 1960, 1962; Dawson, 1963). Dawson also showed that subjects given a six-month training period in 3-dimensional perception improved dramatically as compared with a matched control group without such training, the rate of improvement being highly correlated with performance on Kohs' blocks.

Visual media are used extensively in the Ghanaian educational system, presumably on the assumption that they are readily understood. The primary object of the present study was to test the validity of this assumption, by attempting to answer the question: how do Ghanaian children aged 5–10 years respond to depth cues in pictorial material? Subsidiary aims were to examine the children's interpretations of pictorial items, and to explore the extent to which their answers to questions about pictorial content could be used to study their reasoning.

Method

A total of 122 children were studied, drawn in approximately equal proportions from primary schools in the following centres in Southern Ghana[1]: James Town (Ga), Dodowa (Ga-Adangbe), Koforidua (Ashanti-Twi), Sokode Etoe (Ewe), Anfoega Agatan-yigbe (Ewe), Trede (Ashanti) and Duayaw Nkwanta (Brong Ahafo). There were thirty-six children aged 5–6 years, forty-one aged 7–8 years, and forty-five aged 9–10 years. Selection of subjects was done randomly from lists provided by the head-masters. Examinations were conducted in the precincts of the schools using the vernacular language.

Four pictures from Hudson's (1960) Depth Perception Test were used as stimuli. They were reproduced on 76 mm × 127 mm cards and presented in the order 1, 2, 3, 4 (Figure 1). The pictures on cards 1 and 2 contain the depth cues of object size and super-position, those on cards 3 and 4 perspective as well. All pictures contain the figure of a man aiming a spear, an elephant, a deer[2], and in each the spear is aligned on both the elephant and the deer. The following questioning procedure was adopted, question 1 being asked only with card 1, question 1a only with card 3. The remaining questions were asked with all the cards.

Question 1 (card 1): 'What do you see?' The subject was expected to identify each item, i.e. the man, the spear, the elephant, the deer, the hill and the ground lines. If necessary an item was pointed out and the subject asked: 'What is this?'

Question 1a (card 3): The subject was asked to identify the lines representing the road and horizon.

Question 2: 'What is the man doing?' The answer was expected

1. The predominant tribe is indicated in brackets.
2. Correctly speaking: an antelope. In Ghana, antelope are commonly referred to as 'deer', which term has been used throughout the present text.

Figure 1 Pictures for study of depth perception. (Note that the sizes of figures in card 2 are slightly larger than in the other three cards, also that the actual distance between the man and deer is shorter)

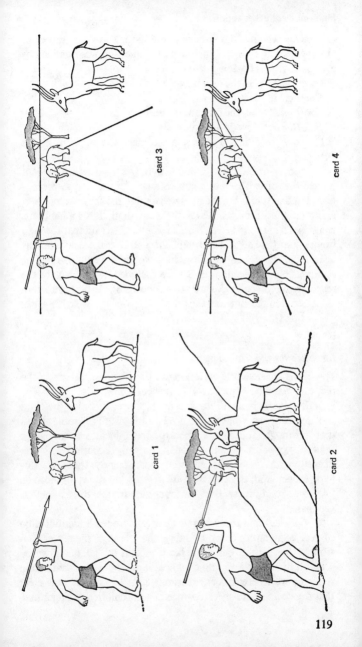

card 1

card 2

card 3

card 4

119

to indicate whether the man was aiming (or throwing) the spear at the elephant or deer. If necessary the question was qualified by asking: 'What is he doing with the spear?'

Question 3: 'Can the deer see the man?'

Question 4: 'How do you know?'

Question 5: 'Can the man see the deer?'

Question 6: 'How do you know?'

Question 7: Which is closer to the man: the elephant or the deer?'

Responses to questions 2 and 7 were regarded as self-evident indications of two or three dimensional pictorial depth perception. If a child said that the man was aiming the spear at the deer, and that the deer was nearer the man than the elephant, his responses were classified as 3-dimensional. If he said that the man was aiming the spear at the elephant, and that the elephant was nearer the man than the deer, his responses were classified as 2-dimensional. Questions 3–6 were included to investigate the reasoning involved in explanations concerning visibility relationships between the man and the deer.

Results

Identification of pictorial items

There was considerable variation in identification of items in the pictures, as shown in Table 1, the percentages in which also include failures in identification, i.e. instances in which the child was unable to say what the item was. Analysis of the table shows that although failed and incorrect identifications, hereafter referred to as misidentifications, generally occurred less frequently with increased age, some, particularly those relating to the deer and the more abstract representations of horizon line and road lines, were encountered frequently in all age groups.

To consider first the objective items, the frequent identification of deer as a goat or sheep is understandable since the representation in the pictures bears a resemblance to the goats and sheep seen on the roads and in the villages in all the regions studied in this survey, whereas deer are rarely seen in Ghana. It is clear that the deer was always recognized by the children as an animal, but that the identification of the animal was dictated by their past experience of animals. Similarly the spear and elephant were generally identified each as belonging to a specific class of objects, which object within the class being determined by the child's past experience of such objects. Thus the man was always identified correctly and the tree almost always. From this it may be concluded that the objective representations in these pictures were recognized correctly in terms of their class, but were identified according to past experience of objects within the class.

With the more abstract pictorial representations, the children's identifications frequently fell within a different class from that intended by the artist, such misidentification often being linked with 2-dimensional interpretations of the pictures. For example, the road in card 3 was frequently described as an object, such as a hill or tree, in which case it was sometimes stated that neither the deer nor the man could see each other, since their view was obstructed by the intervening object. Similarly, the horizon line was almost never identified correctly, usually being described as an object such as stick, ruler or piece of string. Occasionally it was seen as incorporated in a structure provided by the road lines, and identified as a pair of scales or the letter A. Similar misidentifications of the hill lines were also made, although the incidence of these and of misidentifications of the road lines decreased progressively with age. Of interest is the finding that such misidentifications often assumed the form of utilizable objects, the children referring to their function in their responses to the questions. For example, the horizon line might be regarded as a ruler for measuring the tree so that its height might be known, or the hill lines in card 2 as ropes for tying up the goat (deer).

As a general conclusion from these observations, it is proposed that the likelihood of correct identification of pictorial items is greatest if they are realistic representations of familiar objects, least if they relate to abstract concepts. The drawing of the man is an example of the former, the horizon line of the latter. In between these extremes lie the other objects, i.e. tree, spear, deer and elephant, and the hill and road lines. The first four were all recognized in terms of class but were identified in terms of experience. The hill and road lines certainly refer to objective

Table 1
Percentages and Examples of Pictorial Misidentifications

Items	Percentages 5–6 Years	7–8 Years	9–10 Years	Examples of Misidentifications
Horizon line	100	100	96	stick, line, rope, ruler, path, thread, hill, mound, tape, spear, heavens.
Deer	100	91	87	goat, sheep, cow, dog, ass, horse, camel.
Road	61	73	46	sticks, tree, string, table, A, steps, river, rubber gun, triangle, oven, farm, broken stick, hill.
Spear	77	46	10	rod, stick, arrow, pen, gun, pencil, knife, mattock, sword, pistol, iron.
Hill	70	37	15	rope, path, line, river, car, stone, oven.
Elephant	41	17	6	pig, rabbit, goat, sheep, lion, tiger, dog.
Tree	5	0	0	flowers, hand, plantain.
Man	0	0	0	—

reality, but in these drawings are rendered in a highly abstract manner, designed to emphasize distance cues with minimal attention to objective realism. To interpret them correctly requires a knowledge and understanding of both the mode of graphic representation and of the conceptual aspects incorporated in the representations. In the case of the horizon line, these conditions were apparently unfulfilled among the children within the age-range studied, whereas with the hill and road lines there was a progressive increase in correct identifications with age. According to this line of reasoning, the finding that the hill lines were recognized correctly more often than the road lines would be a consequence of the incorporation by the latter of perspective, since this is a highly abstract concept.

As a further conclusion, it may be added that when a child does interpret one of these more abstract items (he may say he cannot), in doing so he tends to regard it in the same way as the objective items, describing it as whatever object he thinks it looks like; furthermore, he will often ascribe to the object a useful function relating to other constituents in the picture.

Pictorial depth perception

An unequivocal result of this study is that very few children responded to the depth cues in the pictures, only one child giving 3-dimensional responses to questions 2 and 7 for all four cards. This was a girl aged 8, daughter of a farmer in a rural community. Her scores on a Gestalt continuation test and design copying test were both more than 2 standard deviations above the mean for her age group in Ghana. Apart from this notable exception, there were occasional 3-dimensional answers to one or other of the critical questions for one or two of the four cards, but there was no evidence of consistent 3-dimensional interpretation.

The following is an example of a transcript in which responses to questions 2 and 7 are all 2-dimensional. The subject was a 10-year-old boy.

Example 1
Card 1 – Q1: Man, elephant, tree, goat, pistol (spear), hill; *Q2:* The man is aiming the pistol at the elephant; *Q3 + 4:* No. Because the goat is behind the tree; *Q5 + 6:* No. Because the hill has blocked his view; *Q7:* The elephant is closer to the man.
Card 2 – Q2: The man has struck the elephant with the pistol; *Q3 + 4:* Yes. Because the goat lifted its head when it saw the pistol. It was then able to see the man; *Q5 + 6:* Yes. Because the goat has lifted its head; *Q7:* The elephant is closer to the man.
Card 3 – Q1a: Horizon = line, road = house; *Q2:* The man is aiming the pistol at the elephant; *Q3 + 4:* No. Because his vision is blocked by the house; *Q5 + 6:* No. Because his vision is blocked by the house; *Q7:* The elephant is closer to the man.
Card 4 – Q1a: Horizon = line, road = ground; *Q2:* The man is aiming the pistol at the elephant; *Q3 + 4:* Yes. Because it has changed its position; *Q5 + 6:* Yes. Because he has also changed his position; *Q7:* The elephant is closer to the man.

As already stated, virtually all the children gave comparable 2-dimensional responses to questions 2 and 7 for all four cards, an understandable consequence of which is that in card 2, the spear was usually seen as sticking into the elephant rather than over-lapping it.

Visibility relationships and causality

As shown in Table 2, a substantial proportion of children in all age groups said that the man and deer were able to see each other, although the relative incidence of positive and negative answers to questions 3 and 5 differed not only from card to card but also in relation to man and deer. An investigation of the causality involved in these visibility relationships was attempted by an analysis of answers to questions 4 and 6.

Table 2
Visibility Relationships Between Man and Deer Percentages of 'Yes' Response to Questions 3 and 5

Age		5–6	7–8	9–10
Card 1	Q.3	76	68	48
	Q.5	71	71	52
Card 2	Q.3	88	75	86
	Q.5	82	89	83
Card 3	Q.3	65	68	52
	Q.5	71	71	59
Card 4	Q.3	82	68	62
	Q.5	82	71	69
Average		77	73	64

Disregarding 'don't know' responses, the incidence of which decreased with age (5–6 years = 25 per cent; 7–8 years = 22 per cent; 9–10 years = 9 per cent), two main agents of causality were evident. One will be referred to as objective, in the sense that it resided in the spatial arrangement of pictorial items; the other will be referred to as subjective, in the sense that it derived from thematic, imaginative projections incorporated in the child's interpretation of the pictures. There was considerable individual variation in the extent to which these two sources were implicated, some protocols yielding evidence only of objective causality, others only of subjective, others a mixture of both.

To consider objective causality first, three objective relations between the man and deer were invoked to account for their ability or inability to see each other. These involved regard, distance, and elevation, as follows.

Regard. (a) Visibility. The commonest objective cause of visibility relationships between man and deer was direction of regard, e.g. 'The man can see the deer because he is looking at it', or 'The deer can see the man because his eyes are looking in that direction', or 'because it is facing him'. The proportion of such explanations ranged between 20 per cent and 40 per cent, there being no significant difference according either to age or to card number. (b) Invisibility. Conversely, the chief objective cause of lack of visibility relationships between man and deer was the presence of other pictorial items between them, which acted as visual obstructions, e.g. 'The man cannot see the deer because the hill (road lines in card 3) is in the way' (see also answers to questions 3–6, cards 1 and 3, p. 294). This category accounted for 50 per cent to 80 per cent of explanations for the deer not seeing the man, 30 per cent to 40 per cent for the man not seeing the deer. The incidence was equal for cards 1 and 3, slightly smaller for card 4, rare for card 2. There were no significant age differences.

Distance. (a) Visibility. Nearness or its equivalent was the objective reason given in 15 per cent to 30 per cent of explanations for visibility relationships, e.g. 'The man can now see the deer because it has drawn nearer', or 'because the deer is standing beside the elephant'. Such answers occurred least often with card 1, most often with card 2, intermediate with cards 3 and 4. It should be noted that the actual or literal distance between the man and deer was equal on cards 1, 3 and 4, shorter for card 2. There were no significant age differences. (b) Invisibility. Only a small proportion of explanations (less than 15 per cent in all age groups) invoked distance as the reason for lack of visibility relationships, e.g. 'The man is too far away to see the deer.' Such responses were given only for cards 1, 3 and 4.

Elevation. (a) Visibility. Height was given as the reason for visibility relationships in 5–25 per cent of the explanations, rather more often among children aged 7–10 years than 5–6 years, and slightly more often in relation to the deer than the man. Examples are: 'The man can see the deer because he is tall and hence can see over the hill and elephant', or 'because the deer's horns are tall and the tips can be seen', or 'The deer can see the man because it is standing on high ground', or has 'climbed the hill'. There was no difference in incidence of this type of response according to card number. (b) Invisibility. As with the distance relation, only a small proportion of answers (less than 20 per cent in the older groups, none in the youngest) gave insufficient elevation as a cause of invisibility, e.g. 'The deer is too low to see the man.' Such responses were limited to cards 1, 3 and 4.

To turn now from objective to subjective causality, the most striking observation of this analysis relates to the influence on reasoning of projected imaginative elaborations, which often extended thematically from card to card in the form of a narrative or running commentary. The incidence of such projection was similar in all age groups, being 36 per cent in the youngest, 40 per cent in the intermediate, and 38 per cent in the oldest. It is possible that a comparable influence was operating in more children than this, but that for one reason or another (e.g. shyness) it was not communicated to the investigators.

Examples of projected imaginative responses are contained in following excerpts.

Example 2 (Boy, 10 years)
Card 1: 'Man can't see goat because his attention is on the lion (elephant), which he wants to kill. The goat is seeing the man because it thinks the man will kill it. The goat will run away when the man approaches.'
Card 2: 'Man has struck the lion and blood will soon come out ... Man looks at goat because he now plans to kill goat too.'
Card 3: 'Oh! Won't you kill goat too? Do you like only lion? ... Man can't see goat because he does not know it is there. Goat sees man because it fears it may be killed.'
Card 4: On seeing picture he says: 'Oh, but what is this that Europeans have drawn like this? ... Man wants to kill lion. Man can't see goat because his attention is on lion. Goat not seeing man; don't know why.'
Example 3 (Boy, 10 years)
Card 1: 'Man can't see camel (deer) because he does not know there is any animal there. The camel can see the man because it is watching

the man so that it can escape when the man rushes on it after killing the elephant.'

Example 4 (Girl, 9 years)

Card 2: 'The man can see the deer because having struck the elephant he is looking to see if the deer will come near so that he can kill it too.'

Example 5 (Girl, 7 years)

Card 1: 'The goat can't see the man because if it could it would run away and not stand there.'

Example 6 (Boy, 7 years)

Card 2: 'The goat has put a stick on its shoulder. It will use the stick for hitting the man (the "stick" refers to the diagonal hill line passing "behind" the deer). This (the other hill line) is a rope which will be used in tying up the goat so that it will not run away.'

Example 7 (Boy, 9–10 years)

Card 1: 'The elephant does not see the man because the man is hiding to get a good aim. The goat can however see the man for since the man is not killing the goat he (the man) is not hiding from it.'

Card 2: 'The elephant is nearer the man than the goat because the man has hit the elephant, and the goat on seeing this will run away.'

Example 8 (Boy, 9 years)

Card 1: 'The man wants to knock the dog (elephant) with the spear because the dog has taken his meat ... The sheep does not see the man because the man is not looking at the sheep.'

In some instances the investigators asked additional questions concerning causality. It was again evident that reasoning was subject to a projective influence, exemplified in the following excerpts:

Example 9 (Boy, 9 years)

Q.: 'Why is the man drawn bigger than the elephant?' *A.:* 'Because there will be no space for a big elephant. The man has been drawn bigger so that he might kill the elephant.'

Example 10 (Boy, 6 years)

Q.: 'Why is the elephant drawn so small when, as you have said, you know that in real life an elephant is bigger than a man?' *A.:* 'It looks smaller in the picture because in ordinary life it is so big that when it walks the ground shakes and because of that it is drawn small.'

No general statements on the development of causality in children can be made on the basis of these results, since they are derived from the application of an unfamiliar test involving a static and artificial display: it does not follow that similar responses would have been elicited in a more realistic and familiar context, such, for example, as used by Piaget (1930, 1954) in his extensive studies on causality in children. Bearing in mind this limitation, it may be concluded that two major agents of causality were operative in the children's interpretation of the pictures. One was objective, invoking relationships consequent on the spatial arrangement of pictorial items; the other was subjective, involving projected imaginative elaborations by the child. There were only minor differences according to age.

Discussion

All the children of this study had attended primary school since their fifth or sixth year. The finding that only one child gave consistent evidence of pictorial depth perception may be compared with the observations of Hudson (1960, 1962) on white primary school children in South Africa. He found that the proportion of children giving consistent 3-dimensional responses increased according to the number of years they had spent at school, the percentage rising from 17 per cent in the lowest primary standards to 72 per cent in the highest. A comparable increase was also found in the incidence of accurate identifications of pictorial items, particularly those incorporating depth cues, such as the hill and road lines. The only other published information on pictorial depth perception in primary school children is also from Hudson (ibid.), who found that 35 per cent of a group of black South African children in the top primary standard gave consistent 3-dimensional responses to the same set of pictures. Hudson (1962, p. 230) concluded that by the time white South African pupils have reached the end of their primary education, the majority are competent at 3-dimensional pictorial perception. In discussing the marked difference between his black and white samples from the top primary school standard, Hudson points out that from an early age the white South African child, both at home and at school, has informal experience in the handling and interpretation of pictorial material, whereas the cultural background of the black South African child offers little opportunity for such informal training. He concluded that culturally determined familiarity with pictorial material is a critical factor in the development of pictorial depth perception, supporting this conclusion by results from studies of adolescent and adult samples with a variety of cultural and educational backgrounds.

The hypothesis that cultural stimulus is critical for the development of pictorial depth perception is supported by the present results. Surveys undertaken in the communities and homes of all the children studied revealed no evidence of activities such as reading, drawing, painting, looking at pictures, pattern-making, or playing with constructional toys, and it was exceptional for a child to have used a pencil prior to going to school; furthermore, most of the parents of the children were illiterate. The opportunity for informal pictorial experience was therefore negligible. The psychological implications of such a cultural influence on the development of pictorial perception are considerable, particularly since there is evidence that lack of the same cultural stimulus may also retard development of visual–spatial functions (Vernon, 1965). It would therefore seem important to test the hypothesis that primary schooling in developing nations would be enhanced by the incorporation of specific training and informal experience in the perceiving, organizing and handling of visual and spatial materials.

Consideration will now be given to the reasoning involved in explanations concerning visibility relationships between the man and the deer. It seems probable that when children gave solely objective reasons to account for their answers concerning visibility relationships, one or other of two attitudes was utilised. Some children gave evidence of imagining themselves in the position of the man and/or deer, and from that vantage point deciding whether or not the other was visible: it is suggested that this attitude is likely to give rise to a negative answer, since it incurs an obstruction of the line of sight between man and deer by intervening objects. However, such negative answers were in the minority, many more children saying that the man and deer could see each other, citing as objective reason a relation by proximity, regard, or elevation. It is tentatively suggested that this conclusion is based on what the child himself could see as he looked at the pictures, a hypothesis which could be tested in the manner of Piaget by experimentation with 3-dimensional models and associated pictorial representations from different viewpoints (cf. Meyer, 1935; Piaget, 1954; Piaget and Inhelder, 1956; Inhelder, 1964).

With regard to subjective causality, study of the projective responses is suggestive of an identification of the child with the various aspects, actions or events which he is describing. However, as he develops his theme, which at times may give an impression of a series of rationalizations accounting for what he has just previously stated about an aspect of the picture, there is little or no attempt to integrate successive answers to form a logically coherent whole. This is at least in part due to the emphasis placed by the child on the needs, motivations and feelings of the characters in the pictures: they are not regarded as static, symbolic representations, but as direct and animated aspects of reality. Causality thus assumes a form which would operate according to the child's conception of what would be happening if the scene he is describing were real. It is evident that this may lead to contradictory statements, since as the child's attention is shifted from one part of a picture to another, so is there a shift of projected actions and intent. For example, statements indicating that between the man and deer there are a number of objects, perhaps a mountain, may be disregarded when the child decides whether or not the deer can see the man. Of importance now are such matters as the man's intent and the significance of this for the deer; for example, if the child feels that the man constitutes a threat to the deer, he may well say that the deer can see the man, but because it fears it may be killed it is hiding from him, perhaps behind the mountain. Following from this he may say that the man cannot see the deer, especially since he is preoccupied with killing the elephant.[3]

In their explanations concerning visibility relationships between man and deer, the reasoning of some children was primarily objective, of others primarily subjective, and of others a mixture of the two. While these variations among the children could be the consequence of differences in temperament and personality, the general pattern of explanation exhibited in this study shows affinities with what Piaget (1937; see also Rapaport, 1951) describes as egocentric thinking, conceived by him as characteristic of a transitional stage in the development of intelligence, stem-

3. See also examples 2–8.

ming out of the earlier sensory-motor stage of infancy, and anticipating the emergence of rational thought. Egocentric thinking is dominated by immediate experience, is more syncretic than deductive, and operates according to special laws of symbolism and immediate satisfactions. Transitions from premise to conclusion occur abruptly without intervening deductive steps, and little heed is given to proving or checking propositions, or to fitting them together into a logically coherent whole. It is submitted that the pattern of such thinking is in most respects comparable to that observed in the present study. This suggestion concerning egocentricity does not imply that the children's thinking would have been the same in a different setting. There is, for example, the interesting possibility that given a culturally relevant context and culturally familiar materials, the older children would have exhibited a shift away from egocentric toward objective, relational thinking. This is a matter for further experiment.

References

DAWSON, J. L. M., (1963), Psychological effects of social change in a West African community, *Unpublished doctoral dissertation, University of Oxford.*

HUDSON, W. (1960), 'Pictorial depth perception in sub-cultural groups in Africa', *Journal of Social Psychology*, vol. 52, pp. 183–208.

HUDSON, W. (1962), 'Pictorial perception and educational adaptation in Africa', *Psychologia Africana*, vol. 9, pp. 226–39.

INHELDER, B. (1964), 'Some aspects of Piaget's genetic approach to cognition', in J. Cohen (ed.), *Readings in Psychology*, Allen and Unwin, ch. 5.

MEYER, E. (1935), 'La représentation des relations spatiales chez l'enfant', *Cahiers de Ped. exp. et de Psychol. de l'Enfant de l'Institut des Sciences de l'Education*, vol. 8.

MUNDY-CASTLE, A. C., and NELSON, G. K. (1962), 'A neuropsychological study of the Knysna forest workers', *Psychologia Africana*, vol. 9, pp. 240–72.

PIAGET, J. (1930), *The Child's Conception of Causality*, Kegan Paul.

PIAGET, J. (1937), *Factors Determining Human Behavior*, Harvard Tercentenary Publication, Harvard University Press, pp. 32–48.

PIAGET, J. (1954), *The Construction of Reality in the Child*, Basic Books. Routledge and Kegan Paul.

PIAGET, J., and INHELDER, B. (1956), *The Child's Conception of Space*, Routledge and Kegan Paul.

RAPAPORT, D. (1951), *Organization and Pathology of Thought: Selected Sources*, Columbia University Press, ch. 6.

VERNON, P. E. (1965), 'Environmental handicaps and intellectual developments: Parts I and II', *British Journal of Educational Psychology*, vol. 35, pp. 9–20, 117–26.

8 W. Hudson

The Study of the Problem of Pictorial Perception among
Unacculturated Groups

W. Hudson, 'The study of the problem of pictorial perception among unacculturated groups' *International Journal of Psychology*, vol. 2 (1967),
pp. 90–107.

The Importance of the Problem for Education

The fact that education is regarded as an art and not as a science
may have something to do with the casual manner in which we
approach the education of the black man in Africa. We take it
very much for granted that methods which are only moderately
successful in our own cultures will prove equally, if not highly,
successful in an alien culture. We fall into the error of thinking of
the black man's mind as a *tabula rasa*, which we have only to fill
with the benefits of our cultural experience in order to promote
whatever objectives we may have in mind. We forget or ignore the
fact that the black man possesses his own indigenous culture. We
shy away from consideration of cross-cultural differences and
difficulties for fear of being accused of racialism. On the other
hand we have come to accept that, in Africa particularly, what is
needed is rapid economic and industrial development and the
provision of virtually universal educational and economic
opportunity, and in accepting this we recognize the black man's
own imperative objective. Yet we find time and again senior
white educationalists, administrators and businessmen comment-
ing adversely on the black man's academic achievement and
operational performance especially in the technological, scientific
and medical fields. Some of this may be due to colour prejudice.
Some of it may derive from the bias which the older generation
holds towards the younger. But this need not discredit entirely
the basic conviction of such experienced men. It seems odd that in
economic and technological development, an area where both
black and white have common objectives, there should be problems and disappointments. In order to grasp technological and

industrial opportunities the black man needs education and training just as does his white counterpart elsewhere. It is precisely here that much of the difficulty and confusion arises. We educate and train, and the trained black man does not match up to our standards. Here we are not concerned with standards of moral and ethical behaviour, but with operational levels and standards of knowledge and practice. This shortfall is not necessarily the black man's fault entirely. It need not predicate an inherent inferiority in any way. It may merely indicate that the white man is a bad educationalist and a worse instructor in so far as he has assumed that subject matter chosen and methods used in its presentation to white people are equally effective without modification for black people. Is it rational of us to expect this? Is it rational of us to shut our eyes to the role that culture plays in education and in the assimilation and association of new concepts and practices? We do not ignore cultural and environmental differences among the national populations of Europe. Why should we do so in Africa? Even in such a limited field as that of pictorial perception, the facts, once we become aware of them, illustrate the gravity and extensiveness of our irrationality.

However, before we come to consider in detail the problems associated with pictorial perception, we must first briefly describe the conditions likely to face the educator in Africa. In European countries there is, if not a homogeneity of education and culture, at least a distinct continuity across the various sub-groups in the population. When we prepare and publish a text book for primary school children for example, we do so in anticipation of its universal acceptability and applicability within the national group for which it was designed. Even if we allow for differences in occupation, opportunity and endowment, cultural distances within a national European community are not so large generally as to require special attention and treatment. To put it in another way, conventional advertisements for whiskey, road safety propaganda posters are equally intelligible and acceptable in the Outer Hebrides and in London, even if their relative urgencies differ. But in Africa the position is radically different and much less amenable to common treatment. In the recent past the bulk of the black male population and the whole of the black female population were illiterate, technologically unsophisticated and marginally acculturated. This position has now changed. The illiterates are still with us in large numbers, but the proportion of children receiving primary schooling is rising rapidly. In the more technologically advanced territories, co-extensive with the widening of economic opportunity, there has been an enhancement of the status and pay of blue-collar jobs, compared with white-collar tasks and the professions. As a direct result of economic expansion, there has been an influx of black work-seekers from the rural areas to the towns, from the traditional way of life to the urban community with its more intimate contact with and dependence upon the material culture of the West. Heterogeneity of education, industrial experience, acculturation and tribal origins is the order of the day. This means that in the case of the primary school child it is impossible to expect a fairly homogeneous standard on entry. Some pupils, particularly in rural areas, may come from illiterate parents. Urban pupils may have one or both parents literate or even educated to university graduate level. In industry the position is more confused. There are intelligent illiterates and unintelligent literates. The older man whose experience merits promotion is often virtually illiterate. The younger literate lacks industrial experience. How does the instructor formulate a training procedure to achieve maximum communication and learning? A further complication is added when the trainer himself is a black man.

If we are going to use pictorial material for didactic purposes, with black pupils and adults in Africa, how effective is it likely to be? Will such material designed in the white milieu evoke the relevant response among black people? In pictorial propaganda, whether for marketing, accident prevention or religious purpose, can we achieve a common presentational mode, or must we present material in different ways to match the various acculturation levels involved? Are our text book illustrations inappropriate and unnecessary therefore by the same token? To what extent are they in need of overhaul, modification or entire rejection? It depends in the ultimate issue on the usefulness of pictorial material as an aid to communication and understanding. So we use it in our own culture. We should expect it to perform a similar function in Africa. Otherwise we must modify or reject it on grounds of expense, irrelevance or misdirection.

The Recognition of the Cultural Factors in Pictorial Perception

Since 1915 psychologists working in Africa or engaged on studies of the psychological test performance of non-white children and adults have become gradually more aware of cultural problems raised by the administration to non-white candidates of tests designed for use with white people. A glance at Andor's annotated bibliography (1966) enables the reader to appreciate the relationship between philosophical thinking and psychological analysis which shaped test design for African samples. Various methods have been adopted in an attempt to meet the cultural difficulties involved in testing. Some testers have been only minimally aware of the problem. Others have been more articulate and have moved from quantitative analysis of innate ability to a study of qualitative differences.

In the study on the development of measures of effective capacity among black mine workers (Biesheuvel, 1949, 1952) perceptual problems arose at an early stage in test construction. At the time these were not examined in detail but since the evidence is cumulative and led to a fullscale investigation later, it is worth describing the findings. Two tests, known as the Block Patterns Test and the Hut Test, were devised. The first test was designed to assess the capacity to manipulate spatial relations after the manner of a simple jigsaw puzzle. The second test was of the serial pattern completion type, resembling a simple form of progressive matrices based upon symmetry.

In the Block Patterns Test material was derived from traditional Bantu patterns. The initial patterns represented complete objects, e.g. beer pot, cut into a small number of sections. The remainder were common Bantu designs abstracted from their natural context. Many candidates failed to recognize the complete pictures shown on the plates on top of which the segments of the patterns had to be assembled. It was not uncommon also for a candidate to superimpose sections upon the plate in what appeared to be a random fashion leaving considerable gaps between edges and often inverting sections. Questioning of candidates

135

showed that such positional errors and inversions did not detract from the representational value in their own estimation. The mere superimposition of sections upon the complete pictorial plate tended to obliterate the need for exact pattern fitting and precise positioning of sections relative to one another. Niessen, Machover and Kinder (1935) report relevant findings on the mannekin and feature profile tests given to children in French Guinea. Apart from the poor appreciation of part–whole relationships, the candidates piled pieces on top of one another or arranged them in some inconsequential pattern. They noticed that insertion of a section of the mannekin test was sufficient to permit recognition of the complete figure to occur.

The Hut Test was a 3-dimensional model of a traditional African round hut. Patterns were hung on both sides of the door with blanks left, requiring correct choices to be made from a multiple choice situation in order to fit and complete the patterns. Recognition of pattern elements and correct fitting of elements were required. In this case candidates might select the correct item or items to fit into the blanks in the total pattern but would position them incorrectly or transpose them.

In the field of projective testing also, perceptual difficulties were encountered. Nadel (1937) described different misperceptions seen by Nupe and Yoruba children. Leblanc (1958) and Ombredane (1954) were critical of projective pictures with African samples. Adcock and Ritchie (1958) recognized the effect of culture difference on Rorschach evaluations. Dennis (1951) and Biesheuvel (1958 a and b) recommended investigation of perceptual habits prior to the construction of projective tests and as an essential tool in their interpretation. The extent to which misperceptions can effect the manifest and latent contents of projective test material is plain from the following examples. The Tomkins–Horn Picture Arrangement Test (Tomkins and Miner, 1959) was administered experimentally to illiterate Bantu adults in South Africa. Plate 4 [This and plate 16 referred to below are not included here.] shows a scene which could be perceuved as a group fighting. According to the authors, neurotic candidates reject aggression in their responses to this scene. The illiterate Bantu adult reports plate 4 as a dancing scene. Plate 16 shows what can be perceived as drops of blood falling from a man's finger as a result probably of an accident as work. Manic-depressives do not see the injury. They describe it as oil dripping from a can. The illiterate Bantu perceives the representation of drops of fluid, i.e. blood or oil, as connected links in a chain. Such deviant responses among illiterate Bantu are symptomatic not of psychiatric syndrome but of perceptual difficulty culturally conditioned. Another study (Hudson, 1960) where structured projective material was employed to study the degree of acculturation of a group of Bantu factory workers in South Africa of different tribal origins, educational levels and degrees of urbanisation, provided corroborative evidence. Two of the pictures, all of which were unambiguous half-tone graphic representations, produced unexpected perceptual responses in twenty protocols. One scene, representing the homecoming of a migrant industrial worker, contained the figures of an elderly couple seated in the traditional way on the ground. Behind, was a thatched round hut with the figure of a worker, clad in overalls, arms akimbo, superimposed upon it. Seven protocols referred to a winged being, a devil, an angel, the temptation of Eve in Paradise. By accident, the artist, in superimposing on the hut the foreground figure of the worker, had placed the ragged thatched roof of the hut in such a position that an observer, who perceived pictures 2-dimensionally, could see the thatch as feathers or wings sprouting from the figure's back just above his shoulders. The posture with arms akimbo aided this perception. Needless to say neither the artist, nor the psychologist who scrutinized the projective material were aware of this perceptual interpretation, until the protocolds were obtained. Perceiving 3-dimensionally, they could not see the picture flat. A second picture was drawn to represent a dema-gogue haranguing a group of workers. As a dominating figure he was placed above the workers, and, in the background, to lend atmosphere to the scene, the artist drew in a long factory building with three tall smoking chimneys. Again by accident, the dema-gogue's outstretched hands were positioned just above the tops of two of the chimneys. Thirteen protocols referred to the madman who had climbed up to the tops of the houses and was warming his hands at the smoke. Given 2-dimensional pictorial convention this interpretation could have been correct. But in this instance, because of perceptual difficulties, candidates were responding to an irrelevant manifest pictorial content and associating it with a latent projective content outside the test's reference frame. Equivalence of perceptually structured stimuli was not achieved and responses could be culturally endemic.

It is only in comparatively recent years that social scientists have turned their attention to the careful study of the effect of culture on pictorial perception. At the turn of the century, Rivers (1901, 1905) did some experimental work on the perception of geometric illusions amongst primitive groups in the Torres Straits. Morgan (1959) using Herskovits's test of geometric illussion and Segall, Campbell and Herskovits (1963) using the same test repeated this work with a large number of samples from Africa and elsewhere, concluding that the intergroup differences obtained supported the hypothesis that a major factor in space perception was the acquisition of habits of perceptual inference. Gregor and McPherson (1965) carried this investigation further by exploring with various Australian aboriginal groups the effect of a carpentered and an uncarpentered environment on the differences in susceptibility to geometric illusion. Thouless in his studies of Indian students showed that they exhibited a greater degree of regression to the real object than did British students. In a study by Beveridge (1940), African students were placed between Indian and European students in respect of this perceptual phenomenon. Pedler (1961) reports on work by Culwick which stressed the deviance from true mathematical perspective which both European and Bantu perception displayed.

The Phenomenology of Pictorial Misperception

Depth perception: Relative object size, overlap and perspective

In 1960 Hudson completed the first of a series of studies on pictorial perception with African samples using composite pictures. The objective was to examine the responses of various cultural groups in Africa to the representational cues of depth. Outline drawings and a photograph of a model scene were constructed so as to depend perceptually on the cues of object size, overlap and perspective. The three objects in the pictures, hunter, antelope and elephant were drawn in a constant relationship to one another in all outline drawings. The first two objects, hunter and antelope were drawn so as to be perceived as lying in the same frontal plane with the elephant in the background. Supplementary depth cues were introduced in the form of a hill on which the elephant was standing, contour lines representing mountains and perspective lines representing a road, vanishing in a horizon. In all pictures the hunter's spear was aligned on both elephant and antelope. Responses to the questions whether the hunter was aiming at elephant or antelope or whether elephant or antelope was nearer the hunter were taken as self-evident indications of 2-dimensional or 3-dimensional pictorial perception. There were ten samples in the original study. A white primary school group formed three samples, viz. beginners, finishers and the total group. A black secondary school group contained two samples, viz. entrants and senior pupils. One group of black graduate school teachers was tested. The remaining four samples were all adult, consisting of one white labourer sample, educated to primary school level, one black illiterate labouring sample, one black labourer sample at primary school level and one black clerical group with secondary school education.

Results showed that white pupils at the beginning of primary school had difficulty in seeing pictures in depth. Even with a photograph, more than one quarter of them should be perceived in two dimensions. By the end of the primary school the majority of the white pupils were competent in 3-dimensional perception of pictorial material. They had no difficulty at all in seeing the photograph in depth. The first conclusion followed that during the primary school period the white pupil acquired competence in pictorial depth perception. But the same conclusion did not appear to hold for black pupils. It was true that black senior secondary school pupils put up slightly better 3-dimensional performance than did black pupils beginning secondary school. On the other hand graduate teachers showed no improvement over them. Statistical analysis showed that there was no real difference among the three black pupil samples. That was an important enough finding in itself, but what was still more important was that the depth perception performance of the more highly educated black samples was not significantly better than that of the white school children in the upper classes of the primary school. In view of the difference in educational level, a perceptual difference in favour of the black samples might have been warrantably anticipated. In this case also all the black graduates had attended multi-racial universities and had taken courses and examinations common for both black and white students. These findings compelled the conclusion that formal education, which had been hypothesized as playing a decisive role in the growth of pictorial depth perception, had no more than a contributive function and was subordinate to other cultural factors in the environment.

Further analysis of the occupational samples led to a further adjustment in hypothesis. Both illiterate and primary educated black labourers saw the pictures flat. So did the white labourers, who had primary schooling. It is not difficult to understand that the illiterate black sample should have failed to see depth in pictures. But in the case of the white sample the performance cannot be explained away on ethnic grounds. Neither can it be accounted for educationally, for the white labouring sample had completed primary school. In this instance the factor of cultural isolation tended to nullify the effect of schooling. On the one hand there was a group from an alien culture, on the other hand there was a sample which had virtually rejected its own culture or belonged at best only marginally. Perceptually, the result was the same. Pictures were seen 2-dimensionally. Hence formal schooling in the normal course is not the principal determinant in pictorial perception. Informal instruction in the home and habitual exposure to pictures play a much larger role.

On four of the test pictures, evidence on additional ethnic samples was obtained (Hudson, 1962 a and b). In addition to the European (white) and Bantu (black) samples previously studied, one sample each of Coloured (mixed blood) and Indian (Asiatic) pupils with comparable educational standard was tested. A much higher percentage of European pupils saw 3-dimensionally. Coloured pupils were superior to Bantu and Indian samples. Bantu and Indian pupils performed equally poorly. For consistency of response over three outline pictures the order was European, Coloured, Bantu and Indian samples with more than two-thirds of the European and fewer than one-third of the Indian pupils perceiving 3-dimensionally. Results on the test photograph corroborated this finding. They showed that European primary school pupils were markedly superior to all other cultural groups in the 3-dimensional perception of a photograph. This conclusion supports the earlier contention that the perceptual determinants are cultural. The Coloured sample is culturally closer to the Western norm than the Bantu sample. It is surprising. however, that the Indian sample had such difficulty and performed at the same level as the Bantu sample. It is worth noting here that the Indian sample, mainly Gujerati-speaking, belong to an alien culture, which unlike that of the Bantu, has its own distinct form of pictorial art with a set of representational conventions peculiar to the Orient.

Although in these studies, the prime data could be quantified and analysed statistically, responses concerned with the identification of items in the pictures showed additional evidence of misperception of the conventional pictorial depth cues. The outline of the hill on which the elephant stood was seen by the two dimensional perceivers as a path or a river. Perspective lines were seen to be an elephant trap or poles. The more educated sometimes saw them as letters of the alphabet. Many of the illiterate Bantu sighted the pictures from side to side to determine accurately the direction in which the hunter's assegai was aimed. A limited number rejected their 2-dimensional percept on logical grounds, claiming that a hunter would never attack an elephant with a spear only. They concluded that the hunter's assegai must therefore be aimed at the antelope. Bantu graduates reported that they could see the picture in two ways, i.e. either flat or in depth, and asked the tester for guidance in deciding their responses.

Foreshortening

Foreshortening is a common convention in western art and represents a form of perspective applied to the figures of humans and animals generally. Three outline drawings were used in the study (Hudson, 1962 a and b). One showed the back view of a man stepping up on a step with one leg. The second presented a back view of a man showing upper arms as far as elbows. The lower part of his body was not visible being cut off by the margin of the picture. In the third plate two plan views of an elephant were drawn. In the one case the legs and trunk were not visible.

It represented a true photographic or foreshortened view of an elephant seen from above. In the other case, all four legs were shown spread out as if the elephant had been flattened out from above. This representation was entirely unnatural and was in fact perceptually impossible. The three pictures were shown to two samples, one of white primary school pupils, the other of illiterate black labourers. Differences in perception were marked. Most of the white pupils saw the two foreshortened drawings of the man in depth. They reported him to be climbing up a step or to be doing something with his hands, which they could not see because his back hid this from their view. The illiterate black sample saw these two pictures flat. In both cases the figure of the man was seen as maimed or injured in some way. In the first case the man stepping up was seen as having a short leg or a broken leg. In the second picture they reported him with a deformed arm, and sometimes as dead, because he had been cut in half (only the top half of his body had been drawn in). To the drawings of the elephants the white children responded as we should have expected. The foreshortened view of the elephant from above was accepted as natural, while the other view showing all four limbs extended was seen as the skin of a dead elephant. The black illiterate sample reported the precise opposite. They saw the foreshortened elephant as dead, since it had no legs. The second drawing (spread-eagled elephant) was seen as that of a live elephant, in spite of the fact that it was perceptually impossible. One of the illiterate candidates tested reported this to be a very ferocious and dangerous elephant indeed, since it was jumping wildly about.

Twisted perspective

In the representation and identification of perceptually impossible objects there appear to be certain philogenetic and ontogenetic parallels. In his cave drawings of fauna, early man used a form of perspective which has become known as Lascaux or twisted perspective. This is a combination of profile and frontal views. Although the body of the antelope is drawn in profile, two horns and two ears are clearly visible. Drawings of cows collected from black students attending an art school in Rhodesia present the same phenomena (Hudson, 1962 a and b). They were asked to draw a cow in profile. Every one drawn had two horns, two ears and four cloven hooves visible. A number of drawings done for a poster competition by black secondary school pupils provided examples of the extension of twisted perspective to inanimate objects such as automobiles. Motor cars drawn in side view showed also the front grille with two head lamps visible. In his early attempts at depicting the human figure the young white child draws full-face views which gradually change to profiles, as he grows older. But there is an intermediate stage where characteristics of the early stage occur in the latter. For example, the profiles are drawn with a pair of eyes visible. Pencil drawings of elephants profile views, collected from illiterate black labourers show similar phenomena (Hudson, 1962 a and b). Irrespective of the shape or size of the drawings, two eyes and four legs were always shown.

The significance of these drawings lies in their demonstration of two distinct representational practices. The white man draws what he sees. If he sees an animal in profile, his drawing of it is perceptually correct. He perceives that a road appears to narrow as it approaches the horizon. So he draws it in this perspective manner although he knows his picture is conceptually inaccurate. When he does draw, the unacculturated black man draws to identify an object. If he depicts an ungulate in profile, he knows that the creature has cloven hoves and he includes this item in a perceptually impossible composition. He draws what he knows and not what he sees.

Absolute object size

These drawings of the illiterate black sample gave further interesting pointers to the problem of pictorial perception. One figure only (elephant profile) was drawn on a *quarto*-sized page. The range of size was striking. It was clear that in his representation of a single object on a blank page, size was unimportant in the perceptual field bounded by the edges of the paper. In Western pictures we use size as a means of indicating distance.

Positioning and orientation

Positioning and orientation of the drawings were unusual. In western art again objects tend to be positioned with reference to a base line at the bottom of the page. The drawings of the black illiterates were scattered randomly over the page, and it was clear that the base line held no special significance for them as a reference point. Orientation of the drawings did not obey western art conventions. Normally objects are drawn standing upon a base line towards the bottom of a page, unless design is intended, in which case objects may be oriented vertically or even inverted. The black illiterates drew elephants rampant, couchant and even inverted. In the case of the inversions, questioning elicited the information that these candidates had seen objects and animals being drawn in sand on the ground by an older man when they had been children. Standing in front of this sand artist, they had always seen things drawn from this standpoint, with the result that when they came to draw themselves they drew objects in an inverted position quite naturally.

It is clear from the evidence obtained from systematic studies of pictorial depth perception and from observation of the drawings of black illiterates that the perceptual cues and representational conventions common in Western pictorial art provide problems of interpretation to the black man. Differences in objective and lack of meaningful exposure to the Western forms of art are largely responsible for these difficulties.

Critiques and the Proposed Psychological Model

These earlier studies have led to discussion by du Toit (1966) and Ferenczi (1966) and have stimulated further research both basic (Deregowski, 1966) and applied (Winter, 1963; Hudson, unpublished). Some account of this work is relevant for an understanding of the perceptual problems involved. Du Toit argued that through concept formation language was responsible for the response pattern of 2-dimensional perception characteristic of the black man in the study (Hudson, 1960). This is an attempt to substitute the principle of semantic deprivation for that of perceptual habituation. The applicability of his principle is suspect in that in Hudson's study the white adult labouring sample's perceptual response was of an order similar to that of the black illiterates. In any event as du Toit noted, the argument does not materially affect the findings. Ferenczi's main discussion on the studies (Hudson, 1960) was concerned with shortcomings in the nature of the test material, experimental design, with sampling desiderata such as age levels, and with incompatibility of the test administration for African samples. Much of his concern is with minutiae. Deregowski's later investigation (1966), which included a repetition of Hudson's work, substantiates on Zambian samples the findings of the original experiment and disposes of most of Ferenczi's objections. Further the design of Hudson's original experiment (1960) stands up to the methodological requirements for cross-cultural research as enunciated by Campbell (1964). In his epistemological considerations he argued that the demonstration of difference is possible only from a basis of similarity. The occurrence of a common pattern as obtained in the experimental findings on depth perception substantiates that the acceptance of differential response as an indication of perceptual differences and not of communication break-down is correct.

One of Ferenczi's comments is relevant to these perceptual studies. He argued that the basic problem was presented in terms of a perceptual aptitude instead of in terms of the educability of perception. It seems possible to reconcile the static hierarchical model of abilities with that of the dynamic nature of their development. The work of Ferguson (1956) and Mac-Arthur (1966) has reference here. In their view, the pattern of abilities stabilised over periods of time as a result of interaction with the environment. This meant that cultural factors played a considerable role in the formation of the mental pattern. The stabilization process took the form of a hierarchical order with those abilities at the highest levels least affected by specific environmental experiences. With this model it is possible to integrate Campbell's theory of analogous preponderance (1964) with the recognition of the formative effect of culture upon effective capacity permitting the observation of differences of performance in such peripheral fields as that of pictorial perception. Mac-Arthur supported his hypothesis from the study of various white, Indian-Meti and Eskimo groups in Canada. Ferguson referred to findings of Burnett in Newfoundland which illustrated the differentiation of ability patterns in terms of environmental differences. He quoted Fleishman also to show that substantial and systematic changes occurred in the factor structure of the learning task as practice continued and that abilities might vary with the stage of learning. Hudson (1962 a and b) demonstrated this statement on four differently educated black samples in Africa, illustrating that the more educated groups (6, 9, 12 years of schooling) would provide a different factorial structure, contingent upon changed dimension of measurement, from the least educated sample (3 years of schooling). What is important here for understanding the implications of perceptual problems in Africa is the concept of stabilization of mental pattern in terms of a cultural mode. To what degree is this stabilization invariant? If the prevalent cultural mode promotes 3-dimensional pictorial perception, can a member of that culture become competent in 2-dimensional perception? Will an adult white man, brought up in the western mode, readily perceive pictures flat? Experience suggests that this is unlikely. This proposition is of course the corollary of the problem under investigation, but both are equally valid propositions. The illiterate black adult and, for that matter, the culturally peripheral white adult are 2-dimensional pictorial perceivers. The educated black adult can be ambivalent. The white child undergoes a perceptual conditioning towards pictorial depth perception in accordance with his cultural requirements.

Schwitzgebel (1962) carried out a comparative study of two South African white and black samples on visual and cognitive tasks, which included length and size estimation and the Gottschaldt embedded figures. Both groups consisted of young adults. His findings demonstrated the difficulty which the black group had in performing the perceptual tasks. He concluded that his findings supported the hypothesis that specific perceptual organisations are culturally characteristic and environmentally dependent, and further that some of the perceptual skills might not be attainable even after extensive education. This proposition has considerable sociological implications particularly in the field of education with heterogeneously schooled and culturally different populations.

Deregowski (1966) in Zambia undertook an analysis of the perceptual basis of the responses of two groups of Zambians (pupils and domestic servants) to pictorial material designed to investigate the effect of the representational conventions of size, superimposition and perspective upon pictorial depth perception. He compared findings obtained in Hudson's pictorial depth perception test with results from a performance type test in which candidates were presented with line drawings of the Necker cube type and asked to construct apparatus models of the drawings as perceived. In addition a drawing experiment was included in which 2- and 3-dimensional models of variations of the Necker cube were presented. Candidates were asked to draw what they perceived. Performances were scored for 2- or 3-dimensional perception. Deregowski found differences between his two samples. School children perceived 3-dimensionally more frequently than domestic servants. No marked differences in depth perception performance were found between Deregowski's results and Hudson's (1960) results on the same pictorial perception test for black primary school samples, except that Zambian pupils gave markedly less frequent 3-dimensional responses to the size cues for depth perception. This result might be due to the lower educational standard of the Zambia primary school sample.

From the fact that a switch from 2- to 3-dimensional response occurred when the same candidates were given both the pictorial depth perception test and the apparatus construction test of the Necker cube, Deregowski hypothesized a restriction of the applicability of Hudson's (1960) findings to the use of conventionalised cues. Two-dimensional responses might occur as a result of the inability of the perceiver to organize the material presented in the test pictures. He confirmed the finding that object identification in a picture did not predicate 3-dimensional perception and he used this information to support the hypothesis that what appeared to be 2-dimensional perceptual response might have occurred not as a result of misperception but either because of a failure to orientate the representation correctly or because of a mode of perceptual integration which relied upon pictorial cues other than depth cues. He reported ambivalent responses when candidates drew a 3-dimensional representation of a 2-dimensional model and constructed a 3-dimensional model of a 2-dimensional drawing. It was not possible to determine whether this finding was due to perceptual ambivalence or to preference for the development type of graphic representation. The fact that Deregowski used performance type responses such as drawing

147

and model-making seems to go a long way to dispose of du Toit's (1966) semantic hypothesis on Hudson's 1960 data. His test-retest design producing no significant response differences refutes Ferenczi's criticism on the score of reliability.

Review of Findings from Applied Research Studies into the Perception of Posters and Symbolic Representations

South Africa

In addition to experimental findings in a controlled pictorial environment, applied studies have been carried out with a view to exploring what happens in the normal course when the black man looks at pictures, designed with a didactic objective in mind. Two such studies have been carried out in South Africa. A study reported by Winter (1963) was concerned with perceptual difficulties in a set of safety posters designed for use in factories. A second study carried out by Hudson repeated the first study but with a different set of posters designed for the mining industry.

In the first study on safety posters for factories, 270 black factory workers in South Africa were questioned on their perception and understanding of six selected posters. This sample contained workers from urban and rural areas, differing in educational level from complete illiteracy to senior secondary school. In terms of exposure to the poster material the group was sub-divided into those entirely unexposed, those with some previous vicarious exposure to them and those to whom the posters had been previously explained. The posters were all printed in colour and contained a variety of representational conventions and techniques, e.g. single scenes, multiple scenes, serial scenes, causal and symbolism. Captions printed on each poster to draw attention to the moral of the illustration were covered during initial questioning, but later exposed.

The first two posters were causal scenes of the 'before and after' type. The first one was concerned with the wearing of goggles when grinding. It contained four sub-scenes. The two top scenes showed a worker at the grindstone wearing his goggles and the worker off duty well dressed and obviously prosperous. The two bottom scenes showed a worker sustaining an eye injury at the grindstone for lack of protective goggles and the same worker now blind and in rags being led around as a beggar. The second poster was concerned with illustrating the danger of stumbling and falling when carrying a load which obscures the view of the worker. Again four scenes were presented, but in this instance the associated sub-scenes were arranged vertically and not horizontally as in the first poster. In both cases the black factory worker had difficulty in associating the man in the 'before' scene with the same man in the 'after' scene. Situation and dress were different and there was no single identification cue visible. The vertical and horizontal association merely confounded an already complicated perceptual task. In the second poster also there was an interesting cultural problem which the artist had accidentally introduced. The last sub-scene in the 'correct' sequence showed the black worker receiving his wages from the paymaster. In the poster the worker was drawn as receiving his pay with one hand only. For the black factory worker in South Africa this has the opposite connotation. It is customary to receive things in both hands and to give things with one hand. So the moral of the illustration tended to be obscured by an accidental breach of custom, since in the poster the recipient of the wage was seen not as a receiver of reward for correct work, but as a donor of money. This was far from the intention of the artist and safety officer. The third poster showed the danger of throwing tools, e.g. a hammer striking another worker on the head. But due to 2-dimensional perception by the black worker, the hammer, intended to be seen as in mid-air, caught in the act of striking another worker, was reported as lying on the window sill. With the prime cue missed, there was a search for the message of the poster, and secondary cues tended then to be exploited inadvertently. In this poster for example, all the human figures shown were looking fixedly into space. Hence it followed for some black perceivers that the message of this poster was that workers should look at what they are working at and that their attention must not be engaged elsewhere. Posters 4 and 5 illustrated the dangers of symbolic convention in Western art. Poster 4 showed how careless behaviour by a worker carrying a heavy wooden plank could injure another worker. The intention of the artist was to portray the actual moment of the accident for he showed the timber striking the victim on the head and obscuring it entirely. The victim is drawn some distance in the background on a smaller scale than the man in the foreground. The impact is symbolised in the form of a star which surrounds the point of contact of timber and head. The victim, being drawn smaller, is seen as a little boy. The impact mark (the star) is taken to be the sun. In the fifth poster which was intended to illustrate the danger of injured toes and fingers as a result of incorrect lifting, impact marks in the form of shock or pain waves were misinterpreted as wrinkles in the man's shirt. The sixth poster was composed to illustrate the danger of standing beneath a loaded crane sling. The artist had drawn a box in a sling of four ropes with one rope broken. Beneath was the figure of the worker with raised arms petrified with horror, presumably as the box descended upon him. The lower half of the worker in the poster was not shown. The artist had surrounded the poster with a broad red oval border and had highlighted the man's face with reddish brown. This was unfortunate. In the first place, the box was not seen as falling. It was clear that three of the four ropes still held it in place. So the danger has to be seen elsewhere. The colour red has acquired a symbolic value for the black worker in South Africa. In lareg quantities it means fire. In smaller amounts it signifies blood. In the case of this poster it was reported as fire. The man was seen as being in a fiery holocaust. This interpretation was heightened by the highlighting of his features. The deciding factor was the fact that the lower half of his body was not visible. It had obviously been consumed in the flames. So the intended message of the posters was lost due to misperceptions and misunderstandings of custom and pictorial convention.

A number of general conclusions derived from this poster study. Oral explanation improved understanding. Captions made no difference since the bulk of the labour force tested could not read well. Visual exposure to the posters with oral instruction increased understanding to the extent of half the sample thus exposed. Educated urban workers gave more correct responses than illiterate rural workers.

The findings also produced proposals for the overhaul of conventional poster design. Single scenes were recommended in preference to multi-scene posters. Conventional depth cues caused confusion. Symbolic convention caused misunderstanding. The colour red had well established significance and diverted attention from the poster's objective if used for mere decorative purposes. Behaviour in the posters should be depicted in accordance with local African custom.

As a result of this study, the safety posters were redesigned bearing in mind these conclusions. They proved to be less attractive from an artistic point of view but more effective in promoting understanding. The revised versions of the posters were extensively tested out before the designs were finalized and printed. Single scenes only were used. Thus the first multi-scene poster studied was simplified to show one man operating a grinding machine and wearing goggles. There were no 'before and after' scenes and no 'right–wrong' techniques shown. Great care was taken to show that the worker possessed all his limbs and fingers even if this meant the loss of perspective and foreshortening. In the case of the 'cranesling' poster the colour red was avoided entirely. The rope sling itself was shown completely severed, the box which it held was in process of descending and the man underneath was running for his life. In all posters background and unnecessary details were eliminated. This produced a rather stark representation, which on test was readily understood. Finally great care was exercised in the composition of the human figure in all the posters. Throughout the figure could be identified as the same person. He wore the same clothes and had a constant physiognomy and shade of complexion. This last point was found to be important. When the figure was depicted in a very dark facial tone, the workers rejected him as a foreign worker from Central Africa. He was too dark and they could not identify themselves with him. On the other hand, if his complexion was shown too light, he was seen as a white man. Consequently the message of the poster was not their concern. Such perceptual details as these become important with variously acculturated African samples, if our objective with pictorial material is didactic.

In the survey of perception of safety posters in the mining industry, three samples were questioned on ten selected posters. Samples consisted of eighty-one supervisors, 111 experienced workers and 100 new recruits. Three of the posters contained two scenes in colour and were read vertically, the top scene showing the scene before the accident and the bottom scene depicting the accident or the result of it. One poster in silhouette contained four scenes read horizontally and was purely instructional in the use of goggles to prevent eye injuries. Analogous symbolism was used in two posters. One consisted of a single scene showing a snake representing a misfire. The other was a dual scene poster, one scene showing the danger of bad roof conditions underground, and the second scene showing an analogous situation from wild life of a bird in front of a trap. Two posters consisted of single scenes. Both were full of irrelevant detail and one relied on foreshortening. One poster was of the minimum presentation type. It contained a coloured representation of a pair of hands held up palms facing. One hand had three fingers or parts of fingers missing with one word in the vernacular meaning 'no spares'. To emphasize the injured hand the artist had drawn blue bands radiating from each amputated finger. The tenth poster included in the test series did not strictly concern itself with safety or accident prevention. It was intended to illustrate cooperation and consisted of nine scenes reading from top to bottom, depicting the old fable of the dilemma of two calves tied together and faced with the problem of drinking milk from two buckets set further apart than the length of the rope which bound them.

It was not surprising to find that the samples tested, typical for the industry in so far as they were mostly illiterates, had perceptual difficulties with these posters. Associations with the dual stage posters were not readily understood with the result that the message of the poster was distorted or lost. Symbolism frequently proved to be an impediment to understanding, in so far as it distracted attention and distorted understanding of the objective of the poster. Since much of the symbolism, e.g. snake, bird, was naturalistic, the relevance for mining tended to be lost. The animal represented was misidentified by some of the sample. The snake, which was a cobra with hood extended, was mistaken for a fish and the calves were seen as hyenas, dogs and even lions. More specific conventions intended to illustrate impact, such as shock waves represented by radiating lines usually accompanied by stars of various colours, were misinterpreted and tended to be taken literally. Where the poster showed an eye accident at the moment of happening, the white stars were taken to be the white parts of the eye, the black stars the black parts of the eye, i.e. pupil of eye, and the red stars blood, according to the common convention. Foreshortening of the human figure produced the response of injury which implies 2-dimensional perception. Plethora of detail and economy of presentation both defeated the objective. In the one instance, the message was lost in a mass of irrelevant background items. In the other case (the poster showing the amputated fingers) there appeared to be too little information provided to permit the objective to be grasped. As it was the blue lines with which the artist surrounded the fingers in an attempt at graphic emphasis proved to be confusing and distracting. They were seen as perspiration, muscles, fingernails and rays of light.

The purpose of each poster was to communicate a specific message appropriate to a specific accident situation. It was true that most of the samples knew that the posters were associated with danger or accidents, but in a vague, general relationship which nullified their specificity. Coloured geometric patterns would have made just as suitable posters and would have been nearly as effective as communicators. As might be expected, supervisors showed more understanding of the posters than the other two samples. Raw recruits had greatest perceptual difficulties. Some examples will serve to show how far off the mark understanding was. The poster showing the hands with injured fingers was intended to show that fingers were irreplaceable and that therefore care should be taken to protect hands by working carefully. Misinterpretations of this message were as follows: 'The poster teaches me how to write', 'The man is counting with his fingers', 'It tells of a man who has open arms', 'I should go and do likewise' (sic), 'I must wash my hands', 'I must give hand signals', 'I must not handle fire'. The poster showing the two calves designed to illustrate the advantages of co-operation gave the following misunderstandings: 'It teaches me how to attend to cattle', 'It shows me how to feed calves', 'It shows me how to bring up calves without a mother', 'It tells me to rest and drink when tired', 'It tells me to work like cattle'. So much for naturalistic analogies among a cattle-owning population!

West and East Africa

Workers such as MacLean (1960) and Holmes (1960, 1963, 1964) have carried out investigations of the comprehension of health propaganda through the medium of pictorial presentation. Mac-Lean discussing findings in a health poster campaign in Nigeria commented on the inappropriateness of posters designed in the western manner. Posters which depended for their impact upon economy of presentation were not understood. She pointed out that posters were unnecessary at this stage of community development in West Africa. Ability to read was counted an achievement not to be hidden under a bushel. Handbills, to us diffuse and tedious, were appreciated and enjoyed in Ibadan. Amateur readers were only too pleased to explain their contents and display their learning to admiring groups in West African towns, where there was still time to stand and listen to someone reading a long printed notice.

Holmes in Kenya stressed the perceptual difficulties found with health posters. He carried out a study on samples of urban youths and women designed to explore certain hypotheses. His findings showed that amount of detail in a picture influenced comprehension. Too much or too little were both detrimental. Lack of understanding of the convention of perspective reduced comprehension and rendered the material of little value for teaching, and pictorial symbols capable of a literal or an extended meaning tended to be interpreted literally by people of limited education. For example, the skull and crossbones symbol for danger was correctly interpreted by less than half of the candidates he tested. The picture of a human eye caused difficulty of recognition due to its symbolic use in dissociation from the other parts of the head. Difficulties with foreshortening were less prevalent than anticipated. Representations of familiar objects were not more easily recognized than those of unfamiliar objects, although generally literal interpretations were received. His attempts to establish whether a familiar object drawn larger than reality was more difficult to interpret than when drawn life size or smaller broke down due to misperception of the stimulus material used.

Central and South America

In Costa Rica and Mexico, Spalding (1961) carried out a study of picture symbols. He found that illustration as such had no assured didactic value and might even prove to be a distraction if its content had not been presented in terms of the past experience of the viewer. Realistic portrayal, reduction of detail and simplification of action were essential to promote a grasp of the idea being communicated. The use of colour might add to the appeal of the illustration, but, unless used functionally, might reduce its communicative value. Captions served to supplement information derived from a picture. Their function was not exegetic, but annotative.

In rural Brazil, Fonseca and Kearl (1960) carried out a study of the comprehension of pictorial symbols. They concluded that age and education were the principal factors affecting comprehension. Their findings on pictorial detail, recognition of familiar objects, realism of representation, literal and figurative meaning of symbols resembled those of Spalding. Sex made no difference to comprehension of symbols of a general nature. Except for symbols very closely related to daily life experience, pictorial interpretation of illiterates was markedly inferior to that of literates. Comprehension was highly correlated with educational level, particularly where symbols had figurative significance or were abstract, serial or divorced from daily life experience. Age was also related to the capacity for comprehending pictorial symbols, though not so markedly as education.

Conclusion

The objective of this paper was to make a brief survey of the recent work done in Africa and elsewhere on the perception of pictorial material with a view to summarizing the findings and relating them to the main issue of communication which confronts the educationalist, whether he be teaching history, health or accident prevention. It is possible to attempt an answer to some of the questions posed above on the didactic use of pictorial material.

How effective will it be? Its effectiveness depends upon two factors, viz. the form of the representation used and the nature of the sample perceiving it. Representation which depends upon specific graphic conventions, upon symbolism or upon serialization will increase the likelihood of misperception and reduce the probability of comprehension. Both pictorial hyperbole and pictorial meiosis will diminish the chances of the didactic objective being achieved. With a homogeneous sample, uniform material can be meaningfully presented. But homogeneity in Africa depends upon the extent of acculturation, of industrialization, of urbanization, of education and ultimately of pictorial experience. It is easiest to attain in a classroom, but is neither automatically nor universally found. The pupils in a given classroom in a given area may differ radically in acculturation level from those in the same educational standard in another area. It is most difficult to attain with the general body of the public. Advertisements and propaganda are directed at the general black public. This concept is mythical. There is no general black public in the same sense as there is a general white public. Rather there exists a series of publics stratified by acculturation. What is pictorially meaningful at one level can be pictorially meaningless at a lower acculturation level. But black people who look at pictures are not usually conveniently stratified. They come in random fashion. Hence at the present time no one mode of representation will suffice. Pictorial presentation must be diversified until such time as by a common educative process perceptual homogeneity has been reached.

In this general statement most of the other questions are answered, viz. the question of the common representational mode, the question of modification or rejection. Finally there is the question of relevance and this has bearing on the decision to retain pictorial material even for unacculturated samples, provided it is properly designed. From this survey of studies it is clear that the picture becomes associated in a generic way with the topic which it is intended to illustrate. This association, though not as specific as the teacher would expect, has its use in that it evokes a mood of receptivity, which is the prime step in the educative process. Provided pictorial material appropriately designed for acculturation level and conceived as a visual aid and not as an independent technique, plays a role in the preparation of the pupil, it is worth the cost of time, effort and money.

References

ADCOCK, C. J., and RITCHIE, J. E. (1958), 'Intercultural use of Rorschach', *American Anthropologist*, vol. 60, pp. 881–92.

ANDOR, L. E. (1966), *Aptitudes and Abilities of the Black Man in Sub-Saharan Africa, 1784–1963*, National Institute for Personnel Research, South African Council for Scientific and Industrial Research, Johannesburg.

BEVERIDGE, W. M. (1940), 'Some racial differences in perception', *British Journal of Psychology*, vol. 30, pp. 57–64.

BIESHEUVEL, S. (1949), 'Psychological tests and their application to non-European peoples', in *Yearbook of Education*, Evans Bros in association with University of London, Institute of Education.

BIESHEUVEL, S. (1952), 'The study of African ability', *African Studies*, vol. 11, pp. 45–57 and 105–17.

BIESHEUVEL, S. (1958a), 'Objectives and methods of African psychological research', *Journal of Social Psychology*, vol. 47, pp. 161–8.

BIESHEUVEL, S. (1958b), 'Methodology in the study of attitudes of Africans', *Journal of Social Psychology*, vol. 47, pp. 169–84.

CAMPBELL, D. T. (1964), 'Distinguishing differences of perception from failures of communication in cross-cultural studies', in F. S. C. Northrop and H. H. Livingston (eds.), *Cross-Cultural Understanding: Epistemology in Anthropology*, Harper, pp. 308–36.

DENNIS, W. (1951), 'Cultural and developmental factors in perception', in R. R. Blake and G. V. Ramsey (eds.), *An Approach to Personality*, Ronald Press.

DEREGOWSKI, J. B. (1966), *Difficulties in Pictorial Perception in Africa*, University of Zambia, Institute for Social Research.

DU TOIT, B. M. (1966), 'Pictorial depth perception and linguistic relativity', *Psychologia Africana*, vol. 11, pp. 51–63.

FERENCZI, V. (1966), *La Perception de l'Espace Projectif*, Didier.

FERGUSON, G. A. (1956), 'On transfer and the abilities of man', *Canadian Journal of Psychology*, vol. 10, pp. 121–31.

FONSECA, L. and KEARL, B. (1960), 'Comprehension of pictorial symbols: an experiment in rural Brazil', *Bulletin, Department of Agricultural Journalism, University of Wisconsin, College of Agriculture*, no. 30.

GREGOR, A. J., and McPHERSON, D. A. (1965), 'A study of susceptibility to geometric illusion among cultural subgroups of Australian aborigines', *Psychologia Africana*, vol. II, pp. 1–13.

HOLMES, A. C. (1960), *Use of Visual Aids in Kenya*, Medical Department, Kenya.

HOLMES, A. C. (1963), *A Study of Understanding of Visual Symbols in Kenya*, Oversea Visual Aids Centre, Publication No. 10.

HOLMES, A. C. (1964), *Health Education in Developing Countries*, Nelson.

HUDSON, W. (1960), 'Pictorial depth perception in sub-cultural groups in Africa', *Journal of Social Psychology*, vol. 52, pp. 183–208.

HUDSON, W. (undated), *Pictorial Depth Perception Test*, National Institute for Personal Research, South African Council for Scientific and Industrial Research, Johannesburg.

HUDSON, W. (1962a), 'Pictorial perception and educational adaptation in Africa', *Psychologia Africana*, vol. 9, pp. 226–39.

HUDSON, W. (1962b), 'Cultural problems in pictorial perception', *South African Journal of Science*, vol. 58, pp. 189–95.

LEBLANC, M. (1958), 'La problématique d'adaptation du T.A.T. au Congo', *Zaire*, vol. 12, pp. 339–48.

MACARTHUR, R. S. (1966), *Mental Abilities in Cross-Cultural Context*, paper presented to Department of Psychology Colloquium, McGill University, Montreal.

MACLEAN, U. (1960), 'Blood donors for Ibadan', *Community Development Bulletin*, vol. 11, no. 2, pp. 26–31.

MORGAN, P. (1959), 'A study in perceptual differences among cultural groups in Southern Africa, using tests of geometric illusion', *Journal of National Institute for Personnel Research*, vol. 8, pp. 39–43.

NADEL, S. F. (1937), 'Experiments on culture psychology', *Africa*, vol. 10, pp. 421–35.

NIESSEN, H. W., MACHOVER, S., and KINDER, E. F. (1935), 'A study of performance tests given to a group of native African negro children', *British Journal of Psychology*, vol. 25, pp. 308–55.

OMBREDANE, A. (1954), *L'Exploration de la Mentalité des Noirs Congolais au Moyen d'une Epreuve Projective, le Congo T.A.T.*, Institut Royal Colonial Belge.

PEDLER, F. J. (1961), 'Characteristics of African populations', *Progress*, vol. 48, pp. 223–32 and 258–65.

RIVERS, W. H. R. (1901), 'Introduction and vision', in A. C. Haddon (ed.), *Reports of the Cambridge Anthropological Expedition to the Torres Straits*, vol. 2, Cambridge University Press.

RIVERS, W. H. R. (1905), 'Observations on the senses of the Todas', *British Journal of Psychology*, vol. 1, pp. 321–96.

SCHWITZGEBEL, R. (1962), 'The performance of Dutch and Zulu adults on selected perceptual tasks', *Journal of Social Psychology*, vol. 57, pp. 73–7.

SEGAL, M. H., CAMPBELL, D. T., and HERSKOVITS, M. J. (1963), 'Cultural differences in the perception of geometric illusion', *Science*, vol. 139, pp. 769–71.

SPALDING, S. (1961), 'Scientific principles of text book design and illustration: A comment', *Audiovisual Communication Review*, vol. 9, pp. 60–62.

TOMKINS, S. S., and MINER, J. B. (1959), *The Tomkins–Horn Picture Arrangement Test*, Springer.

WINTER, W. (1963), 'The perception of safety posters by Bantu industrial workers', *Psychologia Africana*, vol. 10, pp. 127–35.

Part Five **Field Dependence**

It is clear from Part Four that spatial perception is an important factor in the visual organization of non-Western peoples. Two investigators, working more or less contemporaneously, have focused on spatial organization in such disparate populations as the Temne and Mende of Sierra Leone, and the Eskimos. The two investigators are Berry and Dawson; both were interested in spatial discrimination and skill, as evidenced in certain known tests. The chief test which concerns us in this set of selections is that connected with the work, in the United States, of H. A. Witkin. In previous books (1954, 1962), Witkin and his associates had laid the experimental background of what has come to be known as Field Dependence. It is best explained by illustrating basic performances associated with the main test that demonstrates it. This is the Rod-and-Frame Test. The task is to set a rod to the upright condition when the frame against which it is set is tilted. As the test is done in dark-room conditions, with the only cues being the rod and the frame which are illuminated, there is the tendency for subjects to be influenced by the angle of the frame. A paper test which correlates highly with this is the Embedded Figures Test. Here an identified shape is to be picked out from a more complex design in which it is hidden. People are found to behave in certain characteristic ways in tackling these tasks. Those who are influenced by the tilt of the frame and who have difficulty in finding the simple shape in the complex figure are said to be 'field dependent'. Conversely, those who appear to be relatively uninfluenced by the frame or the complexity of the total figure are called 'field independent'. In the original findings Witkin found there was a pronounced sex difference – women being more field dependent than men. In his later book (1962) Witkin found socialization differences in the families of field dependent and field independent children.

Dawson's article (Reading 9) represents a neat connexion with the previous set of selections as he hypothesized that there would be a relation between the ability to correctly perceive pictorial material in three dimensions with the factor of field dependence. In addition he tested out the socialization factors of field dependence with his Sierra Leone samples. Dawson, and Berry too, had used the Embedded Figures Test in their probes into the cultural aspects of field dependence. Wober, working in Southern Nigeria, managed to use the original rod-and-frame apparatus in addition (Reading 10). His findings raise the role of proprioception in the ability to be field independent. Finally Reading 11 by MacArthur is given which supports and emphasizes Berry's (1966) original findings on sex differences in field dependence reported for his Temne, Scottish and Eskimo groups.

References

BERRY, J. W. (1966), 'Temne and Eskimo perceptual skills', *International Journal of Psychology*, vol. 1. pp. 207–29.
WITKIN, H. A. *et al.* (1954). *Personality Through Perception*, Harper.
WITKIN, H. A. *et al.* (1962), *Psychological Differentiation*, Wiley.

9 J. L. M. Dawson

Cultural and Physiological Influences upon Spatial–Perceptual Processes in West Africa – Part I

J. L. M. Dawson, 'Cultural and physiological influences upon spatial-perceptual processes in West Africa – part 1', *International Journal of Psychology*, vol. 2 (1967), pp. 115–25.

Introduction

A number of writers reporting on studies of African spatial–perceptual processes have commented on the apparent difficulty some African *S*s experience in their perception of geometric forms and manipulation of spatial relations. Rollings (1960) comments that 'low ability in Africans to manipulate spatial relations is a common finding in tests and everyday observation.' Jahoda (1956) has stated, 'various investigations in different parts of Africa have accumulated data showing the difficulties Africans experience in manipulating spatial relations and perceiving complex shapes.' McFie (1961) in the course of a Wechsler testing experiment in West Africa 'found contrary to expectation, that the subjects had greater difficulty with Block Designs than with the other subtests.'

Hudson (1960) using a specially constructed test of pictorial perception, demonstrated that Africans with low Western contact tended to be 2-dimensional in their interpretation of pictorial material. In a comprehensive study of African and white samples in South Africa, he found that school-going samples were predominantly 3-dimensional whilst the remainder were mainly 2-dimensional. Hudson considered that,

Formal schooling and informal training combined to supply an exposure threshold necessary for the development of this process. Cultural isolation was effective in preventing or retarding the process, even in candidates possessing formal education of an advanced level. An intelligence threshold also existed for the process, but its development with candidates of average or higher intellectual endowment

161

depended upon cultural characteristics which in Africa might have genetic perceptual determinants.

Of particular interest in Hudson's study was that certain African university graduates even with high intelligence and education, were 2-dimensional in their interpretation of pictorial material. Hudson noted that with the African samples in his study neither intellectual ability nor educational achievement appeared to affect the development of pictorial depth perception to the degree expected from the findings for the white samples. Hudson (1962) summed up his findings in relation to more 2-dimensional African Ss with high education and intelligence, in the following hypothesis:

In a cultural group that has a normal range of intelligence, that in addition possesses high educational qualifications but that is isolated from the dominant cultural norm, pictorial depth perception is not closely related to intellectual endowment or educational achievement. The critical threshold is cultural, and not educational.

It is difficult to understand why Ss with high education and intelligence who have passed through primary school, secondary school and university, should be considered as having insufficient contact with the cultural norm. It is not surprising that Ss who have only moved from a village to a semi-urban way of life should have difficulty with spatial–perceptual tasks, maps, pictures, and diagrams, but what is surprising is that those Ss with high education and intelligence and experience of a carpentered world, should still have not acquired the skills necessary to cope with the spatial–perceptual problems encountered in urban areas. Because of this apparent contradiction it was considered that there might possibly be a limiting spatial–perceptual factor deriving from certain aspects of the African environment which might be influencing individual spatial–perceptual adaptation to the new urban situation.

Of particular relevance in Sierra Leone, appeared to be certain forms of tribal social organization, together with related child-rearing processes which place considerable emphasis on values of conformity, group reliance, maintenance of authority, polygamy, and strict discipline. These particular forms of social organization and child-rearing processes appeared to be likely to develop what

Witkin *et al.* (1954, 1962) have described as a field-dependent more global perceptual style.

Witkin *et al.* (1962) have defined the field dependent person as one who orientates himself by reference to the environment, has a greater need to function as a member of a group, has lower performance on measures of field dependence, whilst individual perception tends to be global. Females tend to be more global and field dependent whilst males tend to be more analytical and field independent. Witkin has found that relevant variables relating to the development of field dependence include harsh parental discipline, strict control, conformity, authority, and the age and extent of psychological differentiation which the developing child achieves from his mother. Mothers of field dependent sons tend to be dominating, emotional, and anxious, whilst the father is generally passive and an inadequate role model.

In Sierra Leone, tribal groups place to varying degrees strict emphasis on values of conformity, authority, harsh discipline, and group reliance, whilst individual competition is discouraged. These social processes described by Dawson (1963a) are considered to be likely to develop what Witkin defines as a field dependent approach. Sierra Leone tribal values tend to be maintained by harsh social sanctions such as 'accusations of witchcraft' and 'swears' which can be used against individuals deviating from group norms.[1] Among the Temne of Sierra Leone, children in villages who are too intelligent and speak up for themselves are said to 'be affected by witchcraft', and are accordingly punished. In this way individual competitiveness tends to be discouraged by these social sanctions and the individual is made to conform with the norms of the group.

In addition the tribal mother in Sierra Leone tends to play a dominant role in the upbringing of her children largely because of the existence of the polygamous family group. In such a situation the father tends to be an inadequate role model not through any personal deficiency, but through lack of contact with his children due to his responsibilities to his other wives and children. Thus

1. The use of 'accusations of witchcraft' as a social sanction among the Temne has been described by Dawson (1963b) whilst the Temne 'swear' which is used in a similar manner by making wrongdoers confess, has been reported by Littlejohn (1960).

the disciplinary pattern within the polygamous family group is in line with Witkin's hypothesis concerning the type of child-rearing processes likely to limit psychological differentiation.

In addition to the cultural variables noted above which are thought to be associated with the development of field dependence, certain physiological variables were also considered to be related to the development of a more field dependent perceptual style. In particular it was thought that the protein deficiency disease Kwashiorkor with its accompanying endocrinal disturbance might be associated with the development in males of a more field dependent approach. Trowell *et al.* (1954) have noted that Kwashiorkor affects the liver which in turn results in a hormonal disturbance involving in males Gynaecomastia (a swelling of the male mammary gland), testicular atrophy, and feminization. It was considered possible that male Ss manifesting this endocrinal disturbance might because of their more feminine traits, tend to develop a field dependent perceptual style.

It was further expected that there might be a certain amount of interaction between the cultural and physiological variables noted above. In this regard it was considered that males manifesting the Gynaecomastia symptom due to their more feminine traits, might be more susceptible to harsh maternal domination, group pressures, and social sanctions. In order to test the hypotheses that certain cultural and physiological variables were possibly limiting the acquisition of spatial–perceptual skills needed in the new urban environment, it was decided to construct a measure of 3-dimensional pictorial perception suitable for use in Sierra Leone. As noted by Gibson (1950) the interpretation of pictorial material in 3-dimensions involves the use of secondary monocular cues and thus constitutes a perceptual task. It was expected that the degree to which individuals in the urban areas of Sierra Leone were able to acquire these perceptual cues to perceive pictorial material in 3-dimensions would be in part a function of individual levels of field dependence. It was further considered that experience of a carpentered environment, educational achievement, intelligence and cultural differences, would be relevant variables in the acquisition of perceptual cues, but only to a certain level beyond which the field dependence variable would be crucial.

The selection of tests to measure field dependence presented something of a problem. Witkin *et al.* (1954) have devised three techniques for this purpose, the Room Adjustment Test, the Rod-and-Frame Test, and the Embedded Figures Test. In addition Witkin (1963) has noted that Kohs Blocks is a measure of field dependence. Due to the complexity of the equipment required for the Room Adjustment and the Rod-and-Frame Tests, Kohs Blocks was used as a measure of field dependence during the initial field-work period, whilst a modified form of the Embedded Figures Test was added after it had been standardized on Sierra Leone populations. The E.F.T. proved to be too complex in its original form. After some experimentation, six cards were retained which gave good reliabilities and validities. In addition to these six cards used for scoring purposes with a time limit of three minutes, two other cards were used for instructional purposes during administration. Considerable care was taken with the administration of all the tests and scales used.

On the basis of the evidence reported in this introductory section the following central hypotheses were established:

Hypothesis 1. It was considered that certain aspects of Sierra Leone tribal culture and related child-rearing processes were likely to be conducive to the development of a more field dependent perceptual style which in turn might be expected to limit the acquisition of spatial–perceptual skills.

Hypothesis 2. It was further considered that feminization occurring in males as a result of the Kwashiorkor endocrinal disturbance would also be likely to lead to the development of a more feminine field dependent perceptual style.

Hypothesis 3. In addition it was considered that there would be a certain amount of interaction between the cultural and physiological variables noted above and that males affected by the endocrinal disturbance would because of their feminine traits, be more susceptible to maternal domination and harsh social pressures, thereby increasing individual levels of field dependence.

Hypothesis 4. It was also considered that educational achievement, intelligence, experience of a carpentered environment and cultural differences, would be relevant variables in the acquisition of cues to perceive pictorial material in 3-dimension up to a certain level, beyond which field dependence was expected to be the major limiting variable. The experiments were carried out in Sierra Leone between 1961 and 1964 to test the above hypotheses.[2]

Construction and Application of the 3-Dimension Test

This initial section is concerned with the construction and application of measures of depth perception used in the study. The use of the term perceptual cue presents something of a problem in pictorial depth perception as Forgus (1966) has pointed out. The term 'cue' is generally used to refer to the triggering of some response whilst the term 'clue' implies some reasoning process. However as the term cue is more widely accepted, it is proposed to apply this term in the present study to describe those secondary monocular cues involved in pictorial perception. Gibson (1950) has distinguished between the primary cues, such as convergence and disparity which are mainly binocular in origin, and the secondary cues which are mainly monocular. Forgus (1966) states that 'the primary (cues) are effective in direct sensory perception, while the secondary cues are used principally, although not exclusively, to create depth effects in drawings and paintings.' Thus the interpretation of pictorial material in 3-dimensions would appear to present a perceptual task involving interacting depth responses to specific cues. As Forgus states, 'depth is immediately a way of perceiving, not merely the addition of something to a picture in varying amounts.'

It was decided to use in the present study the same three cues used by Hudson: Object Size, Perspective, and Superimposition. Again following Hudson (1960) the 3-dimension test was constructed with a number of drawings concerned with horizontal space, and a number concerned with vertical space. A final coloured photograph was included in terms of horizontal space. Two of Hudson's cards, numbers 3 and 7 in the present study, were also included for comparative purposes. The actual cards used, recording form, and details of questions asked are listed in Dawson (1963a). Ss were presented with the cards in a 1 to 9

2. The first three studies constitute the present section of the report, Part 1. The final two (Kwashiorkor, Gynaecomastia and field dependence; factorial analysis) are included in Part II, which appears in the following issue of the *International Journal of Psychology*.

J. L. M. Dawson

sequence. The test was administered orally to one *S* at a time with testing conditions standardized as far as possible. Instructions for illiterate *S*s were given with the aid of an interpreter. *S*s were first required to identify the objects in the pictures and then asked which of a number of objects was closer in distance (not shape or form), to another object. Responses were recorded on the appropriate form.

Table 1
Percentages of 3-Dimensional Responses for Sierra Leone Samples

Sample	N	Horizontal Space*				Vertical Space*			Photograph*	
		O-S (1)	SI (2)	SI (3)	P (4)	O-S (5)	SI (6)	SI (7)	P (8)	SI (9)
Marampa Labourers (Illiterate)	30	6·7	6·7	6·7	3·3	0	6·7	3·3	0	10·0
Kabala Secondary Males (Form I)	22	36·4	36·4	27·3	50·0	27·3	36·4	27·3	36·4	40·9
Marampa Apprentices (Form II–III)	148	55·4	66·9	27·0	51·4	45·27	41·2	29·1	45·9	54·1
Kenama Teacher Training College (Females) 1st Year	38	33·7	58·9	23·7	34·2	15·8	15·8	34·2	41·6	55·8

*O–S: Object–Size; SI: Superimposition; P: Perspective.

In a reliability study involving the 3-dimension test, a test–retest correlation of $r = 0·82$ was obtained. This study involved testing fifty-one West African mine apprentices, and retesting them after a six-month interval. The test–retest correlation of $r = 0·82$ obtained is considered to be quite good and would appear to give some indication of the reliability of the instrument.

The 3-dimensional Test was administered to a number of samples throughout Sierra Leone between 1961 and 1964. 3-dimensional pictorial perception results for three representative male and one female sample are set out in Table 1 showing the percentage 3-dimensional responses by card numbers and the major depth cue used in their construction.

The results in Table 1 give some idea of the relevant sample responses by card numbers and dominant perceptual cues. The results for males show a fairly consistent increase in 3-dimension with educational achievement. However the last sample of females is relatively more 2-dimensional than the males, when considered in terms of educational achievement. Inspection of Table 1 shows that the cards 3 and 7 copied from Hudson's test present slightly more difficulty than the others. The coloured photograph (9), has not elicited significantly more 3-dimensional responses than the line drawing which is in accord with Hudson's findings. Smith *et al.* (1958) also noted that 'work . . . on perceived distance as a function of method of representing perspective showed that judgements of distance in drawing do not vary with the amount of detail included.'

Although the main statistical analysis of contributing variables to field dependence is carried out in Part II of this report [see footnote 2], a preliminary correlation matrix is set out in Table 2 to look at expected relationships between educational achievement, intelligence which is measured by the SL2 group test of intelligence – one of three constructed in terms of indigenous culture, and field dependence as measured by Kohs and the E.F.T. The sample used is a male, Sierra Leone, tribally representative sample homogeneous in terms of age (20–24 years), education (Form 1), and occupation (skilled workers). Ocular bias, visual deficiency, and colour blindness are controlled.

The results in Table 2 show a significant correlation of $r = 0.22$ between education and 3-dimension at the 0.05 level. The relationship between 3-dimension and intelligence is also significant with a correlation of $r = 0.41$. However in line with expectations, the strongest relationship is between 3-dimension and field dependence as reflected in the correlations with Kohs and E.F.T. of $r = 0.64$ and $r = 0.66$ respectively.

Other measures of depth perception constructed for this study included a coloured cine-film, a coloured slide and stereoscopic scenes. The stereoscopic scenes were used to see whether the binocular cues would increase 3-dimension as contrasted with

Table 2
Correlation Matrix (Sierra Leone Male Sample, $N = 99$)

	Educ.	SL2 Intell.	Kohs	E.F.T.	3D
Education	—	0·37	0·21	0·20	0·22
Intelligence SL2		—	0·52	0·43	0·41
Kohs			—	0·73	0·64
E.F.T.				—	0·66
3D					—

$r = 0·20$; $t = 2·01$; $p = 0·05$

results for pictorial material. This was confirmed with a sample of 159 African apprentices who were 46·67 per cent 3-dimensional on pictorial material but 87·20 per cent 3-dimensional on stereoscopic material. The use of the coloured film is noted in the teaching experiment section.

Cultural Variables and Field Dependence

As mentioned in the introductory section, Witkin (1962) has evolved certain hypotheses relating to the type of family environment most likely to limit individual psychological differentiation. It is suggested that this type of family environment is found to varying degrees in Sierra Leone where tribal culture lays stress on conformity, authority, harsh discipline, group reliance, individual initiative is discouraged, whilst due to the existence of the polygamous family group the mother tends to be more dominating and the father often becomes an inadequate role model. In order to obtain a measure of the severity of these family child-rearing processes, an intervening variable was introduced between tribal culture as reflected by child-rearing processes, and measures of field dependence. For this purpose it was decided to use categories of strictness, as these have the advantage of being simple to administer and are not time consuming.

Field Dependence

Table 3
Categories of Strictness and Perceptual Tests (Sierra Leone Sample)

Categories of Strictness	N	Mother 3D	Kohs	E.F.T.	N	Father 3D	Kohs	E.F.T.
Very Strict	32	2·03	14·31	41·23	63	3·54	19·84	71·16
SD		2·4	8·9	11·8		3·3	10·0	15·8
Fairly Strict	35	4·34	21·00	83·40	17	2·82	17·29	60·89
SD		3·4	8·8	9·7		2·6	12·0	17·2
Not Strict	24	3·83	21·96	73·81	9	3·78	14·67	48·07
SD		2·5	11·8	16·6		2·2	8·0	3·8
Analysis of Variance	F	6·073	5·469	7·635		0·428	1·211	0·953
	p	0·01	0·01	0·01		ns	ns	ns

The application of these categories of strictness involved obtaining a measure of maternal and paternal disciplinary dominance, by getting Ss to rate each of their parents as either very strict, fairly strict, or not-so-strict. In order to overcome any possible tribal differences in interpreting these terms, the meanings were explained to all groups. In order to examine these expected relationships between parental disciplinary patterns and field dependence, results are analysed in Table 3 for the same homogenous Sierra Leone tribally representative male sample of skilled workers which was used in Table 2.

In line with expectations the results in Table 2 show a highly significant relationship between degrees of maternal discipline, measures of field dependence, and the 3-dimension test. As expected sons of very strict mothers have significantly lower scores in every case. The analysis of variance F ratios are significant at the 0·01 level for each test. Analysis of variance for father degrees of strictness is not significant for any of the tests. However inspection of the means shows that the trends are in the right direction with the highest means for sons of very strict fathers. The lack of significance for the father category is probably due in part to the small numbers in the not-so-strict category. These results in Table 3 are in line with Witkin's hypothesis regarding the severity of socialization and maternal dominance in limiting the degrees of psychological differentiation achieved by the developing child. The less apparent influence of the father in this situation, is interesting although the trends are in the right direction.

In order to examine more closely the effects of tribal socialization processes on the development of field dependence, an analysis was also carried out of the effects of differences in known Temne and Mende socialization processes, on the emergence of differential tribal patterns of field dependence. It has been pointed out by Dawson (1963a) that there are considerable differences between the two largest tribal groups in Sierra Leone, in regard to tribal values, severity of child-rearing practices, and other socialization processes. These differences have been documented in the above report and relate to the fact that Temne tribal values are much more aggressive than the Western type values of the Mende. The Temne mother is extremely dominating whilst discipline in the Temne home is very strict. Except for the Gpaa-Mende who border on Temne country and who share to some extent Temne cultural characteristics, the Mende people have much less severe socialization processes, the Mende mother is not as dominating, and individual initiative is encouraged to a greater extent than occurs with the Temne.

In view of these known differences in severity of socialization between the Temne and Mende, it was expected that Temne male *S*s would be more field dependent than Mende males. In order to examine the validity of this hypothesis, Temne and Mende male samples were matched in terms of age, occupation, sex, education, intelligence, tribal group, whilst ocular bias, colour blindness, and visual deficiency were controlled. The results for these matched Temne and Mende samples are set out in Table 4 below. Table 4 includes three measures not previously mentioned, linearity and two measures of sexual bias. Linearity which forms part of the somatotype measure obtained for all *S*s, is used in this analysis as Trowell *et al.* (1954) had noted that Kwashiorkor reduces muscularity. Two measures of sexual bias were also used in the study to enable cross-validation: the Franck Drawing Completion Test and the draw-a-person technique, both of which are reasonably culture reduced although not entirely so. A high Franck score indicates more masculine responses. Machover (1957) has noted that when Ss are asked to draw-a-person, if they draw the opposite sex first, there is generally a tendency to identify with the opposite sex. These measures of sexual bias were employed both in regard to the measurement of changes in sexual bias resulting from endocrinal disturbances, and for the analysis of within sex differences relating to perceptual style.

Table 4
Mende and Temne Perceptual Tests and Related Variables

	N	No. Father's wives	Lin-earity	3D	Kohs Blocks	E.F.T.	Franck Sexual Bias	Draw a Person
Temne	49	2·85	4·14	2·92	15·50	55·97	14·46	22·6%
SD		1·5	0·96	2·7	10·3	19·9	1·8	
Mende	49	2·88	3·29	4·00	18·16	75·41	13·77	14·4%
SD		1·8	0·94	2·5	7·4	14·8	1·9	
t		—	4·474	2·076	1·477	7·477	1·917	
p		ns	0·001	0·05	ns	0·001	0·05	

The results in Table 4 show that in line with expectations Temne males are significantly more field dependent on the E.F.T., are significantly more linear, and are significantly more feminine on the sexual bias test, whilst Temne draw 22·6 per cent females first as contrasted with only 14·4 per cent females drawn by the Mende. In addition the more field dependent Temne also have significantly lower scores on the measure of pictorial perception. These results are in line with the hypothesis that the greater severity of Temne child-rearing processes would result in more field dependent characteristics among the Temne. The analysis of these Temne–Mende differences is taken one step further in Tables 5 and 6 below where the comparative effects of Temne and Mende parental categories of strictness are analysed in terms of field dependence and related variables. Temne and Mende mother categories are contrasted in Table 5 whilst father categories appear in Table 6.

Inspection of the Temne–Mende distribution of Ss by the mother categories of strictness in Table 5 shows that whilst twenty-two Temne mothers are rated as very strict, only nine

Mende mothers are classified as very strict. Whilst only eight Temne mothers are rated as not-so-strict, twenty-one Mende mothers fall into this category. The difference between these distributions is significant at the 0.01 level, $(\chi^2 = 11.384, 2 \text{ d.f.})$.

The results for the Temne mother in Table 5 (p. 174) show as expected significantly lower Kohs and E.F.T. field dependence means for the very strict category whilst higher means are obtained in the fairly strict category and the not-so-strict category. The Temne 3-dimensional results follow the same pattern indicating that the acquisition of 3-dimensional cues is closely related to levels of field dependence. Temne Ss in the very strict category are also significantly more linear and have significantly higher feminine sexual bias scores. The results for the Mende very strict mother category show as expected lower more field dependent means than in the fairly strict and not-so-strict categories. However the Mende very strict means are not nearly as low as those obtained with the Temne. Only Kohs and E.F.T. are significant for the Mende mother and these at only the 0.05 level. Linearity and sexual bias for the Mende do not follow the same significant pattern as occurred in the Temne mother categories.

The results for the Temne–Mende Father Categories of strictness using the same matched samples, are set out in Table 6.

Although definite trends are apparent in the Temne father categories for the Kohs and E.F.T. tests, with the highest means as expected in the very strict father category, the results are not significant. The Mende father results are only significant for the E.F.T. at the 0.05 level. It would thus appear that although the trends are in the right direction neither the Temne nor Mende father pattern of discipline appears to significantly influence field dependence to the same extent as occurred with the Temne and Mende mother categories.

The 3-Dimensional Pictorial Perception Teaching Experiment

As part of the over-all research programme it was decided to carry out a 3-dimensional teaching experiment to test the hypothesis that 2-dimensional Ss could be taught to perceive pictorial material in 3-dimension, but within the limits of their field dependence scores. It was considered that if this hypothesis

Table 5
Temne and Mende Mother Categories of Strictness and Perceptual Tests (Male Samples)

Categories of Strictness	Temne Mother						Mende Mother					
	N	Linearity	3D	Kohs Blocks	E.F.T.	Sexual Bias	N	Linearity	3D	Kohs Blocks	E.F.T.	Sexual Bias
Very Strict	22	4·4	0·91	9·9	21·9	15·8	9	3·2	3·7	13·11	39·9	14·3
SD		0·93	1·0	4·4	6·6	1·9		0·76	2·8	6·5	12·9	2·0
Fairly Strict	18	3·7	4·9	19·9	90·1	13·6	20	3·3	4·7	20·8	87·1	13·7
SD		1·0	2·6	6·3	11·8	3·0		1·1	2·9	6·5	14·5	2·5
Not-so-Strict	8	4·2	4·0	20·9	55·9	13·7	21	3·3	3·5	17·9	84·6	13·6
SD		0·68	2·1	11·6	17·6	2·0		0·94	1·9	7·4	12·9	1·6
Analysis of Variance F		11·587	3·421	7·566	17·831	6·531		0·121	1·257	3·723	4·104	0·535
p		0·001	0·05	0·01	0·001	0·01		ns	ns	0·05	0·05	ns

Table 6
Temne and Mende Father Categories of Strictness and Perceptual Tests

Categories of Strictness	Temne Father						Mende Father					
	N	Linearity	3D	Kohs Blocks	E.F.T.	Sexual Bias	N	Linearity	3D	Kohs Blocks	E.F.T.	Sexual Bias
Very Strict	32	4.2	3.1	16.4	66.2	14.1	29	3.4	4.0	18.4	74.6	13.9
SD		1.1	2.7	10.9	16.7	2.5		1.0	2.8	7.4	15.9	1.9
Fairly Strict	13	3.9	2.5	14.7	48.3	14.2	13	2.9	4.3	18.5	85.9	13.9
SD		0.62	2.7	9.3	9.9	2.6		0.75	2.3	4.9	13.4	2.7
Not-so-Strict	3	4.2	2.7	9.0	24.7	12.7	8	3.4	2.4	16.8	47.9	14.9
SD		0.76	3.1	3.5	3.2	1.5		0.91	1.4	8.9	9.9	7.5
Analysis of Variance F		6.609	0.217	0.767	0.887	0.505		1.079	2.049	0.177	4.605	0.83
p		ns	ns	ns	ns	ns		ns	ns	ns	0.05	ns

were confirmed, it would add support to the contention that the acquisition of pictorial depth cues in Sierra Leone, is partly a function of individual levels of field dependence.

The design of the experiment involved selecting 2-dimensional control and study groups, each group consisting of twelve Ss. Ss were matched for intelligence, education (both groups Form II secondary level), occupation (both groups were mine apprentices), sex (both groups were male), age (both groups were between 18 and 19 years of age), tribe (all Ss were Temne), field dependence (both groups had the same Kohs means), 2-dimensional (all Ss were 2-dimensional). Finally ocular bias, visual deficiency, and colour blindness were controlled. Both the control and study groups were initially tested and found to be 2-dimensional in June 1961. The study group was taught the use of pictorial depth cues in eight, weekly, one-hour sessions in August/September 1961. Both groups were retested three months later in December 1961, in order to obtain an enduring effect over time.

The second purpose of the experiment was to test the usefulness of instructional techniques which had been developed for the teaching of pictorial perception. These instructional procedures are outlined below.

(a) Ss from both groups were required to sketch a coloured photograph before and after the experiment to see whether the study group improved over the control group in the application of depth cues to drawing.

(b) It was explained to the study group that depth cues were needed to obtain a sense of depth when representing scenes on a flat surface. This point was demonstrated by getting Ss to sight through a small square cut out of cardboard whilst looking through a window at the outside scenery. Ss were then asked to draw the dominant lines of the scenery on the window. The result was a 3-dimensional representation of the outside scenery on a flat surface, the window. The use of this technique made it much easier for Ss to understand the methods used for representing scenery in 3-dimension on a flat surface. Ss were next required to continue drawing the outside scenery on windows until they were familiar with the technique and could interpret their drawings in 3-dimension using the standard depth cues.

(c) To maintain continuity Ss were also required to sketch their window drawings on to paper, finally, comparing the paper drawings with the outside scenery. After this had been completed Ss were asked to draw the same scenery but without using the window technique.

(d) At this point more elaborate spatial forms were introduced into drawings using illustrations from a simple but clearly illustrated text by Norling (1958).

(e) The final stage of the programme involved the introduction of photographs of the area so that Ss could become familiar with the 3-dimensional interpretation of this medium.

The results for the control and study groups used in the experiment who as noted previously were matched on all possible variables, are set out in Table 7. Inspection of Table 7 shows no significant difference between the two groups at first testing in June 1961, for either Kohs Block means or 3-dimensional Pictorial Perception. However at second testing carried out three months later, the taught study group shows a significant 3-dimensional improvement over the control group at the 0·001 level. The control group showed only slight practice effects. It will also be observed at the bottom of Table 7 that the study group level of improvement as measured at second testing, correlates significantly with the measure of field dependence, $p = 0.884$, significant at the 0·001 level. Both of these results are in line with expectations.

Table 7
3-Dimensional Pictorial Perception Teaching Experiment

Sample	N	Kohs Blocks (June 1961)	3D PP first test (June 1961)	3D PP second test (December 1961)
Study Group	12	16·16	0·50	3·83
SD		11·58	0·52	2·05
Control Group	12	16·88	0·17	0·50
SD		10·56	0·39	0·80
t		—	—	5·286
p		ns	ns	0·001

Rank order correlation
Kohs and second 3D PP $\rho = 0.884$ ($t = 5.790$ $p = 0.001$)
(Study Group)

The coloured cine-film measure of 3-dimension mentioned earlier in this paper was also administered to the two groups in this experiment to see whether as expected study group Ss would show some transfer of perceptual learning from the pictorial material to the cine-film. The results for the cine-film were in line with expectations with the study group 39·1 per cent 3-dimensional on the cine-film medium, whilst the control group were only 11·1 per cent 3-dimensional, a highly significant difference in favour of the taught study group. In addition Ss 2-dimensional on pictorial material were predominantly 2-dimensional on the cine-film.

Discussion and Conclusions

The results of the correlation matrix in Table 2 provided a certain amount of support for Hypothesis 4. Whilst 3-dimension correlated with education ($r = 0.22$) and intelligence ($r = 0.41$), the highest correlations were as expected with the measures of field-dependence, Kohs, $r = 0.64$, and E.F.T., $r = 0.66$.

A considerable amount of evidence was also obtained in the second section to support Hypothesis 1, relating to the effects of cultural influences on the development of field dependence. In looking at the effects of known tribal cultural differences on the development of differential tribal patterns of field dependence, the more aggressive Temne were found to have a significantly more feminine field dependent perceptual style as contrasted with the Mende, whilst Temne were also significantly more linear. These results which support Witkin's hypotheses relating to the effects of severe socialization and maternal dominance on field dependence cannot be attributed to sampling differences as the groups were matched on all relevant variables, tribe, education, intelligence, sex, occupation, age whilst visual deficiency, colour blindness, etc. were controlled.

The two samples used in the pictorial perception teaching experiment were likewise very carefully matched on all possible variables. The results provided considerable evidence for Hypothesis 4 which considered that the acquisition of perceptual skills was limited by the field dependence variable. A correlation of $\rho = 0.884$ was obtained between the original field dependence scores and improved study group scores on the 3-dimension test at second testing, three months after the teaching had been completed. The control group showed only slight practice effects. This experiment also provided evidence to show that 2-dimensional *S*s could be taught to perceive pictorial material in 3-dimension, whilst some transfer of learning to 3-dimensional perception of a cine-film was also obtained. These procedures which were developed in this study have been applied to industrial training. The results obtained with the stereoscopic test for a sample of 159 apprentices showed they were 87·20 per cent 3-dimensional on this medium whilst only 47·67 per cent 3-dimensional on pictorial material. This result points to the possibility that stereoscopic techniques might also be usefully applied in training and education in Africa, to overcome the difficulties often experienced with pictorial material, diagrams, maps, etc.

The results noted above have provided a certain amount of support for Hypotheses 1 and 4 concerned with the differential effects of tribal culture on the development of field dependence and the acquisition of spatial–perceptual skills. Part II of this report takes into account the studies relating to Hypotheses 2 and 3 concerning the effects of the Kwashiorkor induced endocrinal disturbances on field dependence together with the factorial analysis. In addition the over-all results of the research programme are discussed in somewhat more detail.

References

DAWSON, J. L. M. (1963a), *Psychological Effects of Social Change in a West African Community*, Unpublished Ph.D. Thesis, University of Oxford.

DAWSON, J. L. M. (1963b), 'Temne witchcraft vocabulary', *Sierra Leone Language Review*, vol. 2, pp. 16–22.

FORGUS, R. H. (1966), *Perception: The Basic Processes in Cognitive Development*, McGraw-Hill.

GIBSON, J. J. (1950), *The Perception of the Visual World*, Riverside Press.

HUDSON, W. (1960), 'Pictorial depth perception in sub-cultural groups in Africa', *Journal of Social Psychology*, vol. 52, pp. 183–208.

HUDSON, W. (1962), 'Pictorial perception and educational adaptation in Africa', *Psychologia Africana*, vol. 9, pp. 226–39.

JAHODA, G. (1956), 'Assessment of abstract behaviour in a non-western culture', *Journal of Abnormal and Social Psychology*, vol. 53, pp. 237–43.

LITTLEJOHN, J. (1960), 'The Temne Ansasa', *Sierra Leone Studies*, vol. 13, pp. 32–5.

MACHOVER, K. (1957), *Personality Projection in the Drawing of the Human Figure*, Charles C. Thomas.

McFIE, J. (1961), 'The effect of education on African performance on a group of intellectual tests', *British Journal of Educational Psychology*, vol. 31, pp. 232–40.

NORLING, E. (1958), *Perspective Drawing*, W. T. Foster.

ROLLINGS, P. J. (1960), 'A note on the cultural direction of perceptual selectivity', *Proceeding of XVIth International Congress of Psychology*.

SMITH, O. W., SMITH, P. C., and HUBBARD, D. (1958), 'Perceived distance as a function of the method of representing perspective', *American Journal of Psychology*, vol. 71, pp. 662–74.

TROWELL, H. C., DAVIES, J. N. P., and DEAN, R. F. A. (1954), *Kwashiorkor*, Edward Arnold.

WITKIN, H. A., LEWIS, H. B., HERTZMAN, M., MACHOVER, K., MEISSNER, P. B., and WAPNER, S. (1954), *Personality Through Perception*, Harper Bros.

WITKIN, H. A., DYK, R. B., FATERSON, H. F., GOODENOUGH, D. E. and KARP, S. A. (1962), *Psychological Differentiation*, Wiley & Sons.

WITKIN, H. A. (1963), Personal Communication.

10 M. Wober

Adapting Witkin's Field Independence Theory to Accommodate New Information from Africa[1]

M. Wober, 'Adapting Witkin's field independence theory to accommodate new information from Africa', *British Journal of Psychology*, vol. 58 (1967), pp. 29–38.

Theories developed in America hold that the same cognitive style informs both the pattern of an individual's social relations and his performance in certain tests. The tests used in America have largely provided problems in a visual idiom. It is hypothesized that cultures found in Africa may attune skills relatively more highly in an auditory or proprioceptive, than in the visual sphere dominant in Euro-American cultures. Results using a visual, and a mixed visual and proprioceptive test suggest a different pattern of response from African than from American subjects. This is taken to show that the sameness of cognitive style through all fields of an individual's behaviour may not occur for Africans as it may for Americans. Differences of cognitive style for proprioceptive problems may have their own correlates of social behaviour patterns, and these remain to be studied.

A modern rapprochement between theories of personality, and of intellectual development, has been made by Witkin and his collaborators who introduced the concept of field independence (Witkin, Lewis, Hertzman, Machover, Bretnall-Meissner and Wapner, 1954). Receiving support from the work of Bennett (1956), Epstein (1957), Young (1959) and others, though with some equivocal findings as for example from Gruen (1955), the position was thoroughly reviewed and re-stated in terms of the concept of psychological differentiation by Witkin, Dyk, Faterson, Goodenough and Karp (1962).

Recent work in Africa is relevant to refining Witkin's theories,

1. This work was part of a project financed by a grant from the Ministry of Overseas Development, and administered jointly by the Department of Social Anthropology, University of Edinburgh, and by the University of Ibadan, Nigeria.

The experimental work reported, would not have been possible without the able assistance of Mr Otung Etim Ebong.

and it is suggested that the skills involved in the performance of tests used by Witkin need to be more carefully understood than hitherto. Particular skills might be associated with particular cultural backgrounds, and the finding of a given degree of psychological differentiation might not be so generalized throughout all aspects of an individual's functioning as Witkin's theories suggest. Use is made of the idea of 'sensotypes' put forward by Wober (1966) to suggest that in the field of visual perception and the exercise of allied powers of psychological differentiation, Witkin's schema associating social and psychological test data may hold good; but that it remains to be shown if it also holds good for transactions in the field of proprioception, which may be culturally of salient importance in parts of Africa.

Theory of Field Independence and Psychological Differentiation

Field independence was defined by Witkin *et al.* (1962, p. 47) as the ability to separate an item perceived from its context. Most experiments used visually presented material which was described in the context of the 'visual field'. An extension of the theory linked visual with social and maturational phenomena. The ability to separate visual items from their context was shown to be aligned with the development of a sense of distinct personal identity. The person is considered to be an item, set in the context or 'social field' of his family and the society around him.

Witkin *et al.* (1962) describe two extremes of practices in the socializing of children. The first tends to produce a conformist child through strict punishment and by preventing the assumption of individual responsibility. Such children are said to 'perceive globally'; they do not structure the perceived world actively and hence they tend not to deal skilfully with problems of visual analysis. The other extreme produces the individualist, who is considered to have to assess the world for himself; because he develops the habit of analysing structure, he is able to do well at certain types of problem. In this way, the theory becomes a theory of psychological differentiation: tests of field independence, social conformity and general ability all measure activities which can be described in similar terms.

Dawson (1963) was the first to apply field independence theory to findings in Africa. He noted that socialization practices in certain African tribal societies resembled the situation producing the classical extreme of Witkin's field dependent type. People were taught to respond to social standards, to be 'other-directed' in Riesman, Glazer and Denney's (1953) nomenclature rather than individualistic. Further, tests of field independence of the kind used by Witkin evoked very poor performance from Dawson's subjects (Africans from the Temne tribal group), suggesting a lack of habits of analysis for some types of visual material.

Two kinds of reason were suggested for these poor performances of Temne subjects. One was Witkin's orthodox explanation, that a high degree of socialization as distinct from individualization underlay a low level of psychological differentiation which was responsible both for poor test performance and for the patterns of social behaviour observed. The second explanation concentrated on the lack of familiarity which Temne subjects had with Western modes of communication, especially print, diagrams and transactions in visual codes; this lack of familiarity would explain poor test scores, and socialization practices and social behaviour would remain to be accounted for separately. This second explanation, however, received no support from the observations of Preston (1964) and the experiment of Berry (1965). They showed that Eskimos, as unlettered as Temne and with equally little contact with Western cultures, did much better on tests such as Block Designs than did Temne. The findings left the orthodox Witkin–Dawson explanation of Temne socialization practices and resultant psychological differentiation in a strengthened position.

This was the stage at which the present refinement to the above theory was introduced. It was noticed that the tests used by Witkin of field independence and of psychological differentiation involved transactions and skills in the visual field. Certain tests also involved the subjects in integrating data from visual and proprioceptive fields, though the term 'field' appears to have been used by Witkin et al. (1962) ambiguously to refer to sources of both modalities of perception. It appeared possible that American subjects, brought up in a culture emphasizing visual values and codes for communicating information, might be a valid population in which the Witkin theory could stand. However, African (Temne) subjects were brought up in a culture emphasizing proprioceptive values and skills, and thus their relevant field of psychological differentiation might be that of proprioception or audition and, at any rate, not so much the field of visual transactions. Evidence on the nature of Temne and other West African cultures includes the absence of writing previous to Western or Muslim contact, the shortage of colour terms, and even of analysis of stars into constellations by pattern. On the other hand, Temne and other West African cultures include an elaboration of the proprioceptively and aurally perceived world. Thus, music is an extension of speech, rhythm an extension of movement, beauty a function of grace of movement as much as of configuration of visage, and dance is a regular and favoured form of elaboration of activity, started at an early age.

The idea of sensotypes has therefore been put forward by Wober (1966), that is, that the prevailing patterns of childhood intake and proliferation of information from the various sense modalities differ according to culture. Thus, while Witkin's whole work was done among Americans largely of one sensotype, the application of his theories and tests might not be valid for Africans of another sensotype. The use of one of Witkin's tests involving proprioception might therefore be a more appropriate index of psychological differentiation among Africans of the type tested by Dawson (1963) and Berry (1965) than the use of the entirely visual tests.

The following hypotheses need to be tested as a preliminary to future work on the question of the appropriate sensory modality for tests of differentiation:

(1) That in the sensotype common in certain West African cultures, proprioceptivity is (still) relatively more elaborated with respect to visuality than would be the case in Western cultures;

(2) That, therefore, West African subjects would have better scores on tests where proprioceptivity was important: (a) relative to their scores on tests dependent on visuality; and (b) relative to scores of Westerners on similar tests;

(3) That results of West African subjects would approximate

more towards those of any Western groups in whom proprioceptivity was highly trained than to results of normal Western groups.

Method

Two tests of the group described by Witkin *et al.* (1962) as being indices of field independence were included in a battery given to subjects in Southern Nigeria. The mean scores of the Nigerian subjects have been compared with mean scores found by American workers, and correlations between test scores and an index of educational level have been examined for the Nigerian subjects.

The tests

The rod-and-frame test (R.F.T.). The subject is seated in a totally dark room and views a display consisting of a luminous square frame and a luminous rod mounted centrally within it. The frame has its bottom edge parallel to the ground, but it can be tilted about a horizontal axis so that either of the bottom corners can be pointing almost towards the ground. The rod is mounted on the same axis and can be pointed towards the ground ('vertical') or tilted away from the vertical with or against the tilt of the square. In the apparatus used, the dark room was a 6 ft 6 in cube internally. The luminous square had sides 13 in long, and the width of the slit actually visible was $\frac{1}{4}$ in. The rod was 11 in long and also bore a slit $\frac{1}{4}$ in wide. An arrangement was made with bulbs, a rheostat and a battery charger, whereby just enough current was supplied to make the slits comfortably visible.

The subject deals not only with a visual display, but in a sense also with a proprioceptive display, as he sits in a high-backed armchair which is tiltable to right or left by wedges placed under the legs. A footboard is attached to the chair, which keeps the subject's feet off the ground. Both the subject in his chair, and the square frame and rod may therefore be tilted (see Figure 1).

The task for the subject is to tell the experimenter to move the rod which has been tilted away from the vertical before the illumination is made, back to a vertical position. When the subject believes the rod is resting in a vertical position, its actual displacement from the vertical is read off by an assistant outside the dark room, who views a suitably arranged pointer and scale.

This error from the true vertical constitutes the score. A high score thus indicates a poor performance.

The embedded figures test (*E.F.T.*). The subject is shown a simple geometrical figure on a card. He then sees a complex figure which contains the original simple figure as a part of it (the first card having been removed). The task is for the subject to find where the simple figure is 'hidden' and then to point it out. The present version of the test used eight items from those of Witkin (1950). These items were A–3, A–4, C–1, C–4, D–1, D–2, F–1 and G–1 (see Figure 2). The time taken to find each item is noted (with a maximum of 5 min allowed) and the total for the test found. The selection of these particular items and their order had been determined by pre-testing among school-children. The procedure in testing was to show each simple figure for 15 sec and then to start timing the period required to find it in the complex figure. If

Figure 1 The rod-and-frame test

subjects asked to see the simple figure again the complex figure was removed and the simple one shown again for 5 sec, the stop-watch being stopped. No subject asked for more than four repetitions; some asked for one or two, but most often none was requested. The time reckoned was the total search time, without counting time for repetitions of the simple figure. As with the R.F.T., a high score indicated a poor performance.

The test is clearly one of transactions entirely in the visual field and similar in the skills required for it to Raven's Matrices and the block of designs test (used by Dawson, 1963 and Wober, 1966) with which significant correlations were reported.

The subjects

The eighty-six subjects were all male employees of a large company in Southern Nigeria. They were chiefly from Ibo tribal groups, with Edo groups furnishing the others. Both these tribal groups have had similar exposure to Western influences, and both live in geographically similar conditions; both depended for livelihood on subsistence farming and evolved cultures lacking literacy but with intense development of music, dancing and tonal language. All the men were manual workers ranging from completely unskilled to skilled artisans. Literacy ranged from nil to fair and was influenced by formal education which was assessed by a four point scale. All those with no school experience were marked 1, and those who had only completed 'Primary VI', which was a long established watershed in common educational experience in Nigeria, were marked 3. Those with school experience less than Primary VI were marked 2, and those who had gone on from Primary VI to secondary modern, grammar schools, colleges for teacher training or the Company's apprentice school were marked 4. The scale thus did not attempt to represent equal intervals by educational criteria, but the categories were occupied by numbers not greatly skewed in any direction. The average age of the men was 32·2 years.

The testing situations

All the tests were given individually. The instructions were spoken in English or pidgin English appropriate to the understanding of each subject. Before the R.F.T. the author, aided by a Nigerian

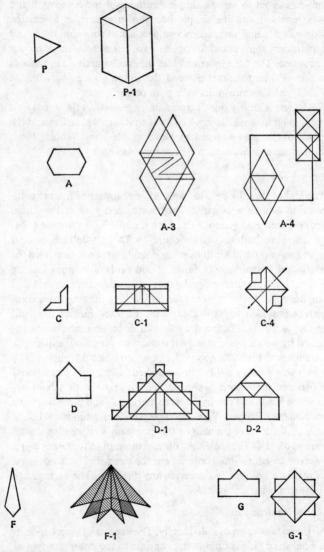

Figure 2 The selection of items that was used from the embedded figures test of Witkin (1950)

188

assistant, carefully explained the meaning of the idea 'vertical' to each subject with the aid of a plumb-line and other demonstrations. During trials of the R.F.T., the author remained in the dark room with the subject, and the assistant stayed outside to re-align the rod after each trial and to read off scores on a scale provided. The room became exceedingly hot quite rapidly, and the door was opened and air and light were admitted twice during each run of trials for each subject; during the pauses the tilt of the chair was also adjusted. There is no doubt that social conditions differed in the Nigerian work from what has been described as the setting in American laboratories; if any systematic differences likely to affect good performance occurred, it seems likely that the Nigerian subjects had the less favourable conditions.

In the case of the E.F.T., the author gave all the tests individually. The preceding explanations were thorough and the subjects were motivated as keenly as possible to work without delay. Though it is probable that some of the slowness of performance among Nigerians was due to a lack of the competitive zest that subjects often bring to such tasks in Western countries, it is nevertheless thought that subjects' difficulties with this test were very real. Several men failed nearly every item, while the quickest finished the eight items in under four minutes. Encouragement was given in between items to those failing items early on.

Rigid orthodoxy in keeping to printed instructions for test administration was not the guiding principle of the test administration. The two chief points were held to be: to explain the nature of the problems, and to create and sustain maximum motivation. It is believed that the subjects were thus showing their best available performances in each of the above tests.

Results

The scores on the R.F.T. gained by Nigerian subjects are first compared with two other sets of American results. Only those conditions of the test where the square frame was kept straight are considered here, for reasons explained after the table.

Table 1
Scores for Nigerian Workers Compared with American Subjects on
R.F.T. with Frame Kept Straight
(Scores in mean degrees displacement of rod from true vertical)

Frame	Body position			n	Source of data
	Right, 28°	Straight	Left, 28°		
Straight	—	—	4·53	53	Witkin and Asch (1948)
	Right, 30°	Straight	Left, 30°		
None	3·30	—	2·64	75	Comalli et al. (1959)
	Right, 28°	Straight	Left, 28°		
Straight	1·20	1·18	1·29	86	(Present data)

The conditions experienced by subjects whose results are in
Table 1 are those where the proprioceptive problem is of comparative prominence. In the present experiment, and in that of
Witkin, the frame-straight condition was used; in the investigation
of Comalli, Wapner and Werner (1959) no square frame at all
enclosed the tilted rod. In all three investigations, however, the
subject's body was tilted considerably. The result is that in both
cases of American subjects, the level of error was greater than
that found for Nigerians. Where the body was tilted to the right,
the mean Nigerian score was significantly better than for Comalli's
subjects ($t = 7·60$; d.f. 159; $p < 0·01$). Where the body was
tilted left, the mean Nigerian score was again significantly
better than for Comalli's subjects ($t = 4·65$; d.f. 159; $p < 0·01$);
and the same superiority held good over Witkin's subjects ($t = 3·54$; d.f. 137; $p < 0·01$).

The conclusion is clear that, in circumstances of what Witkin
terms 'analytic functioning' where proprioceptive information
(body tilt) is more prominent than the visual inconsistencies, the
Nigerians were better than the Americans. One possible interpretation could be that the testing situation was easier for the
Nigerians. It has been suggested that this was unlikely owing to
social disparity between subjects and English investigator, and to
physically hot and stressful conditions; the data of Tables 2 and
3 also argue against this possibility.

Table 2
Scores for Nigerian Workers Compared with American Subjects on
R.T.F. with Frame Tilted
(Scores in mean degrees displacement of rod from true vertical)

Frame	Right, 28°	Straight	Left, 28°	n	Source of data
		Body position			
28° Left	—	6·2	9·4	53	Witkin and Asch (1948)
28° Left	11·08	10·86	11·47	86	(Present data)
28° Right	—	5·7	11·98	53	Witkin and Asch (1948)
28° Right	11·16	11·8	12·06	86	(Present data)

The situation giving rise to the results in Table 2 had both proprioceptive and visual displacements for the subjects to deal with. Comparison of Witkin's results for his American subjects with the performance of Nigerian subjects in the body-tilted condition showed no significant differences (for the condition with both frame and body tilted left, $t = 0.072$; d.f. 137; $p > 0.05$; and for the condition with frame tilted right and body tilted left, $t = 0.04$; d.f. 137, $p > 0.05$). In the condition where the body was straight, however, and the task was primarily one of having adjustments made to a tilted visual display, the Americans made less error than Nigerians.

The findings in Tables 1 and 2 tend to support hypotheses 2 (a) and 2 (b) and therefore, by implication, hypothesis 1. It is also damaging to the argument that the testing situations were unequal and in favour of the Nigerians, to find that they systematically did worse in the body-straight situation shown in Table 2.

A further test of hypothesis 2 (b) may be made by comparing the results of the Nigerian subjects with those of two groups studied in America by Gruen (1955). One of these groups was of dancers, highly trained in proprioceptive sensitivity; the other was of normal subjects (non-dancers). Gruen classified her results slightly differently, and the present data have been rearranged in Table 3 to parallel her classification.

Gruen stated that there were no significant differences in performance between normals and trained dancers. As in the comparison with Witkin's data, Nigerians were better when body-tilt was involved (proprioceptivity becoming important) and worse than Americans when the body was straight. (Gruen's data were not presented in a form in which significance of differences could be readily estimated.) This is additional support for hypothesis 2 (b).

Among the Nigerian subjects only, comparison of performance in conditions where the frame was straight and body tilted, with performance when the frame was tilted with the body kept straight, show that the former elicited much more accurate judgments, i.e. it was easier for them to resolve a proprioceptive than a visual displacement from normal conditions. This supports hypothesis 2 (a).

Table 3
Comparison of R.F.T. Scores Between Nigerians, Americans and American Professional Dancers
(Scores in mean degrees displacement from true vertical)

Group	n	Body and frame tilted same way, 28°	Body and frame tilted opposite, 28°	Body straight, frame tilted, 28°	Source
Normals	46	12·33	14·14	7·07	Gruen (1955)
Dancers	30	13·57	15·00	6·58	Gruen (1955)
Nigerians	86	11·32	11·57	11·02	(Present data)

Table 4
Product-Moment Correlations Between R.F.T. and E.F.T. Results for Gruen's American Subjects (Gruen, 1955)

Group	Body and frame tilted, same way	Body and frame tilted, opposite ways	Body straight, frame tilted
Normals	0·47**	0·43**	0·75**
Dancers	0·32	0·32	0·36*

* $p < 0.05$ for difference from zero. ** $p < 0.01$.

Gruen gave her two groups of subjects the E.F.T. as well as the R.F.T., and the correlations between the tests are available. The

Table 5
Product-Moment Correlations Between R.F.T. and E.F.T. and
Educational Level for Nigerian Subjects ($n = 86$)

Variate	R.F.T.	Educational level
E.F.T.	0·21	—0·37*
R.F.T.	—	0·08

*$p < 0·05$ for difference from zero.

Nigerians also did both tests, and so the patterns of inter-correlations can be compared.

The evidence from these correlations can be interpreted as support for hypothesis 3. Thus in Gruen's investigations, for those parts of the R.F.T. involving body-tilt (proprioceptive problems) the dancers showed no significant correlation with their performance on the E.F.T. That is to say, the two tests posed to them problems which were dealt with in basically different ways. In the condition where the body was kept straight (the problem principally visual) there was a significant correlation for dancers with their E.F.T. results. In any case, the situation for normals was different from that for dancers. The Nigerian subjects showed no significant correlation between E.F.T. and R.F.T. results, thus showing their closer similarity to American professional dancers than to other American subjects. This appears to be good support for hypothesis 3. It is also shown among Nigerian subjects that formal (Western) education has more bearing upon E.F.T. than upon R.F.T. results.

Discussion

It has been argued that Witkin's rod-and-frame test contains a proprioceptive component which makes it essentially different from tests involving purely visually mediated transactions. This being so, groups of subjects who might by culture or by training be especially sensitive to the proprioceptive field would show characteristically different patterns of scoring on this test. This has been found to be the case. American dancers, and especially Nigerian manual workers, have shown that for them the R.F.T.

193

does not measure the same skills or analytic style as the E.F.T.

This finding has two areas of applicability. The first is that there exists a test of 'analytic functioning' (Witkin's term, 1962) in which Africans have been shown to do as well as, or better than Americans or Europeans. This is a rare finding that has occurred once only before in the work of Beveridge (1939) who compared fifty-two Ghanaian students with twenty Europeans on a test of adjusting a rod to the horizontal, inside a tilted room. Though half the Europeans were women and their average age nearly twice that of the Africans, rendering the results equivocal, nevertheless in this task involving action in a proprioceptive field the Africans did better than the Europeans. Beveridge wrote (op. cit.) 'their perception is guided less by visual and more by other cues than is that of the European.'

The second application of the present findings is the modification of Witkin's theory of psychological differentiation. It would appear that 'style of cognitive functioning' is not so uniform throughout all fields of an individual's expression as had originally been supposed by Witkin. The finding in America that the E.F.T. and similar visual tests indicated a person's level of psychological differentiation was supported in Sierra Leone by Dawson (1963) using visual tests. However, visual tests appear not to be sole indicators of psychological differentiation. The evidence here is that such differentiation may occur in sensory fields other than the visual one. Using the idea of sensotypes introduced by Wober (1966) it may be suggested that suitable tests in visual idiom indicate levels of differentiation implying certain sorts of socialization experience and social behaviour. Tests in proprioceptive idiom, however, may be more appropriate for measuring differentiation among those of a less visual sensotype and may be associated with experiences of socialization and with social behaviour in patterns that have not as yet been worked out.

References

BENNETT, D. H. (1956), 'Perception of the upright in relation to body image', *Journal of Mental Science*, vol. 102, pp. 487–506.
BERRY, J. W. (1965), A study of the Temne and Eskimo visual perception, *Preliminary Report, University of Edinburgh, Department of Psychology*, no. 28.

BEVERIDGE, W. M. (1939), 'Some racial differences in perception', *British Journal of Psychology*, vol. 30, pp. 57–64.

COMALLI, P. E., WAPNER, S., and WERNER, H. (1959), 'Perception of verticality in middle and old age', *Journal of Psychology*, vol. 47, pp. 259–66.

DAWSON, J. L. M. (1963), Psychological effects of social change in a West African community, *Unpublished MS, Department of Social Anthropology, University of Edinburgh*.

EPSTEIN, L. (1957), The relationship of certain aspects of body image to the perception of the upright, *Unpublished doctoral dissertation, New York University*.

GRUEN, A. (1955), 'Dancing experience and personality in relation to perception', *Psychological Monographs*, vol. 69, no. 14, whole no. 399.

PRESTON, C. E. (1964), 'Psychological testing with Northwest Coast Alaskan Eskimos', *Genetic and Psychological Monographs*, vol. 69, pp. 323–420.

RIESMAN, D., GLAZER, N., and DENNEY, R. (1953), *The Lonely Crowd: A Study of the Changing American Character*, Doubleday.

WITKIN, H. A., and ASCH, S. E. (1948), 'Studies in space orientation, IV: Further experiments on perception of the upright with displaced visual fields', *Journal of Experimental Psychology*, vol. 38, pp. 762–82.

WITKIN, H. A. (1950), 'Individual differences in ease of perception of embedded figures', *Journal of Personality*, vol. 19, pp. 1–15.

WITKIN, H. A., DYK, R. B., FATERSON, H. E., GOODENOUGH, D. R., and KARP, S. A. (1962), *Psychological Differentiation*, Wiley.

WITKIN, H. A., LEWIS, H. B., HERTZMAN, M., MACHOVER, K., BRETNALL-MEISSNER, P., and WAPNER, S. (1954), *Personality Through Perception*, Harper.

WOBER, M. (1966), 'Sensotypes', in *Journal of Social Psychology*, vol. 70, pp. 181–9.

YOUNG, A. H. (1959), 'A test of Witkin's field dependence hypothesis', *Journal of Abnormal and Social Psychology*, vol. 59, pp. 188–92.

11 R. MacArthur

Sex Differences in Field Dependence for the Eskimo: Replication of Berry's Findings

R. MacArthur, 'Sex differences in field dependence for the Eskimo: Replication of Berry's findings', *International Journal of Psychology*, vol. 2 (1967), pp. 139–40.

Witkin (1966) reported clear-cut and pervasive sex differences in field-dependence in numerous studies in the United States, England, Holland, France, Italy, Israel, Hong Kong and Sierra Leone, women tending consistently to be more field dependent than men. With such pervasiveness he found it tempting to think of these sex differences as dictated by biological factors, but he also considered that the cause may lie in the encouragement of a more dependent role for women in many cultures.

Berry (1966) found similar sex differences in his Temne and Scottish samples, but for his samples of Eastern Eskimo from Baffin Island there were no significant differences between male and female scores in field dependence. Berry saw this as consistent with the fact that 'Eskimo women and children are in no way treated as dependent in the society; very loose controls are exercised over wives and children'. An embedded figures test has been one of the main measures of field dependence used.

In connexion with other studies, we administered Vernon's Embedded Figures Test to two samples of Western Eskimo pupils at Inuvik and Tuktoyaktuk, about 1800 miles from Berry's Frobisher Bay samples. Near-zero point-biserial correlations between sex and Embedded Figures were found, as shown in Table 1. While reliability checks on Embedded Figures were not made for these samples, the correlations between this test and Raven's Standard Progressive Matrices were 0·70 and 0·68 for the respective samples, suggesting reasonable reliabilities. This replication of Berry's findings for the Eskimo adds evidence suggesting that observed sex differences in field dependence in other cultures may be shaped largely by social or other environmental influences.

R. MacArthur

Table 1
Correlations of Sex and Embedded Figures[1]

	Age	Boys N	Girls N	Point-biserial r with sex Prog.Mat.	Emb.Fig.
Sample 1	9–12 yrs	60	27	0·18	—0·01
Sample 2	12½–15½ yrs	38	42	—0·08	0·05

1. High scores are male and field independent.

References

BERRY, J. W. (1966), 'Temne and Eskimo perceptual skills', *International Journal of Psychology*, vol. 1, pp. 207–29.
WITKIN, H. A. (1966), 'Cultural influences in the development of cognitive style', in *Cross-Cultural Studies in Mental Development*, Symposium 36. XVIIIth International Congress of Psychology, Moscow, pp. 95–109.

Part Six Conservation

We turn now from studies of perception proper to the transition in childhood from perception to conception. The derivation of the studies reported here stem from the classic work of Jean Piaget on Swiss children (best summarized in Flavell, 1963). The particular notion that is selected here is that of the concept of conservation. How does a child acquire the concepts of quantity, substance, weight and volume? On this problem of the development of invariance the work of Piaget has given us certain answers. The following three papers deal with the same problem in different cultural contexts. Actually the first person to apply Piaget's methods outside the Western world was Hyde, who reported her observations in a doctoral dissertation in 1959. In that same year Price-Williams carried out a series of tests on the concept of quantity on children of the Tiv tribe in Central Nigeria, reproduced here as Reading 12. When Bruner and his associates at Harvard made a large scale survey of cognitive processes in such different areas of the world as West Africa, Mexico and among the Eskimos, conservation was one of the main targets of inquiry. Patricia Marks Greenfield's study among the Wolof of Senegal concentrated on the development of conservation, comparing literate and illiterate populations. It is to be noted that both Price-Williams and Marks Greenfield conducted their investigations in the native language – an important methodological element in work on thinking in a cultural context. The similar methods used in both these investigations with somewhat different results has generated further work on this topic. Reading 14 by Goodnow gives a useful survey to the cultural studies of conservation, and suggests useful lines of inquiry.

References

FLAVELL, J. H. (1963), *The Developmental Psychology of Jean Piaget*, Van Nostrand.

HYDE, D. M. (1959), An investigation of Piaget's theory of development of the concept of number, *Unpublished Ph.D. thesis, University of London.*

12 D. R. Price-Williams

A Study Concerning Concepts of Conservation of Quantities
among Primitive Children

D. R. Price-Williams, 'A study concerning concepts of conservation of
quantities among primitive children', *Acta Psychologica*, vol. 18 (1961),
pp. 297–305.

I. Introduction

In the volume entitled *La Genese du Nombre chez l'Enfant*
published in English in 1952 as *The Child's Conception of Number*
(6), Professor Piaget traced through the principles involved in the
concept of number from early beginnings regarding the conservation of quantities, through the notions of cardinal and
ordinal correspondence, to additive and multiplicative compositions. Research on the same lines as the book by other
workers is limited. Estes (2) published a study which claimed to
refute Piaget's theories in this field, while Dodwell (1) has produced evidence partly in favour of Piaget's conclusions as regards
young children, though not unequivocally. The present research
deals with only one section of *The Child's Conception of Number*
(Part I of the book), namely that to do with the conservation of
continuous and discontinuous quantities. Any originality that
the present study may have lies not so much in the type of
investigation or techniques employed as in the nature of the
subjects. These were illiterate bush West African children, living
in conditions which can be called primitive in the social sense of
the word.

In the book referred to, Piaget maintained that the child progressed through three stages regarding the notion of conservation.
First the child obeys merely perceived characteristics and is not
influenced in his responses to the experimental situation by any
notion of identity of quantity. As he puts it, 'Perception of the
apparent changes (in the experimental material) is ... not corrected by a system of relations that ensures invariance of quantity.
The second stage is characterized by an emerging of the idea of

conservation, though not wholly, while the third stage consists of an immediate postulation of conservation of the quantities involved. The transition from the first stage to the third can be looked upon as a dependency on the immediate, perceptual and concrete to a fully detached and abstract mode of operations. In the present study this equivalence allows us to test a relevant side issue. Levy-Bruhl in his book *How Natives Think* (3) stressed what he called the prelogical mentality of primitive peoples. His writings covered a great many examples; what is pertinent here are his theories regarding the concept of number. On this he wrote: 'They [i.e. primitive peoples] count and even calculate in a way which, compared with our own, might properly be called concrete.' He noted that in a certain tribe (the Abipones) 'when they return from an excursion to hunt wild horses or to shoot tame ones, none of the Abipones will ask them "How many horses have you brought home?" but "How much space will the troop which you have brought home occupy?" ' He goes on to state that 'Prelogical mentality does not distintcly separate the number from the objects numbered.' Now this apparent lack of differentiating number from space or objects is precisely the kind of thinking which Piaget has called egocentric, and in the case under review constitutes stage one regarding conservation. It is a kind of thinking which is rigidly bound by the apparent perceptual manifestations. Therefore in bringing evidence to bear on Piaget's findings on Swiss children from a collection of West African children, we are also testing Levy-Bruhl's conclusions. However, it must be noted that the latter postulated that the 'native' never progressed beyond what we can now call the egocentric stage.

II. Subjects

This investigation was conducted while the writer was on a field research among the Tiv of Central Nigeria. The particular area in which the work was done was partly influenced by the British administration and by Roman Catholic and Protestant missionaries to the extent that there were bush schools and dispensaries. However, in the immediate neighbourhood of the compound in which the writer was living, in a native hut in the manner of an anthropologist, the ratio of illiterates to literates was great. This particular investigation concerning ideas of conservation was done in a very informal manner with these illiterate children, either in the investigator's own hut or in the huts of the various children involved. By the time this research was carried out the investigator had mastered a sufficient knowledge of the language to conduct the questioning without the assistance of translators. However, the questions were prepared in advance with the help of the teachers in the nearby bush school, so as to prevent, as far as possible, inappropriate questions. Nevertheless, it has to be admitted that a thorough mastery of the language was not sufficient to allow follow-up questions of the type which Piaget asks, other than the question 'why?'.

The matter of determining the age of the children presented a major difficulty. No child or adult reckons his age by the year, so that in order to ascertain age groups one is compelled to go to a somewhat roundabout and inevitably rough procedure. What was required, in order to make comparative estimates with previous findings, was an age range from 5 to 8. Now the official age for entry to the school was 6 years. This is still of course an approximation but it allowed the teachers to form a basis of half-yearly intervals, from 6 to 8. Certain children were selected by the teachers as being clearly in each of these four groups, even if they were unable to state precisely the number of months involved. With these children as a starting point, interrogation of illiterate children in the various compounds from which the literates came, was done. Each child and its parents (or, as is usual with Tiv, practically everybody in the compound) was asked whether a particular boy X was the same age as his fellow, the selected schoolboy. In this somewhat arduous manner nine illiterate children were chosen as subjects for each of the four groups. This still left the under-sixes. Here we were compelled to rely on physical characteristics of height, teeth and verbal fluency, but had to be content with an estimate of between five and six. The five age groups are as follows:

Gr. 1   Between 5 and 6
Gr. 2   6·0 to 6·6

Conservation

Gr. 3	6·6 to 7·0
Gr. 4	7·0 to 7·6
Gr. 5	7·6 to 8·0

It is no use denying that this is inevitably a rough grading, but what is relevant to Piaget's theories is the *relative* age, and although the absolute age here is open to query, there is a stronger reliance on the *comparative* ages.

A number system exists in Tiv. Most of the elder children tested could count, as indicated by making strokes on the ground, up to twenty or thirty. It is an interesting point, in view of the concreteness thesis, that when Tiv say a number up to and including ten, a manual gesture particular to each of the ten digits always accompanies the spoken term. Even when a two or three digit number is spoken, the last always has its characteristic gesture.

III. Method

Piaget's techniques were followed as closely as possible.

Conservation of continuous quantities

Two glasses of equal dimensions (A1 and A2) were each three-quarters filled with fine earth. The contents of A2 were then poured into two smaller glasses of equal dimensions (B1 and B2) such that the level was identical. The child was then asked whether the amount of earth that had been in A2 and now was in B1 and B2 was more than (the Tiv term used is *hemba*), less than (*dahar*) or the same as (*kwagh mom*) that in A1. There were two variants of this procedure:

(1) There were two initial glasses, A1, A2. The contents of A1 were poured into two *tall* identical containers, B1 and B2, and the contents of A2 poured into two *short* containers, B3 and B4. The level of the former therefore was relatively low, while that of the latter was relatively high. In this way the question of *level* was probed.

(2) Two initial glasses as before, A1, A2. The contents of A1 were poured into *three* identical containers, such that the level was approximately equal, while the contents of A2 were poured into

six identical containers. Both sets of containers were of similar shape and size. Thus the question of *number of containers* was tested.

In both conditions the child was asked whether one set of the new containers held more, less, or the same quantity of earth as the other set. In all three cases the child agreed that there was an equal amount of earth in the initial glasses.

Conservation of discontinuous quantities

Exactly the same procedures as with continuous quantities described above were performed with nuts. In this case the subjects saw the experimenter put in the nuts, one at a time, in each of the two initial glasses in one operation, so that they agreed that each vessel contained the same number of nuts. One additional experiment was performed with the nuts, to test the ability of number from space. A row of nuts was strung in a line of 24 inches, and another row, composed of the same number of nuts, alongside the former in a line of 12 inches. The subjects saw the experimenter place the nuts alternatively in each row, so that a one to one correspondence was observed. The children were then asked whether the longer line had more, less, or the same number of nuts as the shorter line. This experiment was not meant to pursue the further subject of cardinal one-to-one correspondence (though in passing it does throw light on this aspect of the concept of number) but merely to see whether the perceptual appreciation of length tended to overcome the idea of constancy of quantity using these discrete elements. In Piaget's original experiments, he had asked his subjects whether necklaces made up of the beads in the containers would be of the same length. I attempted this but ran into difficulties of explanation, so performed the above task instead.

In all these experiments reasons for the answers were noted.

IV. Results

Quantitative

The results of the various combinations of the transpositions of both earth and nuts are seen in Table 1.

Conservation

Table 1
Responses to the Transposition of Continuous and Discontinuous
Quantities

		Gr. 1 N = 9		Gr. 2 N = 9		Gr. 3 N = 9		Gr. 4 N = 9		Gr. 5 N = 9	
Task	Answer	C	D	C	D	C	D	C	D	C	D
I	A1 > B1, B2	5	4	6	5	4	3	2	3	—	—
	A1 < B1, B2	4	5	3	4	4	4	3	3	—	1
	A1 = B1, B2	—	—	—	—	1	2	4	3	9	8
	(tall) (short)										
II	B1, B2 > B3, B4	—	—	—	—	—	—	—	—	—	—
	B1, B2 < B3, B4	9	9	9	9	8	5	4	3	—	—
	B1, B2 = B3, B4	—	—	—	—	1	4	5	6	9	9
III	6 > Containers	9	9	9	9	9	9	7	4	—	—
	6 < Containers	—	—	—	—	—	—	—	—	—	—
	6 = 3 Containers	—	—	—	—	—	—	2	5	9	9

C=Continuous quantities (earth)
D=Discontinuous quantities (nuts)

The results of the experiments with placing nuts in unequal
rows are seen in Table 2.

Table 2
Responses to Discontinuous Quantities in Lines

Answer	Gr. 1 N = 9	Gr. 2 N = 9	Gr. 3 N = 9	Gr. 4 N = 9	Gr. 5 N = 9
24 > 12	9	9	8	3	—
24 < 12	—	—	—	—	—
24 = 12	—	—	1	6	9

Qualitative responses

In Table 1, task I results did not discriminate between the level or
the number of containers. Task II and III posited these two
dimensions separately. But during the first task, when the child
was questioned why he thought A1 had more or less earth or nuts
than B1, B2, his answer was either in terms of level or the number

of containers. In fact when A1 was judged to have more than B1, B2 it was on the basis of level that he was operating, and when he judged it to be less, it was on the basis of number. It was quite clear that it was these factors that were operating and not any others. The child would point to the level of earth or nuts and indicate that there must be more as it was higher (or less as it was lower). When numbers were involved, the subjects would clearly claim that there must be more earth or nuts as there were more containers. As regards these subjects who judged the various examples to be equal, their explanation was in terms of the actual operations which the experimenter performed. The experimenter had taken the glass and poured the earth into two other glasses – it must be the same. These subjects would spontaneously actually perform the operation themselves, and a great majority of them appeared as if the question demanded of them was one that only a European would ask. Furthermore, they would reverse the sequence of operations, by, for example, pouring back the earth from the second containers to the first. The same reaction, among the older children, came with the task of laying out the nuts in rows. Supporting their answer of 'ka kwagh mom' (it's the same), was a manual re-arrangement of the nuts in the two rows so as to make a direct one-to-one correspondence. With those children that thought the longer row contained more nuts there was a gesture that indicated there was more distance involved in one row than another.

V. Discussion

There seems little doubt from the results that the progression of comprehension concerning conservation postulated by Piaget is evident in these African children. Piaget, however, maintained that there was a stage of intermediary reactions (between the stage when the child relied wholly on perceptual cues, and the concept of conservation proper), in which for example the child acknowledges that the quantity of liquid will not change as it is poured from glass to glass, but will regress to the purely perceptual stage when three or more glasses are used. In order to give further evidence on this intermediary stage, it is necessary to inspect the figures in Table 1 of tasks II and III. In those groups which are relevant to intermediary reactions, namely 3 and 4, the following Table 3 shows the distribution of correct responses according to the question of level and according to the question of number of containers, as brought out by tasks II and III. It is unnecessary to introduce a statistical technique merely to point out that there are fewer correct responses when there are more than two containers involved and when there are two. It

Table 3
Correct Responses to Tasks Relating to Level and Number

	Continuous	Discontinuous
Level	33%	56%
Number	11%	23%

would of course be instructive to see whether there was a critical ratio of number of containers, but the main point is satisfied. Table 3 also discloses that the number of correct responses for these two groups is higher for discontinuous quantities than it is for continuous quantities. It would seem therefore from the relatively small sample tested, that at this intermediary stage the child has less trouble in conceptualizing conservation when he is presented with discrete phenomena as when he is confronted by a continuous mass.

The supporting evidence for the same stages that Piaget postulates concerns, of course, only the conservation point. The present study cannot throw light on the other subjects which one finds in *The Child's Conception of Number*, on seriation and the like. It will be recalled that Dodwell found considerable variations in the different test situations that he tried out, so that he was unable to generalize the three stages over the entire range of concepts: that is over conservation, provoked and unprovoked correspondence, seriation and cardinal–ordinal properties. His evidence on conservation, however, as shown in the graph of the children from 5 years 6 months to 8 years and 10 months, appears to agree with the original findings of Piaget, and is in line with the results of the present study.

On account of the difficulty of obtaining precision in age, this research can only be taken, in this regard, with some degree of approximation. It is clear that the general *sequence* from 'global comparisons' to 'concrete operations' occurs in these African children. Whether the change over occurs at the age of seven, as Piaget maintains, and which Lunzer (4) supports as regards the conservation of volume, is more difficult to say. The results of Table 1 suggests that this is the case with number in these illiterate children. As these children have had no formal instruction in abstract numbers, there is much to be said for the neurophysiological interpretation of readiness for dealing with such concepts. It is true that the subjects of these experiments were familiar with a game, known throughout Africa, concerning the placement of pebbles in two rows of holes. Proper playing of this game entails a good understanding of many of the concepts which are considered under the general category of number. Other than this the children tested had very little experience of the kind of topic which was performed.

It is interesting to note further that the children who performed these tasks successfully spontaneously carried out the operations and reversed the procedure. This is an essential element, as Mays (5) has pointed out in his review of Piaget's recent studies, for any form of mental experimentation and logical inference.

Concerning the adjacent thesis which was incidentally put to the test, namely Levy-Bruhl's ideas of 'native' concepts of number, it is quite clear that this is an excessive over-generalization. At least by the age of 8, the kind of thinking that Levy-Bruhl envisaged, has tended to disappear. In a further paper (in preparation) concerning approaches to classification I have shown that this kind of concrete thought also disappears in the formation of categories, among the Tiv. It may of course be true that what goes under the heading of 'pre-logical mentality' may be more evident in other so-called primitive societies. If this is found to be so, then the direction of theory would be steered towards the relevant varying experiences which children undergo. As regards Tiv children, in the particular fields explored, there seems little difference to the sequence which has been found in European children.

Summary

Five groups of nine illiterate bush West African children of the Tiv tribe were tested on the question of conservation of continuous and discontinuous quantities. The techniques employed were similar to those worked out by Piaget, reported in his book *The Child's Conception of Number*. Earth and nuts were used as examples of continuous and discontinuous quantities respectively. Results indicated that the progression of the idea of conservation followed that found in European and other Western children by previous investigators. On account of the difficulty of precision of absolute age among the children tested, there is some hesitation in claiming that the change over from a purely perceptual to a conceptual reliance regarding conservation takes place exactly at the age which it is found in Western subjects, but it would seem to be approximately so. The results are discussed in the light of Piaget's theories and speculations concerning the mode of thought in so-called primitive peoples.

References

1. DODWELL, P. C., 'Children's understanding of number and related concepts', *Canadian Journal of Psychology*, vol. 14 (1960), pp. 191–205.
2. ESTES, B. W., 'Some mathematical and logical concepts in children', *Journal of Genetic Psychology*, vol. 88 (1956), pp. 219–22.
3. LEVY-BRUHL, L., *How Natives Think*, English Translation, London 1926.
4. LUNZER, E. A., 'Some points of Piagetian theory in the light of experimental criticism', *Journal of Child Psychology and Psychiatry and Allied Disciplines*, vol. 1 (1960), pp. 191–202.
5. MAYS, W., 'Development of logical and mathematical concepts: Piaget's recent psychological studies', *Nature*, vol. 174 (1954), pp. 625–6.
6. PIAGET, J., *The Child's Conception of Number*, Routledge & Kegan Paul, 1952.

13 P. Marks Greenfield

On Culture and Conservation

P. Marks Greenfield, 'On culture and conservation', in J. S. Bruner, R. R.
Olver and P. M. Greenfield, eds., *Studies in Cognitive Growth*, chapter 11,
Wiley, 1966, pp. 225–56.

Both too much and too little have been said about 'primitive
mind' – too much in that the descriptions given us by anthropologists have been for the most part rather global generalizations
based on inference from language, myth, ritual and social life.
Such accounts are not founded upon the observation of 'mind
in action', upon an analysis of behavior in concrete situations.
So, we know very little indeed about 'primitive minds' at
work, and their operation remains largely to be explored. In
fact, it is not unreasonable to ask in what sense the label
'primitive' is even applicable to the thinking of non-Western
peoples.

What has been implicit in the work of such anthropologists as
Boas, Durkheim, Mauss, Mead and Whorf is the assumption
that different modes of thinking are characteristic of different
cultures. It is a bold hypothesis that variations in cognitive
functioning are formed by cultural influences. Unfortunately,
from the point of view of testing the hypothesis, the study of
intellectual development has been confined almost entirely to
members of our own Western societies. Our richest picture of
cognitive development, that drawn by Jean Piaget, is based
entirely on experiments in which age alone is varied. In his view,
cognitive maturation is made to appear like a biologically determined and universal sequence. While Piaget admits that
environmental influences play a role, the admission is *pro forma*,
and inventive experiments remain confined to American and
European children, usually middle class children at that. Where
Piaget's work has been extended to non-Western societies, the
emphasis has been almost entirely quantitative. Such work
has been confined largely to timetable studies, to the time 'lag'

in the development of 'foreign' children in contrast to children in Geneva or Pittsburgh or London (Flavell, 1963). Qualitative differences between Western thinking and that of traditional societies have rarely been explored. Psychologists, when they have gone abroad, have usually approached their work in other cultures as though they were dealing with familiar phenomena, present in greater or lesser quantity (usually lesser). Hence the equation of 'primitive' adult with 'civilized' child.

Cambridge has steadily disagreed with Geneva on the fundamental 'how' of intellectual growth. Our own work has emphasized the role of internalized, culturally transmitted technologies. One way of exploring this role is to establish the manner in which an enriched (or impoverished) environment affects growth. This approach uses instruction in its broadest sense as its instrument of exploration. A second approach is to study development in societies in which the culturally given 'technologies' are radically different from our own, with the hope of finding and analysing differences in cognitive functioning. This is the major strategy of the research reported in this chapter, though we shall at the same time study the effect of instruction on children in the different cultures.

The experiments to be described were done in Senegal, the western-most tip of former French West Africa. The subjects were Wolof, members of the country's dominant ethnic group. The Wolofs, who are Moslem, constitute over one-third of Senegal's total population of 2,300,000. The basic experiment was the familiar one developed by Piaget to study the conservation of quantity and is described in Chapter 9 [not included here]. It consisted in equating the quantity of water in two identical beakers, then pouring the contents of one beaker into one of a different size and inquiring whether the amount of water is now the same. Particulars will be set forth in a later section. For theoretical purposes the experiments could have been done almost anywhere. Many other preliterate traditional societies would provide as dramatic a contrast with our own milieu as this one did.

The Wolof group was selected from those found in Senegal largely because its children are to be found not only in the French-style schools of Dakar, the cosmopolitan capital city, but also out in the bush, sometimes receiving the beginnings of a French education, more often not.

The children were constituted into nine groups, the better to discern the effect of cultural differences: three degrees of urbanization and education were represented, with three age levels within each. As in all under-developed countries, the contrast between urban and rural life is enormous in Senegal, independent only since 1960. In the city one finds the accoutrements of Western industrial life; in the rural village, no matter how close, there is virtually none. School itself represents a new world of French culture and the written word, a world in almost dizzying contrast to the oral traditions of traditional West African society.

The cultural milieu of our first group, the rural unschooled children, had neither schools nor urban influence. Their setting was Taiba N'Diaye, a traditional Wolof village of about a thousand people. Its economy, like that of the whole country, is based on oil-producing peanut cultivation, although millet is grown for local consumption. Still, undernourishment is the general rule. Socially, residentially, and economically, the village is divided into fifty-nine compounds, each surrounded by a wooden palisade and inhabited by an extended family unit. Within each compound are several small, round, thatched huts inhabited by various members of a patrilocal family.

The village, located in the Cayar region of Senegal, is fifty miles by a good road from the country's coastal capital. It is found in the midst of bush, Senegal's dominant rural landscape. Flat expanses of grass are broken only by scattered baobab trees. The grass is mostly brown and dead during the cool, dry season (November through June). The landscape returns to green after the first rain, when the year's cultivation begins. The two sharply divided seasons are typical of the subtropical climate which covers most of the country.

Although the village has an elementary school, the children of our first group had never attended it. As already noted, they were subdivided into three ages: six to seven, eight to nine, and eleven to thirteen (seventeen, twenty, and twelve children respectively). Our age data are, alas, approximate. African children, especially in the bush, have only the vaguest idea of how old they are in terms of years; and parents stop counting age after a child receives his Moslem baptism, which happens on the eighth day after birth. Fortunately for us, however, the French government a number of years ago instituted civil status for all with its prerequisite census, a source from which reasonable age estimates can be obtained for children born since 1950. Any child not on the census rolls of Taiba N'Diaye was automatically eliminated from the study. Still, the census is far from perfect, and it is probably more accurate to say that our age data are accurate on the average, rather than in the particular case.

The cultural setting of the second major group – rural school children – was identical with that of the first with respect to the rural Wolof milieu in which its members lived. In fact, many of the children came from the same village of Taiba N'Diaye, and in at least ten cases from the same families. These children, however, unlike the first, were receiving a French-style education. Taiba N'Diaye's own school provided the two oldest groups of children, who were in the third and sixth grades. These groups (twenty and twenty-four children respectively) matched the two oldest unschooled rural groups. To find a group corresponding to the youngest unschooled children, it was necessary to go to a very similar Wolof village nearby where the school included a first-grade class. Twenty-three first-grade children from Méouane participated in the experiment.

Finally, the cultural milieu of the third group was characterized by the presence of both aspects of Western culture, urban setting and schooling. This group came from Dakar, the cosmopolitan capital of Senegal and the former capital of French West Africa. The children in this group came from three of the city's public schools. As with the rural-school children, the Dakar group was selected from the first, third, and sixth grades. Thus the two school groups were matched exactly with respect to the number of years of schooling as well as approximate age. Grade level and age are only roughly correlated in Senegal because of the vagaries which result from attempting the relatively sudden conversion to literacy of an entire population. For this reason, the ages of the school groups were more variable than those of the unschooled groups, and at least some of the school groups had a slightly higher average age. (There were twenty-three first-grade children, twenty-two third-grade, and twenty sixth-grade.)

According to a Wolof informant, children in the bush are *not* chosen to go to school on the basis of their intelligence. In fact, if a child shows promise at the Koranic school to which all boys and girls are first sent, he may be kept there and never sent to the national school. Such a selection factor would preclude an imbalance of native intelligence in favor of the school group. In general, certain families elect to send their children to school. If one child is sent, all usually go, except that girls, in line with the Moslem attitude toward women, are often not sent to school at all. Thus, there is no reason to believe that the rural children in school and out were not equivalent with respect to native endowment, and we can confidently attribute differences between the two groups to the school experience itself. Traditionally, school attendance has been linked with caste membership, with low-caste members of the society being the most willing to give their children a French education. In this village, however, school attendance was not related to caste.

The academic program is based on a French model and, as in France, is under the central control of the Ministry of Education. Indeed, the curriculum is specified in such minute detail by a booklet entitled *L'Education Sénégalaise* that, for all practical purposes, our two school groups were having the same educational experience; and consequently the differences between the two groups must therefore be attributed to other distinguishing features of urban and rural milieu.

The school children went through the experiments individually at their school. Though every effort was made to hold things constant from school to school, there were some inevitable and considerable variations. In one city school the principal occupied the office adjoining the room in which the experiments were being carried out, and his callers periodically passed through the room, unannounced except by the long compulsory series of Wolof salutations. In the bush schools, at the other extreme, privacy was fairly complete, but the exigencies of space were such that the experimenting was done outdoors rather than in. Sampling in general was systematic. In a given school class every nth child would be taken from the roll in order to arrive at a sample size close to the target of twenty children per subgroup.

The unschooled bush children were examined at the author's

compound in the village, one much like all the others. Its combined dining-room-and-kitchen building served as the experimental room, and a rough thatched shelter in the middle of the compound provided a 'waiting room' for the next subject, who was usually accompanied by a good number of curious children from his own extended family. While an official document from the Minister of Education aided us in securing school children as subjects, it was necessary to obtain permission from every family head individually so that the children under his jurisdiction might participate. Although none refused, there was an initial suspicion that an attempt was being made to conscript their children into school. For these children, the sampling unit was the residential compound, and the selection of children within a compound was made on a systematic basis from among those enumerated in the census rolls.

The experimental situation, in so far as it consists of an interview of one child by one adult, is unheard of in the traditional culture, where almost everything occurs in groups, and adults command rather than seek the opinions of children. The children, nevertheless, whether attending school or not, seemed at home with the tasks, and many seemed to be enjoying themselves thoroughly. Although they talked much less than Western children do and restricted themselves to answering questions, their patience was monumental and, correlatively, their attention span seemed to surpass by far that of American children.

The author carried out all the experiments in the Wolof language. A young Senegalese girl served as recorder, taking verbatim transcripts of the children's responses in a highly individualized phonetic system, for Wolof is an oral language and the recorder was not a linguist.

The exact conservation task was based on the most unambiguous translation of the American and Swiss procedure as could be formulated in Wolof. Although the school children were at various stages in learning French, the language of all formal instruction, the use of French in the experiments would have annulled their value by destroying the comparability of the groups. Among the subgroups of the school sample, for instance, the developmental progress between the first and sixth grades which is simply due to an increased ability to understand and express oneself in French would be indistinguishable from that due to an actual shift in modes of thought. Moreover, the school groups responding in French would in no way be comparable either to their unschooled Senegalese comrades or to their European counterparts, both of whom would have the advantage of being interrogated in their native tongue. At least one previous study of conservation in Africa suffered from this methodological flaw (Flavell, 1963).

In the basic conservation task (pre-test, Figure 1) a child was presented with two identical beakers partly filled with water. The child equalized the water levels of the two beakers. The water of one of the beakers was subsequently transferred to a second longer, thinner beaker, causing the water level to rise, of course. The child was then asked whether the two beakers still had the same amount of water. In the second part of the experiment six shorter, thinner beakers replaced the long, thin one and this time the water was divided among the six. The child compared the water in the original beaker with the total contents of the six small ones and judged whether or not the amounts were equal.

A major linguistic difficulty that had to be overcome was the inherent ambiguity in the Wolof language surrounding the two words for 'equal' (*tolo* and *yem*). Both have the double sense of equal level and equal amount. Since the correct solution of the conservation problem depends on recognizing the distinction between these two 'equalities,' the cognitive implications of this linguistic difficulty are substantial.

Adult Wolofs agreed, however, that the version finally used referred unambiguously to the quantity rather than the level of water. In Wolof, the key conservation question was asked this way:

Ndah sa verre bi ak suma verre bi nyo yemle ndoh; wala suma verre bi mo upa ndoh; wala sa verre bi mo upa ndoh?

A literal translation into English yields the following:

Does this glass of yours and this glass of mine have equal water; or does this glass of mine have more water; or does this glass of yours have more water?

217

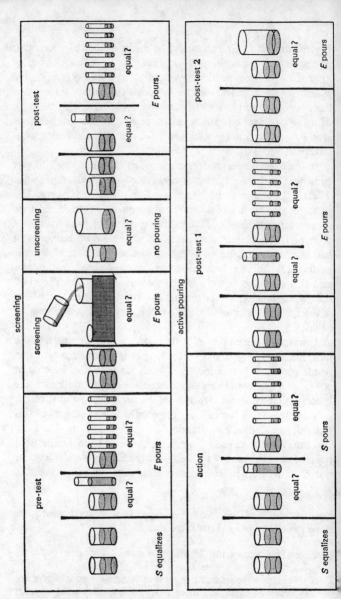

Figure 1 Procedures used in experiments

218

An interesting problem arose when it came to asking the unschooled children to justify their answers to this question. A previous experiment had shown that whereas the question, 'Why do you *think* or *say* that thus and such is true?' would meet with uncomprehending silence, the question, 'Why *is* thus and such true?' could often be answered quite easily. So the question asked of American children, 'Why do you *think* this glass has more (or equal) water?' was modified to, 'Why *does* this glass have more (or equal) water?'[1] It would seem that the unschooled Wolof children are lacking in Western self-consciousness: they do not distinguish between their own thought or a statement about something and the thing itself. Thought and the object of thought seem to be one. Consequently, the idea of explaining a *statement* is meaningless; it is the external event that is to be explained. The relativistic notion that events can vary according to the point of view may therefore be absent to a greater degree than in Western culture.

The Pattern of Conservation

The development of the conservation of a continuous quantity, as a maturational achievement, is said by Piaget to be but one manifestation of more general and fundamental changes that occur in the course of cognitive growth. The first question we must ask is whether conservation does in fact develop among the Senegalese and whether this development relates to chronological age.

The achievement of conservation was said to be present when a child gave equality responses to both quantity comparisons with the standard beaker, that involving the long, thin beaker and that involving the six small beakers. A child who changed his mind was given credit for his final answer. The data on conservation are presented graphically in Figure 2. The most striking thing here is the one point at which conservation *ceases*, for all practical purposes, to be related to age. The oldest unschooled bush children (eleven- to thirteen-year-olds) show no significant in-

1. The question actually asked was, 'Lu tah nyo yem?' (literally, 'What reason they are equal?') or 'Lu tah bi mo upa bi?' ('What reason this one has more than this one?').

crease in conservation over the eight- and nine-year-olds. Only half of the unschooled bush children attain conservation at this late age. It is possible, of course, that development is simply slower without school, so that an adult group might manifest 100 per cent conservation behavior. Other results, however, obtained

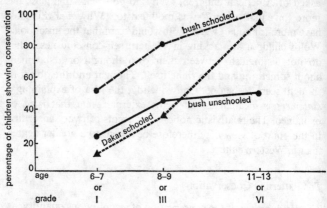

Figure 2 Percentage of children of different backgrounds and ages exhibiting conservation of a continuous quantity

both from these subjects and from subjects in other cultures do not make it seem likely. Chapter 13 shows a study of conceptualizing done with unschooled adults when eleven- to thirteen-year-old children were found to respond in essentially the same manner as the eight- and nine-year-old group [study not included in this excerpt]. No further changes in the pattern of conceptual thought were observed in the adults, save for a decrease in the variability of response from subject to subject. That experiment and this one suggest that, without school, intellectual development, defined as *any* qualitative change, ceases shortly after age nine. An investigator in Niger has made the same observation among unschooled African children on a completely different type of activity – drawing.[2] And another investigator who worked with conservation tasks (albeit different ones) found no difference between minimally schooled Chinese adolescent boys and a

2. Evelyn Pierre, personal communication.

matched group of adults in Hong Kong in the percentage of subjects with conservation Goodnow (1962). It would appear at first glance that the technologies and skills absorbed from the school experience may indeed strongly affect the question of whether some children in Senegal (and perhaps elsewhere) even achieve conservation of a continuous quantity.

In contrast, the school children of bush and town yield the familiar developmental sequence, with conservation virtually always attained by the sixth grade. Note one point. The interviews were all in Wolof, as mentioned; but schooling is in French. It is interesting that the skills being learned in French do in fact carry over into thinking and speaking in Wolof. Bush school children, indeed, are almost indistinguishable from American or Swiss children. The studies reported elsewhere in this book, using much the same procedure as was used in Senegal, report conservation in half the children at ages six and seven (first and second grade) among American children. Other investigators have reported 75 per cent conservation behavior at age eight (third grade) (Flavell, 1963). Bush school children show 52 per cent conservation in the first grade (probably an average age of eight) and 80 per cent in the third grade (average age between nine and ten). In terms of grade level, the Senegalese figures are close to being identical to the Western ones, although the Wolof children are behind in terms of chronological age. The parallel findings certainly cast strong doubts on any simple maturational notion of development. Rural Wolof children exposed to a certain set of cultural influences, namely, the school, differ more from other rural Wolof children raised without school than they do from European children. As the two groups of Wolof children are from the same gene pool, whereas the Europeans represent a non-overlapping gene pool, this finding casts deep doubt on any biological–genetic point of view.

As for the performance of the Dakar school children, it is markedly inferior to that of the bush children in terms of the proportion of children showing conservation, until the sixth grade, when the two school groups are virtually indistinguishable in this respect and the unschooled group falls dramatically behind. We could attribute this difference to the globally disrupting effect of urbanization. Yet a look at the reasoning behind the children's amount judgments indicates that such an explanation is not only too general to have much explanatory value, but is also untrue. In any case, we cannot talk about these children's lives as being 'disrupted' by urban influences, for the overwhelming majority were born in Dakar and have been children of the city from the start. So let us go on to the children's reasoning, which is in any case more interesting than the percentage attaining conservation at each age.

There are basically three types of justification. These can be ordered according to how much they reflect *directly perceptible* features of the current situation. First, *perceptual* reasons do so to the highest degree. This class of reason refers to the features of the display in front of the child; it includes any description of the beakers and their contents. Perceptual reasons can be classified according to analyticity and complexity. In addition, one type of perceptual reason expresses a conflict between the appearance ('It looks like more') and the reality ('But it's really the same') of the situation. This type of reason occurred in the conservation responses of American children shown in Chapter 9 [not included here], but did not manifest itself in the African protocols. If any conflict between the 'appearance' and 'reality' of the situation exists for these African children, it is expressed in different ways. In fact, previous pilot work at the Institut d'Etudes Pédagogiques at the University of Dakar had indicated that there is no conventional way of translating into Wolof the question oriented towards an appearance-reality conflict – 'Is the water in the second glass "really" different or does it "just look" different?' – and that when the translation is made the children do not understand what it means.

Second, *direct-action* reasons refer to the act of pouring the water from one of the standard beakers into a test beaker (or beakers). Note that these reasons are still rather closely tied to the situation, for the act actually takes place in the experiment and is the most recently observed physical action. Nevertheless, a direct-action reason can also be considered a Piagetian operation. Piaget states that an operation is an action that is both *internal* and *reversible*. We shall keep only the former part of the definition, leaving the latter for empirical investigation and later discussion. Still, it is an open question whether the direct action has in fact been internalized. If so it has been retained *exactly as it happened*.

The third category of reasons is called *transformational*. These reasons go beyond the 'givens' of the present situation and represent a transformation of that situation in the child's head. For this reason they are truly 'operational' in Piaget's sense, for they are by definition the products of *internalized* (or mental) *action*. In the present experiment, the transformations utilized in reasoning were of two main sorts: action and identity. The action transformations were sometimes inverse, also called negative or reverse ('If you were to pour it back . . .'), sometimes correlative ('If you were to pour the other one . . .'). These action transformations will be called *indirect-action* reasons, so as to emphasize the fact that they are not directly observed in the experiment. Note that the correlative action creates a *hypothetical* state of equality in the two sets of test beakers (for example, two long, thin beakers) while the inverse action recreates the *initial* state of equality in the two standard beakers. The inverse thus reestablishes the original state produced by the first equalizing operation. Reference to the original state of the system, in this case the state of equality in the two standard beakers, constitutes, the third and most important type of transformation argument, the *identity* reason (for example, 'This one [full standard beaker] and this one [empty standard beaker] had equal water'). Identity is the 'null' transformation: nothing is changed. Logically, the identity argument is the most basic, because it is in fact the initial equalizing operation that determines the correct answer to the conservation problem. But logical primacy cannot be automatically equated with psychological primacy, as Piaget is wont to do; therefore let us examine the psychological status of the identity argument.

In America, younger children rely much more heavily on perceptual reasons than do older children. This is also dramatically the case among the Wolof school children (Figure 3). Indeed, we find a drop from 79 per cent perceptual reasons in the first grade of the bush school and 63 per cent in the first grade of the Dakar school to 27 per cent in both sixth grades. But the unschooled bush children, identical to the bush school children in every respect save one, use *more* perceptual reasons as they grow older. Yet note that the unschooled children start out less perceptually oriented than those in school. It seems, then, that the *first* effect of schooling is to increase their analytic attention to the perceptible features of situations such as our experiment, and that this effect is then followed by a systematic and drastic reduction in the importance of such features. This result, shown in Chapter 8, finds an interesting parallel in the American children,

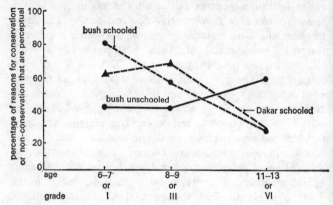

Figure 3 Percentage of reasons for conservation or non-conservation that are perceptual

who, in developing the relational idea of a proportion, first become *more* perceptual with age, in the sense of learning to utilize more than one perceptible attribute at a time [not included in this excerpt]. Only after this stage do they unify these attributes by means of the 'fraction' schema. This simpler, more symbolic 'theory' in turn eliminates the need for the plural perceptual reasons out of which it arose.

Let us now look at reasons in relation to conservation judgments. Do Wolof children fail to conserve for the same reasons as Western children, and do they attain conservation by the same paths? In most cases the Wolof children use a transformational or direct-action reason as the basis for justifying conservation, just as American children do; see Chapter 9 [not included here].[3]

3. References are often made to other chapters of *Studies in Cognitive Growth*, not reproduced in this volume. Consult the original work for full information – *Editor*.

However, direct action assumes greater importance in the conservation reasoning of these children than it did in the American children's proconservation arguments. Price-Williams (1961), working with Tiv children in Nigeria, also found that justifications for equality judgments were in terms of action. The over-all totals of the reasons used by all one hundred eighty-one children studied were:

40 per cent based on perceptible features,

16 per cent based on direct action,

44 per cent based on transformation (identity and indirect action).

In support of non-conservation, they were:

78 per cent based on perceptible features,

20 per cent based on direct action,

2 per cent are transformations.[4]

These figures indicate that transformation reasons are a sufficient, if not a necessary, condition for conservation. A closer look at the actual transformation arguments reveals that 95 per cent of them contain a reference to the identity 'transformation'. Therefore, we may conclude that the identity argument is not only *logically* but also *psychologically* sufficient for a conservation judgment. On the other hand, the psychological results do not confirm the logical idea that an identity reason is also *necessary* to conservation of amount.

As for reversibility, that is, the possibility of inverse action, it is secondary to the identity element in two ways. First, it usually does not appear as a reason in isolation, but is accompanied by an identity argument (e.g. 'If you were to pour this water [long, thin beaker], here this one [full standard beaker] and this one [empty standard beaker] would be equal'), whereas identity alone often appears as an argument for conservation. Thus, it would seem that identity is a necessary condition for the use of reversible action as a conservation argument. One could say that reversibility without identity yields the kind of result obtained by Carey (Chapter 9): a change in level obtained by pouring the liquid into a beaker of a different shape is seen as reversible;

4. Seventy-eight per cent of the children contributed two reasons, corresponding to the two parts of the conservation task. Only three out of the one hundred eighty-one children gave as many as four reasons, the maximum number possible.

but, although the young child may realize that the change is temporary, it is no less 'real' to him, for the change in level implies a correlative change in quantity. In brief, Carey finds reversibility without conservation.

Second, it is *identity* rather than *reverse* transformations that cause direct-action reasons to be associated with an 'operational' or correct solution to the conservation problem. In other words, direct-action reasons are *always* in support of conservation when they contain an identity element. When they do not, they frequently support an incorrect judgment. Reverse action, in contrast, is rarely even associated with direct-action reasons. In consequence, it seems more accurate to say that it is identity, and not reversibility, that turns actions into operations, at least in the conservation situation.

One final observation concerning the role of identity in conservation. As action reasons become more operational, both in the sense of supporting conservation judgments and in the sense of being more internal (that is, indirect), identity arguments increase in a rather dramatic correlation (Table 1). Thus identity would seem to be an accurate index of operationality defined according to these two Piagetian criteria.

Before leaving the discussion of reasons in support of conservation judgments, we must point out an interesting difference between American and Wolof justifications. The older American children participating in Frank's screening experiment sometimes spontaneously remark upon the *necessity* of equality (e.g. 'It must be the same'). There is not one instance of such an appeal to necessity among all the Wolof children, although the language does contain the requisite vocabulary.

Turning now from equality to inequality judgments, we see that the general picture of nonconservation reasoning is also very similar to that found in the United States, for the overwhelming conservation block is a perceptual one. The Wolofs deviate from the American pattern in one major respect, however: there is a significant minority (20 per cent) of inequality judgments that are supported by *direct action* reasons. That is, Wolof children often say things like, 'There is more in this glass because you poured it.' American children only use such reasons to support a conservation position, although Piaget (1952) reports one instance of an action reason for a non-conservation response in a four-year-old. This seemingly bizarre reasoning did not come as a complete

Table 1
Percentage of Action Reasons that Include a Reference to the Identity Justification

	Direct-Action Reasons for Non-conservation	Direct-Action Reasons for Conservation	Indirect-Action Reasons for Conservation
Reference to identity	0%	47%	75%
Number of reasons	19	75	20

surprise, since pre-tests conducted in the Senegalese bush in 1963 by Bruner and Valantin had underlined the importance of definition by action. They had found that one glass would be called 'the same' as another by virtue of the fact that each had 'been poured into'. But here was something different: inequality based on an action.

It could not be simply a matter of equating actions rather than amounts of water, for different children gave the same action answer in the same situation, sometimes to justify a judgment of equality and sometimes to justify a verdict of inequality. A control procedure also cast doubt on the idea that equality would be based on identical actions when the quantities of water were different. More likely, the children are utilizing *action* reasons to explain a *perceptual* discrepancy between the appearance of the water in the two glasses. The contrast between the initial appearance of equal quantities of water and the later appearance of inequality is perhaps resolved by recourse to the experimenter's action. It is that form of 'magical' thinking in which natural phenomena are explained by attributing special powers to intervening human agents.

School suppresses such thinking with astonishing absoluteness. There is *not one instance* of such reasoning among the children who have been in school seven months or more. Urban life itself exerts no influence in this direction, for among the first-graders in Dakar (who had completed no more than four months of school at the time of the experiment) one finds the most 'magical' reasoning of all – 80 per cent of these children's action reasons are of this type.[5] So, Wolof children who have not been to school differ from American children in the reason why they do not have conservation. Their reasons reflect less 'perceptual seduction' than 'seduction by the experimenter's actions'.

As just described, direct actions are less likely than indirect actions to bear the mark of an operation (internalization), for their origin is to be found in external physical action. And note that it is also *direct*- rather than *indirect*-action reasons that are used by the unschooled children to support inequality judgments. This finding is in line with Piaget's general point that conservation demands internalized operations.

In Senegal, as in the United States, perceptual reasons support both conservation and non-conservation judgments. Although perceptual reasons are relatively infrequent among both the youngest unschooled children and the oldest school children, the former group uses them to support *non-conservation*, the latter, *conservation*. Can we then find an observable difference between the two types of perceptual reason, a difference that will set off the thinking of Senegalese children who have conservation from those who do not? It would seem so. When perceptual reasons reflect attention to *several* perceptible aspects of the conservation situation, they are likely to back up a conservation position; when they indicate that the child is centering on only one aspect of the situation, they are likely to go along with nonconservation. However, the two perceptible aspects do not have to be the two dimensions of height and width that Piaget claims are of crucial importance to conservation through compensation. In fact, a reference to the *same* dimension of two *beakers* is more effective than a reference to two *dimensions* of one or two beakers.

Returning now to the city-school children, we must note that it is precisely in this respect that the younger city-school children fall behind the rural groups. That is, their transformation reasons are associated with conservation about as often as in the bush.

5. These children had had less schooling than the first-grade bush children, as they had to wait several months for their parents to construct a classroom. In fact, the few months of schooling they had received were probably ineffectual because of conditions of extreme overcrowding and disorganization.

But many more of their perceptual reasons are reasons *against* conservation. It turns out that, correlatively, the city children are much less inclined to focus on more than one aspect of the situation when they give perceptual reasons; they more often think in terms of *one* attribute of *one* of the beakers, never mentioning other attributes of the same beaker or the other beakers involved in the experiment. Nor are they inclined to relate two features of the displays even implicitly through the use of a comparative descriptive word – e.g. 'thinner', 'taller'. The importance of getting away from a single salient perceptible cue if an American child is to develop conservation was also commented upon in Chapter 9. Thus, the rural–urban difference in the percentage of younger children showing conservation is *not general*, but is concentrated among those children who give perceptual reasons.

Exposure to the more diverse sensory impressions of the city seems not to make children more perceptual; quite the opposite – their perceptual impressions of the experiment (as reflected in their reasons for judgment) were *less* diverse, *more* restricted to a single impression. We may hypothesize, however, that linguistic conditions produce this poverty of perceptual description in city children. Wolof as spoken in Dakar has become much simplified, owing to its status as the African *lingua franca* there. And, indeed, the descriptive language of the city children was less varied than that of their rural counterparts, particularly the school children. The importance of symbolic coding in fostering a conflict was discussed in the preceding chapter.

A Screen against Perceptible Cues

One of the strategies for discerning what produces a particular reaction is to try to alter it. In the screening studies carried out with American children (Chapter 9), it was argued that conservation depends for its attainment on the development of a sense of conflict between how things appeared and how they 'really were.' If such were the case, the argument continued, one should hasten conservation by shielding the child from initial exposure to the perceptible inequalities by carrying out the pouring with beakers behind a screen. This is to say, one would first show the identical beakers with an equal amount of water in them. Then the contents of one of the beakers would be poured into a taller, wider beaker – with all beakers covered almost to their tops by an opaque screen. This procedure worked in the United States and, indeed, it succeeded strikingly in getting the children to say that the same amount of water was present in both beakers, not only while the screen was in place but also after it was removed. The screen was a success, pedagogically.

Would the same procedure prove successful among children whose language indicates little concern with noting and reconciling self-consciously the differences between appearance and reality? It would seem unlikely. In any case, a screening procedure similar to that used in Massachusetts was employed in Senegal (see Figure 1), including a request for the reasons for amount judgments both before and after the removal of the screen (see pp. 193 ff of *Studies in Cognitive Growth*).

As for gross results, only 30 per cent of the eighty-one Wolof children who did not have conservation on the pre-test discussed before showed an improved performance on the post-test, in contrast to 61 per cent improvement among comparable American children. These results are in terms of shifts among three categories of response: (1) *conservation*, which means an equality reaction on both parts of the pre-test; (2) *fluctuation*, or giving a conservation response to one part of the pre-test and a non-conservation response to the other; and (3) *non-conservation*, with inequality answers on both parts of the pre-test.

While screening was not totally ineffective with the Wolof children, the effect was trivial on closer inspection. For it turned out to be nothing more than a threshold phenomenon. What screening did was to induce conservation in those children who were already on the verge of conservation, as indicated by their fluctuation on the pre-test. Those who had shown no previous signs of conservation were helped little. The change wrought in the fluctuating subjects was virtually the same as with American children: in Massachusetts 65 per cent of such subjects were moved to conservation, as compared with 55 per cent in Senegal. In addition, 73 per cent of the American children who had shown no conservation on the pre-test showed improvement (either to fluctuation or conservation) on the post-test. In Senegal, only 13 per cent of the comparable group of thirty-eight Wolof children improved on the post-test; and only one of them moved all the way from non-conservation to conservation. In sharp contrast, 36 per cent of the children giving non-conservation judgments in Massachusetts moved all the way to conservation on the post-test as a result of screening. In short, if a Senegalese child was not already uncertain on the pre-test, he was not likely to be helped by the screening procedure. The same was not true of the American children. The data are summed up in Table 2.

It would be helpful to relate that one could easily tell on the basis of the reasons proffered during the pre-test which fluctuating subjects would be moved toward conservation by screening. Alas, the number of subjects shrinks as one seeks to isolate justification patterns. However, some suggestive results can be given. The first is that, if the subjects show any tendency to justify incorrect judgments in the language of identity, they are certain to be in the conservation group after screening. At the other

Table 2

Percentage of American and Senegalese Children who Showed Various Degrees of Improvement from Pre-test to Post-test as a Result of Screening Experience

	Pre-test			
	No Conservation		Fluctuation	
Post-test	United States	Senegal	United States	Senegal
No conservation	27%	87%	12%	7%
Fluctuation	37	10	23	38
Conservation	36	3	65	55
	100%	100%	100%	100%
Number of children	11	38	17	42

extreme, those fluctuating subjects who show any sign of action magic in their justification are almost sure not to benefit from screening. Finally, fluctuating subjects who use any form of perceptual analysis to back up incorrect quantity judgments are more likely to benefit from the screen than those who use non-analytic perceptual arguments in the same situation. Perceptual analysis involves any effort to describe particular attributes of the water or of the beakers.

In the main, however, we are prepared to believe that screening was of very little help to those who had not yet achieved conservation and that the help it afforded the fluctuaters was non-specific, the result of an opportunity to practice. It is doubtful whether much is due to special features of the screening technique itself. Other findings support this conclusion. For example, screening does not affect the reasons given by Wolof children without conservation either after unscreening or in the later post-test. Most notably, *perceptual* reasons are not reduced one whit, *even during the time that the water level is hidden by the screen*. In Massachusetts, on the other hand, there is a sharp decline in perceptual reasons with the introduction of the screen (in all age groups) and a further decline in perceptual reasons on the post-test (among all but the youngest group).

What is there in Wolof thinking that renders screening so ineffective as an instructional technique? Certainly, it would appear that school children, particularly Dakar school children, have perceptual barriers to conservation just as American children do. It might be that the screen does indeed shield them from a quick misleading ikonic rendering of the situation (Chapter 9, p. 199 of original volume), but that the symbolic representation substituted for the perceptual image and designed to serve as a guide for organizing their perceptions in a new way (Chapter 9, p. 201 of original volume) actually organizes these perceptions by means of a conceptual framework foreign to their thinking. This important pedagogical point will be more fully documented following the presentation of some additional relevant data.

As for the Wolof children who do not go to school, it is not so difficult to understand the failure of the screen as an instructional technique, for perceptual difficulties did not seem to be their problem in the first place. They do not justify non-conservation by a perceptual rationale. Action reasons more often serve that purpose. In this group, moreover, perceptual reasons do not decrease as conservation increases with age. Quite the contrary: an increase in perceptual reasons is associated with an increase in conservation. So it seems reasonable to suppose that a procedure designed to eliminate reasons based on perceptible cues would not be particularly relevant for this group. Consequently, a second training technique, specially planned to combat 'magical' thinking about action, was developed for unschooled children. The results of this second experiment should also bear upon the question of whether screening was in fact relevant to the difficulties of our group of unschooled children. Consider this second training technique before we draw any final conclusions about the children's reaction to screening itself.

Combating Action-Magic

In this version of the conservation procedure, everything remained basically the same with one exception: the child did all the pouring himself. The rationale was this: the child, while perfectly willing to attribute 'magical' powers to an authority figure like the experimenter, would not attribute any special powers to himself. A discrepancy in the apparent amount of water was not so likely to be rationalized as having been produced by adult magical power. Any child, moreover, is bound to have more accurate cause–effect notions with regard to his own action than with regard to the actions of others. The child with little experience in manipulating environmental objects – as would be truer of children in the passive Wolof culture than of children in America – might also be more prone to attribute puzzling changes to extrinsic powers. Experience in producing effects on the physical world might combat this tendency.

As before, the child began by equalizing the water levels in the two standard beakers, pouring into one to match the other. Then, unlike the first procedure, the experimenter told the subject to pour the water from one of the beakers into the long, thin beaker used in the first experiment (Figure 1). He was then asked if the two beakers contained the same amount of water and why. The wording of the two questions was exactly the same as in the previous experiment. After giving his explanation, the child was told to pour the water back into the standard beaker and finally to distribute the water among the six small beakers. Once again, he was asked if the standard beaker and the six small ones contained the same quantity of water and why. The rest of the

233

experiment consisted of two post-tests, with the experimenter pouring, to see whether conservation would carry over to the standard situation. The first post-test, exactly like the post-test of the screening experiment, used the same tall, thin beaker and the six small beakers into which the child poured in the first part of the present experiment. The second post-test substituted a new beaker, the tall, wide one. In this way there was an opportunity to observe whether conservation would prevail in a situation the child had not met while pouring the water himself. (The sequence of events is made clear in the bottom half of Figure 1.)

This 'active' version of the conservation experiment can be considered both as a test of conservation and as a training technique for the traditional conservation task. As there was no pre-test, we can first of all ask whether the conservation rate and the reasoning when the child pours differ from when the experimenter pours. A comparison with the pre-test of the screening experiment yields this information. In the second place, we may ask whether this procedure is effective as a training technique. A comparison of the post-test results of the two training experiments answers this question. A different group of rural unschooled children participated in this experiment, but the two groups were comparable and from the same village. Essentially the same selection procedures were used, but the children doing the 'active' version of the conservation test represented only half of the village's extended family units, rather than all of them, as in the first experiment. All the children from a given family who were going to participate in either conservation experiment did so at the same time, so that any contaminating communication was kept to a minimum. Because of the smaller sample in this experiment, the two oldest groups had to be lumped together for purposes of analysis. The formation of a single group of eight- to ten-year-olds seemed perfectly justified by the homogeneity of the pre-test conservation results from the two oldest unschooled groups (discussed before) in the screening experiment. There were nine six- and seven-year-olds and eleven eight- and ten-year-olds.

That pouring makes a difference to the unschooled children is evident. Among the younger ones, two-thirds of the group who transfer the water themselves have conservation; only a quarter of the other group had conservation when the experimenter poured. In the older group, the contrast is equally dramatic: 82 per cent of those who do the pouring themselves show conservation, as compared with slightly less than half of the group placed in the standard testing situation. So much for the pre-test.

The 'do-it-yourself' procedure has surprisingly strong effects on later behavior as well. Recall that there are two post-tests to compare, each corresponding to a post-test on the screening procedure. The first post-test is comparable to the unscreening. This one is carried out with the same beaker as was used in the 'do-it-yourself' condition – the taller, thinner one and the six small ones. The second post-test involves, as in the screening post-test, a change to a different beaker. The two procedures are compared in Figure 4. As far as the older children are concerned, it turns out that it does not matter which post-test we compare. Active participation by the child is superior to screening as a pedagogical experience. In the older group, all the children show conservation in both post-tests. Screening had produced it in only two-thirds of the older children, according to post-test figures.

Among the younger subjects, there is a little backsliding on the first post-test, and no difference between the effectiveness of screening and pouring as training techniques. The young unschooled bush children show an effect comparable to that in the youngest group of American children who succeed under optimal training conditions with screening, but who cannot withstand the misleading cues in the post-test. But on the second post-test, eight of nine of the bush youngsters regain conservation, a proportion considerably higher than the half who had shown it after screening in the earlier study of unschooled children in Taiba N'Diaye. This increase is mostly due to the greater difficulty of maintaining conservation when the water is divided among several beakers, a task that was included on the first post-test, but not on the second. The reasons for the greater difficulty of this task will be taken up later.

Could the rather dramatic effects of 'doing it yourself' be the potentially universal result of activity *per se*, or do they occur because this training technique undermines the 'magical' mode of causal thinking peculiar to unschooled bush children? Or might the superiority of 'pouring' over screening stem from a procedural artifact – in other words, the children who poured had no pre-test on which it was easy to err, and thus they had no 'commitment' to an incorrect solution. To test these two possibilities, an additional control experiment was run with some Dakar school children attending a girls' school. Although the other

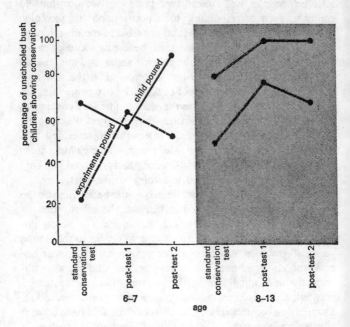

Figure 4 Percentage of bush unschooled children showing conservation after pouring and screening

groups tested had included boys, this aspect seems unimportant, since no consistent sex differences had shown up in the first conservation experiment in Dakar.

The control experiment comprised two conditions – a 'pouring' condition and a 'screening' condition. There was no pre-test under either condition. Fifteen Wolof children from the first and third grades took part in the pouring experiments, seventeen in the screening experiment. The screening experiment was exactly like that already described, minus the pre-test. The pouring

236

experiment was like the first one, except that the six small beakers were completely eliminated.

The proportion of children showing conservation (41 per cent) when the screen separated subject from beaker was between that obtained on the *pre-test* of the previous experiment and that obtained while the screen was in place during the same experiment. But the post-test result was clearly inferior to that produced by the first screening experiment. This suggests again that screening itself is not effective, but rather that it permits a repetition of the conservation tasks. The control experiment, lacking a pre-test, permitted less repetition and produced inferior results. We may also eliminate the issue concerning the effect of initial error on the pre-test, leading to an interfering commitment that diminishes the effects of training. Initial error does not reduce the effect of screening: the screen promotes conservation no better, even when it is the child's first experience with the conservation problem.

The results of the pouring experiment do indeed suggest that the effectiveness of the 'active' form of the conservation task is based on its 'anti-magic' capability. Pouring does not work at all among the city-school children who do not have the 'magical' thinking that the procedure was designed to combat. Only one child showed conservation under this condition, a performance that is even markedly inferior to the level of the Dakar school children operating under standard conditions in the first experiment. It may well be that pouring for the city children may have an interfering effect, but time did not permit a fuller examination of the matter.

The success of an instructional method in one group of children and its failure in another strengthens our conviction that differently enculturated children have basically different schemata for approaching conservation, schemata which go beyond mere verbal differences. Indeed, the variation from group to group in response to 'screening' and 'pouring' indicates the presence of greater subcultural differences in thinking than might have been concluded from the differences in the verbal reasons they gave in defense of their judgments. For example, more than half of the nonconservation reasons given by the two older unschooled bush groups in the pre-test of the screening experiment were perceptual rather than action ('magical'); yet the act of pouring was followed by conservation in all of a matched group of rural subjects. In contrast, there is no reason to think that any subject in Dakar was moved from non-conservation to conservation as a result of transferring the water from beaker to beaker, though the verbal justifications of these children were also highly perceptual.

Price-Williams' (1961) study of conservation of both continuous and discontinuous quantities among unschooled Tiv children in Nigeria gives further indication of the importance of active manipulation. This investigator found that 100 per cent of the Tiv children had achieved both types of conservation by age eight, in sharp contrast to our upper limit of 50 per cent with much older children. However, his description of the children's behavior during the experiments indicates that the Tiv culture is quite different from the Wolof one in promoting an active manipulative approach to the physical world. Price-Williams describes the children's behavior like this:

These children would spontaneously actually perform the operation themselves ... Furthermore, they would reverse the sequence of operations, by, for example, pouring back the earth from second container to the first (Price-Williams, 1961, p. 302).

Such self-initiated action was *never* observed among unschooled Wolof children, and it may well be the key to the great disparity between the two cultures in spontaneous conservation results.

How shall we know directly that the unschooled child's act of pouring infirms his 'magical thinking'? If such were the case, a child's reasons for his judgments should reflect it. They should differ according to whether the experimenter or the child pours. We have, after all, drawn conclusions about the ineffectiveness of screening on the grounds that the children's reasons were the same before and after the procedure. And indeed, we find that when the child pours, his reasons are dramatically different from those he gives when an adult does. Magical-action reasons, which constituted a quarter of all reasons when an adult pours, are non-existent when the unschooled older children themselves pour. Responses like, 'The water is not the same because you poured it', disappear. In the younger group, action reasons drop from 42 per cent with an adult pouring to 8 per cent when the children pour. What emerges in place of action justifications are identity reasons. The child who pours on his own now uses his initial equalizing operation as the basis for his justification of conservation. 'I made them the same.' In the oldest group we find that identity reasons account for 64 per cent of all justification when the child does the pouring. When the experimenter pours, only 20 per cent of all reasons are based exclusively on a return to the initial situation of equality ('logical identity'). In the younger group comparable figures are 50 per cent and 4 per cent. There is an interesting difference between the reasoning of older and of younger children. Among the younger ones, the proportion of perceptual reasons stays the same, no matter who pours. Identity reasons replace magical-action reasons when the child pours. In the older group, perceptual reasons as well as action reasons decline when the child takes over the pouring.

How, finally, shall we explain the fact that among the Wolof children who have not been to school, those who pour the water from beaker to beaker have conservation, while those who only watch the experimenter pour do not. Why is this the case? Two possibly related reasons suggest themselves. One stresses motoric experience and its resultant sensory feedback, the other the removal from the task of a powerful authority figure. If the effect were due to feedback from the action of pouring, one would hardly expect action reasons (which refer to this new experience of transferring the water) to decrease. In fact, they do decrease, and drastically. Our view, rather, is that the intervention of an authority figure in the standard experiment attracts attention; whatever that person does is important, even if irrelevant to the solution of the problem. The attention of the child is drawn away from his own action and from the intrinsic nature of the task itself. The child, in a way, is trying to solve the experimenter rather than the problem. Only when the authority figure withdraws does the child turn fully to the logically essential parts of the action, beginning with equalizing the water and carrying through to a recognition that the initial act establishes an identity throughout.

Once again identity – a return to the beginning – turns out to be not only the logical but also the psychological heart of conservation. It seems as though identity may be the 'invariant' in conservation itself. At least, identity appears to be as necessary to the attainment of conservation for these unschooled Wolof children as it was for American children (Chapter 9). But if the psychological 'essence' of conservation begins to take on an aspect of universality, the techniques by which it can be implanted are not, as these experiments show. Indeed, the variation in successful instructional methods from group to group is nothing more than a sharply focused reflection of the diversity of pre-conservation schemata that we have been describing.

Lest it appear that action alone plays a part in the preconservation schema that is corrected by 'pouring', we might consider a very revealing observation. It was often the case that a child, when asked to match the amount of water that the experimenter had poured into one standard beaker, would pour *all* the water from the pitcher into the second standard beaker, although the pitcher contained too much. The reason for his mistake seemed to be that he had initially watched the experimenter pour *all* the water from her pitcher into the first standard beaker and that he was doing likewise. Yet he was perfectly capable of realizing afterwards that he had poured too much and of correcting his mistake. The child was not merely matching the perceptual end state, as he was asked to do, nor was he matching only the action of pouring. What he was doing was making an erroneous causal connexion between the two, just as in the experiment proper. He was assuming that, if he performed exactly the same action as the experimenter, the end result would also be the same.

Piaget would say something like this: 'Actions are still not dissociated from the objects upon which they bear. He does not yet apprehend interrelations among objects *per se*; what are grouped are the action-object amalgams' (Flavell, 1963, pp. 137–8). Although this description fits, Piaget uses it to refer to the development of the sensori-motor state that takes place before age two and limits it to the child's representation of his own actions. Thus Piaget's child, in this instance, is said to organize his world in terms of practical space, a space that cannot be represented by symbolic means. But our Wolof children can, and certainly do, represent their world symbolically and in a very complicated language indeed! It makes much more sense to think in terms of an interaction between levels of representation, as these have been discussed throughout these pages. In the present case, we have a symbolic means of coding (language);

but in terms of content, i.e. what is coded, the representation does not go much beyond the capacities of the enactive mode – sensori-motor phenomena (actions) are represented by symbolic means. These sensori-motor phenomena differ from concrete operations, for they are not reversible. What this group of Wolof children is coding in language is a sequence of acts in the order they occur; the transformational possibilities of language are not utilized, and we are left with the symbolic analogue of an action sequence.

Consider now whether the unschooled children's lack of response to the screen bears out this view of the achievement of conservation. To do so, we must first look at the school children. The school children, recall, differed from the unschooled young Wolofs and, as we noted, were much closer in their conservation responses to American children than to their own countrymen. Yet they did not learn conservation from the screening procedure, as American children had. We have delayed a closer look at the failure of screening until now. At this point, however, it becomes especially appropriate.

When the screen is put in place before the American children, 82 per cent of them agree that the hidden beakers contain equal water. In Senegal 62 per cent of the unschooled rural children respond in this way, 67 per cent of the rural school children, but only 42 per cent of the city children. Why is this the case, if the school children are most like American children in their approach? In fact, it turns out that in certain respects they are even more perceptual than American children, particularly the Dakar children, and far more so than the unschooled bush children. With the beakers hidden behind the screen, they persist in wondering about where the water level is. American children almost always give their judgments when the screen is in place with not an apparent thought for the water levels. Not so the Dakar children, of whom several had to be eliminated because they peeked behind the screen – behavior never encountered in America. The Dakar children often predicted the water level by the compensation principle and then gave the judgment of inequality on that basis.

What happens when the screen is removed? The results are exactly what would be predicted from the preceding analysis of the reasoning in different groups (Table 3; Figure 4). Unschooled children, using action cues more than the school groups, are not affected by the new perceptible cues revealed when the screen is taken away. Conservation responses are more frequent without the screen than they were with it, in sharp contrast to the response of the three school groups (bush, Dakar, and American), in which removing the screen results in a sharp decline of conservation answers. Note that unscreening involves no new 'pouring' cues which might lead the rural children astray. It is just such

Table 3
Percentage of Children with No Conservation on Pre-test who Give Conservation Responses during and after Screening

	Cambridge	Bush No School	Bush School	Dakar School
Screen present	82%	62%	67%	42%
Unscreening	61%	69%	33%	16%
Post-test	54%	38%	33%	19%
Number of children	28	29	15	31

cues that make the second part of the standard conservation situation – where the water is divided among the six small beakers – more difficult for this group of children than the first part, as has been mentioned before. When the water is poured into the six small beakers, it is particularly easy to explain the perceptual discrepancy by action inequality. The child is presented with an action contrast of six pouring motions to one. For children sensitive to action, this inequality situation must be much more compelling than the one in which water is poured once into the standard beaker and once into a beaker of a different shape.

As for the post-test, the school children who survived unscreening also survive the post-test, the unschooled children less well. It may well be that the unschooled children, given their tendency to action-magic, more easily fall prey in the post-test to all the pouring done by the experimenter, whereas perceptible cues, the nemesis of the school children, are no more misleading than on the previous unscreening condition.

Some Conclusions

We have covered much ground and examined in fine detail the

responses and reasons of our Senegalese children. Several points stand out consistently.

The first is that there is a wider gap between unschooled and schooled Wolof children from the same rural village than between rural and urban school children. By the eleventh or twelfth year virtually all the school children have achieved conservation. Only about half of those not in school have done so.

The school children, moreover, show the typical early reliance on perceptible cues in justifying their judgments and a later decline in such judgments. In contrast, unschooled children in the bush show a gradual rise in perceptual reasons over the same age span.

Screening the children from perceptible cues has a relatively minor effect on children who have not yet started to fluctuate. It has its effect principally by virtue of giving the fluctuaters a chance to practice. In general, screening has a minor pedagogical effect in contrast to its effect in hastening conservation in American children.

A principal difficulty with the unschooled Wolof children was their tendency to 'explain' the changed (to them) amount of water in terms of action-magic – it was different because the experimenter had poured it. The specific cure for this was having the children pour for themselves. But it is noteworthy that such a do-it-yourself expedient helped the unschooled children and not the school children, who were much less given to such reasoning.

In fact, the most characteristic thing about the unschooled children is the extent to which action is crucial to their representation of the world and the degree to which symbolic representation is, for them, a sequential account of a train of actions. What is striking about the African child who is exposed to Western education is the degree to which he rapidly becomes perceptualized, almost overperceptualized. This is so much the case that the interposition of a screen between him and the 'misleading' beakers of liquid, rather than freeing him to carry on a symbolic equation of the liquid, only tempts him to look behind the screen to see how it looks.

Conservation, it would seem, depends for its development on the presence of a sense of identity, the idea of a potential return to an initial state, in this case, the state of equality. It is identity which must be used to integrate the other cues provided by the situation. The American child often does so through an 'appearance-reality' schema which allows him to deal *simultaneously* with the 'appearance' of level and the 'reality' of identical substance. When the definition of equal quantity shifts from the former to the latter, conservation is achieved.

The Senegalese child, however, cannot use the idea of identity to integrate conflicting cues through cross-classification of the situation according to both 'appearance' and 'reality'. To him this distinction does not exist, and one has more than a little difficulty even communicating the contrast in the Wolof language. When American children use identity as a justification for an equality judgment, they often say, 'It's the same water', or 'It *looks* like more but really is the same'. They make identity a *present* phenomenon. But the Wolof child says, 'This one and this one [the two standard beakers] are [or were] equal.' Note that one of these is now empty. Therefore he expresses identity through describing a past state rather than a present one; this is identity by recapitulation. The conflict for the Wolof child is between the initial and the later appearances of the water. It is resolved by the recognition of the identity of something observed a moment ago and something observed now. It is perhaps for this reason that the reference to two beakers is the most effective single type of perceptual reason with respect to conservation, for it is the standard beaker that provides a tie with the 'past' equality of the initial situation. Similarly, the 'action' experiment perhaps integrates conflicting cues by providing continuity of action between the past and the present.

It follows that a training technique for the 'perceptually seduced' school children of Senegal would also be one that stresses a continuity of past and present, promoting an easier integration of the two, and one that draws particular attention to the past and its crucial equality cues.

If these experiments indicate one thing of special importance, it is the way in which different modes of thought can lead to the same results. It has too often been assumed that different intellectual means must of necessity lead to different cognitive ends. This might occur in the case of problems which have no objectively definable 'right' answer. But where there are action

constraints and consequences for behavior (as with the phenomena of conservation), a disparity in results is not necessarily the
case. We have shown how an identity schema is as crucial to
conservation in Senegal as in the United States but that it can
develop by different means. Senegalese children do not utilize
the language of identity ('same') or the classification of the
present situation according to both appearance and reality to express identity. Both these modes of expression when employed by
American children make the equality of the past simultaneous
with the present inequality of appearance. The Wolof children, by
contrast, achieve conservation by establishing identity between
the *successive* states of past and present. Their link might be
either the continuity of action from one part of the experiment to
another, or the constant appearance of the standard beakers.

It is obvious that in order to survive all peoples must somehow
come to terms with a few basic laws of the physical world, despite
profound differences in 'world view'. Certainly, the conservation
of a continuous quantity across transformations of appearance
is one of these basic facts. Nevertheless, certain ways of thinking
may be more powerful than others as a means to the discovery of
new laws, laws which may be 'optional' to survival under certain
conditions. Thus Newtonian thinking is fine for some purposes,
but Einstein can do the same thing and more. Consequently, it is
well to bear in mind that intellectually too there is more than one
way to skin a cat – regardless of whether all ways are equally
effective for skinning twenty cats, or for that matter, dogs.

References

FLAVELL, J. H. (1963), *The Developmental Psychology of Jean Piaget*,
Van Nostrand.
GOODNOW, J. J. (1962), 'A test of mileau differences with some of Piaget's
tasks', *Psychological Monograph*, no. 555.
PIAGET, J. (1952), *The Child's Conception of Number*, Humanities Press.
PRICE-WILLIAMS, D. R. (1961), 'A study concerning concepts of conser-
vation of quantities among primitive children', *Acta Psychologica*,
vol. 18, pp. 297–305.
Studies in Cognitive Growth:
Chapter 8: On Relational Concepts, by J. S. Bruner and H. J. Jenney.
Chapter 9: On the Conservation of Liquids, by J. S. Bruner.
Chapter 13: On Culture and Equivalence, by P. M. Greenfield, L. C. Reich
and R. R. Olver.

14 J. J. Goodnow

Cultural Variations in Cognitive Skills

J. J. Goodnow, 'Cultural variations in cognitive skills', *Cognitive Studies*, (in press).

In recent years there has been a considerable increase in studies conducted with children who are not from the same cultural background as our usual middle-class *S*s. The backgrounds have varied, sometimes being pre-literate societies, sometimes cultures that are literate but still of a village type, and sometimes milieus that are urban and educated but not Anglo-Saxon in tradition or style.

My aim is not to provide an extensive review of these studies. Rather, I hope to use some illustrative studies as a way of asking some general questions, questions about the nature of cross-cultural variations and the implications for our ideas about how intelligence develops, and how differences in skills arise.

We may start with the question: Why be interested in children from other cultures? It is often said that different cultures provide some ready-made variations in environment that would be impossible to produce in the laboratory or in a planned experiment. This is true, but it is also true that we are not as yet skilled in specifying the critical points of difference between one environment and another – critical, that is, for the performance we have in mind. As a result, it is often difficult to interpret results in any fine way, to know what the environmental conditions are that give rise to the similarities and differences we find. How much of a problem this represents depends, of course, on the state of our knowledge. There are times when we have so little data that all is grist to the mill, and times when we need data of a particular type in order to advance. At our present state of knowledge, however, the problem is large enough to give a special point to questions about what one can learn from cross-cultural studies that cannot be learned in other ways.

In a broad sense, each cross-cultural study provides a piece for a developmental puzzle. The puzzle lies in accounting for the fact that we change as we grow older, that at 2, 5, 20 and 40 we are not identical when it comes to remembering, classifying, or problem solving. The fact that we change with age is easy to observe. What is difficult is answering those perennial questions: Just what is the difference? And how does it come about?

For this general puzzle, cross-cultural studies can supply pieces we did not have before, variations in method we did not think were possible or significant, upsets in relationships we had come to think of as constant. As in all puzzles, of course, the pieces are not all equally valuable at any one time, and on occasion we have to set a piece aside until we reach a point where it can be fitted in.

From the puzzle point of view, the biggest difficulty with cross-cultural studies has been the lack of overlap between pieces – each study a new culture, and, very often, a new task. Now we are a long way from being able to plan for critical points of overlap between cultures, i.e. we do not know as yet how to match culture X and culture Y on the features that affect performance Z, or on all the features save one. Overlaps between tasks, however, can be planned, and such overlaps are much to the fore in a number of recent cultural studies. To give some examples:

Segall, Campbell and Herskovits (1966) have gathered results from a wide variety of cultures, using the same visual perception tasks throughout. Their results have been so intriguing that other psychologists, such as Jahoda (1966) have been taking the same tasks to still more cultural groups, trying to pin down just what produces the variations in performance.

A group with a Harvard core has used the same classification task with children from several settings – Boston, Senegal, Alaska and urban and rural Mexico. This is the work of Olver and Hornsby, Greenfield, Reich, Maccoby and Modiano, all branching out from the Harvard Center of Cognitive Studies (Bruner, Olver and Greenfield, 1966).

Vernon (1965, 1966) has used the same extensive battery of tasks with several samples of 11-year-old boys – English, West Indian, Canadian Indian and Eskimo. In a rare step, he has also made ratings on a number of environmental variables and is attempting a set of direct relationships between the environmental differences and the patterns of test performance.

Lesser, Fifer, and Clark (1965) have given the same tasks to lower and middle class American children with varying ethnic backgrounds – Chinese, Negro, Jewish, and Puerto Rican. Class variations, it turned out, lowered the level of performance but not the pattern of abilities; ethnic differences varied the pattern.

The last example is a group of people who have come to overlap through no deliberate intent on their part, but through a shared interest in tasks developed by Piaget and his colleagues. It is this group I shall emphasize. It offers some nice overlaps in several respects: in the sample of tasks, the sample of Ss, the environmental variable, and happiest of all, in some of the results.

The group of studies has the following points in common:

1. Two or more tasks have been used. This similarity is critical, since what is often most informative for the developmental puzzle is not the absolute level of performance so much as the relationships among performances.

2. Some of the tasks have been the same. In particular, at least one of the tasks has been a Genevan conservation task, i.e. a task where a change is made in the perceptual appearance of an object and the child is asked whether there has been a change in some invariant quality like weight or length.

3. On the environmental side, the studies have all been strongly concerned with variations in the amount and quality of schooling.

To run through the list quickly, the set of studies includes three where the children have had no formal schooling or practically none – studies by Siegel and Mermelstein (1965) with Negro children in Prince Edward County, Virginia; by Magali Bovet[1] with Algerian children; and by myself in Hong Kong. In addition, there are two studies by psychologists primarily interested in the difference between types of schooling – by Peluffo (1962, 1964, and personal communication), working in Italy with children coming up to the urban North from southern villages; and by Vernon (1965) comparing English schoolboys with West Indian schoolboys.

1. All references to the work of Magali Bovet are based on personal communication.

What has come out of these overlapping pieces?

1. As we move away from a technological society there is not any over-all lag or retardation across tasks, but rather what Vernon has called a series of 'peaks and troughs'. Some tasks shift their difficulty level more than others.

2. Fortunately, there is some consistency to the tasks that stand up well throughout. If we list tasks in terms of the extent to which performance changes as we shift away from our traditional S, some of the conservation tasks appear at the top of the list as showing either no change or the least degree of change. Only some of the conservation tasks are sturdy in this sense, namely the tasks for amount, weight, volume, and surface, but not tasks for the conservation of length (Vernon, 1965) or time and speed (Bovet).

3. Again fortunately, there is the beginning of consistency in the tasks not handled so well outside the traditional group. This consistency is harder to define, but in a rough fashion they seem to be predominantly tasks where the child has to transform an event in his head, has to shift or shuffle things around by some kind of visualizing or imaging rather than by carrying out an overt series of changes. The spatial or perceptual aspect of these tasks comes as something of a surprise. It used to be thought that 'disadvantaged' groups would be most handicapped on verbal or abstractive tasks and that imaging or spatial-type tasks would be the fairest. This seems not to be so, and a division of tasks into 'verbal' and 'non-verbal' seems not to be the most fruitful that could be made.

The three results warrant some special attention. They provide a set of focal points for looking at cross-cultural variations, both in terms of the way they parallel the results of other studies and in terms of the problems and implications they bring with them.

The first result – no over-all lag but a differential shift – has its parallels in several studies. To span a time range, Nissen, Machover and Kinder pointed out in 1935 that children in French Guinea gave varying performances on a number of tasks. They were, for instance, much closer to Western norms in reproducing a sequence of moves made by a tester (touching a set of cubes), than in reproducing designs. Recently, this kind of effect has been taken further by results showing that differential patterns of skill

are more likely to occur among children of similar formal schooling with differences in ethnic background than with differences in
class (Lesser, Fifer and Clark, 1965), and more likely to occur
with major differences in schooling than with differences of class
or ethnic background (Goodnow, 1962), or differences in intelligence (Goodnow and Bethon, 1966).

Whenever such differential shifts are found, they challenge
assumptions we may hold about general factors underlying performance. It is easy to assume that tasks with the same difficulty
level, especially if they have some surface similarity, are based on
the same abilities and processes, or on a general and unitary
intelligence. This assumption requires a closer look when we find
the tasks we work from do not necessarily hang together. From
the particular set of studies cited, for example, one would become
cautious about assuming 'conservation' to be a skill more general
than it is content-specific. Equally, a closer look may need to be
made at some of our global descriptions of environments. In
recent years, for example, there has been a great deal of interest
in 'amounts of stimulation', in searching for an 'optimal amount'
that will neither 'under-stimulate' nor 'over-stimulate'. To this
pattern of search, differential shifts are a reminder that 'stimulation' is a variable constantly in need of definition and specifica-
tion, in terms of kind as well as amount. The critical factors may
equally well turn out to be some specific experiences,

The second and third results – areas of agreement on the skills
that unite and divide children from different backgrounds – are
the ones that help most towards specifying what kind of experience leads to what kind of skill. They are the points from
which we can start a sharper analysis of just what it is that a task
demands and a society provides. These analyses are, for me, the
heart of cross-cultural studies, and some examples of them form
the major body of this paper.

Pinning Down Differences in Skills

Matches between the features of a task and the features of an
environment may well start from an analysis of tasks, either by
asking what it is that some tasks have in common or what it is
that gives rise to uneven performances. Typically, the focus is

either on the content of the task or on the operation that is to be carried out. One may start, for example, from the fact that the scores of Negro children on a number of intelligence tests are by and large lower than those of middle-class white children, and set up the hypothesis that the difficulty stems from the content, from varying degrees of familiarity with the words used and the objects portrayed. Alternatively, one may look not so much to features of the material as to what the child has to do with the material, the operation he is asked to carry out. This is the direction taken in the suggestion that poorly schooled children have particular difficulty with tasks calling for some kind of imaged change in material. And finally, one may look for the solution in some interaction between content and operation – children from a particular background may well be able to carry out a particular operation with one kind of material but not with another.

From any direction, it is never easy to specify and prove just what it is about a task that makes it easier for children of some cultures than for others. But the effort is critical if we are to make any meaningful connexions between skills and experiences. For a particular example, I would like to turn to the data that suggests the importance of 'imaged transformations'. I have suggested that children with little schooling may be especially handicapped on tasks calling for imaged changes, for transformations that have to be carried out in the head. In stressing this kind of difference among groups, I am not alone. Vernon (1965, 1966) has suggested a similar kind of task area in his stress on an 'imaging' factor, affecting performance on a number of perceptual–spatial tasks. Vernon looks to an environmental variable other than schooling, namely the extent that the background is, for boys, purposeful, planful and male-oriented. For the moment, the important thing is the stress on a common area as highly vulnerable to group differences, whatever its source. Despite the common stress, however, neither 'imaging' nor 'imaged transformations' nor 'mental shuffling' are definitive descriptions of what underlies the vulnerable tasks, and I would be the first to admit that these identifications of the vulnerable area are tentative.

To give a closer look at an identification in terms of 'imaged changes', I shall take two sets of results. The first set comes from a combination of some Hong Kong data with some American data gathered by Gloria Bethon and myself. The second set is drawn from Vernon's work with West Indians. From these results and the nature of the tasks they are based on, others may draw hypotheses different from the one presented here. Whatever the hypotheses, the overlap in results is striking enough and rare enough to call for some detailed attention.

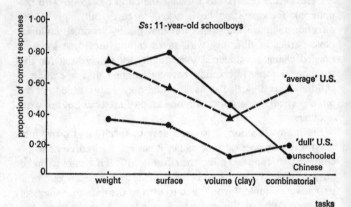

Figure 1 Patterns of task difficulty for Ss varying in nationality, schooling and intelligence (adopted from Goodnow and Bethon, 1966)

Figure 1 presents data adapted from Goodnow and Bethon (1966). There are three groups of boys, all 11 years old. One group is Chinese with little or no schooling. The other two are American schoolboys, with known levels on an intelligence test – the California Test of Mental Maturity. The median for the group labelled 'dull' is 81, with a top of 88; the median for the group labelled 'average' is 111, with a top of 120.

The interesting features to these results are:

1. First of all, the pattern or order of difficulty is the same for the dull and the average American groups. We can eliminate the possibility that any change in pattern with a non-schooled group is the result of a simple drop in general intelligence.

2. On the first three tasks, there is very little difference between the Chinese group and the average American group. These tasks are all conservation tasks. The first is the well-known task for

conservation of weight, with two pieces of clay. The second – conservation of surface – is perhaps less well-known. The child starts with two equal pieces of green paper, each one a grassy field with a cow on it. The child agrees that one cow has as much to eat as the other, and then the experimenter starts putting down twelve houses on each field, one on each field at a time. In the end the two fields look quite different with the houses on one arranged in two rows of six, and the houses on the other scattered widely. Again the child is asked if one cow has as much to eat as the other. The third task is conservation of volume, with displacement of water. Two balls of clay are shown to displace equal amounts of water. Then, with one ball changed to a pancake-shape, comes the question: What about now? Do both push the water up by the same amount, or does one push the water up more than the other?

3. The only task on which the Chinese boys fall below the 'average' Americans is the Genevan task of combinatorial reasoning. The child has to make pairs of colors, repeating no pairs and omitting none. He starts off with practice on three colors, then on four colors, and he is helped to get all pairs. Finally, he is asked to work with six colors. The point of this request is to encourage him to figure out something in advance. He is asked to try and figure out a trick or a system that will make the task easy, will help him to repeat none and omit none. The task is scored for the presence of a systematic approach to the problem, and this is what the unschooled group had trouble with. A number of them ended with fifteen pairs, and some of them became aware that they had to have the same number of each color, but they relied a great deal on moving the pieces around physically, shifting them from here to there in actual movements and then looking at the moved-around pairs.

My first hypothesis for these results (Goodnow, 1962) was that there might be something special to conservation tasks in general. But that hypothesis is set aside by Vernon's (1965) results with conservation of length, and by Magali Bovet's results with con-servation of time – both conservation tasks but both poorly handled in contrast with conservation of amount. For the com-binatorial task, I had the feeling that the trouble was in the request to work it out in advance, in the head, so to speak; but one task provided a poor bias to work from. The result in itself seemed a stable enough one, in that Peluffo (1964) also found the combinatorial task harder than conservation of volume for rural but not for urban school children in Sardinia.

A much wider base was offered by Vernon's (1965) results. I have taken out some of his West Indian results to illustrate again a pattern of strengths and weaknesses, and to show how they raise again a theme of mental rather than physical shuffling of material. Figure 2 shows the material selected.

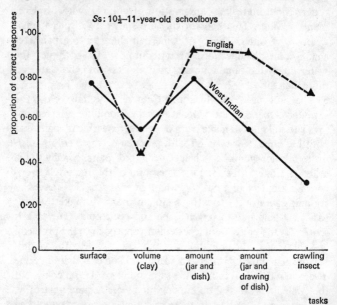

Figure 2 Patterns of task difficulty for English and West Indian schoolboys (adapted from Vernon, 1965)

In one of those happy overlaps, Vernon was also working with boys about 11 years old. In his case the Ss were schoolboys aged $10\frac{1}{2}$ to 11, one group Jamaican, the other English. And he had used some of the same tasks as were given in Hong Kong – conservation of surface, with the cows in the fields, and conservation of volume, with water displaced by two balls of clay. On neither of these tasks, as Figure 2 shows, was there a difference between the two groups. What is more, the absolute levels of performance on these two tasks by all four groups of boys (American, English, Chinese and Jamaican) do not vary widely. All the scores on the volume task, for example, are between 40 per cent correct and 60 per cent correct at this age level.

Both the third and fourth tasks selected from Vernon (1965) ask about conservation of amount with liquids. The third task starts with two transparent jars, half filled with water. The child adjusts them until they are equal. Then the experimenter presents a small dish and says, 'Now I'll pour mine into this dish. Have we the same, or have you more, or less than me?' On this task, the two groups were equal. On the fourth task, however, the Indian group falls well below the English group, even though the task seems to involve only a minor change. The tester now used one tall jar and the drawing of a dish, and asks: 'If I poured the water from this bottle into this dish, would there be more water in the dish than in the bottle, or less, or the same?'

The difference between the two forms of the amount task may be simply a difference in content. It has often been said that children from less technological societies have trouble with drawings and diagrams. The difficulty could also be a combination of content and operation. The child not only has to cope with a drawing rather than an object – a difference that should not confuse schoolboys too greatly – but he must also imagine the water transferred from bottle to dish without the benefit of first adjusting for himself the level in two jars or of seeing the experimenter actually pour all the water from the jar to the dish.

That the difficulty may lie in the operation as much as in the content is suggested by some other tasks used by Vernon. One of these is shown in Figure 2 – the task of the crawling insect. Vernon showed the child a circle $2\frac{1}{2}$ inches in diameter and said, 'Here's a drawing of a jar on its side. I'm going to draw a little insect on top.' The drawing shows a clear head and tail, with the head pointing left. 'Now,' says Vernon, 'the insect starts walking around the outside edge, like this. You draw for me what he would look like when he gets round to here.' 'Here' is a dot on the bottom rim of the circle. If we ask how many Ss draw the insect with his head pointed correctly, the answer is 71 per cent of the English group and 28 per cent of the West Indians.

Again the task seems to have two parts to it. The child must attend to direction or orientation as a critical part of a drawing and he must make a transformation in his head. Orientation in a drawing does appear to be a feature that is made salient by learning. McFie (1961), for example, points out that student nurses and boys entering high school in Uganda were very different from English *S*s in their attitude towards orientation in copying designs or on the Kohs Block Test, so that on the first encounter with the tasks inversions and rotations were common.

Paying inadequate attention to direction may be part of the Jamaicans' difficulty. There is as well, however, the need to image the reversal in position, and it seems to be this part of the task that links it with the poorer Jamaican performance on two further tasks. On one of these, the child is shown a string of cards, each containing a number, so that what he sees is 3 2 5, or 2 0 4 9 3. He is asked, 'What is the biggest number you could make with these?' He is not allowed to shift the cards around by hand. On this task, the English and the Jamaican schoolboys are again widely apart: 86 per cent and 58 per cent respectively with three numbers, 73 per cent and 32 per cent with five numbers. The two groups are equally apart on a last task, where they have to think through some left–right relationships. The tester places a pencil, a penny and an eraser in a line, and asks such questions as: 'Is the rubber to the left of the penny or to the right? Is the rubber to the left of the pencil or to the right?' With six questions like these 61 per cent of the English schoolboys make no errors, but this applies to only 30 per cent of the West Indians.

No one of these tasks is conclusive in itself, but taken together they suggest that one of the sharpest differences among cultural groups may lie in tasks where the child has to carry out some spatial shuffling or transforming, in his head, without the benefit of actually moving the stimulus material around. This suggestion, we may add, is in line with a recurring comment on a difference in task approach among groups with varying degrees of formal schooling in the Western sense. *S*s with less formal schooling often impress their highly educated observers as making greater use, even excessive use, of action and direct manipulation of material. This kind of comment has been made for non-Western groups by

Maistriaux (1955), McFie (1961), and Richelle (1966), and for Western adults by Hanfmann (1941).

I have looked at the role of 'transformations in the head' in some detail for several reasons. There is a need for working hypotheses in comparing cultural groups and differences in 'imaging' or 'imaged transformations' have now appeared often enough and with enough specificity to qualify as a promising working hypothesis (cf. Vernon, 1965, 1966; Goodnow and Bethon, 1966; Goodnow, 1968). And as we come closer to such specific skills, we may begin to ask more sharply whether there are experimental differences that might match the differences in skill. I do not wish to suggest, however, that the picture is in any way final. Very recently to hand, for example, is the first major statement of Vernon's results with Canadian Indians and Eskimos (Vernon, 1966). Both groups were surprisingly weak on conservation tasks, perhaps, as Vernon suggests (1966, p. 192), because of linguistic factors. (Vernon's Ss were all tested in English, a language more familiar to the Jamaican than to the Canadian Ss; Goodnow's Chinese Ss were tested, through an interpreter, in their own dialect.) Whatever the explanation for the poor conservation performance, a good performance, by the Eskimos especially, on most of the perceptual-spatial tasks remains surprising. On these, the Eskimos were close to the English norms. This kind of result means that good spatial or imaging performances occur without high-level schooling, a result that sharpens and spices considerably the question of what kinds of experience help in producing particular kinds of skill.

Matching Skills to Experience

Suppose for a moment that varying degrees of skill in mental shuffling or in imaging transformations do account for the recurring performance differences we have noted among several cultural groups. This would represent one of the two aims in cross-cultural research – pinning down the nature of a difference in skill. The other aim is to connect the difference in skill to a difference in experience. How could it come about that the children in our usual samples have developed some kinds of imaging skills more fully than the children in some other groups have?

And how is it that there is so much less variation in performance on tasks like the conservation of amount?

At this point, we must lean to some extent on conjecture, and on some general points in the literature on spatial skills. To start with, we may note that 'spatial' skills – often imaging skills – seem to be a highly variable area of performance in general. Piaget, for example, rarely comments on a great deal of variability in the age at which a child can master a task, but it is for a spatial task (predicting the flat shape of a folded or rolled piece of paper, for example) that he notes a considerable effect from specific experiences: 'The child who is familiar with folding and unfolding paper shapes through his work at school is two or three years in advance of children who lack this experience' (Piaget and Inhelder, 1967, p. 276). And Sherman (1967) has recently argued that many of the sex differences on cognitive tasks stem from the stress on spatial visualization in the tasks: visualization that girls, because of sex-typed activities, are poorly prepared for. It seems unlikely, then, that there will be any simple or single explanation of how differences arise in skills at mental shuffling or transforming. In a broad sense, the explanations that have been suggested can be placed into two groups, one emphasizing the role of general attitudes, the other stressing more specific experiences.

An example of a general factor is Vernon's argument for a relationship between performance on perceptual-spatial skills and the degree of purposefulness and planning shown in the home (Vernon, 1966). Vernon points out that the relationship is yet to be fully tested. It seems quite reasonable, however, to expect that a general readiness to stop and plan ahead would make a considerable difference to tasks where premature action can lead to difficulties that are hard to undo (as in many mazes), or where there is a premium on a systematic approach to a task (as in the Genevan task of combinatorial reasoning). In fact, Richelle (1966) considers the reluctance to 'inhibit action' as the chief cause of poor scores by a large group of Congolese children on many of Rey's performance tasks.

Even if a child has the readiness, however, to stop and think ahead, he needs the tools to do so. It is here that specific experiences would appear to be most critical. Such experiences have often been pointed to. Vernon (1966), for example, mentions the training that Indian and Eskimo children have in tracking and in locating objects spatially. Porteus (1931) felt that tracking helped some primitive peoples achieve a better performance on his mazes, and Havighurst, Gunther and Pratt (1946) considered that experience in drawing and painting played a similar role for the draw-a-man task. These identifications of critical experience are highly plausible, but two things are needed. One is some *a priori* identification; the other is some clear demonstration of a difference in skill between two groups selected to vary in terms of some specific experience.

Price-Williams' recent study of conservation of amount is a case in point. From the Mexican town of Tlaquepaque he selected boys with two kinds of family background. One group came from pottery-making families; the other from non-pottery-making families of a similar social class. Out of several conservation tasks, the former group is significantly better on only one: conservation of amount with clay. Price-Williams is currently conducting a replication of this kind of study. Whatever its outcome, his study is a nice example of the kind of research needed to make explicit and testable any matches between experiences and skills.

Even given demonstrated matches between experiences and skills, we shall still have to ask how the specific experiences can give rise to the skill we have in mind. How, for example, do certain past actions or experiences lead on to skill in thinking a problem through in one's head, without benefit of some reminding or testing action? One of the general effects of repeated and varied actions may be an atmosphere in which magical explanations do not easily survive. Beyond this, past actions may provide an 'action model', a pragmatic model that serves as a landmark, reference point, or mnemonic device for pinning down a relationship and holding it in mind. An example of this comes from a Chinese boy explaining conservation of weight. He pointed out that sometimes when he bought rice it came in a bag like Figure 3a, and sometimes it came in a bag like Figure 3b, but it was always the same weight: he knew because he had carried them.

Another function actions may have is to provide the opportunity

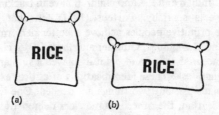

(a)   (b)

Figure 3

for translating a problem into terms other than actions. For a translation from actions to some map of relationships, we may simply need a fair amount of practice. This is, for example, the argument Mandler (1954) makes for maze-learning. Ss at first find their way through a maze mostly by feel and in terms of a sequence of actions. With more and more practice, however, they begin to have some kind of mental map of how the maze might be laid out. The same sort of learning seems to occur in mastering the layout of a new city. It takes a considerable amount of actually going to places and actually consulting a map before we have some independent picture of how things are arranged, clear enough to realize that such and such a street ought to be able to provide a detour if a familiar path is blocked. I am not suggesting that this translation into units that can be mentally shuffled around takes place automatically. Part of it must depend upon a certain amount of general practice in 'mapping things out', a certain amount of learning to drop unessential details out of the mapping.

That translation with 'maps' does not take place automatically is suggested by some actual maps – drawn maps – gathered by Dart and Pradhan (1967) from Nepalese children. Even for a familiar route, these children gave maps that marked places by pictures rather than points, where the path reflected more the sequence of actions than a set of relationships. They were, comment Dart and Pradhan, essentially 'like a string of beads, list(ing) in correct sequence the places we should pass through without giving any clues as to distance, trail intersections, changes of direction, and so on' (1967, p. 653). One can find such

260

directions outside of Nepal, but at least we are usually aware that there is another kind of map, and by and large the difference between cultures is not in complete presence and complete absence, but in frequencies of occurrence and in the content to which an idea or a principle is applied.

I have suggested so far that in order to move from a physical to a mental shuffling of objects and events, we may need practice with actually moving the objects around, or seeing them move, and we may need general practice in mental shuffling and mapping. To close the argument, we may turn back briefly to the shared and unshared skills described earlier.

For the argument to be reasonable, we would have to argue that most cultures provide the practice and the pragmatic models needed for judgments of properties like amount, weight, surface and displacement of water – or at least that practice for these judgments is more widespread among cultures than is practice for judging properties like length or time; that seems feasible. Amount and weight especially seem to be areas that meet Price-Williams' criteria (1961, 1962) for good task performance: a variety of actions for practice and a high value placed on the accuracy of judgement.

We would also have to argue that cultures differ more among themselves in the practice they provide in mental as against physical shuffling, that also seems feasible. There are almost certainly culture and class differences in attitudes towards impulsive or unnecessary action, in the number of times that a child is told: 'You didn't have to do it that way, or you didn't have to ask me that; you could have worked it out.' Formal schooling is very likely to be another source of differences in restraints on unnecessary or impulsive action, and of differences in amount of time spent constructing things, putting them together and taking them apart, or matching a drawn shape – often schematic – against the memory of an object. There is a world of difference, as McFie (1961) points out, between the American or British middle-class child who has played with 'shapies' and jig-saw puzzles, and the child who has few construction toys, or toys at all, and who sees few diagrams or schematic representations of things. The Nepalese children referred to, for example, 'use no other kind of map; they do not use drawings or spatial representations at all (except for records of land ownership, which do not change very frequently), and the lack of spatial models may be very natural' (Dart and Pradhan, 1967, p. 653). Vernon's Eskimo boys, however, are a reminder that 'familiarity with the spatial products of white civilization' (1966, p. 193) is not a necessary condition for developing spatial skills and that the road to a set of nicely specific ties between skills and experiences is likely to be a long one.

One last remark needs to be made about ties between skills and experiences. If the ties are likely to be so specific, how is it that so often one cultural group is poorer than another on a large number of tasks? And is the over-all goal to be simply a long list of specific ties? For such questions Ferguson (1954, 1956) offers a provocative argument. There is, he argues, considerable transfer among skills, and the lack of one which normally opens the road to developing several others can easily create a picture of generally lower performance. If we can ever identify such cornerstone skills, or firm hierarchies of skills, then the task of describing how differences in skill develop is likely to become much easier.

References

BRUNER, J. S., OLVER, R., and GREENFIELD, P. M. (1966), *Studies in Cognitive Growth*, Wiley.

DART, F. E., and PRADHAN, P. L. (1967), 'Cross-cultural teaching of science', *Science*, vol. 155, pp. 649–56.

FERGUSON, G. (1954), 'On learning and human ability', *Canadian Journal of Psychology*, vol. 8, pp. 95–112.

FERGUSON, G. (1956), 'On transfer and the abilities of man', *Canadian Journal of Psychology*, vol. 10, pp. 121–31.

GOODNOW, J. J. (1962), 'A test of milieu differences with some of Piaget's tasks', *Psychological Monographs*, vol. 76. no. 36, whole no. 555.

GOODNOW, J. J. (in press), 'Problems in research on culture and thought', N. J. Flavell and D. Elkind, eds., *Festschrift for Piaget*, Oxford University Press.

GOODNOW, J. J., and BETHON, G. (1966), 'Piaget's tasks: The effects of schooling and intelligence', *Child Development*, vol. 37, pp. 573–82.

HANFMANN, E. (1941), 'A study of personal patterns in an intellectual performance', *Character and Personality*, vol. 9, pp. 315–25.

HAVIGHURST, R. J., GUNTHER, M. K., and PRATT, I. E. (1946), 'Environment and the draw-a-man test: The performance of Indian children', *Journal of Abnormal and Social Psychology*. vol. 41, pp. 50–63.

JAHODA, G. (1966), 'Geometric illusions and environment: A study in Ghana', *British Journal of Psychology*, vol. 57, pp. 193–9.

LESSER, G. S., FIFER, G., and CLARK, D. H. (1965), 'Mental abilities of children from different social groups and cultural groups', *Monographs of the Society for Research in Child Development*, vol. 30, no. 102.

MCFIE, J. (1961), 'The effect of education on African performance on a group of intellectual tests', *British Journal of Educational Psychology*, vol. 31, pp. 232–40.

MAISTRIAUX, R. (1955), 'La sous-évolution des noirs d'Afrique. Sa Nature – ses causes – ses remedes', *Revue de Psychologie des Peuples*, vol. 10, pp. 167–89 and 397–456.

MANDLER, G. (1954), 'Response factors in human learning', *Psychological Review*, vol. 61, pp. 235–44.

NISSEN, H. W., MACHOVER, S., and KINDER, F. (1935), 'A study of performance tests given to a group of native African Negro children', *British Journal of Psychology*, vol. 25, pp. 308–55.

PELUFFO, N. (1962), 'Les notions de conservation et de causalité chez les enfants prévenant de differents milieux physiques et socio-culturels'. *Archives de Psychologie*, vol. 38, pp.75-90.

PELUFFO, N. (1964), 'La nozione de conservazione del volume e le operazione di combazione come indici di sviluffo del pensiero operatorio in soggette appartenente al ambiente fisici e socioculturali diversi', *Rivista di Psicologia Sociale*, vol. 11, pp. 99-132.

PIAGET, J., and INHELDER, (1967), *The Child's Conception of Space*, Norton.

PORTEUS, S. D. (1931), *The Psychology of Primitive People*, Longmans Green.

PRICE-WILLIAMS, D. R. (1961), 'A study concerning concepts of conservation of quantities among primitive children', *Acta Psychologica*, vol. 18, pp. 297-305.

PRICE-WILLIAMS, D. R. (1962), 'Abstract and concrete modes of classification in a primitive society', *British Journal of Educational Psychology*, vol. 32, pp. 50-61.

PRICE-WILLIAMS, D. R., and GORDON, W. (no date), Manipulation and conservation: A study of children from pottery-making families in Mexico, unpublished paper. [See Further Reading for full reference.]

RICHELLE, M. (1966), 'Etude génétique de l'intelligence manipulatorie chez des enfants africains à l'aide des dispositifs de Rey', *International Journal of Psychology*, vol. 1, pp. 273-87.

SEGALL, M. H., CAMPBELL, D. T., and HERSKOVITS, M. J. (1966), *The Influence of Culture on Visual Perception*, Bobbs-Merrill.

SIEGEL, I. E., and MERMELSTEIN, E. (1965), Effects of nonschooling on Piagetian tasks of conservation, *Paper presented at A.P.A. meeting, September*.

SHERMAN, J. A. (1967), 'Problem of sex differences in space perception and aspects of intellectual functioning', *Psychological Review*, vol. 4, pp. 290–99.

VERNON, P. E. (1965), 'Environmental handicaps and intellectual development', *British Journal of Educational Psychology*, vol. 35, pp. 1–12, 117–26.

VERNON, P. E. (1966), 'Educational and intellectual development', among Canadian Indians and Eskimos', *Educational Review* vol. 18, pp. 79–91, 186–95.

Part Seven Achievement Motivation

The concept of achievement motivation and its related techniques is probably the most culturally pursued idea that we have yet seen in cross-disciplinary research, other than the superordinate concept of personality itself. The disciplines of anthropology, sociology and psychology have all been concerned with it. Achievement motivation has become recognized as a socialization system, turning on parental or societal standards of excellence inculcated in early childhood. The American way of life has been recognized as encouraging striving attainment and competitiveness (McClelland *et al.*, 1953). One way of measuring achievement motivation – pioneered by McClelland – is to analyse stories made through application of the Thematic Apperception Test (T.A.T.) by way of coding for achievement imagery. A modification of this technique is to use folk-tales as the index for achievement, and this was done on a cross-cultural basis by McClelland and Friedman (1952). Further methods include the study of achievement imagery in dreams and content analysis of achievement themes in written essays, both of which have been used by Levine (Reading 16).

When this notion of achievement is taken outside the context of an obviously competitive culture such as the United States, a number of questions arise. First, is the method of analysing the T.A.T. for achievement imagery one that is culture free? This is really the main target of Angelini's paper using Brazilian subjects (Reading 15). Second, to what socialization factors, if any, is achievement motivation related? McClelland and Friedman (1952) had reported that it was produced by early severe independence training, though this was not supported by Child, Storm and Veroff (1958), who used a larger sample of societies than had McClelland and Friedman. However it is more probable that achievement motivation is due to a number of socialization practices, which would include independence training, but also include direct achievement training, the teaching of self-reliance and a certain amount of freedom from parental control (see Rosen, 1961; Winterbottom, 1958).

Another question relates to the connexion of need achievement with the place of entrepreneurial differences in society; Levine addresses his discussion to this theme, as well as to the concomitant problems of ideological and sociological factors associated with entrepreneurial enterprise in Reading 16.

References

CHILD, I. L., STORM, T., and VEROFF, J. (1958), 'Achievement themes in folktales related to socialization practices', in J. W. Atkinson, ed., *Motives in Fantasy, Action and Society*, Van Nostrand.

MCCLELLAND, D. C., ATKINSON, J. W., CLARK, R., and LOWELL, E. (1953), *The Achievement Motive*, Appleton-Century-Crofts.

MCCLELLAND, D. C., and FRIEDMAN, G. A. (1952), 'A cross-cultural study of the relationship between child-training practices and achievement motivation appearing in folk tales', in G. E. Swanson, T. M. Newcomb and E. H. Hartley, eds., *Readings in Social Psychology*, Henry Holt, revised edn.

ROSEN, B. C. (1961), 'Family structure and achievement motivation', *American Sociological Review*, vol. 26, pp. 574–85.

WINTERBOTTOM, M. (1958), 'The relation of need for achievement to learning experiences in independence and mastery', in J. W. Atkinson, ed. *Motives in Fantasy, Action and Society*, Van Nostrand.

15   A. L. Angelini

Measuring the Achievement Motive in Brazil

A. L. Angelini, 'Measuring the achievement motive in Brazil', *Journal of Social Psychology*, vol. 68 (1966), pp. 35–40.

Introduction

This paper summarizes research done in Brazil employing the projective technique for the measurement of human motivation developed in the United States by McClelland, Atkinson, Clark and Lowell (3). For this technique, the present author has used the name 'Projective Method of Motive Evaluation' (Método projetivo de avaliação da motivação) and refers to it as M.P.A.M.

The general purpose of the research was to evaluate the new technique by applying it to individuals who belong to a culture different from the one in which the method was developed. *E* wanted to ascertain whether or not a method that is projective and that involves the analysis of imaginative stories operates as satisfactorily in a Brazilian environment as it does in the one in which it was originally proposed.

The design involved checking to see whether manipulating the achievement motive experimentally, as in the United States, has the same effects on achievement imagery in fantasy in Brazil. A point of particular interest was to see if the arousal effects were the same in women as in men, since previous work in the United States had shown that they were not the same (1, 3, 4, 5, 6).

E selected the interruption-of-tasks technique as the means of arousing achievement motivation, the effects of which could then be measured projectively (through the M.P.A.M.) rather than through recall, as in Zeigarnik's and others' studies. It was assumed that success in completing tasks tends to reduce achievement motivation and that failure tends to intensify it. The effects on fantasy of such experimental manipulations could then be compared with the effects of a neutral condition in which the motive was not aroused at all. Furthermore, including a neutral condition permits comparison of need-achievement scores obtained by Brazilian students with those obtained by American students under similar test conditions.

Method

The subjects were three groups of each sex selected at random from among university students in two schools in the city of São Paulo. The groups of male Ss were composed of thirty individuals each; the female, of forty each.

Because E wanted to compare Brazilian with American need-achievement scores, he used for the male Ss four pictures for eliciting stories employed in the United States, originally identified as B, D, G, and H (3). The pictures for the female Ss were devised anew because E did not find adequate pictures among those used in the United States. In designing pictures, E tried to create situations characteristic of the sex and which presumably were 'suggestive' in arousing achievement motivation in women. The themes chosen were a woman sewing, a woman handing a paper to a seated girl, a girl in a chemistry laboratory, and a young girl seated in front of a book.

Short tasks and long tasks, accompanied by simple instructions such as 'put the words in order', 'cross out letters or numbers', 'add', 'substitute by code', etc. were chosen. The long tasks were identical with the short ones except that they included a greater number of items.

The procedure did not vary with the sex of the Ss; but the three male groups were designated A, B, and C and the three female groups A', B', and C'. For group A or A' the M.P.A.M. was administered under neutral conditions, i.e. each S was asked to cooperate in the study of a 'new test of creative imagination'. For the other two groups (B and C, or B' and C'), experimental conditions were introduced to intensify motivation. Groups B and B' were given the short tasks; C and C', the long ones. These tasks were presented to the student as *general-intelligence tests, already applied in the United States, composed of various subtests which, besides general intelligence, also measured the capacity of promptly understanding and executing, in writing and without mistakes, certain instructions. For this reason although the tests were relatively easy, the time taken for their solution was considered to be important.*

The time limit was just sufficient for the individuals whose tasks were short to complete them. As the two groups worked in the same room and did not know that they were being given tasks of different length, Ss whose tasks were short enjoyed a success situation for invariably they had more time than they needed to solve all the items in each subtest; while Ss whose tasks were long experienced frustration or failure since the time limit was never sufficient. The first condition (short tasks) is indicated as the *success condition;* the second (long tasks), as the *failure condition.* After administration of the tasks, which (according to the instructions given to the Ss) constituted the chief purpose of the research, the M.P.A.M. was given with the comment that it was a creative-imagination test under study, being administered to them only to take advantage of the fact that they were assembled. Each slide of the M.P.A.M. was presented 20 seconds and was followed by a four-minute interval during which each S was to write a story suggested by the slide.

Results

The stories were scored for need-achievement according to the third revised system proposed by McClelland *et al.* (3) and yielded the results shown in Table 1. Table 2 summarizes the analysis-of-variance results. Need achievement for the experimental groups (both men and women) is significantly greater than for the neutral groups, as the F ratios show.

Table 1
Mean Need-Achievement Scores

Test condition	Male subjects			Test condition	Female subjects		
	N	Mean	SD		N	Mean	SD
A. Neutral	30	6·43	3·24	A′. Neutral	40	7·55	3·56
B. Success	30	7·93	4·11	B′. Success	40	9·35	3·57
C. Failure	30	9·73	4·39	C′. Failure	40	11·05	4·01

Table 2
Analysis-of-Variance Results

Source of variance	Male subjects				Female Subjects			
	Mean square	df	Variance estimate	F	Mean square	df	Variance estimate	F
Experimental conditions	164	2	82·0	5·09*	245	2	122·5	8·63**
Individuals	1399	87	16·1		1661	117	14·2	
Total	1563	89			1906	119		

*$p < 0.01$.
**$p < 0.001$.

The significance of the differences among the three groups of each sex can also be tested by pairs. Because the groups had the same numbers of subjects (thirty in each male group and forty in each female group), a critical difference can be computed, as suggested by Lindquist (2), for a given degree of significance. At the 0·05 level, the critical difference is 2·06 for the male groups and 1·67 for the female groups. The differences between the means in the case of the male groups (1·50, 1·80, and 3·30) for the groups A and B, B and C and A and C, respectively, show that only the difference between the groups A and C is significant. In other words, the mean need-achievement score for male Ss in the failure condition is significantly higher than that for male Ss in the neutral condition. For Ss in the success condition, the difference is in the same direction, but is not significant. In the case of the female groups, each of the three differences between groups A' and C', A' and B', and B' and C' (3·50, 1·80 and 1·70) is significant. Both groups of 'aroused' Ss scored higher than Ss in the neutral condition, and Ss who 'failed' scored higher than those who 'succeeded'.

The scores obtained in group A (Brazilian male students – neutral condition) can be compared with the scores of a group of thirty-two American male college students, obtained under the same experimental condition by Atkinson (3). For the Brazilian group, the mean need-achievement score is 6·43 ($SD = 3·24$); for the American group, 6·63 ($SD = 4·26$). The difference between these means is not significant ($t = 0·206$).

Discussion

The results confirm the hypothesis that the projective method of measuring achievement motivation under study yields results similar to those obtained in the United States. More specifically, giving Brazilian students experiences of success and failure has similar effects on their achievement imagery, when it is defined in terms of competition with a standard of excellence. In spite of the cultural determination of such standards, the scoring definition is apparently sufficiently general to detect the same experimental effects on fantasy in Brazil. Of course the universal applicability of the scoring definition can only be admitted after satisfactory results have been obtained in a number of cultures. On the other hand, the results of the present study are sufficiently encouraging to support the belief that it will be possible to study the intensity of the achievement motive itself as it varies from culture to culture.

A new finding of this study is that achievement imagery can be increased by experimentally manipulated success and failure in women. Previous results obtained by Veroff (4), Wilcox (6), Field (1), and Veroff, Wilcox and Atkinson (5) with women did not confirm the arousal effects obtained with men. As the present author was especially interested to ascertain whether the M.P.A.M. technique was applicable to women, he profited from the earlier negative results in the United States and paid particular attention to factors that may not have been sufficiently considered by American experimenters. First, he tried to create greater ego involvement for the success and failure conditions by stressing the achievement instructions for the long and short tasks. Second, for the female groups he used pictures with only female figures in them. This fact is important because in the American research the so-called 'female plates' contained at times figures of each sex. While this difference may seem trivial, it might provoke notable alterations in the projections of women. Because of the higher prestige attached to male figures, female Ss (while not identifying themselves with the male figures) may start to tell stories about men that do not reflect their own motivation but simply cultural attitudes toward work and achievement in men. This is, of course, only a hypothesis which cannot be definitely confirmed with the data available; but it suggests an interesting line for future research with the M.P.A.M. On the other hand, it is possible that the differences observed between this study and the American studies are not due to differences in the way the pictures were made but to real differences between Brazilian and American female students. It is possible that, as Brazilian culture does not totally accept the attendance of women in university courses and as the reduced number of university courses limits opportunities and creates competition with the male sex for entrance into these schools, the woman who succeeds in entering a university in Brazil might represent a motivational type nearer to the male.

The results for the three experimental conditions demonstrated almost always a significant increase in mean need-achievement score for both sexes in the passage from the neutral to the success condition and from the success condition to the failure condition. These results give support to the validity of the method of measurement, but if one considers that the achievement motive can be *satisfied* by success and *aroused* by failure, the results from the groups that worked under the success condition might seem contradictory, for success in the previous tasks (by satisfying the achievement motive) should produce the lowest need-achievement mean and not the intermediate one. But one must remember that in the neutral condition *E* gave instructions that would not arouse motivation other than that existing, and that with the success and failure conditions the instructions insured an ego involvement in the situation (before the application of the M.P.A.M.) that was enough not to be totally reduced by the success arising from the completion of the short tasks.

As to the comparison between Brazilian and American students, the results showed a small and insignificant difference between the means of the two groups. The equivalence of the means, however, must be evaluated with caution. The scoring was done separately by judges belonging to the same culture as the *S*s; so it is possible that a real difference between the groups was cancelled by a systematic bias in the judges due to the fact that these belonged to different cultures. The comparability of the means, therefore, should be checked by larger researches specifically planned to compare the intensity of the achievement motive in the two countries. The present finding may be taken as a suggestion that there is no difference in the average achievement score of Brazilian and United States male university students.

References

1. FIELD, W. F., The effects on thematic apperception of certain experimentally aroused needs, *Unpublished Doctoral dissertation*, University of Maryland, 1951.
2. LINDQUIST, E. F., *Design and Analysis of Experiments in Psychology and Education*, Houghton Mifflin, 1953.
3. McCLELLAND, D. C., ATKINSON, J. W., CLARK, R. A., and LOWELL, E. L., *The Achievement Motive*, Appleton, 1953.
4. VEROFF, J. A., Projective measure of the achievement motivation of adolescent males and females, *Unpublished Honor's thesis*, *Wesleyan University*, 1950.
5. VEROFF, J., WILCOX, S., and ATKINSON, J. W., 'The achievement motive in high school and college age women', *Journal of Abnormal and Social Psychology*, vol. 48, pp. 108–19.
6. WILCOX, S., A projective measure of the achievement motivation of college women, *Unpublished Honor's thesis, University of Michigan*, 1951.

16 R. A. Levine

Dreams and Deeds: Achievement Motivation in Nigeria

R. A. Levine, *Dreams and Deeds: Achievement Motivation in Nigeria*, University of Chicago Press, 1966, chapter 8.

The most significant empirical findings reported in chapters 5, 6 and 7 [not included here] are summarized in the following paragraphs.

In a study of Nigerian male secondary school students:

1. The frequency of achievement imagery in dream reports was greatest for the Ibo, followed by the Southern Yoruba, Northern Yoruba, and Hausa, in that order, as predicted by the status mobility hypothesis. The Ibo–Hausa and Southern Yoruba–Hausa differences are statistically significant. The order of the groups does not correspond to their ranking on frequency of educated parents. Differences between groups comprised on the basis of mothers' education are extremely small in the sample as a whole and in the Ibo and Southern Yoruba subsamples. Moslem–Christian differences are highly significant but almost entirely confounded with ethnic group membership. Among the Northern Yoruba, the only group with enough adherents of both religions, there is no difference in frequency between Moslems and Christians.

2. The frequency of obedience and social compliance value themes in essays on success written by the students was greatest for the Hausa, followed by the Southern Yoruba and Ibo, in that order. The Ibo–Hausa and Yoruba–Hausa differences are statistically significant.

In a nation-wide public opinion survey of Nigerian adults:

1. The proportion of persons mentioning self-development or improvement as a leading personal aspiration was greatest for the Ibo, followed by the Southern Yoruba and Fulani–Hausa, in that order. Ibo–Fulani–Hausa and Southern Yoruba–Fulani–Hausa differences were highly significant statistically.

2. The proportion of persons mentioning improvement of standard of living or national prosperity through technological advance as a leading aspiration for Nigeria was greatest for the Ibo, followed by the Southern Yoruba and Fulani–Hausa, in that order. Ibo–Fulani–Hausa and Southern Yoruba–Fulani–Hausa differences were highly significant statistically.

The Ibo have moved into higher education and professional occupations, formerly dominated by the Yoruba, very rapidly and in large numbers since 1920.

In the rest of this chapter we shall discuss these findings in relation to the three questions fundamental to psychological anthropology raised at the beginning of chapter 2 [see original source]. We shall attempt to draw conclusions regarding the reality of the group differences revealed in this study, their sociocultural causes or determinants, and their consequences for the functioning of the Nigerian social and political systems.

The Validity of the Findings

Do the data presented above demonstrate a real psychological difference between the populations studied? We raise this question in its most extreme form because we believe it has been too often overlooked by culture–personality investigators, who have not paid enough attention to the validity of their measures of group differences. We have attempted to solve this problem by methods of cross-validation – that is, by developing independent lines of evidence that can be checked against one another in the way a historian checks several documentary sources or an ethnographer checks informant's accounts of the same events. Correspondence between facts independently arrived at makes it more likely that they represent an objective reality and less likely that they are derived from a bias of the instrument used to collect them. In this study, three methods of cross-validation were used: checking different measures of the same factor against one another, checking theoretically opposite factors against one another, and comparing contradictory predictions concerning group differences on one factor.

Identical group differences in achievement motivation were found in the analysis of the dream reports and in the public opinion data. These two measures were alike in giving the individual a relatively free opportunity to express his needs and wishes, but they were unlike in most other ways. The request for a dream report elicited an elaborate personal fantasy in narrative form without asking directly about personal desires; the survey questions asked directly about personal aspirations focused specifically on self and nation. The two different methods were employed by different administrators with different samples of the ethnic groups under different conditions. Thus their concordant results cannot be attributed to similarity in method of approach, investigators, samples, or conditions of administration. Their independence and diversity make the identical group differences less likely to be due to errors of measurement in either.

The differences between the Hausa and the two other groups are supported by statistical tests in both bodies of evidence. The Ibo–Yoruba differences are so consistent in these data and in the information on achieving behavior that we are inclined to accept them as real (although of lesser magnitude) despite their consistent lack of statistical significance. The likelihood of such differences being due to chance is lessened by their replication in diverse sets of data.

The validity of the findings in this study can also be assessed by examining the relation of achievement motivation to a behavioral disposition that is theoretically opposed to it, authoritarianism. In theory, n Achievement is closely linked to self-reliance and individualism as personal attributes; hence, individuals and groups high on n Achievement should be low on submission to, and dependence on, authority. The more a man is disposed to yield to the commands of others, the less he is likely to set his own goals and strive to achieve them. It is logical, then, to predict that n Achievement should be inversely related to a measure of authoritarianism. The failure of our measure of achievement values in the schoolboys' essays prevented our running this correlation across individuals, but we did find the order of groups on obedience and social compliance values to be the reverse of their order on n Achievement. Furthermore, the same group differences were statistically significant on both variables. This predicted reversal on an independently defined and scored factor confirms the concept of n Achievement as antagonistic to authoritarianism as a personality dimension; it also indicates that our methods of assessing achievement motivation were measuring what they purported to measure, a dimension inconsistent with strong obedience values. This is another independent line of evidence supporting the likelihood that our group differences in n Achievement were not due to chance.

Finally, we can examine the validity of the findings by comparing the results predicted by the status mobility hypothesis, which involves real differences between ethnic groups, with those predicted by rival hypothesis, stating that apparent ethnic differences are masking underlying differences in acculturation, religion, examination anxiety, or temporary conditions of administration. These findings are presented in detail for the dream report data in chapter 5 [see original source]; they show that none of these factors accounts as adequately for the variations in achievement imagery as the assumption of genuine ethnic differences. The acculturation factor (as measured by parents' education) is most effectively examined by multiple comparisons: across groups, across individuals for the sample as a whole, and within two subsamples. None of these comparisons yielded results predicted on that basis. The hypothesis that factors of examination anxiety or other temporary conditions of the schoolboys accounted for the group differences are made less likely by the convergent data of the public opinion survey, conducted with adult respondents in normal community settings. The religious factor cannot be ruled out, although subsample comparison among the Northern Yoruba did not support it. Thus the testing of hypotheses that cast doubt on the reality of ethnic group differences did not support the idea that nonethnic factors could better account for the revealed differences in achievement motivation.

On the basis of the convergent support for the ethnic group differences from several independent and diversely varying bodies of evidence, and with the additional knowledge that data casting serious doubt on the ethnic nature of these differences have been sought and not found, we conclude that a strong likelihood has been established for the reality of the differences between Hausa, Ibo and Yoruba reported above. This means that we find the evidence convincing enough to say that the differences found between the samples studied are probably characteristic of the populations and would manifest themselves in further studies using other samples and other instruments of measurement.

Explanations of the Group Differences

Assuming that the differences in n Achievement among Hausa, Ibo and Yoruba are real, what caused them? Since we predicted these differences from the status mobility hypothesis, we tend to see proof of them as confirmation of that hypothesis. But do the findings constitute an adequate demonstration of the validity of that hypothesis, or are they susceptible to explanation on other theoretical grounds?

We are convinced that the results of the predictive study support the status mobility hypothesis but leave some relevant questions unanswered. The full theory assumes that a system of status mobility affects parental values (concerning the ideal successful man), which in turn affect their child-rearing practices, which in turn produce a certain level of n Achievement and other personality characteristics relevant to successful mobility. The findings presented in this study do not include data on parental values as such or on child-rearing practices, thus leaving open the question of whether these factors are necessary to explain the ethnic group differences. A more conclusive study would show correlations of n Achievement with child rearing, and parental values, both within and between groups. Furthermore, although we had hundreds of individual instances of n Achievement, there were only three instances of status mobility systems, and the Hausa, Ibo and Yoruba differ in many other ways apart from status mobility: religion, population density, colonial history and so forth. We cannot at present be certain that it is not one or more of these latter group differences that might account for the variation in achievement motivation. With a set of fifty diverse ethnic groups varying in both status mobility patterns and n Achievement scores, we could make comparisons that did not confound status mobility with other cultural or structural properties of groups. In such a sample it would be possible to examine the relation of religion and population density to n Achievement independently of status system, and to discover which of these group characteristics was the best predictor of n Achievement and what proportion of the variance in n Achievement each accounted for. Until this larger scale comparison is undertaken, our conclusions concerning the relation of status mobility to achievement motivation will remain tentative.

In the absence of a more conclusive study confirming the status mobility hypothesis, we can nevertheless compare that hypothesis with alternative explanations of the present findings. If we find these alternatives less plausible, we might retain our original hypothesis as the best explanation in light of the available facts; if we find one or more of them equal or superior in plausibility, we might reject or modify the status mobility hypothesis. Our examination of alternative explanations has as its aim not only the decision of which to accept but also a deepening insight into the problem of accounting for achievement differences between ethnic groups. The only determinant of these differences mentioned so far has been the degree of conduciveness of the traditional status mobility system to the self-made man. We now review three other possible determinants of n Achievement in groups: population pressure; withdrawal of group status respect; contemporary status mobility patterns. The discussion of each determinant separately is followed by a consideration of complex interactions of factors and of possible research designs for answering the empirical questions which have been raised.

Population pressure

The basic point here is that the Ibo homeland in Eastern Nigeria is one of the most densely populated regions in Africa, and overpopulation has been held responsible for Ibo activity in non-agricultural occupations. We are fortunate in having the case for this determinant stated by Horton as part of a theoretical argument concerning psychological explanation in anthropology and as applied knowledgeably to the Ibo.

Perhaps the most prevalent form of naïveté is the psychologist's readiness to accept certain obvious purposes and attitudes as ultimate, and to search at once for their causes. The social anthropologist, in many, cases, would point out that these purposes and attitudes had 'reasons'. That is, he would show that they were not really ultimate, but on the contrary, were rationally justified by other purposes and attitudes lying beyond them.

The Ibo people of Eastern Nigeria have become renowned in recent years for the value they set on aggressive competition, the struggle for achievement, and the willingness to explore new avenues of power and status. A culture-and-personality theorist, whom I talked to about them, took this value as an obvious 'ultimate', to be interpreted as the effects of certain causes – possibly in the realm of child training. As a social anthropologist, I was suspicious of this. I pointed to the fact that over much of Iboland there is acute land shortage, that anxious parents quite 'reasonably' encourage their children to struggle for a school success that will fit them for some career other than farming, and that when the children grow up, their own 'reason' tells them that their only hope of a comfortable existence lies in continuing the struggle in outside trade, or in jobs in government or the big commercial firms. To back up this interpretation, I pointed to the fact that in pockets of adequate land supply like Nike and Abakiliki, where everyone can still get along comfortably in a farming career, this syndrome of aggressive competition and readiness to exploit new avenues of advancement is not at all obvious (Horton, 1963).

This position deserves serious consideration not only because the population pressure argument has a great deal of face validity for anyone acquainted with Nigeria but also because it presents a familiar and important challenge to psychological anthropology. Horton's hypothesis is that Ibo achievement behavior is a conscious, rational adaptation to an obviously difficult economic situation. The implication is that the Ibo response is that of any rational man in a coercive environment, and therefore needs no more complex psychological assumptions about the Ibo than that they can perceive their environment and are reasonable enough to want 'a comfortable existence'. We believe this rationalistic view does not help explain the most important aspects of the Ibo 'syndrome of aggressive competitions'.

The first important aspect of Ibo achievement behavior overlooked by Horton is that it was not the only 'reasonable' course of action open to them. When a rural family is faced with a decline in income such as that caused by overcrowding on the land, there is a choice between lowering standards of consumption and finding new sources of income. The former alternative, which involves becoming accustomed to increasing poverty, is in fact adopted by families in economically depressed areas all over the world. Such families operate on a principle of least effort in which the comfort of remaining in familiar surroundings and doing familiar things, even when faced with starvation, outweighs the future economic benefits that might be gained from drastically changing their way of life. So long as their impoverishment is gradual, they will put up with it, for it affords known and immediate gratifications that would be missing were they to seek new productive activities. Their behavior is by no means totally irrational; it is based on a short-run hedonistic calculus into which long-range considerations do not enter. To persons predisposed to adopt this course of action (or inaction), the Ibo willingness to uproot themselves and give up accustomed if reduced rewards, seems unreasonable and unnatural.

Another path available to the Ibo was that followed by the Hausa. The latter have not been reluctant to leave their land in search of nonagricultural income; Hausa traders are everywhere in West Africa. Their pattern of trade, however, is traditional, and no matter how long they stay in modern cities like Accra and Lagos, they remain conservative with regard to education, religion and politics, and aloof from modern bureaucratic and industrial occupations. This does not seem to be an unreasonable adaptation, but it is very unlike that of the Ibo migrants to the same cities. There were, then, at least three possible courses of action open to the Ibo in response to their acute land shortage: to accept impoverishment at home, to extend traditional trading patterns while remaining as unWesternized as possible, and to pursue Western-type economic activity with the changes in ways of life that were required for it. Other peoples have adopted the first two alternatives in response to economic adversity; although some Ibo undoubtedly did too, many chose the third course. The difference is not one of rationality but of energy and effort.

In simplest terms, the successful pursuit of a novel occupation involving a high degree of enterprise or education is not for a lazy man, no matter how hard pressed he is financially. To be as successful as so many Ibo have been they had to have adopted long-range goals of self-improvement, renounced immediate comfort and consumption in order to pursue these goals, applied themselves mentally and physically to this pursuit over a long period of time. Such efforts require extraordinary energy, of which many men are not possessed, no matter how poor they are initially; it is this energy factor that we call achievement drive or motivation.

Even if it be granted that population pressure caused the Ibo to seek employment in the cities, this would not explain why they strove to excel when they gained these opportunities. Every evidence we have indicates that Ibo, unlike many others, have not been content with 'a comfortable existence'; they have restlessly worked toward the top in their new fields of endeavor. This crucial difference between simply making a living and persistent striving for long-range success is another point overlooked by Horton and unaccounted for in his rational adaptation hypothesis.

In our opinion, then, this hypothesis is unconvincing because it fails to explain those aspects of Ibo economic behavior that indicate a consistent pattern of success strivings above and beyond the need for subsistence. We do not reject as implausible a relationship between population pressure and economic achievement, but only Horton's account of the mediating psychological factors involved. Achievement-oriented responses to overpopulation seem to be more common in Africa than in many other parts of the world, since a number of the apparently most enterprising African peoples, for example, the Kikuyu, are also among the most overcrowded in their rural homeland. This is a subject worthy of comparative research. If measures of n Achievement and achieving behavior could be obtained for a sample of African ethnic groups varying widely in population density or in capacity to subsist by agriculture, we could determine whether population pressure is related to achievement. Following Horton's suggestion of local differences in overcrowding and achieving behavior in Iboland, we could compare more and less crowded Ibo rural populations on n Achievement. Finally, we could carry such study one step further by comparing highly achieving Ibo individuals with their less enterprising fellows from the same areas on the amount of land to which they or their families had access. Until such investigations are carried out, we cannot be certain about the relationship of population pressure to economic achievement. Such a relationship would not be incompatible with our general formulation. It seems to us quite plausible that population pressure is translated into economic achievement in Africa through the child training practices of anxious parents which produce higher levels of n Achievement in

their children. Investigation of the amount of time elasped between the onset of severe land shortage and the rise in achieving
behaviour would be crucial to the testing of this hypothesis.

This brings us to Horton's argument about 'ultimates', by
which he presumably means enduring behavioral dispositions
which have a driving force of their own, as opposed to adjustable
perceptions of the changing environment. Although mentioning
Ibo encouragement of children's academic achievement, Horton
clearly does not believe that this encouragement produces in the
individual a disposition to achieve that is later applied to economic behavior; the economic achievement is seen as based
independently on a perception made in adulthood concerning
available occupational opportunities. This implies that the adult
achieving behavior is a specific economic response to an economic
challenge or incentive; there is no reason or pressure for Ibo to
manifest achievement strivings outside the economic sphere. There
is evidence, however, that Ibo manifest such strivings in a variety
of non-pecuniary activities. Mrs Ottenberg (1965, p. 6), discussing
the values of the rural villages of Afikpo, mentions achievement
in connection with athletic contests, a feature of traditional Ibo
village life that has remained important. The efforts and accom-
plishments of many individual Ibo in art, literature, science, and
nationalist politics have been conspicuous and cannot be reduced
to pecuniary motives. Their tendency to achieve seems as strong
in athletic, cultural, and political activities as in business, civil
service, and the professions. The generality of this disposition can
be seen also in the data of this study, in which samples of their
behavior ranging from dream reports to hopes for the future of
Nigeria showed the Ibo ahead of other groups on achievement.
This consistent performance suggests an internal drive that
seizes the opportunity for expression in any type of situation
rather than a specific adjustment to economic necessity. As
Horton's hypothesis fails to account for the suprarational energy
involved in Ibo achieving behavior, so it cannot explain the
generality of that behavior, particularly in nonpecuniary spheres
of activity.

To return to our original consideration, does population
pressure vary concomitantly with n Achievement in the three
ethnic groups of our study? There can be no question that popula-

tion pressure among the Ibo is more severe than in the other two groups. With rural densities ranging above one thousand per square mile (cf. Ottenberg, S., 1958), the Ibo home country is one of the most overcrowded in Africa. The Southern Yoruba have an average density of three hundred to four hundred per square mile (Galletti *et al.*, 1956), and their rural homeland has been one of the most prosperous agricultural areas in West Africa. Cocoa cultivation in particular has provided a high income yield from land, and there is arable land available that has not been farmed. The situation among the Hausa is not strictly comparable to that of the other two, since they inhabit a different vegetation zone with less rainfall; the densities vary greatly from one local area to another. It is clear, however, that the Hausa have not experienced the severe population pressure that the Ibo have. Thus the difference in *n* Achievement between the Ibo and Hausa might be accounted for in terms of population pressure, but the consistently significant differences between Yoruba and Hausa cannot be explained in this way. The Yoruba and Hausa are closer to one another in their ability to subsist adequately through agriculture, but the Yoruba are much closer to the Ibo in achievement motivation. The effect of rural population pressure on *n* Achievement cannot be ruled out, but does not account for the results obtained herein. It is to be hoped that the questions raised by the population hypothesis receive the systematic research attention they deserve.

Withdrawal of status respect

Hagen (1962) has raised the question of why a 'traditional society' or some group within it will suddenly abandon traditional ways and turn its 'energies to the tasks of technological advance'. His theoretical answer is that 'the basic cause of such change is the perception on the part of the members of some social group that their purposes and values in life are not respected by groups in the society whom they respect and whose esteem they value' (Hagen, 1962, p. 185). The group so affected by 'withdrawal of status respect' is first demoralized and then prompted to find alternative means of righting itself with the disparaging wider society. In so doing – a process which Hagen believes to involve changes in child rearing and personality development – the group assumes a role as technological and economic innovator, thus promoting economic growth in a hitherto stagnant society. Can this concept of withdrawal of status respect account for the differences in *n* Achievement among our three Nigerian groups? We must examine their history under colonial administration to find out. The Ibo could certainly be considered to have suffered a withdrawal of status respect during the early colonial period. Before British administration they constituted a relatively isolated cluster of societies, although they traded with coastal groups and some of their other neighbors. Once they came under British rule, however, various factors – their traditional entrepreneurial energies and/or population pressures – induced many of them to move to coastal towns like Lagos and Calabar and other centers of population. In those places they found peoples, like the Yoruba and Efik, who had had much more Western contact and education and were firmly entrenched in the best civil service jobs and professional positions. These sophisticated peoples despised the Ibo not only as bush people lacking in Westernization but as savages whose traditional culture lacked cloth and clothing, urbanism, and political centralization, and allegedly involved cannibalism. Being regarded as naked savages from the forest with an inferior culture must have hurt many Ibos profoundly. Coleman has mentioned both the resentment and the ethnocentric Western scale of values which gave rise to the disparagement:

Educated Ibo leaders have been particularly resentful over the cliché that Africans have no culture and no history. ... Many early European observers glorified the cultures, traditions, and histories of the Hausa states, and, to a lesser extent, of the Yoruba kingdoms, to which the Ibo, and other groups similarly placed, were invidiously contrasted (Coleman, 1958, p. 338).

Out of their resentment at being despised as a backward people, and also at being discriminated against in jobs and housing in towns dominated by other ethnic groups, may have come the tremendous Ibo determination to get ahead, to be more modern than anyone else, to favor technological advance, and to succeed in every field individually and as a group.

It can be argued with equal cogency that the events since 1900 have afforded the Hausa maximal protection from the withdrawal of status respect which often accompanies colonialism. In the system of indirect rule they were allowed to retain their own rulers and continue the traditional life fostered by those rulers. Lord Lugard's agreement insulated them from Christian missionaries and Western education (Coleman, 1958, pp. 133–40), so that they never suffered the jolts to cultural self-esteem which are inflicted on a non-Western people by mission Christianity, by knowledge of the outside world, and by a new scale of educational values. In other words, they could continue to see as undiminished in splendor their traditional culture with its monarchy, orthodox Islam, orientation toward Mecca, and Koranic schooling. They did not suffer the invidious comparison with European culture or Europeanized Africans which southern Nigerians did. Furthermore, they maintained their autonomy until they were able to enter into a federation with the southern regions with themselves as the dominant leaders, having a majority of the voting population under their control. Hence, when the Fulani–Hausa political leaders came to Lagos, they came as the rulers of the Federation of Nigeria, without having to bow their heads to the Nigerians who had acquired European sophistication. Although the history of the Ibo indicates they were maximally exposed to disparagement in terms of the European scale of values introduced by colonialism, Hausa history indicates that they were maximally insulated from it.

The Yoruba were intermediate on withdrawal of status respect; although they were not insulated from the inevitable disparagement involved in intensive missionization and Western schooling, they received these blows to their cultural self-esteem so early, relative to the other groups, that they were able to view themselves as superior to the less Westernized peoples. Furthermore, although their traditional culture did not receive the respect paid by the British to Hausa culture, its monarchical tradition and associated cultural complexity protected the Yoruba from a low evaluation of their own group as contrasted with Europeans.

If, then, we view the three ethnic groups in terms of the hypothesis derived from Hagen that withdrawal of status respect leads to something like *n* Achievement, we can indeed find support for such a hypothesis. The Ibo, leading in *n* Achievement, certainly suffered the most complete group loss of respect during the colonial period; the Hausa, lowest on *n* Achievement, were most insulated from the conditions producing social disparagement in a colonial society; and the Yoruba, in a sense, had it both ways. On the basis of our Nigerian comparison, we cannot reject the theory which views achievement striving as a reaction to group disparagement, and we must admit it as a plausible explanation of our findings. The only fact it cannot explain is the greater achievement orientation of the precolonial Ibo as compared with Hausa and Yoruba.

Contemporary status mobility patterns

A final alternative hypothesis arising in the course of analysing the data is that the ethnic group differences in *n* Achievement are due to variation in the *contemporary* situations in status mobility in the three groups. Since the contemporary status mobility system of the group is a complex precipitate of the traditional system, its modification under colonial administration, and the present state of economic opportunities, this hypothesis is an eclectic one in which there is room for several of the factors hitherto considered.

The basic idea in this hypothesis is that the frequency of *n* Achievement in a group is determined primarily by the more or less accurate perception of the growing male child as to the chances of his rising socially and the behavior which leads to success in the status system. His perception is determined by the information concerning the state of the system which he receives from various individuals and institutions, including older members of the family, school teachers, religious instructors, books and mass media. Let us assume that he forms a fairly stable image from these diverse sources of information by the time he is fourteen years old. If his image is that the chances of his rising socially are good and that individual competition with a standard of excellence is what leads to success, then he will manifest the achievement motive. If his image is that he has little chance of rising socially and that obedience and social compliance lead to what success is available, then he will not manifest the achievement motive. Intermediate examples will vary between these extremes, according to the amount of the perceived opportunities and the strength of the perception of achievement behavior as instrumental in success. Thus the frequency of n Achievement in a population will co-vary with the strength of the incentives for achievement behavior perceived by the men as being offered by the status mobility system during the years in which they were growing up. In this theory there is little time lapse between changes in status mobility system and changes in n Achievement, at least in the younger generation, and neither parental values nor child-training practices are involved as mediating variables – only the transmission of information to the child.

How does such a theory explain the findings of this study? Beginning with the Hausa, we can say, following Smith, that both the hereditary privilege of the Fulani and the institution of clientage have strongly survived into the present (at least as of 1950, when he did his study), and determine the magnitude and nature of opportunities in the contemporary Hausa status mobility system. This is, of course, because the colonial policies of indirect rule, prohibition on Christian missions, and slow development of Western education had enabled the traditional system to survive almost intact into the present. Thus a Hausa boy who was nineteen in 1962 would have grown up with an image of the possible in status mobility which was not drastically different from that of a boy growing up in 1865, the date for which Smith provides a picture of the traditional system. Our analysis of that latter system, then, holds good for the present, uncontaminated by notions of local democracy, the individual Christian conscience, and achievement of high status through successful education, and reinforced by Islamic injunctions of obedience as the highest virtue. The conclusion is that our sample of Hausa students, and the Fulani-Hausa adults surveyed in the national poll, had their level of achievement motivation formed by a status system which, now as in the past, does not offer strong incentives for independent achieving behavior.

Making the same assumption about the perceptual relationship between contemporary status mobility patterns and level of n Achievement, we have to consider rather different social factors in the Ibo case. Let us assume that the traditional Ibo system at very least predisposed Ibo children to be unusually sensitive to information about opportunities for alternative paths of rising

socially and, specifically, opportunities for rising through occupational performance. The overpopulation and consequent
decline in local agricultural opportunities forced adults to seek
increasing amounts of information about outside opportunities
in a variety of types of work, information which in the normal
course of events was passed on to children. The flow of this type
of information was vastly increased by the work of Christian
missions and Western schools, which furthermore operated –
along with the development of Western bureaucratic institutions
in government and commerce – to create new institutional settings
for the advancement of achievement-oriented persons through the
acquisition of education and modern technical skills. The current
generation of Ibo (including those whose behavior was sampled in
1962) reached maturity with a high level of n Achievement aroused
and reinforced by the strong incentives for achieving behavior
which they perceived by being exposed to an extraordinary
amount of information concerning opportunities outside their
local and traditional horizons. Thus the status mobility system
which incites their achievement motivation is that of all modern
Nigeria, not that of their local environment.

The Yoruba occupy the intermediate position, according to this
theory, because, although they were exposed even earlier than the
Ibo to a great deal of information about modern occupational opportunities and advancement through schooling (because of
Christian missions, widespread Western education, and the
introduction of Western bureaucratic institutions), the other
side of the picture was balanced by local agricultural prosperity
(primarily through cocoa farming) which reinforced not only the
traditional occupation of farming but also many segments of the
traditional sociopolitical status system. Since opportunities for
wealth and status enhancement existed in agriculture, and land
tenure was traditional, it was possible for ascriptive aspects of the
traditional status system to be bolstered directly or indirectly
through agriculture. A Yoruba youth would reach maturity with
the perception that opportunities existed locally and in old-
fashioned institutions as well as in the translocal world of modern
achievement. Although he would perceive many incentives in the
latter – hence his much greater level of n Achievement than that of
his Hausa contemporaries – he would be more likely than his Ibo

counterpart to be attracted to reliance on modified forms of local clientage, which have managed to survive in the contemporary Yoruba social structure.

This theory of contemporary status mobility and achievement motivation does plausibly account for the ethnic differences in *n* Achievement which form the core of findings in the study. Its central difference from the theory of traditional status mobility presented in chapters 2 and 3 [not included here] is that the latter involves parental values of individualism and specific training of the child in independence and achievement to develop the achievement motive, whereas the former assumes that a status mobility system can communicate its incentives to the child fairly directly and cognitively, without the familial manipulation of his motives. It is possible to devise research designs which would pit these theories against one another in contradictory predictions. The theory originally proposed predicts that, regardless of the contemporary system and its incentives, only those individuals who have been subjected to certain routines of independence and achievement training will manifest *n* Achievement; the other theory predicts that *n* Achievement will vary from one group to another concomitantly with the contemporary state of opportunities and incentives, independently of specific training routines in the individual life history. The next step is to conduct comparative studies of *n* Achievement with measures of child rearing and the perception of opportunities as part of the data collection procedures.

We believe that our discussion has illuminated the problem of finding determinants for the ethnic group differences in *n* Achievement, but it has not led us to reject as implausible all of the alternatives to our traditional status mobility hypothesis. More definite conclusions must await further research.

Social and Political Consequences of the Group Differences

Whatever their origins, the motives, attitudes, and behaviors reported on here seem to have some clear implications for the directions of social change in Nigeria. This investigation indicates that associated with well-known regional variations in levels of economic development and Westernization in Nigeria are individual behavioral dispositions of a deep-seated nature which are probably resistant to change. If this is true, they will continue to influence Nigerian social life, at least in the foreseeable future.

The behavioral dispositions studied are not randomly or uniformly distributed among the three major ethnic groups of Nigeria; they vary significantly, and form a distinctive cluster. The cluster consists of achievement motivation, concern with self-improvement, non-authoritarian ideology (here measured through obedience and social compliance values), a favorable attitude toward technological innovation, and rapid advancement in Western education and the Western type of occupational hierarchy. The Ibo and, to a lesser extent, the Yoruba are high on all of these dimensions; the Hausa are low. This should not be interpreted as a simple absence in the Hausa instance, but rather as an attachment to an authoritarian ideology probably strongly reinforced by continued training in Islamic orthodoxy, a personal fatalism (probably also reinforced by the Hausa version of Islamic doctrine), and a conservatism in educational and economic affairs.

One effect of this clustering of dispositions is that those individuals most prepared to occupy the positions of professional, technical, and bureaucratic leadership in the newly formed Nigerian nation are persons favoring the modern advance symbolized by technological innovation and antagonistic to traditional authoritarian government and doctrines of passive obedience. As the southern Nigerians (Ibo and Yoruba) race forward in preparing themselves for these positions, the inevitable conflicts between them and the Hausa leaders of the North (who dominated the federation politically until 1966) have assumed an ideological as well as a sectional flavor. It is not simply Hausa versus the ethnic groups of southern Nigeria, but conservatism versus modernism, authoritarian versus democratic ideology, and Islamic obedience versus Christian individualism. For example, post-independence measures to exclude job-hungry educated southern Nigerians from civil service and teachings posts in the North for which few Hausa are qualified, were based not only on a desire not to be dominated by other regions but also on a rejection of the values which the educated southerners represent and might propagate. The overproduction of achieving individuals in southern Nigeria and their underproduction in the North thus result not simply in a problem of ethnic allocation of jobs but in a confrontation of contradictory ideologies of modernization and authority. This confrontation played an important part in the Ibo officers' revolt of 1966, which was inspired by sentiments similar to those of Chike Obi described in chapter 7 [see original source].

The Yoruba, in their intermediate position on these dimensions of individual disposition, have been pulled in both directions. The Yoruba ethnic group contains within it individuals who are among the most Westernized and attitudinally modern in tropical Africa, but it also includes a large rural population which has had to change little in order to survive effectively in the contemporary period and which is still strongly oriented toward traditional patterns of leadership as represented by the *obas* (kings) and chiefs. For a while the Yoruba were able to operate as something of a political unit, but since early 1962 they have been torn by a severe political schism. What is notable from the viewpoint of this study is that the schism increasingly took on the flavor of a fundamental ideological conflict. Despite numerous countertrends, the main thrust of the split involved one faction appealing to traditional and less educated elements in the population, whereas the other gained support from modernizing intellectuals, professionals, and urban militants. Significantly, in 1964 the former became allied with the Hausa-dominated Northern Peoples' Congress, and the latter with the Ibo-dominated National Council of Nigerian Citizens. Thus the contemporary political behavior of the Yoruba, like their responses as measured in this study, shows them torn between the ideological poles represented by the more extreme Ibo and Hausa.

None of this will come as a surprise to the student of Nigerian politics. We present it in order to suggest that there is a consistent pattern of group differences revealed in unconscious imagery, explicit value-attitude formulations, educational achievement, and economic and political behavior. Although there are other ways of viewing it, we propose that the latter behaviors are the outcomes of culturally determined differences in the incidence of personality characteristics such as n Achievement and authoritarianism among the three ethnic groups. If this view is correct, then personality differences between ethnic groups are factors deserving more attention in the analysis of contemporary African social behavior than they have heretofore received.

References

COLEMAN, J. S. (1958), *Nigeria: Background to Nationalism*, University of California Press.

GALLETTI, B., *et al.* (1956), *Nigerian Cocoa Farmers*, Oxford University Press.

HAGEN, E. E. (1962), *On the Theory of Social Change*, Dorsey Press.

HORTON, W. R. G. (1963), 'The boundaries of explanation in social anthropology, *Man*, vol. 43. pp. 10–11.

OTTENBERG, S. (1958), 'Ibo receptivity to change', in W. R. Bascom and M. J. Herskovits (eds.), *Continuity and Change in African Cultures*, University of Chicago Press, pp. 130–43.

OTTENBERG, P. (1965), 'The Afikpo Ibo of Eastern Nigeria', in J. L. Gibbs (ed.), *Peoples of Africa*, Holt, Rinehart and Winston.

Part Eight Freudian Hypotheses

The impact of psychoanalysis and derivative schools soon made its impact on the social sciences generally. In the cross-cultural field, the first steps began with psychoanalytically minded anthropologists who were inclined to look at cultures with the conceptual tools of the clinician. Freud himself made some incursions into the field of what is now called cultural anthropology: *Totem and Taboo* (1912) being the main result. This movement was met in turn with another tendency, which demanded from the cultural data statements which tended to modify universal Freudian theories. Scholars began to point out that Freudian generalizations about humanity at large had their genesis in a select and perhaps narrow sample of Central Europeans. It was recognized that family structure, child upbringing and interpersonal behaviour dynamics differed widely across the world. What influence did this variance have on the classical psychoanalytic statements about human nature? All of the Readings in this final part originate from this kind of reasoning. They are concerned with Freudian hypotheses about symbolism, about dreams, slips of the tongue, relationships of the the child to his mother, weaning and defence mechanisms.

The first Reading (17) deals with Freudian symbolism. In the writings of psychoanalysis reference is often made to common objects, animals and certain types of people, that are said to pertain to anxieties and complexes of both neurotic and normal persons. Some of these objects have sexual connotations. They may crop up in dreams or in daily speech. Now Minturn takes as her starting-point the well-known fact that some languages have a sex-linked grammatical gender. She asks whether this is associated with that kind of object which Freudian symbolism would identify as male or female. In other words, a word that is recognized in psychoanalytic lore as a symbol referring to female sex characteristics, should have a feminine gender, and the same principle would apply to male symbols. The following paper by Lee

Freudian Hypotheses

(Reading 18) delves into the dreams of Zulus, and through them he
finds material with which to test Freudian interpretation of dream
symbols in a culture which, of course, Freud himself never touched.
Lee's analysis of Zulu dreams shows not only the influence of
wish-fulfilment, but also shows the influence of unresolved conflict on
symbol formation as it occurs in dreams. As Zulu culture is poles
apart from the kind of mileau in which Freud formed his theories,
such attesting material makes for interesting confirmation of this
segment of Freudian theory.

The next contribution (Reading 19) represents a neat example of
Freudian substitution of words, such as occurs in slips of the
tongue or pen. Freud's little book, *The Psychopathology of Everyday
Life* (1914), provides plenty of examples. Here, Devereux gives an
instance from Indochina (as it then was), which reveals the same
kind of mechanism among the Sedang people, as Freud originally
showed among Europeans.

The next two Readings (20 and 21) shift to another aspect of
Freudian theory. Possibly no other segment of Freudian theory
excited so much comment and concern, when it first was made
known, as the Oedipus complex theory. Freud had made clear that
the manifestation of sex did not suddenly emerge at puberty,
but had its characteristics at a much earlier age. Accordingly the
Oedipus complex theory maintains that boys are sexually attracted
to their mothers (the complement of this, namely that girls are
attracted to their fathers is known as the Electra complex). This is
recognized as a normal stage of the development of sex and affection
and occurs at about the age of four or five, thereafter
disappearing and developing into normal attachments in later life
to the opposite sex. A consequence of the Oedipal attraction is
difficulties in the relation of the boy to his father, emerging as
hostility and rivalry. If the stage is not assimilated properly, then
damaging properties to the later personality are encountered.
Quite apart from any clinical evidence that might support or
alternatively invalidate this theory, it is clear that certain
environmental conditions should be investigated. First of all there is
the type of family. The Western nuclear family is composed of a
mother, father and children, in which the father is generally the
biological parent of the offspring. The coincidence of 'genitor' and
'pater' which we have in our kind of society, does not, however,
occur in those societies in which descent is through the female
('matriliny'). Here the biological father (genitor) is one man and
the pater, who is the chief male authority figure, is the mother's
brother. Among the Trobriand Islanders there is an arrangement of

296

this kind, and the anthropologist Malinowski (1937) showed that there is an analogous Oedipus complex in a family type of this kind. It is not identical with the Western situation though. Rivalry exists between the male child and his uncle, the mother's brother; there is close affection between the child and his biological father; taboos are encouraged towards the feelings of the male child towards his sister.

By making a global investigation of Oedipal-type situations, attention can be given to factors which are either minimal or lacking or not clear-cut because they are not institutionalized, in our own society. One of these is sleeping arrangements of the infant or small child with the mother. Reading 20 from Whiting pursues the consequences of this in some detail. He shows that sleeping arrangements are linked with such institutional practices as the couvade and male initiation rites, but more relevant to the Oedipus complex theory, is that close sleeping arrangements between the child and his mother encourage dependency and strong identification in that child towards his mother.

In a similar cross-cultural survey Stephens (Reading 21) correlates prolonged postpartum sex taboos (the taboo on sexual intercourse for women after the birth of a child) with the sexual attraction between mother and male child, which in turn has certain consequences. These consequences, such as menstrual taboos and relationships with certain kin, are put forward as general global evidence for the Oedipus complex.

Cross-cultural work on children and adolescents covers a very wide spectrum of interests, and we can only provide one example in this volume of readings. Ever since the early days of the classic studies by Margaret Mead (1928, 1930) in Polynesia, the various forms of child rearing and its consequences in later life have been given much attention both by psychologically minded anthropologists and by culturally minded developmental psychologists. The larger part of the early literature focused on the relation between child rearing and personality dynamics. This has constituted the majority of the evidence underpinning personality and culture theories. In this the clinical hypotheses of psychoanalysis played a major role. Under this direction the early experiences of sucking and weaning, toilet training and the transition from dependency upon the mother to independency of the child, were all emphasized. As a result of the influence of learning theories, and analysis of habits generally, other socialization systems such as aggression and achievement were given due attention. We have already seen in the section on achievement motivation how socialization factors are introduced.

Psychoanalytic assertions have it that weaning experiences are a major frustration in the growth of the infant. Now it is the custom among Zulus to wean their children on a day set in advance, so we have in this instance no gradual diminution of this practice over time, and thus it might be thought from theoretical considerations that such an abrupt transition would have traumatic effects on the Zulu child. Albino and Thompson compared an experimental group of nine males and seven females in their pre- and post-weaning behaviour. Interviews with the mother and observation of the children were the main methods used. An evaluation of the results is presented here as Reading 22.

Psychoanalysis showed that individuals had characteristic ways of coping with the vicissitudes of life such as frustrations, lack of fulfilment, guilt feelings and aggressive impulses. Subsequent research on societies indicated that various institutions adopted characteristic customs which resembled such coping strategies on the part of the individual. For example the activity of witchcraft could be interpreted as deflecting aggression away from between the members of the society that practice it, to some mutually agreed scapegoat. From a sociological point of view this is one way of preventing internal disruption in a society. Displaced aggression is a common phenomenon in ordinary daily life and it is an important mechanism in the interaction of individuals with their society. In their book on *Child Training and Personality* (1953), Whiting and Child showed that there was a correlation between those societies which encouraged severe training in the control of aggression and which entertained the belief that spirits could cause illness. Displacement was indicated as the spirits were defined as animals rather than humans. In Reading 23 Wright shows that the hero in folk-tales directs his aggression towards strangers or enemies and not towards friends, in those societies in which control of aggression is maximized in childhood.

References

FREUD, S. (1912), *Totem and Taboo*, Kegan Paul. [Penguin edition, 1938.]

FREUD, S. (1914), *Psychopathology of Everyday Life*, Ernest Benn.

MALINOWSKI, B. (1937), *Sex and Repression in Savage Society*, Harcourt, Brace.

MEAD, M. (1928), *Coming of Age in Samoa*, William Morrow. [Reprinted in Penguin.]

MEAD, M. (1930), *Growing up in New Guinea*, William Morrow. [Reprinted in Penguin.]

WHITING, J. W. M. and CHILD, I. (1953), *Child Training and Personality*. Yale University Press.

17 L. Minturn

A Cross-Cultural Linguistic Analysis of Freudian Symbols

L. Minturn, 'A cross-cultural linguistic analysis of Freudian symbols', *Ethnology*, vol. 4 (1965), pp. 336–42.

The Freudian theory of dream symbolism assumes that a wide variety of objects, animals, persons, or situations may symbolize significant persons or events in the life of the dreamer. Objects or events which provoke anxiety or guilt are particularly likely to appear in the form of disguised symbolism, rather than realistic representation. Since sex drive and ideas associated with it are among the ideas and images likely to provoke anxiety or guilt, Freud and later psychoanalysts assumed that many dream symbols refer to sexual content. While Freudian theory assumes that many symbols may be idiosyncratic to particular individuals, and that dreams must therefore be interpreted in the context of the individual's use of symbols, it also assumes that a number of symbols are used by large numbers of people, either because their shape, function, or other characteristics are inherently similar to the objects they represent, or because the symbols are used in the mythology, folklore, or literature of a society and are therefore learned by most people in that society.

Some authors have taken issue with the Freudian interpretation of symbolism, but their discussions are usually limited to one language, or one kind of grammatical distinction. De Wit (1963) presented English-speaking male and female subjects with a series of symbolic words and recorded their responses. He concluded that his results do not support Freud's theory. Kahane and Kahane (1948) interpreted the augmentative feminine in Romance languages as a discriminative device essentially unrelated to the femininity of the words. Hasselrot (1957) concluded that this distinction between augmentative and diminutive nouns comes about because the augmentative feminine was developed from the plural feminine, which in turn developed from the neuter plural. Levy (1954) failed to find evidence of sexual symbolism in subjects' responses to line drawings. Lessler (1962) however, using some of Levy's material and a somewhat similar procedure, found that elongated objects are classified as masculine and rounded objects as feminine. Lessler's results show that the sexual associations are stronger for masculine than for feminine symbols.

The sexual referent of words is doubtless not the only factor determining their classification. Furthermore, one would not expect sexual symbolism to influence large numbers of words which do not have such symbolic associations. The relevant questions, then, include: Is the linguistic classification of words, which Freudians designate as male or female symbols, influenced by their symbolic referent, and does this influence appear in a variety of languages? The present study is specifically concerned with symbols that presumably have a sexual referent. Freud mentioned a number of such symbols; while some of these may symbolize either sex, others are presumed to be exclusively masculine or feminine in their symbolic referent.

The hypothesis to be tested is that, in languages with a sex-linked grammatical gender, nouns representing objects that are either male or female symbols, but not both, will tend to have the gender of the sex they symbolize. Since a number of other linguistic considerations determine gender, it is unlikely that this trend will be emphasized in most languages, but in so far as the symbols are used by large numbers of people speaking a variety of languages, the direction of the gender relationships should be consistent across languages. We therefore based the test of the hypothesis primarily on a sign test of the direction of gender classification of symbol words in several languages, rather than on the magnitude of the relationships for individual languages, although the latter will be considered.

Assuming the validity of the hypothesis – that words will be classified according to the gender of the sex they symbolize – there appear to be three logical alternatives for the extensiveness of such a relationship:

1. The relationship between gender classification and symbolic significance is a universal phenomenon and will appear in all languages tested.

2. The relationship is peculiar to Indo-European languages. A more restricted version of this hypothesis is that the relationship is peculiar to German, since Freud spoke this language, but this will not be seriously considered since the same phenomena have been found by other European and American clinicians in languages other than German, and since our list of symbols comes from the dreams of English-speaking Americans.

3. The relationship is peculiar to Judaic-Christian culture and will appear in languages spoken by Christians, Hebrews, and, perhaps, Moslems, since Islam also shares the Old Testament.

Method

Word sample

The list of symbol words was taken from a list of dream symbols, which were obtained by Calvin Hall from the dreams of college students. This source of symbols, rather than those in Freud's writings, was chosen for a number of reasons: they came from the dreams of a sample of normal subjects rather than neurotics; the subjects are contemporary rather than Victorian; the subjects are both male and female, while the majority of Freud's patients were female; the list was readily available. Probably the most important of these considerations is that the symbols were drawn from a non-neurotic population. Since language is the property of an entire population, it seemed unwise to test a linguistic hypothesis with symbols drawn exclusively from the dreams of therapy patients. There is, of course, considerable overlap between Hall's list of symbols and the dream symbols mentioned in other psychoanalytic writing.

Hall divided his list into male and female symbols on the basis of his analysis of his subjects' dreams. In order to obtain a list of symbols that could be classified by sex with some reliability, proper names, phrases, and general object classifications were deleted from the list. Hall's list, with his sex classification, was then presented to four clinical psychologists in the Psychology Department of the University of Illinois, with instructions to exclude any words that seemed ambiguous. A word was eliminated if two of the four judges agreed that it was ambiguous. The linguistic analysis is thus based on a list of nouns containing fifty-four male symbols and sixty female symbols that the judges agreed were classified unambiguously by Hall.

Language sample

Since sex-linked gender classes occur chiefly in Indo-European languages, there was some question of their independence of one another. To minimize the possibility of non-independence, only one language was selected from any one branch (see Table 1) of the Indo-European languages: French from Romance; German from Germanic; Russian from Slavic; Greek from Hellenic; Irish from Celtic; Maharata from Indic.

The analysis also includes four non-Indo-European languages: Arabic, a Semitic language; Tunica, an American Indian language of the Tunican family; Nama, a Khoisan language; Hausa, a Chad-Hamitic language. This does not exhaust the number of independent non-Indo-European languages with gender, of course, but data on others have been difficult to obtain.

Procedure

The list of English symbol words was translated by native speakers of the foreign languages who were fluent in English for all but the last three languages in Table 1. If two words were given in translation, one masculine and one feminine in gender, the case was not counted; if one word was either masculine or feminine and the other one neuter, the word with the sex-linked gender was counted. Stratified random samples of 500 nouns in each language[1] were drawn – by recording the gender of the first noun on every nth page of the dictionary, so that the entire alphabetic range was covered – to determine the expected frequency of the different genders.

Results

Table 1 presents the results of this analysis. The first three columns on the left indicate the number of words in the list of male and female symbols that were translated into each language. The Nama, Tunica and Hausa data are based on numbers considerably smaller than those of the other languages, since trans-

1. The Nama word count is based on 410 words.

Table 1
Analysis of Masculine versus Feminine Gender Classification of Male and Female Symbolic Nouns

Language	Number of words translated male	female	total	Female Symbols expected %	observed %	observed-minus-expected difference %	probability of difference	Male Symbols expected %	observed %	observed-minus-expected difference %	probability of difference	Male v. female χ^2 probability
French	54	57	111	52	56	+4	ns	48	54	+6	ns	0·30
German	52	56	108	43	56	+13	0·06	57	60	+3	ns	0·20
Russian	52	59	111	51·5	47	−4·5	ns	48·5	55	+6·5	ns	0·90
Greek	52	60	112	65	57	−8	ns	35	23	−13	ns	0·70*
Irish	49	67	116	37	24	−13	0·01	63	67	+4	ns	0·30*
Maharata	47	48	95	40	59	+19	0·03	60	59	0	—	0·20
Arabic	51	58	109	36	38	0	—	64	68	+4	ns	0·70
Tunica	23	23	46	53	64	+11	ns	47	81	+34	0·001	0·01
Nama	19	12	31	37	67	+30	0·09	63	63	0	—	0·10
Hausa	31	25	56	37	36	0	—	63	71	+8	ns	0·70

*Wrong direction.
Differences of less than 3 points are not counted.

lations for many of the symbol words were not available. In the other languages, we were able to translate almost all fifty-four male and sixty female symbols. The next eight columns contain the results of the comparison of the expected frequencies of gender, as determined by random word counts, and the obtained gender frequencies of the female and male symbols. These genders were omitted in computing the expected frequencies in languages with a neuter or common gender, so that the expected frequencies for male and female genders always total 100 per cent.

The probabilities of the differences between observed and expected frequencies were calculated using the sign test. Four tests have high probabilities in the predicted direction. For the female symbols, the observed-minus-expected differences for German and Maharata have probabilities of less than 6 per cent and that for Nama has a probability of 9 per cent. For the male symbols, the difference for Tunica has a probability of 0·1 per cent. Only three of the observed-minus-expected differences are in the wrong direction for female symbols (Russian, Greek, and Irish) and only one for the male symbols (Greek), and the magnitude of these differences is significant for Irish female symbols only.

Another way of testing this hypothesis utilizes chi-square analysis of the comparative frequency with which male and female symbols are classified as masculine or feminine in gender, ignoring the expected frequencies of random noun samples. The results of chi-square analysis are presented in the last column of Table 1. The results are in the predicted direction eight out of ten times. The probability of obtaining this result is 5 per cent. The chi-square for Tunica has a probability of 1 per cent, and chi-square value for Nama has a probability of 10 per cent.

We have said that the consistency of gender classification of symbol words probably will not be great for most individual languages, since variables other than the symbolic significance of words determine their gender. Important to this prediction is the consistency of the direction of the results. The differences between observed and expected frequencies are in the predicted direction five out of eight times for the female symbols. The sign test indicates a probability of 36 per cent that five-eighths of the predictions will be in the right direction. For male symbols, the observed-minus-expected differences are in the predicted direction seven out of eight times – a probability of 3 per cent. The hypothesis, therefore, is confirmed for masculine symbols only.

It appears, then, that there is a consistent tendency to classify masculine symbolic nouns according to the gender of the sexual referents, and a less consistent tendency – but in the predicted direction – for the classification of feminine symbolic nouns. These results are consistent with Lessler's finding that associations are stronger for masculine symbols. Since the strongest relationships occur in Tunica, Nama and Maharata (an Indo-European language spoken primarily by Hindus), this tendency is not limited to either Christian cultures or Indo-European languages.

Table 2 presents the results of the expected versus observed frequencies of the neuter gender for four Indo-European languages and for common gender for Tunica and Nama. In Greek, the only language in which the observed-minus-expected differences are not as predicted for both male and female symbols, symbolic nouns are classified as neuter much more frequently than

Table 2
Analysis of Neuter Gender Classification in Male and Female Symbolic Nouns.

| Language | Female Symbols | | | |
	neuter expected %	neuter observed %	observed -minus- expected %	probability of difference
German	18	23	+5	ns
Russian	30	17	−13	0·04
Greek	22	53	+31	0·00006
Maharata	28	40	+12	0·08
Tunica	41	4	−37	0·00009
Nama	5	8	+3	ns
German	18	13	−5	ns
Russian	30	10	−20	0·001
Greek	22	53	+31	0·00006
Maharata	28	32	+4	ns
Tunica	41	9	−32	0·0006
Nama	5	5	0	ns

would be expected by chance ($p < 0.00006$). The explanation seems to be that, since the neuter gender in Greek is grammatically the simplest, common nouns tend to be neuter in gender. Since many of the symbol nouns are fairly common names, they are more often neuter than is a random sample of nouns. In Maharata, the female symbol nouns that are not of feminine gender also tend to be neuter rather than masculine gender – a probability of 8 per cent. Russian symbol words, on the other hand, are less often neuter than would be expected by chance, i.e. symbol nouns that do not have the gender appropriate to their sexual referent tend to have the gender of the opposite sex.

The third gender classification for Tunica and Nama is not neuter. In Nama, a small percentage of nouns are classified as neither masculine nor feminine. In Tunica, 41 per cent of the nouns may be either masculine or feminine, depending upon whether the noun referent is singular or plural. It is of particular interest that the symbol nouns rarely fall into this category. The probabilities of both differences are very high, i.e. the symbolic nouns maintain an invariant gender class far more frequently than do Tunica nouns in general.

The hypothesis being tested is that nouns representing male or female sex symbols will be classified by the gender appropriate to their symbolic value. The data indicate that such a tendency does exist, particularly for masculine symbols, and, although it is not usually prominent in individual languages, it is consistent across a number of unrelated languages.

References

DE WIT, G. A. (1963), *Symbolism of Masculinity and Feminity*, New York.

HASSELROT, B. (1957), *Études sur la Formation diminutive dans les Langues Romanes*, Uppsala.

KAHANE H., and KAHANE, R. (1948), 'The augmentative feminine in the Romance languages', *Romance Philology*, vol. 2, pp 135–75.

LESSLER, K. (1962), 'Sexual symbols, structured and unstructured', *Journal of Consulting Psychology* vol. 26, pp. 44–9.

LESSLER K. (1963), The anatomical and cultural dimensions of sexual symbols, *Unpublished Ph.D. dissertation, Michigan State University.*

LEVY, L. H. (1954), 'Sexual symbolism: A validity study', *Journal of Consulting Psychology*, vol. 18, pp. 43–6.

18 S. G. Lee

Social Influences in Zulu Dreaming

S. G. Lee, 'Social influences in Zulu dreaming', *Journal of Social Psychology*, vol. 47 (1958), pp. 265–83.

Introduction

To the Zulu, as to depth psychologists, dreams are of great importance. They can greatly influence the life of the individual Zulu – mainly because it is held by the people that dreams are, to parody Freud, 'the royal road to the ancestors'. The ancestral spirits, venerated in the indigenous religion, are believed to use the dream as their chief means of communication with this world. In dreams they can convey both approval and disapproval of the actions, past, present, and future, of their descendants. In addition, dreams are held to be of both diagnostic and prognostic significance in the tribal medical system – particularly where psychogenic disorders are concerned.

The *Isangoma* diviner – diagnostician, soothsayer, and interpreter of the ancestors – most highly regarded medical consultant in Zulu society, is only admitted to his profession when he has developed a 'soft head' and become 'a house of dreams', 'the new home of the ancestors'. This process is seen to have begun with his symptoms of emaciation, fugue states, and disturbed dreams. *Ukuthwasa* (emergent possession by the ancestors) having been diagnosed, the afflicted person will receive, usually for some 18 months to two years, an intensive training in the traditions and craft of the cult from a senior diviner. His dreams will be analysed in terms of fairly stereotyped interpretations which have been handed down in this 'apostolic succession' for several hundred years. Finally, he will experience the 'Great Dream' in which he will go out to the river and then go under the water in a deep pool. There he will meet with a huge python who will give him his future power by allowing him to collect white earth from beneath it. He will then emerge from the water as a new person – the home of the ancestors – 'with his ways now clear' (1, 5, 16). The whole of the dream, within its life context, is obviously one of symbolic re-birth, using symbols found in many parts of the world (10, 14). In the light of the findings reported below it is of interest that the great majority of *Isangoma* diviners (circa 90 per cent) are women. Male diviners are frequently transvestite and are generally regarded as being 'feminine'. In Zululand the marriage of a male diviner is regarded with Rabelaisian incredulity.

Lastly, many dreams are held to be of prophetic import, and may indicate a course of action to be followed by the dreamer. The one complication here is that the real portent of the dream may be either similar or opposite to its manifest content. For example, the relative of a sick man may dream that he has died. The diviner may, under certain circumstances, predict his death – under others, his recovery (5). The situation, despite the difference of time relationships involved, has some of the elements implicit in the interpretation of dreams in the West, where 'dream reversal' is suspected (9).

This paper, however, does not deal with the more specialized dreams of Zulu life and the comments above are given merely to show that the Zulu have been, for centuries, concerned with the content of dreams. The findings reported below show how the dreams of ordinary men and women are themselves, in their turn, circumscribed and influenced by the social pressures and sanctions of the culture.

Procedure

The field work was done in the Nqutu district of Zululand, over some two years. I was forced to use fairly direct question and answer methods for the eliciting of information, as free association methods were impracticable. Rural Zulu see no sense in the latter and I found it impossible adequately to convey the idea to them. Despite these limitations of method some clear differences emerged when differing groups of dreamers were compared. It must be remembered throughout, however, that the findings are concerned with the manifest content of remembered dreams. As I asked questions about dreams, I soon found that I had been allotted a role as a kind of 'white *isangoma* diviner', in contrast to the surgeons and physicians of the hospital, who fell into the general class of 'white herbalists' in the methods that they used.

The main investigation was concerned with the incidence and aetiology of certain local psychogenic disorders common in the area and the relationships of these states with marital status, age, obstetrical history, dreaming, etc. In the course of this some 600 subjects, a fairly representative sample of the population, were asked: 'How much do you dream?' and: 'What do you dream about?' In this way the central manifest content of a large number of dreams was obtained, together with a rough estimate of the amount of remembered dream activity. This formed part of the extensive investigation. In the intensive research, carried out on some 120 women subjects, the same questions were asked about dreams, but later free interrogation by the interviewer was allowed, and the individual subject was asked to describe two recent dreams in detail. For a detailed discussion of the area, method, sampling procedures, etc. see Lee (18).

The results, in general, lent themselves readily to quantification and statistical handling, as stereotyped dreams (in terms of their central imagery or themes) were very common. All dreams collected could be readily classified under less than fifty main 'content' headings. It would, I think, be next to impossible to secure this degree of limitation and uniformity in dreams collected from any sections of a complex Western society. Of additional assistance was the apparent lack of latent content in many of the dreams:

The case of young children affords us a convenient test of the validity of our theory of dreams. In them the various psychical systems are not yet sharply divided and the repressions have not yet grown deep, so that we often come upon dreams which are nothing more than undisguised fulfilments of impulses left over from waking life. *Under the influence of imperative needs, adults may produce dreams of this infantile type* (Italics mine) (Freud, 11).

The purpose of this paper is certainly not to show that Zulu dreams are 'childish', but to illustrate the imperative nature of some motives which underlie the dreams of this people. It is always difficult, if not impossible, to prove the lack of latent content in a reported dream especially where method is as restricted as in the present investigation. Nevertheless the probability that such dreams may occur in adults, under certain circumstances, will be shown in the body of this paper.

Two last possibilities must be taken into account. That the dreams reported were merely not culturally conditioned answers to questioning – 'The proper thing for a person of my age and sex to say' – was, I think, shown by the great variety found in the detailed dreams of the intensive group. Despite close correspondences in main themes and images, genuinely individual detailed dreams were reported, though many common symbols were shared. Also, as dreams are important to the Zulu, it might be that stereotyped interpretations were common currency in the area, and the reports would follow the interpretations relevant to the life circumstances of the dreamer. In fact, less than 10 per cent of all women claimed to know the 'meanings' of any dreams, and these were mostly older women. The interpretation of dreams is very much the prerogative of the diviner. Laymen do not feel entitled to express any definite opinions in this field.

Results. Firstly, women showed a much greater amount of reported dream activity than did men. Of 389 women, 52 per cent said that they had 'many' dreams, and 48 per cent reported 'few' or 'no' dreams. Comparable figures for 136 men were 40 per cent and 60 per cent, the difference being significant at better than the 0·01 level of confidence. These figures confirm the general impression gained from many clinical interviews with subjects who were not included in the quantitative study. 'Many dreams', in the above context, meant 'much dreaming', as not much variation in central content was found. A woman would often report dreaming one stereotyped dream at least three times a week for some months. She would report this as 'many dreams'. It is of interest that despite women's aversion to nearly all dreaming (in the vernacular, they complained of being 'worried' or 'stabbed' by dreams), they were less likely to show serious and incapacitating symptoms as the result of dreaming any particular dream repeatedly. Men, on the other hand, regarded nightmares, particularly those of the classical 'suffocation' type, with a very deep horror and often had to be hospitalized as the result of ensuing anxiety symptoms. The dream affect was sufficiently strong to precipitate a full scale anxiety neurosis.

Between the sexes, there were great group differences in terms of the central imagery or themes of reported dreams. Table 1 illustrates these. This table, abstracted from the extensive investigation, included virtually all the dreams volunteered by rural Zulu. A very small number of other very rare themes were elicited by questioning in the intensive investigation. So that it will be seen that the number of different dreams, at any rate in terms of central imagery, is very restricted. It is also apparent that more women dream of intrinsically terrifying objects, such as 'monsters', than do men. That the latter, in general, tended to enjoy dreaming more than did women was confirmed in interviews with individual subjects. The only dreams liked by women are those of 'a baby', flying, money, and, in a very few cases, sexual intercourse or lovemaking.

Table 1

Central Theme or imagery of Dream	Explanatory Notes	Percentage of women (N = 114) Reporting the Dream	Percentage of men (N = 114) Reporting the Dream
Dead people	These are usually dreams of the ancestors	32	18
Water	Ponds, lakes and still water generally	32	5
Snakes		17	3
Flooded rivers		16	6
Crowds of people	Usually tribal gatherings	10	10
Spooks (*Izipokwe*)	Ghosts (not ancestral spirits), often believed to have been sent by a sorcerer	10	4
Meat		10	3
Tokoloshe	Short, hairy, priapic, very muscular men, believed to live in rivers and to attack women sexually	7	2
Food, eating and beer	The local beer is made from the staple food, maize	9	3

Central Theme or imagery of Dream	Explanatory Notes	Percentage of women (N = 114) Reporting the Dream	Percentage of men (N = 114) Reporting the Dream
'A baby'	Dreamer is usually suckling or caring for a small baby	7	Nil
Children	Apart from the specific mention of 'a baby'	7	1
Being chased	By crowds, cattle, 'someone', cars or 'a man'	6	1
Fighting	The dreamer fighting somebody else	5	9
Motor cars		5	4
Dogs		4	2
Izilwane	Literally 'small wild beasts', an avoidance term for 'monsters'	4	1
Trains		3	1
Thunder		3	1
Being attacked	Someone trying to kill the dreamer	3	4
Cattle		2	10
A wedding		2	5
Precipices		2	1
Europeans		2	1
Imikhovu	short, resurrected and 'doctored' men. The familiars of sorcerers	1	3
Flying	Dreamer flies through the air without mechanical aid	1	1
Baboons	Commonly regarded as the familiars of sorcerers.	1	1
Being stabbed	By a man, or people	1	Nil
Money		1	4
Being attacked	By women	1	Nil
Sexual intercourse or lovemaking		Nil	4
A bicycle		0·25	1
Cats		Nil	1

But the most important fact that emerges from Table 1 is that dream content, for the particular sex, is derived almost exclusively from areas of social experience permitted by the culture *in the indigenous system of sanctions*, of some 50 to 100 years ago. Thus women, acting under a traditionally very strong cultural imperative, dreamt of babies and children, while cattle, the acquisition of which is their chief economic goal and source of prestige, appeared in the dreams of men. Zulu women, in the nineteenth century, were allowed no part in the handling of cattle. This was a very strong taboo, relaxed for only one day in the year. Nowadays, however, most of the women must perforce work with the cattle, as the majority of the men are away from home for some 10 months of the year as a result of the migrant labour situation. The women show no conscious guilt over this handling of cattle, so far as could be ascertained in personal interviews.

Traditionally the one exemption from the cattle taboo occurred on the day of the *Nomkumbulwana* festival.[1] On this day the women and girls were allowed to dress in male clothing – the men being confined to their huts – and to drive the cattle, at the same time singing obscene songs and assaulting, by privilege, any men found straying from the huts.

Now the transvestite and possibly wish-fulfilling nature of the *Nomkumbulwana* celebrations led me to ask the women subjects of the intensive investigation: 'Have you ever wished that you were a man?', and to this from some 50 per cent of the women, I elicited strongly affirmative answers. This result has been duplicated in a recent predictive study the full results of which are still being assessed.

Briefly, the position is: modern Zulu women, handling cattle daily, and often very jealous of the life situation of men, are unable in their dreams to take over the symbols which, by traditional social sanction, are the prerogative of the male. This tends to confirm the Freudian hypothesis of the early introjection of the parents (8) – the parents also, presumably, having relatively 'time-lagged' super-ego values – and would mean that the super-ego content of the individual, at any rate in its more unconscious

1. *Nomkumbulwana* – 'The Princess of the Sky' was, in effect, a Zulu Ceres. A detailed account of the festival can be found in Asmus (1).

aspects, may have relatively little to do with contemporary values. In a previous study (17) it was found that educated Africans tended to assimilate the technology of the West before acquiring its moral codes, and this result can, I think, reasonably be attributed to processes in the individual similar to those discussed above.

In the present study it is clear that not even the conscious wish to be a man, on the part of a female dreamer, can break down the prohibitions of the past. A final point concerning the cattle dreams, again reflecting the social situation, is that the very occasional woman's 'cattle' dream found was usually of being pursued and gored by an ox or bull, whereas those of men were pleasant wish-fulfilment dreams of the ownership of large herds, the inspanning of superb teams of oxen, etc.

More males dream direct dreams of fighting – traditionally a male activity in this warrior society. The showing of aggression by women is strongly deprecated. All such aggression is found only in the covert patterns of the culture. In this connexion it is of interest that the answer to the question: 'When have you wished that you were a man?' was frequently 'When I am annoyed, I would be able to fight', and that the crying fits that were the main subject of the whole investigation were often precipitated, in individual girls or women, by feelings of rage which could not be expressed in violence. Here again we see the operation of a traditional taboo in the circumscription of manifest dream content.

One possible breaking down of this 'symbol' division between the sexes can be found in the dreams listed. Meat feasts and beer drinking are usually more the prerogative of males, though there are no very general taboos on these as feminine gratifications. It is possible that the greater incidence of these dreams among women reflects their desire for maleness, though this interpretation must, for the present, remain hypothetical.

In areas of experience permitted equally to both the sexes – exemplified by dreams of tribal gatherings, the appurtenances of sorcery, or ancestors – no great differences appeared. Men did not reflect their greater amount of contact, relatively, with Western civilization in their dream content and this may serve to emphasize that the great majority of remembered manifest themes are, culturally, out of date.

Certain dreams, notably those of Flooded Rivers, Water, Snakes, and *Tokoloshe*[2] are predominantly dreamt by women. Let us take the Flooded River and Water dreams first. The local interpretations, by diviners or knowledgeable laymen, is: 'to dream of flooded rivers means that you will give birth to a baby.' Allowing for a difference in time relationships and purpose of interpretation, this is an orthodox Freudian interpretation (9). The Zulu are cognisant of the part played by the amniotic fluid in parturition and, in the language, as a reinforcement of this interpretation of the symbol, there are many links between the ideas of water and of childbirth. For example, the word *isiZalo* means both the uterus and the mouth of a river.

Babies themselves sometimes appear in river dreams, though this is not common. For example, one 25-year-old woman who had a stillborn child said:

I dreamt that one day we went to the river to wash. When we had finished we collected our clothes. I had a young baby and it fell into the water. I put my arm in the water and rescued the baby, just at the point of death. After I gave it first aid treatment it became better. We went home. I woke up.

But the great majority of river dreams are of the river in spate. The dreamer is being swept away, or attempting to avoid the flood water when half way across, or is standing on the bank unable to cross.

2. The *tokoloshe* is a small, muscular, priapic and hairy being who is reputed to live in rivers, emerging to wreak mischief in general and, in particular, to attack women sexually. In dreams his role is aggressively sexual. Cf. Boerner (quoted by Jones, 13): 'Sometimes voluptuous feelings are coupled with those of *Angst;* especially with women, who often believe the night-fiend has copulated with them (as in the Witch trials).'

A useful account of the tokoloshe can be found in Kohler (16). This being may also be referred to (as a form of avoidance of the dreaded name) as '*ilwane*' or 'small wild animal' by women, and this usage may form an interesting symbolic link in the language with the nature of the beings concerned. Cf. Jones (13): 'Animals lend themselves to the indirect representation of crude and unbridled wishes. Analytical experience has shown that the occurrence of animals in a dream regularly indicates a sexual theme....'

Direct dreams of giving birth to, suckling, or caring for a baby are also interpreted locally as meaning that the dreamer is pregnant. These dreams are liked, in contrast to the anxiety dreams of flooded rivers. Dreams of still water are neither liked nor disliked to any great extent, and bear a similar local meaning of pregnancy.

So much for these dreams and their local interpretations. We must now examine the situation of the dreamers more closely. The obstetrical history of over 400 women was collected at the same time as the dream material. (The obstetrical memories of Zulu women are extremely detailed and accurate as the bearing of children is vitally important to them.) Table 2 gives the results for the dreamers of six common dreams.

It must be remembered that none of the dreams was, for the individual dreamer, necessarily exclusive of others – thus it would be perfectly possible for one and the same woman to report dreaming, on different occasions, of, say, water and ancestors or crowds and flooded rivers. We are here concerned with the group characteristics of collectivities selected on the basis of similarity of particular responses. The procedure is actuarial, and the dangers of applying actuarial procedures to the individual must be kept in mind. Though, to quote Meehl (20): 'As to Allport's emphasis upon the distinction between prediction from categories and predictions from the individual, it should be clear that in principle all laws even of the so-called dynamic type refer to classes of events.'

It will be seen, in Table 2, that dreamers of 'a baby' had very much the worst record of married infertility, both complete and partial (cols. 6, 10, 11). Even those who had borne children had subsequently lost more than half of them (col. 12). Also of significance is that this group were the youngest in terms of mean age, the distribution being normal (cols. 4, 5). Had they been older it might have been expected that more of their children would have predeceased them.

Now these obstetrical characteristics of the group are the very ones, in their society, which would cause, in the individual, the greatest psychological need for 'a baby.' In Zululand, the young bride must bear a child early in marriage or be despised of all

Table 2

Dream (Central Imagery)	No. of Women Reporting Dream	Married, Widowed, Single			Mean Age	S.D. of Ages	% Dreamers (Married or Widowed) Having Borne No Child	% Dreamers (Single) Having Borne No Child	% Dreamers (Married, Widowed & Single) Having Borne Children but with None Still Living	% Dreamers (Married, Widowed & Single) With Children Still Living	Total No. of Children Borne	Average No. of Children per Married or Widowed Dreamer	Ratio of Living Children to Total No. of Children Borne
		M	W	S									
'A baby'	27	24	—	3	25	6·4	33	8	7	52	59	2·4	0·49
Flooded rivers	64	49	10	5	31	10·5	11	8	8	74	222	3·8	0·61
Still water	129	88	14	27	30	13·8	20	18	9	53	295	2·9	0·61

(The above are all 'birth' dreams. Comparable 'control' figures for three other common dreams are given below.)

Dream (Central Imagery)	No. of Women Reporting Dream	Married, Widowed, Single			Mean Age	S.D. of Ages	% Dreamers (Married or Widowed) Having Borne No Child	% Dreamers (Single) Having Borne No Child	% Dreamers (Married, Widowed & Single) Having Borne Children but with None Still Living	% Dreamers (Married, Widowed & Single) With Children Still Living	Total No. of Children Borne	Average No. of Children per Married or Widowed Dreamer	Ratio of Living Children to Total No. of Children Borne
		M	W	S									
Dead people	128	92	23	13	35	15·0	16	8	7	70	466	4·0	0·62
Crowds	40	22	7	11	31	15·0	17	28	7	47	99	3·4	0·61
Spooks	38	25	4	9	32	14·2	13	21	16	50	124	4·2	0·56

Columns 6, 7, 8, and 9 total to all dreamers of any particular dream (i.e. 100% for each instance.)

other women. The migrant labour situation – 80 per cent of the young married men are away from home for an average of some 10 months in the year – together with high venereal disease rates (partly a function of the same migrant labour situation) makes conception early in marriage less likely, nowadays, than in the traditional subsistence economy. So, probably, dreams of 'a baby' are commoner than they were, as are the 'new' psychogenic disorders of women which have arisen in the last 60 years or so (18).

Be this as it may, it seems that these dreams of 'a baby' are certainly of a wish-fulfilling nature. They are dreamt chiefly by young married women on whom the social pressure to prove their fertility is very great. The dreams appear to lack latent or symbolic content and to fall under the classification of highly motivated dreams cited by Freud above. Now Eysenck (7) states: 'On the basis of detailed observation of the dreams of many patients, we arrive at the hypothesis that "dreams are wish-fulfilments." From this hypothesis we deduce (sic) that starving men should dream of food. If this can be shown to be so, our hypothesis is supported; if this can be shown not to be so, our hypothesis is decisively disproved.' Eysenck then goes on 'decisively to disprove' the Freudian hypothesis by citing evidence to show that subjects starved in the *laboratory* did not dream more of food than did controls, and continues: 'Thus experimental procedures show Freud's anecdotal evidence up as inconclusive and irrelevant; they also disprove his fundamental hypothesis regarding the nature and purpose of the dream.' In effect, however, Eysenck has *actually* tested the hypothesis 'All wishes will be reflected in dreaming.' Not part of the Freudian canon.

The present study has tested the hypothesis that women dreaming of babies should have more need of them than women not dreaming of babies, and the Freudian hypothesis of dreams as wish-fulfilments has been partially confirmed for one particular dream in Zulu society.

Further confirmation of this finding exists in other material collected. Subjects with a history of pseudocyesis, commonly found in the area, also tended to dream the direct 'baby' dreams. Also, in the intensive investigation, in an attempt to elicit dominant wishes, the open ended question was asked: 'What would you like most in the world?' Of twenty-one subjects who had volunteered the information that they dreamt constantly about 'a baby', nine gave 'a baby' as their wish and four said 'children'. Of ninety-seven subjects who volunteered other dreams or claimed not to dream at all, only eight gave 'a baby' as their wish, and ten said 'children'. The difference is significant at the one per cent level of confidence.

So much for the dreamers of 'a baby'. By comparison, the group dreaming of 'still water' contains many more single women who have borne no child, and married or widowed women who have borne relatively few (cols. 3, 7, 10). The age distribution is much more scattered than in the case of 'baby' dreamers (cols. 4, 5). There is no great amount of complete married infertility (col. 6). The probability is, in terms of obstetrical characteristics (compared, say, with the dreamers of 'dead people'), that a wish for offspring is still likely to be present in the group, though not in as strong a form as among 'baby' dreamers. But here it is necessary to try to explain the use of the water symbol in the place of the direct birth dreams.

Before we do this, however, let us first take into account the third type of 'birth' dream, that of the flooded river. This group contrasts, in terms of its concomitant characteristics, strongly with the other two above. Mostly married women [like 'baby' dreamers but unlike 'still water' dreamers (col. 3)] they show, comparatively, a very low rate of complete married infertility (col. 6), in contrast to all other groups, including those groups reporting the 'control' dreams. They are a normally distributed age group, significantly older than 'baby' dreamers. They have borne many more children than either of the other two 'birth dream' groups. The dreams are dreams of great anxiety, often involving fear of the loss of the dreamer's life in the flood water.

With these facts before us it seems possible to construct a model, using ethnographic evidence, which will satisfactorily account for the facts of symbol formation in the 'water' and 'flooded river' dreams, and for the specific nature of the symbols adopted.

The married Zulu woman who has borne no child has her

conflict – in this case, fear of childbirth and the economic difficulty of rearing children[3] versus the biological need for children allied with the very strong cultural imperative to prove herself fertile and so justify the bride-price paid for her – resolved by the strength of the latter motives. She dreams directly of 'a baby'.

The Zulu girl, unmarried, with a high premium set by the society upon the value of her technical virginity, fears marriage, but expects to bear children as a mark of her attainment of adult status. She dreads the discipline that will be imposed by her future husband's relatives, particularly his mother, when, as is customary she goes to live in the man's household. Of 114 women asked, in the intensive investigation: 'What time of your life was the happiest?' seventeen replied 'When I got my first baby', but ten said 'Before I married', and seventeen 'When I was a girl', or 'Schooldays'. Two local sayings are pertinent here: '*Akuqhalaqhala lahlul' isidwaba*' – literally 'No proud girl ever had the better of the skin skirt (of marriage)', and also 'to be treated like a bride', a phrase expressing the epitome of contemptuous maltreatment.

The married woman who has borne two or three children no longer has a very strong motive for bearing many more, although the cultural pressure to do so is still, in a very mild form, there. She is not, however, in the disgraceful position of the childless wife. She has proved her fertility and justified her existence.

With these two groups, unmarried girls and moderately fertile wives, we still have unresolved conflicts about childbirth, although they are not very intense. In the case of the former, fear of marriage and childbirth versus her own biological nature and the long term expectations of the society. In the case of the latter fear of further childbirth and increased economic strain versus a fairly mild social demand. From all the evidence available, these con-

---

3. In parenthesis, the situation as to these motives must be given very briefly here. Childbirth, in Zululand, is frequently very difficult and dangerous because of bad primitive and 'magical' midwifery practices and also of anatomical difficulties – the pelvic formation of the average woman making easy birth unlikely.

The cost of childbirth is often of grave importance. The people of the area are very poor – the district being about ten times overpopulated for its carrying capacity for healthy human beings. Infant mortality, largely as a result of malnutrition, is about 400 per 1000 live births.

flicts are very equally balanced, and the cultural imperatives are not strong enough to produce a direct wish-fulfilment dream. The dream is the dream of 'still water', and little anxiety attaches to it in the mind of the dreamer. This dream is, in some senses, intermediate between the two other 'birth' dreams. Symbolism is present, but the affect of the specific image adopted is relatively innocuous.

Finally, we get the nightmare dream of the flooded river – often with the life of the dreamer threatened within the compass of the dream. This is dreamt by married women with considerable experience of childbirth. Here the fear of further deliveries and childrearing is very intense and is still in conflict with social pressure to continue bearing children for as long as possible. This latter motive may be reinforced by competition with younger co-wives in the polygamous situation. Fear of childbirth and rearing is still socially unacceptable, and again we get the formation of a dream symbol, but with a heightened emotional affect – horror in the dream – and anxiety symptoms upon awakening. Even menopause does not necessarily bring release from this dream, as there is still conflict between the motives conditioned by years of social pressure and the new-found status of 'a man' granted by the society. The post-menopausal woman is allowed many hitherto masculine prerogatives, but must relinquish any desire for more children and may have to suffer the sexual competition of younger wives.

Generally, then, this evidence seems to confirm the hypothesis that symbol formation in dreams is dependent upon a state of unresolved conflict in the dreamer, and that anxiety shown by the choice of a frightening symbol will be a function of the anxiety aroused by one or more of the factors of the original conflict.

Cf. Jones (13): 'It is a general law that the more intense is the "repression", in other words the greater is the conflict between the repressed desire and the conscious mind, the more distorted will be the dream that represents the fulfilment of that desire.' In the light of the present findings, it is more difficult to agree with the same author when he writes: 'Broadly speaking, there is an *inverse* (italics mine) relationship between the amount of distortion present in the ideas (condensation, symbolism, etc.) and the amount of *Angst* present.' This rule might apply as

between the two symbolic birth dreams above (in that the idea of
'flooding' is closer to the reality), but it does not seem to hold if
we compare both of these with the direct dreams of 'a baby'.
In the latter case less *Angst* or continuous conflict is experienced
by the subject, both in real life and in the dream. Greater need –
yes. Greater *Angst* – no.

The snake and *tokoloshe* dreams are frankly sexual in character
– and are often of violent sexual attack by either of these. The
local interpretation of the snake dream is frequently: 'This
means that there is a man that you fear.' Again a remarkable
parallel with Freud, in his view of snakes as 'those most important symbols of the male organ'. With both these dreams,
those of 'Izilwane' – the 'small wild animals' discussed above,
must be linked.

Now pleasurable direct dreams of sexual intercourse and lovemaking are dreamt by men, and by a very few unmarried girls.
Sexual intercourse, among the Zulu, is largely directed to the
satisfaction of the male. Most men have few strong conflicts here,
and there is little cultural prohibition. The migrant labour
situation exacerbates the need as there are few women available
in the towns, and again we have a direct wish-fulfilment dream,
without symbolism or apparent latent content. The question that
remains to be answered is how these dreams can also occur in
young unmarried women.

Pre-marital sex play (the only prohibition being on the actual
physical penetration (3, 15)), is greatly enjoyed by the Zulu girl.
The sweetheart of her particular choice will take care to exercise
skill in his lovemaking, aware of the threat of possible rivals. The
relationship is both exciting and physically satisfying, unlike
sexual congress in marriage. As a result, at this stage, the prospect
of full sexual intercourse is inviting enough, and the way is open,
in the absence of anxiety and unresolved conflict, for the direct
wish-fulfilment in the dream.

Married women, however, tended to dream of snakes and
tokoloshe more frequently when their husbands – normally
away – were home on holiday. From all the clinical evidence
available, it would seem that the sexual difficulties and frustrations of married women are increased by the physical presence of
the husband. Here we have a symbol formation in the dreams, to-

gether with very great anxiety. These are regarded as being the most horrible and terrifying dreams of all. They are, in type, analogous to the dreams of 'flooded rivers'.

At the beginning of the research I had thought it probable that the migrant labour system would subject women to intolerable psychic as well as economic stress, but in the event this was not in fact confirmed. The situation even seems to give a certain amount of relief from the fear of sex in marriage. Women who might have been expected to show psychic traumata as a result of having to do men's work formerly taboo to them were, in fact, the less likely to be nightmare ridden. Women 'worried by dreams' belonged, by and large, to the more traditional elements of the population, closely tied to their feminine roles, and were not as common among those who had achieved a certain measure of 'masculine' function in such things as money matters, dominance in the homestead, etc.

Rough correlations also appeared between the ages of dreamers and the particular dreams dreamt. Ancestor dreams occurred in women of all ages from 14 to 70 years. Snakes, *tokoloshe*, and flooded river dreams were practically limited to women under the age of 50 – while dreams of 'a baby' and children were reported by women of ages when childbearing might be considered very probable, between 18 and 35. Dreams of 'a wedding' were found in an even younger group, mostly unmarried. 'Fighting', a comparatively common dream in men, was a dream of a few unmarried women under 22. Overt aggression, after marriage, is forbidden the Zulu woman by her culture. Briefly, then, the dreams of Zulu women may be said to be generally appropriate to their age, status, and role.

Further evidence, throwing some light on dream content, emerged from other aspects of the investigation. *Tokoloshe* and babies were frequently hallucinated by non-psychotic Zulu women. Some 30 per cent of all women studied showed a history of auditory or visual hallucinations. None of these were gravely deranged, though anxiety attacks and 'crying fits' sometimes followed the experiences. Some women indeed, seemed to have an affection for their particular *tokoloshe*, though they tended to report, when in hospital, that it was the patient in the next bed that had been brutally raped. An amusing example of 'displacement'! In a form of the Thematic Apperception Test that I used in the intensive investigation, three of the pictures were derived from Zulu dreams. These were: (a) a snake lying on a sand spit in the middle of a river, (b) a flooded river, with a vague figure upon the farther bank, (c) a *tokoloshe* approaching some huts. For all three stimuli a definite pattern of reaction emerged. The anxiety-ridden group – sufferers from the local 'crying fits' which I was investigating – and very closely corresponding to the individuals 'worried by dreams' tended to avoid, in their stories and descriptions, the real nature of the unpleasant stimuli. To them the flooded river was 'a forest'; the *tokoloshe*, a harmless old man or madman. The snake, though recognized for what it was, was dead, harmless, or asleep. The control group, on the other hand, which contained many 'non-dreamers', recognized the pictures for what they were, and commented freely upon their horrible nature. This latter group appeared to use fewer perceptual and/or apperceptual verbal defences than did the anxious group. Differences here were statistically significant.[4]

Finally, there is some evidence that Zulu dream content is changing, at any rate superficially, as a result of the culture contact situation. Better educated women sometimes made use of Western imagery. When I met members of the nominally Christian separatist and syncretist sects (cf. Sundkler, 21), I found that the ancestors – the 'dead people' of the traditional dreams – had suffered a sea change into '*Ingelosi*' (Angels). These angels, on further investigation, proved to be the selfsame ancestors, dressed in white robes and with wings attached.

It is sometimes found that whole sequences of a dream may follow a traditional theme, but be superficially clothed in modern dress. For example, the following one, dreamt by a Christian woman:

I dreamt I was ill. I was on my way to Church. I was told to make my offerings. I was to pay sixpence, and to pay a shilling for my dead relatives. I did this. After I had done this I recovered from my illness.

4. It would be of interest to present these pictures of unpleasant dream content tachistoscopically, to see whether the relationship between anxiety and failure to report recognition can be explored in this way. Lack of equipment in the field prevented this being done at the time (cf. 4, 12, 19).

Advice was given that I must never give less then sixpence in my offerings.

Here we have the traditional propitiation of the ancestors (they are believed to show their displeasure at the actions of their descendants by visiting them with illness) by the giving of a sacrificial gift. All this within the modern framework of the Christian religious usage.

One last example of the more 'modern' type of dream comes from a relatively highly educated woman who had lived with her husband in Johannesburg – a rarity in the Reserves. In this dream we see something of the stresses of town life and labour for the African, together with a great nostalgia for the country:

I was with my husband. We were walking together in a street in Johannesburg. We were lost and could not find our room. We had forgotten our room number. He also told me that he was sacked from work. We walked until we came to a place with fine vegetables, all green. I asked my husband to come to me so that he might sleep in the greenery. He went into some thick grass. I called him but he did not answer the call. I was worried and woke up.

I have not touched, in this paper, on the great mass of material found in Zulu dreams which illuminated the ethnography, value systems, and witchcraft systems of the area. Changes in witchcraft beliefs, folktales, etc., which are to be found almost yearly in the accounts of informants, are often absent in the dream. In the dream the *tokoloshe* is always a *tokoloshe* and behaves as a traditional *tokoloshe* ought to do. In descriptions, or in Thematic Apperception Test responses, he may often be confused with the *Umkhovu* – another short man, a doctored and resurrected corpse (6, 16) – whose traditional function is solely that of familiar to a witch. In the nineteenth century this would have been unheard of, a display of crass ignorance of the facts of life. Now it is common. It would appear that the unconscious minds of individuals are very stable repositories of the past, and can be used as a valuable source of ethnographic material.

The collection of dreams from large samples of populations, even by crude question and answer methods, may materially assist the psychologist or anthropologist to penetrate the screen of 'ideal culture' so easily supplied by obliging informants, and may throw considerable light on the actual operation of the values of any society.

In parenthesis, one dream that I stumbled upon is of rather exotic interest. In an earlier field trip I found that dreams of 'graves' were reported by a few women. I asked for a description of these 'graves', and was told that they were made of four flat stones, making a rectangular box, with another stone as a lid. At the time this description struck me as most peculiar, as it bore no relation at all to traditional Zulu burial methods. It was only later that I realized that I had been given a perfect description of a burial kist, common in Neolithic Europe. Dream graves, then, among the Zulu, do not differ from the ones used by the people since times immemorial. Whether we have here a genuine museum piece of an archetype or not is beyond all useful conjecture, though the occurrence seems very difficult to explain in terms of cultural diffusion.

Summary

For centuries, dreams have been important to the Zulu people. They have been regarded as a channel of communication with the ancestors, and as such have been interpreted by the local diviners. The field work for the present research was carried out in two stages: (a) the extensive investigation of some 600 subjects, (b) the intensive investigation of some 120 female subjects. The manifest content of remembered dreams was elicited from all subjects by question and answer methods. In the intensive investigation these were supplemented by a form of the Thematic Apperception Test.

Zulu dreams were found to be very limited in content, and stereotyped in terms of central imagery. This fact enabled quantitative comparisons between groups of dreamers to be made.

The dreams of men and women were compared, and it was found that the dream content of women was largely circumscribed by prohibitions from the indigenous system of social sanctions of the last century. Super-ego values would appear to be 'time-lagged'.

Local interpretations of symbols were found to coincide with orthodox psychoanalytic interpretations.

Groups of women, representing the dreamers of different

dreams, were compared against the background of their obstetrical histories. A lack of symbolism in highly motivated dreams was found – a phenomenon reported by Freud. In addition, the Freudian hypothesis of the dream as a wish-fulfilment was partially confirmed.

When groups dreaming various types of 'birth' dreams were compared, against an ethnographic background, a hypothetical model could be set up to account for the specific content of each type of dream. It would appear that symbol formation in dreams may be dependent upon a state of unresolved conflict in the dreamer, and that the *Angst* shown by the choice of a frightening symbol will be a function of the anxiety aroused by one or more of the factors of the original conflict.

Certain terrifying dreams of sexual meaning lent themselves to the same type of quantitative and explanatory procedure. Generally, the dreams of Zulu women would appear to be appropriate to their age, status, and role.

Supplementary evidence was gained from clinical interviews and the use of a Thematic Apperception Test. Hallucinations and test responses, particularly those of 'defence', fitted well the overall pattern of unconscious mental activity investigated.

Dream content is beginning to be affected, superficially at any rate, by the culture content situation, though, in the main, it seems to be more invariant than verbal accounts of folklore, witchcraft beliefs, etc. The unconscious minds of individuals would appear to be a very stable repository of the past, and a valuable source of ethnographic material.

References

1. ASMUS, G., *Die Zulu*, Essener Verlanganstalt. 1939.
2. BRYANT, A. T., *Olden Times in Zululand and Natal*, Longmans, Green, 1929.
3. BRYANT, L. A. T., *The Zulu People*, Shuter and Shooter, 1949.
4. BRUNER, J. S., 'Personality dynamics and the process of perceiving', in R. R. Blake and G. V. Ramsey, eds., *Perception, an Approach to Personality*, Ronald, 1953.
5. CALLAWAY, C., *The Religious System of the Amazulu*, Blair, 1868.
6. *The Collector*, Marianhill Mission Press, Pinetown, 1911.
7. EYSENCK, H. J., *Uses and Abuses of Psychology*, Penguin Books, 1954.
8. FENICHEL, O., *The Psychoanalytic Theory of Neurosis*, Norton, 1945.
9. FREUD, S., *The Interpretation of Dreams*, Allen and Unwin, 1954.

10. FREUD, S., *Introductory Lectures on Psychoanalysis*, Allen and Unwin, 1922.
11. FREUD, S., *An Autobiographical Study*, Hogarth Press, 1935.
12. HOWES, D., and SOLOMON, R., 'A note on McGinnies' "Emotionality and perceptual defence"', *Psychological Review*, vol. 57 (1951), pp. 229–34.
13. JONES, E., *On the Nightmare*, Hogarth Press, 1931.
14. JONES, E., 'The theory of symbolism' in *Papers on Psychoanalysis*, Baillière, Tindall and Cox, 1950.
15. KOHLER, M., *Marriage Customs in Southern Natal*, Ethnological Publications, 4. Department of Native Affairs, Pretoria, 1933.
16. KOHLER, M., *The Izangoma Diviners*, Ethnological Publications, 9. Department of Native Affairs, Pretoria, 1941.
17. LEE, S. G., A preliminary investigation of the personality of the educated African, by means of a projective technique, *M.A. Thesis, University of Natal*, 1949.
18. LEE, S. G., A study of crying hysteria and dreaming in Zulu women, *Ph.D. Thesis, University of London*, 1954.
19. MCGINNIES, E., 'Emotionality and perceptual defence', *Psychological Review*, vol. 56 (1949), pp. 244–51.
20. MEEHI, P. E., *Clinical vs. Statistical Prediction*, University of Minnesota Press, 1954.
21. SUNDKLER, B. G. M., *Bantu Prophets in South Africa*, Lutterworth Press, 1948.

19 G. A. Devereux

A Primitive Slip of the Tongue

G. A. Devereux, 'A primitive slip of the tongue', *Anthropological Quarterly*, vol. 30 (1957), pp. 27–9.

Data on the psychopathology of everyday life[1] have become increasingly rare in psychoanalytic publications, and are almost nonexistent in psychoanalytic studies of primitives. The following slip of the tongue is, so far as the writer knows, the only one reported from a primitive tribe.

The data about to be presented concern the village of Tea Ha, Sector of Dak To, Annam, Indochina, inhabited by members of the Central branch of the Sedang, a Mon-Khmer speaking agricultural and headhunting jungle tribe. The slip was made by Mdat, a youth in his late teens, son of the widowed sorceress A-Rua. Ndat was probably the most outstanding young man of his generation, whose vigorous character, eloquence and natural leadership assured him a position in the tribe which was out of proportion with his age. Ndat had been in love with, or had at least been very interested in marrying, A-Hloa, eldest daughter of the headman of another one of the three longhouses composing the village. A-Hloa was a singularly attractive but somewhat reticent girl, and somehow the marriage never came off. She eventually married, under circumstances which are not quite clear, the writer's headboy and interpreter, who may have taken advantage of his 'prestige' to persuade the girl to marry him. At any rate relations between the writer and his headboy on the one hand, and Ndat on the other, remained cordial. Ndat frequently visited the writer's house and was usually among the first to see new batches of photographs, whenever they were returned from the coast developed, printed and ready to be pasted in an album. It should be added that since the Sedang have no painting, and

1. Sigmund Freud, 'Psychopathology of everyday life', in *The Basic Writings of Sigmund Freud*, Modern Library, New York, 1938.

are therefore not trained to translate a 2-dimensional representation into a 3-dimensional image, few of them ever learned to recognize photographs. Ndat was one of those who did learn this trick and was therefore eager to inspect each new batch of pictures.

On one of these occasions the headboy was showing his friend and unlucky rival the latest batch of photographs, which included a picture of the girl in question. On being shown that picture, Ndat said: 'That is A-Hlèrl.' The writer corrected him, saying: 'No – it is A-Hloa,' but was promptly informed that A-Hlèrl had been A-Hloa's former name, which she had discarded several years earlier.

It is extremely noteworthy that on no other occasion had the writer heard Ndat or anyone else refer to this girl otherwise than as A-Hloa. In fact, the writer recalls no occasion on which anyone else ever miscalled a person who had changed his name by his or her former name.[2]

The slip is rather easy to interpret. It seeks to deny that there is a girl named A-Hloa who is married to a man who had enough authority to defy even energetic and ambitious young Ndat, and restores an earlier state of affairs, when there was a girl named A-Hlèrl whom Ndat had confidently expected to marry.

The timing of the slip may be interpreted at least tentatively. It occurred at a moment of *sudden recognition*, witness the fact that the utterance 'This is A-Hlèrl' was almost an exclamation. We already noted that the Sedang had to learn to recognize photographs, and that not all of them had acquired this skill. Hence, in a sense, the timing of this slip was determined by the startling suddenness of the recognition. This facilitated 'the return of the repressed', at a time when most ego functions were monopolized by Ndat's effort to 'recognize' the photograph, i.e. to translate a 2-dimensional object into a 3-dimensional image.

A further determinant of the timing of this slip can be mentioned only in the most tentative manner. The slip, denying

2. Slips of this nature occur, however, in other tribes, where people change their names rather frequently. Thus, when the writer's old Mohave informant changed his name from Civi: to Hivsu: Tupo: ma, a good many Indians and almost all whites continued to refer to him for years by his old name. The Havasupai, who are related to the Mohave, are reported to resent being called by their discarded names. See Leslie Spier, 'Havasupai days', in E. C. Parsons, ed., *American Indian Life*, Viking, New York, 1925.

present reality and restoring the *status quo ante*, occurred in the presence of the two persons who, one directly and the other indirectly, were responsible for the present situation: the head-boy who married the girl, and the writer whose prestige the headboy *may* have exploited to bring about this marriage. It may therefore represent also an almost wholly unconscious attempt to defy and challenge the 'guilty parties', indicating that some day the *status quo ante* would be restored ... presumably when the writer's field work came to an end.[3] It is hard to say whether or not this hope was a realistic one. Some Sedang, in discussing A-Hloa, thought she would never remarry after this present loveless marriage, especially since they felt that she was quite reticent and not especially interested in men. If this estimate of A-Hloa's character is correct, then Ndat's slip of the tongue was also an attempt at self reassurance – a kind of 'whistling in the dark.' The plausibility of the admittedly speculative inferences as to motivation contained in this last paragraph is increased by the fact that Ndat had repressed his understandable resentments quite effectively and was on unusually friendly terms with the writer and the headboy. Under such circumstances an indirect and unconscious outbreak of hostility, in the form of a slip of the tongue, or of some other parapraxis, was almost predictable.

3. There were indications that the marriage between A-Hloa and the headboy was, from the point of view of the latter, a temporary arrangement, for the duration of the field trip. The headboy, a Sedang borderer – or so-called 'Reungao' – often criticized the marital set-up among the true Sedang: 'In my village the men clothe their women; hence they are the bosses. But the Sedang women weave clothes for their men and therefore they are the bosses.'

20 J. W. M. Whiting

Socialization Process and Personality

Excerpt from J. W. M. Whiting, 'Socialization process and personality', in F. L. K. Hsu, ed., *Psychological Anthropology*, Dorsey Press, 1961, pp. 360–65.

[...]

Exclusive Sleeping Arrangements and Cross Sex Identity

The over-all indulgence of infants discussed above is concerned with how a child is treated during the day. The relation of a child to his parents at night has also been shown (Whiting *et al.*, 1958) to be an important child-rearing variable. In most societies over the world infants sleep in the same bed or on the same sleeping mat as their mothers. Even where an infant has a cradle or cot of his own, this is generally placed next to the mother's bed within easy reach. The sleeping distance between a mother with a nursing infant and her husband, however, is more varied. In slightly over half of the societies of the world the husband sleeps either in a bed in the same room but at some distance from his wife, or in another room. This may be called an 'exclusive mother–infant sleeping arrangement.'

Whiting and co-workers (1958) showed that exclusive mother–infant sleeping arrangements are strongly associated with male initiation rites at puberty. They offered three different interpretations of this association. They assumed that such sleeping arrangements (a) increased the Oedipal rivalry between son and father and that initiation rites served to prevent open and violent revolt against parental authority at a time when physical maturity would make such revolt dangerous and socially disruptive, (b) lead to excessively strong dependence upon the mother which initiation rites serve to break, and (c) produced strong identification with the mother which the rites serve to counteract.

Although the first interpretation was favored by these authors, later research (Whiting 1960a; Burton and Whiting 1960;

Stephens, 1962) has favored either the third or a modification of the second, the incest hypothesis to be discussed below. The first interpretation has been rejected for a number of reasons. The assumption made by Whiting and his associates (1958) that exclusive mother–infant sleeping arrangements exacerbate rivalry between father and son is not supported if one looks more closely at the facts. In the first place, since such sleeping arrangements usually occur in polygynous societies, the father has sexual access to his other wife and, hence, should not be particularly frustrated by the infant or see him as a rival. In the second place, at the time of weaning when the exclusive sleeping arrangements terminate, the father usually does not move in to sleep with the mother, since in more than half such societies a man never *sleeps* with his wife and in most of the remaining societies he sleeps with each wife in turn and, thus, sleeps with any one wife at most but half the time.

Campbell has in this volume suggested another version of the rivalry hypothesis, namely, that a younger sibling may be seen as the person responsible for the infant's fall from grace at the time of weaning. Although this hypothesis has considerable plausibility, the fact that in societies with exclusive mother–infant sleeping arrangements the mother is under a sex taboo during the nursing period should mean that the younger sibling would ordinarily not appear until at least nine months after the previous child's displacement. The mother, herself, therefore, seems to be the best candidate as the person who is perceived by the child as the one responsible for the termination of his exclusive relationship with her. It is she who at the same time both weans him and refuses to let him sleep with her.

In a recent theoretical paper Whiting (1960b) has formulated a series of hypotheses concerning identification as it relates to the control and mediation of resources. One hypothesis in this formulation has bearing upon the analysis in the preceding paragraph. This, the so-called 'status-envy hypothesis', is stated by Whiting (1960b, p. 18) as follows: 'If a child perceives that another has more efficient control over resources than he has; if, for example, he sees another person enjoying resources of high value to him when he is deprived of them, he will envy such a person and attempt to emulate him.'

If the status-envy hypothesis be applied to sleeping arrangements, the father should be seen to occupy an envied position if he sleeps with the mother, particularly if the infant is in a cradle. Contrariwise with the exclusive mother–infant arrangements, when the mother withdraws this exclusive privilege at the time of weaning, she should be seen as the most envied person. This should lead a boy to see his mother's status, and that of women in general, as being all important and powerful, and, hence, lead to cross sex identification.

A preliminary test of this hypothesis was presented by Whiting (1960a) and has been summarized by Burton and Whiting (1960). A more detailed report is in preparation and will be published under the joint authorship of Whiting, Fischer, D'Andrade and Munroe. In this study the following evidence is presented in support of the status-envy hypothesis.

First, members of the societies in which male initiation rites occur often define these rites as death and rebirth – the death of a person in a 'woman–child' status and rebirth into the status of an 'adult male'. This suggests that an initial cross sex identification in boys is recognized.

Second, exclusive mother–infant sleeping arrangements are associated with the couvade as well as male initiation rites. The couvade can be interpreted as a cultural device which permits the acting out of the female role. Since initiation rites and couvade rarely occur in the same society, some reason must account for the choice between counteracting and permitting the expression of cross sex identity. Residence patterns serve this purpose. Societies with exclusive mother–infant sleeping arrangements and patrilocal residence tend to have initiation rites, whereas those with exclusive sleeping and matrilocal residence generally have the couvade. It has not been settled as to whether residence operates as another factor relating to status envy and identification or whether it requires a differential role for adult males.

Third, totemism was also shown to be associated with exclusive mother–infant sleeping arrangements. This fact leads to the interpretation that totemism serves to establish a male's relationship to his male progenitors where his early life creates some doubt about it.

Finally, in a recent study Bacon, Child and Barry (MS.) showed that the rate of personal crime (assault, murder, rape, suicide, sorcery, and the making of false accusation) is highest in societies with exclusive mother–infant sleeping arrangements. They interpreted this as an attempt, in part at least, to express masculinity in societies where there is a need to deny an underlying feminine identity.

As has already been suggested, polygyny is the maintenance system variable most strongly associated with exclusive sleeping arrangements. In nearly 80 per cent of societies with strict monogamy the mother and father sleep in the same or adjacent beds, whereas this is only true of 3 per cent of those households where a husband has more than one wife. Whether polygyny has an influence upon the various projective consequences of exclusive mother–infant sleeping arrangements is now under investigation and cannot be reported upon here. Residence, however, as was reported above does, in interaction with sleeping arrangements, have a direct association with both male initiation rites and the couvade.

Infant Seduction and Mother–Son Incest

Whiting and his co-workers (1958) found that another child-rearing practice relating to infancy was strongly associated with male initiation rites at puberty. This practice consists of a prolonged post partum sex taboo lasting for at least a year. This practice is often associated with the belief that sexual intercourse will sour or alter the mother's milk in a manner that would be dangerous to a nursing infant. The taboo is generally coterminous with the nursing period which often lasts in these societies for nearly three years. Whiting's group (1958) interpreted this factor as having much the same effect as that of an exclusive mother–infant sleeping arrangement. Stephens (1962), however, assumed that a mother, deprived of her normal sex life during such a prolonged period, will gain some indirect sexual satisfaction from her infant, particularly during the act of nursing. If this interpretation is correct, a strong incestuous bond between mother and son should be established in societies with a prolonged post partum sex taboo.

Stephens (1962) argued that since the expression of mother–son incest is not permitted in adult life in any society, this early tendency must be strongly opposed and that strong sex conflict and anxiety should be induced. As a projective index of such conflict, ue chose the degree to which menstrual taboos were elaborated in a society. He established a scale which indicated the degree to which women were isolated from men while they were menstruating and argued that this measured castration anxiety in the males. He then showed that societies with a prolonged post partum sex taboo tended to have elaborate menstrual taboos as measured by this scale. The fact that the Whiting and Child (1953) measure of the severity of sex training in later childhood was also related to Stephen's menstruation scale lends support to the interpretation that it is an indicator of sex anxiety.

These results suggest that male initiation rites serve to oppose mother–son incest as well as to counteract cross sex identification. The fact that severe menstrual taboos were not found by Stephens to be independently related to male initiation rites is puzzling, however.

Stephens and D'Andrade (Stephens, 1962) report still another consequence of a prolonged *post partum* sex taboo. They showed that societies with this practice tend to have formal avoidance patterns between a woman and her daughter's husband, between a man and his son's wife, and between a brother and a sister. They argue that these avoidances result from sexual conflict produced by the seductive and incestuous relationship between mother and infant consequent upon the prolonged *post partum* sex taboo.

Polygyny is again the aspect of the maintenance system which is highly predictive of a prolonged *post partum* sex taboo. Stephens (1962), however, found that polygyny alone is not significantly related to the degree of elaboration of menstrual taboos. Thus, a pattern similar to that reported for the nature of the gods emerges, where a maintenance system variable is related to a projective system variable by common linkage with a personality variable implied by a child-rearing practice. [...]

References

BACON, M. K., CHILD, I. L., and BARRY, H. (no date), A cross-cultural study of crime in pre-literate societies (typescript).

BURTON, R. V., and WHITING, J. W. M. (1960), The absent father: effects on the developing child, *Paper presented at the A.P.A. Meeting*, September.

STEPHENS, W. N. (1962), *The Oedipus Complex: Cross-Cultural Evidence*, Free Press.

WHITING, J. W. M. (1960a), Social structure and identification, *Mona Bronfman Shenkman Lectures delivered at Tulane University*.

WHITING, J. W. M. (1960b), 'Resource mediation and learning by identification', in I. Iscoe and M. Stevenson, eds., *Personality Development in Children*, University of Texas Press.

WHITING, J. W. M., and CHILD, I. L. (1953), *Child Training and Personality*, Yale University Press.

WHITING, J. W. M., KLUCKHOHN, R., and ANTHONY, A. S. (1958), 'The function of male initiation ceremonies at puberty', in *Readings in Social Psychology*, Holt, pp. 359-70.

21 W. N. Stephens

The Oedipus Complex Hypothesis

Excerpt from W. N. Stephens, *The Oedipus Complex Hypothesis: Cross-Cultural Evidence*, Free Press of Glencoe, 1962, pp. 16–18 and 182–5.

[...]

The Oedipus Complex Hypothesis

I shall first define what I mean by 'Oedipus complex'. Through-out this work, the term has a very limited meaning – limited mainly by what can be tested and measured here, and what can't be. *By Oedipus complex, I mean the sex attraction of a boy for his mother.* I do *not* mean rivalry felt toward the father. I shall always refer to the Oedipus complex of boys; I shall have nothing to say about girls.

To get a better understanding of this definition, and on the hypothesis it leads to, we had best review what psychoanalysts have meant by the term 'Oedipus complex'. Here is a very brief and simplified account of the Oedipus complex and its effects, according to Freud and Fenichel:

1. Young boys customarily become sexually attracted to their mothers.

2. As a result, they feel hostile and rivalrous toward their fathers.

3. This has lasting effects on their personalities. Here are some of the results of the Oedipus complex:

(a) Unconscious fantasies, which continue to influence a man's motives and view of the world. Largely through the action of unconscious fantasies, the Oedipus complex also influences:

(b) Attitudes towards sex, particularly sexual fears, inhibitions and avoidances.

(c) Moral standards and guilt.

(d) Mental illness.

In these studies, I shall test only statements 1, (a) and (b).

Nothing will be said directly about mental illness, moral standards or guilt. Also, I do not have substantial evidence on father–son rivalry. I *do* have considerable evidence that bears these questions:

Do boys become sexually attracted to their mothers?
Does this have lasting effects on their attitudes toward sex?
Are these effects mediated by unconscious fantasies?

In other words, in this work the following general hypothesis (or, if you like, hypotheses) will be tested: *Young boys – at least under optimal conditions – become sexually attracted to their mothers. This generates lasting sexual fears and avoidances. These fears are (at least in one instance) mediated by unconscious fantasies.* 'Optimal conditions' refers to factors that make the mother more seductive – primarily, the long postpartum sex taboo. 'In one instance' refers to castration anxiety, as reflected in menstrual taboos. [. . .]

Conclusion

The main job of this book [i.e. *The Oedipus Complex: Cross-Cultural Evidence*] was to document the Oedipus complex hypothesis, as formulated in the first part of this Reading. Along the way there have been a good many incidental findings. The research also raises a number of implications, which could be speculated upon at great length. I shall not discuss incidental findings any further. Neither shall I draw implications; I leave this job to you, the reader. I shall devote this passage merely to a summary of the cross-cultural evidence bearing on the Oedipus complex hypothesis.

Here, once again, is the hypothesis of this work: *Young boys, at least under optimal conditions (long postpartum sex taboo), become sexually attracted to their mothers. This generates lasting sexual fears and avoidances. At least in one instance (castration anxiety), these fears are mediated by unconscious fantasy.*

The hypothesis is documented by correlational evidence. Most of these correlations were predicted in advance of the facts. The following are the added assumptions as to the 'meaning' of cross-cultural variables, required for the predictions:

Freudian Hypotheses

The long *postpartum* sex taboo intensifies the son-to-mother sex attraction, thereby intensifying (and making more likely) castration anxiety, phobic attitudes toward incest, and (for initiations) Oedipal rivalry.

Extensiveness of menstrual taboos is partly caused by frequency and intensity, in a population, of castration anxiety.

The nine child rearing variables, correlated with menstrual taboos, reflect indirectly, conditions that intensify castration anxiety.

Severity of kin-avoidance is caused to some degree by frequency and intensity, in a population, of phobic attitudes toward incest.

The occurance of initiations for boys is partly determined by frequency and intensity of Oedipal (father–son) rivalry. (This prediction was made by Whiting, Kluckhohn and Antony.)

Table 1 lists all correlations that bear on the hypothesis: first all the correlations that were formally predicted, and then all the correlations that were not.

Once, out of a total of fourteen times, the direction of trend was not predicted. Nine of the sixteen predicted correlations are statistically significant. Six of the eight non-predicted correlations are significant.

Table 1
Summary of Correlations Bearing on the Oedipus Complex Hypothesis

Variables Correlated		Direction of Correlation	Was Correlation in Predicted Direction?	P Value*
1. Correlations formerly predicted				
Duration of post partum sex taboo	Presence of initiations for adolescent boys	positive	Yes	0·01
	Severity of mother-in-law avoidance	positive	Yes	0·01
	Severity of son's wife avoidance	positive	Yes	0·05

340

Variables Correlated		Direction of Correlation	Was Correlation in Predicted Direction?	P Value*
	Severity of brother–sister avoidance	positive	Yes	0·01
	Extensiveness of menstrual taboos	positive	Yes	0·02
Extensiveness of menstrual taboos	Diffusion of nurturance	negative	Yes	0·28
	Severity of punishment for masturbation	positive	Yes	0·01
	Over-all severity of sex training	positive	Yes	0·05
	Severity of aggression Training	positive	Yes	0·18
	Importance of physical Punishment	positive	Yes	0·07
	Pressure for obedience	negative	No	0·65
	Severity of punishment for disobedience	positive	Yes	0·18
	Strictness of Father's obedience demands	positive	Yes	0·20
	Whether or not father is the main disiplinarian	positive	Yes	0·02
	Frequency of severing in folktales	curvilinear	—	0·30
	Frequency of all types of physical injury in folktales	curvilinear	—	0·001
2. Correlations not formerly predicted extensiveness of menstrual taboos	Composite predictor of castration anxiety	positive	—	0·000001
	Intensity of sex anxiety	positive	—	0·01
Duration of the postpartum sex taboo	Intensity of sex anxiety	positive	—	0·03

Variables Correlated		Direction of Correlation	Was Correlation in Predicted Direction?	P Value*
	Severity of sex training	positive	—	0·25
	Change of residence for adolescent boys	positive	—	0·002
	Breasts not considered Sexual stimuli	positive	—	0·04
	Totemism with food taboos	positive	—	0·10
	Importance of sorcery as an explanation for illness	positive	—	0·01

*All P values are based on a two-tailed test of significance.

These do not constitute twenty-four *independent* pieces of evidence, because some of the measures are contaminated by each other. The correlations have added limitations: the 'variables' represent the Oedipus complex in only an indirect fashion; none of the correlations directly indicate the direction of causation.

Making allowance for this, I feel that the massive evidence leaves a rather small margin for doubt. The probability is high that this hypothesis, embodying several of the coreassumptions of psychoanalytic theory, is approximately valid.

22 R. C. Albino and W. J. Thompson

The Effects of Sudden Weaning on Zulu Children

Excerpt from R. C. Albino and W. J. Thompson, 'The effects of sudden weaning on Zulu children', *British Journal of Medical Psychology*, vol. 29 (1956), pp. 194–7.

[...]

There is little doubt, in view of our previous arguments, that weaning in our sample is mainly psychological and that, therefore, its observed effects are not due to nutritional disturbance. It is important, also, to note that in addition to the weaning there is a rejection of the child by its mother, and that she may be the source of the observed effects.

Because of the difficulty of making inferences from behaviour to psychological states in an alien group, on account of linguistic and other obstacles, we have restricted ourselves almost entirely to a discussion of observed behaviour. We have not, as result, been able to confirm the psychoanalytic views on the psychological effects of weaning, which refer specifically to states of mind. Our findings do, however, in a general way, confirm the general hypothesis of the psychoanalysts that weaning is disturbing and that the intensity of the effect is proportional to age.

The reaction to weaning varies from child to child in form and intensity. Every child was disturbed, but the disturbance could be a transitory upset lasting only a week or so, or a gross change in the personality of the child which was still present at the end of seven weeks after weaning. The constancy of the weaning procedure implies that the variability is due largely to the previous history and constitution of the child, and we must assume that the effects of weaning cannot be considered without reference to those factors.

It is also evident that the immediate gross disturbance from weaning is usually short lived. Most of the children in our sample were normal in the sense of being fairly well, though not fully, adapted members of their society seven weeks after weaning.

If any permanent changes do occur as a result of weaning they are not due to the persistent effect of immediate reactions, such as aggression, but are rather the readjustments of the organism to the effects of weaning. The event of weaning seems to force upon the child the necessity of altering his behaviour in certain ways. That this is so is clear in the case of the child's personal relationships. In all the children the mother comes to be regarded in a different way, the previous close attachment to her, which has existed from birth, being replaced by an apparent indifference which lasts for some weeks. Also, the child develops new relationships of both a positive and negative kind with siblings which in many instances persist and, together with the new attitude to the mother, form a new matrix for the child's social behaviour.

The particular manner in which the relationship becomes reorganized varies from child to child. So far as the mother is concerned, the child in some cases not only renounces her but is at some time very hostile towards her, although in some the child apparently merely renounces his mother; in others it is difficult for him to renounce her altogether and he makes attempts to regain her affection.

Most children were ambivalent, being alternatively hostile and affectionate towards their mothers. Together with the ambivalence, and perhaps being part of it, are attempts to overcome the hostility. Child no. 8, for example, who, the mother asserted, was 'trying to be good', showed this clearly. Further evidence of ambivalence is seen in the fact that all but five children continued to sleep with their mothers after weaning, though they tended to sleep facing away from her. One child, who had previously slept with a sibling, went to its mother on the night of weaning.

It is interesting to note that the aggressiveness towards the mother spreads into the environment. In this respect again weaning must be regarded as not merely affecting the child as an isolated organism, but as an event which disturbs both it and all of the small society in which it lives.

Thus, it seems that weaning is an event which produces great changes in the child's social relationships. The important question is how permanent are these changes. For the majority of our sample the change towards the mother is permanent in its form – the child never again recovering the close pre-weaning attachment to her. And their permanence is also seen in the changed relationships to the siblings.

After this readjustment of family relationships, the most interesting finding is the increased maturity of the child. The independence, greater facility in the use of language and the appearance of concern for strangers, all of which persist, give the impression (which the mothers also have and which they seem to expect) that the child has grown up and is no longer an infant. It would seem as if weaning, far from being a merely disorganizing experience at this age, is also a socializing and maturing influence. In earlier weanings, so far as can be inferred from our few reports, this does not appear to be the case. In them the disorganization of behaviour is very gross and would appear to outweigh any socializing influences. Also these early cases do not appear to be able to adjust so easily to the loss of the mother as the later cases, for they continue to be greatly disturbed for a longer period.

If one looks at the nature of the socialization and of the changed social relationships of the child, it appears that they are the result of two factors. A replacement of the mother as a love object by others in the environment (there is perhaps also an aggressiveness towards any object that is identified with the mother, as we observed in twelve cases). That is, the attitudes to the mother are displaced to the environment. The second factor is the isolation of the child from the environment. He sits alone and goes off on expeditions of his own and also takes note of strangers who previously were not part of the family. It would seem as if the child has given up his close dependence upon others and on the family as a result of his mother's rejection and has been forced, by his hostility, to isolate himself and to become an independent being. It may be, if this interpretation is true, that the child in adapting to the effects of weaning undergoes a sudden increase of ego development. That is, he becomes more aware of himself as an independent entity separated from this environment, and takes active steps to adapt himself to this environment, and it to him.

The one symptom which showed the greatest tendency to continue was the aggressiveness. Taken in conjunction with the increased maturity of the child, it implies that weaning produces an individual both more mature and more inclined to make active demands upon his environment than the unweaned child.

The two immediate reactions of apathy or of 'excitement' are interesting in that they appear very similar to reactions observed by Ribble in children deprived of maternal support and which Bowlby has also observed in deprived children. The determinants of the two reactions are not evident from our data, and neither is it clear whether the later behaviour of children showing the two reactions differs. The variability of pre- and post-weaning behaviour within the two groups is as great as that between them, and with such a small sample using qualitative methods it is impossible to be definite. It seems, however, that these two reactions are fundamental in the reaction of infants to deprivation, and it would be worth investigating whether there might not be genetic as well as environmental factors present.

Aggressiveness, besides being the most persistent of all the immediate reactions, seems to tend to increase rather than to diminish and may, or may not, be accompanied by an increased naughtiness. It begins very soon after weaning, usually on the first night, and may be considered the most immediate reaction to weaning. It is, also, the most disturbing reaction, as it is the main cause of the disturbances in the child's social relationships, and especially of his relationship with his mother. Its continuance and its frequency both seem to imply that it is of very great importance. Naughtiness, on the other hand, appears later than aggression and must be regarded as a secondary effect resulting from an organized attempt to control the situation. One may, perhaps, interpret the aggressiveness as a non-specific reaction directed at first against the mother and then the environment and the naughtiness as a more specific and controlled direction of the aggression. If this is the case, then we again have evidence that weaning intensifies, after an initial disorganization, the controlling mechanisms in behaviour, The undifferentiated and more primitive aggression gives place to the performance of acts with an aggressive aim, but of a kind which are known by the child to cause greater disturbance in the family. (It will be noted that all the naughty acts are highly directed in that the child chooses just those forms of behaviour, such as spilling water, which are very disturbing in the society in which he finds himself.) There may be a further reason for the persistence of aggression. It seems that so far as the aggression is not directed to the mother and does not disorganize the social relationships of the child or its own activities it may be regarded as a socially useful form of behaviour, for it enables the child to gain its own ends. This, and the fact that a certain amount of aggression is encouraged and tolerated in Zulu society, may be the reason why this change exists; as well as being the main initiator of the changes, aggression may eventually become a valuable result of weaning, once it is directed in a socially approved manner.

The changes tend to show a cyclic character which is particularly evident in the relationship of the child to its mother. We have already noticed that he may, after a period of attacking his mother, change his behaviour to a more demanding form. This is replaced later by attacks, and the alternation continues for a period, when, in most cases, the child gives up these responses to its mother. This alternation, which was characteristic of all the behaviour we observed, makes it seem as if the child is attempting, in an active way, to adapt himself to the situation of being rejected by his mother. He does not merely react by frustrated behaviour, but undertakes various activities which may be regarded as attempts, first, to restore the mother to her original position, and, later, to exist without her support. Again, it seems as if the child is compelled by the weaning to become a mature and independent person, and achieves this only after a period of readjustment involving several trial solutions; for example, demanding the mother, trying to please her, attaching himself to another person, aggressively trying to influence his mother by naughty behaviour. The immediate reaction seems to be one of attack and aggression which, in the face of the frustration received, is to be expected. It is only after this preliminary disorganized form of behaviour that the attempt at adaptation occurs. It is important to emphasize here that weaning does not appear to be simply a disturbance in response to frustration which gradually settles down, but that it involves, after a preliminary disturbance, a series of active adaptive changes in the organism, and may, at the age of about eighteen months, be a most powerful stimulus to ego development.

23   G. O. Wright

Projection and Displacement: A Cross-Cultural Study of
Folk-Tale Aggression

G. O. Wright, 'Projection and displacement: A cross-cultural study of folk-
tale aggression', *Journal of Abnormal and Social Psychology*, vol. 49 (1956),
pp. 523-8.

The study of societies reveals many examples of the use of folk
tales and rituals which are aggressive in content. In varying
degrees this aesthetic aspect of culture seems to provide a device
by which aggressive feelings can be displayed in fantasy without
the disruptive effects which otherwise would result from their
direct expression. This fantasy aggression, however, presumably
has some correspondence with real-life aggression. In order to
understand folk-tale aggression, therefore, we will attempt to
discover the relationship between specific antecedent conditions
and the specific outcomes with which they are associated in folk
tales.

Part of the theoretical framework for the study of folk-tale
aggression grows out of the approach–avoidance theory of
Dollard and Miller (1). This theory gives us a scheme for ap-
praising the joint effects of approach and of avoidance in conflict
situations. While the experimental evidence supporting the approach – avoidance theory originally came from work with
animals, a reasonable elaboration will transform its application
from psychophysical phenomena to those which are psycho-
cultural.

One of the important elaborations of the approach-avoidance
theory is the result of the work of Whiting (see 3, 4). Whiting's
hypothesis asserts that the intensity of the displaced responses,
as well as the cultural distance of displacement, is a function
of anxiety. This hypothesis is confirmed in the doll-play investigations in which it was found that the display of large amounts
of aggressive behavior in fantasy is connected with a high degree
of anxiety arising from previous punishment for aggression (2).

Another elaboration of the approach–avoidance theory is the

result of the work of Whiting and Child (4), in which the original theory as it applied to displacement is extended to projection. This work, which examined the relationship between aggression anxiety and the theories held by members of the society regarding the causes of disease, attested the validity of the theory and provided further evidence that such a theory, in fact, could be useful in understanding cultural phenomena.

The work of Whiting and Child did not independently test displacement and projection. This present study, however, does make this independent test by analysing folk-tale behavior. The choice of folk tales for study was somewhat dictated by the fact that such an analysis could be carried out on the basis of classifying the behavior of the characters in the folk tales as either displacement (qualities of the objects of aggression) or projection (qualities of the agents of aggression).

Procedure

The material used in this study has been developed from an analysis of folk tales from thirty-three societies, including selections from Oceania, Asia, Africa, North America and South America. Since the child-training data of Whiting and Child (4) were to be used as one of the variables, folk tales had to be assembled for the societies that were among the seventy-five used in their study. The folk-tale literature of these seventy-five societies was examined, and preliminary selections on the basis of available material from thirty-seven societies were made. At the outset it was decided not to include origin legends because of their lack of comparability with ordinary folk tales. For the same reason, those folk tales told exclusively in the third person with the ethnographer as narrator were excluded, since they were likely to be overlaid with the cultural bias of the ethnographer. In consequence of one or the other of these restrictions, the folk tales from four of the initial selections were discarded. These societies were the Ainu, Arapesh, Azande and the Maori.

In order to provide sufficient data for analysis, twelve folk tales were selected from each society. Moreover, in order to eliminate the inclusion of fragmentary tales, each of the folk tales selected was required to be a complete episode. An episode was defined as a sequence of action having a definite beginning and proceeding to some definite action climax.

In order to carry out the study, a scheme permitting quantitative analysis of the folk tales was needed. In addition, it was necessary that the scheme comprise objective scoring categories so that the subjective estimates of the investigator would be minimized. These requirements are met in the scoring scheme used by the doll-play investigators. Their scheme was modified for use with folk tales.

Central to the scoring system is the concept of *interaction units*. As the term implies, an interaction unit is a complete behavior sequence between two persons. In order to be complete, the sequence must contain at least two action elements. First, a person must initiate an action toward some other person. Second, this initiated action must be responded to by the other person. For example, a mother initiates action by calling her child to lunch. The child responds to this action by stopping his play and coming into the house. The first element we can call *initiation*; the second *response*. The person starting the action we can call the *initiator*; the person responding to the action we can call *respondent*.

Now, since many of the actions are likely to be more than simple action–reaction, we have decided on a convention for complex actions. In our example of the mother calling the child to lunch, how will the action be scored if the child were to say, 'I'm busy, mother, and can't come in now'? What is the action of the mother to be called if she in turn responds to the reply of the child by a threat of spanking? The convention adopted is to score the calling of the mother and the reply of the child as one interaction unit, with mother as initiator and child as respondent. In turn, the reply of the child and the threat of the mother are scored as the second interaction unit, with the child as initiator and the mother as respondent. If the threat of punishment causes the child to come into the house, this is scored as the third interaction unit, with mother as initiator and child as respondent. Allowing a reaction to be both a response and an initiation solves our scoring dilemma.

When the interaction unit is used as the vital measure in the scoring system, it is possible to build additional classifying measures around this unit. For example, it is possible to classify the status of the initiator, the status of the respondent, the nature of the initiation, and the nature of the response. It is possible, moreover, to make comparisons from folk tale to folk tale by the use of the quantitative measures.

The interaction sequences were scored as aggressive or non-aggressive; each aggressive act was scored for intensity (ranging from a score of 1 for non-accomplishment of aggressive intent to a score of 5 for killing); and finally, each sequence was classified as to the agent and object of the act.

In order to test the reliability of the scoring system, four students at the Wilberforce State College (Ohio) were asked to score thirty-six folk-tale episodes selected at random from the collection. These students were trained in the use of the system for five hours prior to the scoring. An index of reliability was computed as follows: the sum of the agreements for a pair of the student scorers was divided by the total number of items scored by them; the scores of the writer and of the students were randomly paired in all possible combinations for each of the scoring categories; the resultant index of reliability was 0·83, with 1·0 representing perfect agreement.

The scoring of the folk tales provides a comprehensive set of data on the display of aggressive feelings in folk tales. This is our consequent variable. Data also were needed for the child-training practices, our antecedent variable. For this antecedent variable, the child-training data of the study of Whiting and Child (4) were used. These data, in the form of ratings on seven-point scales, were available for twenty-six features of child-training practices. The details of the rating scale for the practice that is relevant to the present study are as follows (the numbers indicate the ends of the rating scale):

Severity of Aggression Training

7 – Child severely punished for any form of aggression; fighting, disrespect or disobedience not permitted.

1 – All but the most severe forms of aggression permitted; fighting encouraged.

In analysing the data, the societies were divided into two groups, high and low, on the basis of the ratings for the child-training practice. The data were then analysed for significance of difference between means.

The Effect of Punishment Anxiety on Displacement

The first hypothesis to be tested is that objects of displaced aggression are chosen farther and farther out on the generalization continuum as a function of the amount of aggression anxiety.

This hypothesis is derived from the approach–avoidance theory, which considers the joint habit strength of aggression and aggression anxiety to be the algebraic difference between the two tendencies. As the degree of anxiety is increased, this anxiety function shifts the point of maximum response toward objects less and less like the original object.

The approach–avoidance theory specifies *where* on the generalization continuum the maximum response is likely to occur, but Whiting's theory specifies also *how strong* this maximum response is likely to be. This theory asserts that anxiety is frustrating, that is to say, it interferes with the initial response, and that this interference is itself drive-producing. Consequently, the joint effective habit potential is a function of the product of the joint habit strength (i.e. of the difference between the aggression and the aggression anxiety) and the strength of frustration as indicated by aggression anxiety.

In order to translate this hypothesis into terms that can be tested with the folk-tale data, the punishment of children for aggression will be called aggression anxiety; the Hero will be called the point of original response; the similarity dimension will be considered as beginning at the Hero and extending through friends, relatives, and acquaintances to strangers at the least similar position; and finally, the frequency of aggressive acts involving a given category along the dimension of similarity will be called strength of response. Further, we will consider our hypothesis supported if the following conditions are found:

1. In the folk tales of a society in which the child-training practice is low severity of punishment for aggression, the frequency with which friends of the Hero are used as objects of aggression should be higher than it is in the folk tales from societies in which the practice is high severity of punishment for aggression. This condition should be found because our theory predicts that the lower the anxiety, the more like the original object will be the displaced objects.

2. Conversely, in the folk tales of societies in which the child-training practice is high severity of punishment for aggression, the frequency of the use of strangers as objects of aggression should be higher than in those of societies in which the practice is low severity of punishment for aggression. This condition should be found because our theory predicts that the higher the anxiety, the less like the original object will be the displaced objects.

The data used for this analysis were the antecedent child-training measures of severity of punishment for aggression versus the frequency of use of the friends of the Hero as objects of aggression. The scores of frequency of use of friends as objects of aggression were obtained by counting the number of times the friend is used as the object of aggression in the folk tales, and dividing this frequency by the total aggressive acts.

Analysis of the data indicates that for the group of societies in which aggression anxiety is low (low severity of punishment for aggression), the mean frequency of the use of friends of the Hero as the object of aggression is 13·3, whereas the mean of the group of societies in which aggression anxiety is high (high severity of punishment for aggression) is 8·67. The difference is significant at the 0·005 level (obtained $t = 3·8$).[1] The results of this and the following tests are shown in Table 1.

The use of the measures for the friends of the Hero as the object of aggression instead of the Hero himself is a question that naturally arises. In applying the test of the hypothesis, it was felt that the Hero as the object of aggression actually represented self-aggression, and that this fact might introduce this effect as an uncontrolled variable. Consequently, the objects considered closest to the Hero, namely, his friends, were chosen.

In order, however, to provide information that might be useful in refining the hypothesis, the analysis of the data on the Hero was carried out. In this analysis, the means of the frequency of use of the Hero as object of aggression were compared for the high aggression–anxiety group of societies and the low aggression-anxiety group of societies. The difference is not significant – that is to say, the difference in the means which we observed are likely

1. In all of the results reported, only one tail of the t distribution is used, since all of the results are in the predicted direction.

to have arisen by chance. The obtained t is 0·47; the significance level is approximately 0·30.

The test of the converse condition, that of comparing the frequency of the use of strangers as the object of aggression under the conditions of high aggression anxiety and of low aggression

Table 1
Summary of Findings

| Mean Frequencies of Aggression | Aggression Anxiety | | | |
	High N = 12	Low N = 14	t	p
Agent of aggression				
Hero as agent	22·3	23·0	0·21	0·25
Friend as agent	15·33	18·54	1·18	0·13
Stranger as agent	30·5	25·43	2·46	0·01
Object of aggression				
Hero as object	27·33	29·43	0·47	0·30
Friend as object	8·67	13·3	3·8	0·005
Stranger as object	31·66	26·58	2·21	0·015
Intensity of aggression	19·58	15·7	2·02	0·035
Hero triumphant	2·14	4·85	2·86	0·005

Note. – This table shows mean scores for frequences of various categories of agents and objects of aggression, for intensity of aggression, and for fate of the hero in the folk tales. (Societies are dichotomized on the basis of two degrees of aggression anxiety, high and low.)

anxiety, discloses that the mean of the frequency of use of strangers as the object of aggression for societies in which aggression anxiety is high is higher than in societies in which aggression anxiety is low. The means are respectively 31·66 and 26·58. The difference between the means is significant at approximately the 0·02 level (obtained $t = 2·21$). Thus, in sum, the societies in which children are severely punished for aggression, as compared to the mild societies, represent friends of the Hero *less* frequently and strangers *more* frequently, as would be expected from the displacement hypothesis.

The Effect of Punishment Anxiety on Projection

The second hypothesis to be tested is that the agents of projected aggression are chosen farther and farther out on the generalization continuum as a function of the amount of aggression anxiety.

In order for our theory to be consistent, the findings for displacement should have their counterpart in projection. The child-training measures of punishment aggression, used as indices of aggression anxiety, should be related to projection in such a way that the folk tales of societies in which punishment for aggression is severe should display more aggression performance that uses the stranger as agent, since the tendency to express aggression under these conditions should be projected far out on the generalization continuum. Stated another way, high aggression anxiety should be associated with a more frequent use of stranger as aggressive agent.

The folk-tale data translated into terms of our theory are analysed, using severity of punishment for aggression as the degree of anxiety about aggression, and the frequency of the use of various categories as agents of aggression; these were considered an index of the strength of the joint effective habit of aggression and aggression anxiety. We will consider our hypothesis as supported if the following conditions are found:

1. In the folk tales of societies in which the child-training practice is low severity of punishment for aggression, the frequency of use of the Hero as agent of aggression should be higher than in those of societies in which the practice is high severity of punishment for aggression. This condition should be found because our theory states that the lower the anxiety, the more like the original object will be the projected agents. This condition should also be found for the use of friends of the Hero as agents of aggression.

2. In the folk tales of societies in which the child-training practice is high severity of punishment for aggression, the frequency of use of strangers as agents of aggression should be higher than in folk tales from societies that practice low severity of punishment for aggression. This condition should be found because our theory states that the higher the anxiety, the less like the original objects will be the projected agents.

The data used for this analysis were the antecedent child-training measures of severity of punishment for aggression versus the frequency of the use of the Hero as agent of aggression. The scores of frequency of use of the Hero as agent of aggression were obtained by counting the times the Hero was used as agent of aggression in the folk tales, and dividing this by the total aggressive acts.

Analysis of the data indicates that the mean frequency of use of Hero as agent of aggression in the high aggression-anxiety societies is 22·3, whereas it is 23·0 in the low aggression-anxiety societies. The difference between these means, though in the predicted direction, is not significant (p is approximately 0·25; obtained $t = 0·21$).

Analysis of the data for the use of friends of the Hero as agent of aggression, using a procedure similar to that for the Hero, indicates that the difference between the means of frequency of use of friends as agents of aggression is also in the predicted direction, but is not significant (p is approximately 0·13; obtained $t = 1·18$).

In the converse condition, namely, high aggression anxiety accompanied by the more frequent use of the stranger as agent of aggression, analysis of the data indicates that for the group of societies in which aggression anxiety is high, the mean frequency of use of stranger as agent of aggression is higher than that of the group of societies in which the aggression anxiety is low. The mean frequencies are, respectively, 30·5 and 25·43. The difference between the means is in the predicted direction and is significant at the 0·01 level (obtained $t = 2·46$).

The findings discussed here tend to support the theorems and to suggest that the individual may, in fact, use psychologically harmless ways to express his aggression in the presence of aggression anxiety. It is suggested, moreover, that the individual apparently chooses harmless agents and objects of aggression on the basis of their categorical differences from the agents and objects associated with the initial anxiety. The findings also suggest that two qualifications are essential in the interpretation of these data. Both relate to the discrete placement of the cultural categories along the dimension of similarity.

The first qualification is that the present theory, which relates anxiety to projection and displacement, is not refined enough to predict the characteristics and the behavior of the Hero in folk tales as a function of the anxiety of the society. The explanation proposed is that the position which the Hero occupies on the generalization continuum is theoretically influenced by the transition between real life and fantasy and that more things must be known about the influence of complex psychological factors in this transition area before our predictions will gain accuracy.

The other qualification is that a precise placement of the intermediate categories of relatives and acquaintances cannot be made with the use of our presently developed theory. The explanation of this condition probably lies in the complexity of meaning which various societies attach to cultural categories. It is possible, for example, that in one society the similarity of relatives to strangers might be perceived to be greater than between acquaintances and strangers, while in another society the opposite might be true.

The Effect of Aggression Anxiety on Intensity of Aggression

Another aspect of the relationship of aggression anxiety to fantasy aggression is of interest, namely, the apparent influence of the strength of anxiety on the intensity of aggression in folk tales. Our theory suggests that the aggression anxiety will diminish at a more rapid rate than the intensity of the aggression as displacements and projections are made farther and farther out on the generalization continuum. We should be able to foretell from this theory that fantasy, since it represents situations in many ways dissimilar from real life, should provide a vehicle for the expression of aggression, and should do so with an intensity which is directly related to the amount of real-life punishment for aggression.

An examination of this theory is made in the third hypothesis to be tested, namely, that punishment for aggression increases the intensity of aggression in situations which are distinctly dissimilar from those in which the punishment occurs.

This hypothesis, translated into terms which are applicable to the folk-tale data, states that the punishment of aggression leads to aggression anxiety. This anxiety reduced the display of aggressive behavior toward objects similar to those associated with the

357

initial punishment. As we have seen, in such situations displacement and projection of aggression are likely to occur. Moreover, the strength of the joint effective habit of the aggression and of the aggression avoidance is thought to be the product of the difference between the two tendencies and the degree of avoidance. We should expect, therefore, that the greater the anxiety, the greater the intensity of the fantasy aggression.

Our hypothesis will be supported if it is found that the folk tales of societies in which high aggression anxiety is generated by severe punishment for aggression show a greater intensity of aggression than exists in the folk tales of societies in which low aggression anxiety is generated.

The data used for this analysis were the same child-training measures of severity of punishment for aggression used in the previous analysis related to the intensity of the folk-tale aggression. The scores for intensity were obtained by taking the sum of the intensity measures for each act of aggression in the folk tales of a given society and dividing this sum by the total acts of aggression in the folk tales.

An analysis of the data indicates that the mean of the intensity of aggression for the group of societies practicing high severity of punishment for aggression is 19·58, whereas the mean for the group practicing low severity of punishment for aggression is 15·7. The difference between the means is in the predicted direction and is significant at approximately the 0·03 level (obtained $t = 2·02$).

The Effect of Aggression Anxiety on the Fate of the Hero

There is one additional analysis by which information may be disclosed about the fantasy structuring of the aggression in folk tales, namely, the relationship between aggression anxiety and the fate of the Hero in the folk tales. Actually, such an analysis provides another test of the kind and amount of projection and displacement which develop as the consequent variable of aggression anxiety. The fate of the Hero, moreover, is likely to be a more sensitive measure of the expression of fantasy aggression than those involving secondary characters.

An examination of this theoretical position is done in the

fourth hypothesis to be tested, namely, that the Hero should triumph less often in folk tales of societies in which the child-training practices include severe punishment for aggression. This hypothesis is a restatement of the second hypothesis that high aggression anxiety results in projection far out from the Hero on the generalization continuum. This theorem is built on the assumption that the behavior of the Hero is understandable as a projection of the individual. Consequently, in cases of high aggression anxiety, it is to be expected that having the Hero triumphant is likely to be accompanied by large amounts of anxiety, so that triumphant characters of the folk tales are likely to be less like the Hero. In short, a small degree of triumphant-Hero aggression should accompany high aggression anxiety.

The data used for this analysis were the child-training data of severity of punishment for aggression versus the frequency of Hero triumphant in the outcomes of the episodes.

An analysis of the data for the fate of the Hero shows that the Hero is triumphant less frequently in the high aggression anxiety group of societies. The means are 2·14 and 4·85. The difference between the means is significant at the 0·005 level (obtained $t = 2·86$).

This finding is in accord with the earlier results in which it was seen that a comparable relationship was true, namely, that of the more frequent use of the stranger as agent of aggression in folk tales of societies in which aggression anxiety is high. In both cases, the theoretical assumptions underlying the functioning of the phenomenon of generalization in conflict are found to be valid.

Summary

1. The analysis of the folk-tale data supports the essential features of the theory which was developed to supply insight into the consequences and outcomes of action and behavior in folk tales. The approach–avoidance theory of Miller, restated in terms of Whiting's modification of it for the influence of conflict-produced drives, provides a coherent basis for the explanation of the phenomena of projection and displacement in folk tales. Admittedly, the predictive powers of such a theory are not perfect,

but the results obtained for the tests of the hypotheses are all in the predicted direction.

2. In general, it is found that high punishment anxiety, when it is connected with the expression of aggression, leads to the kind of folk-tale behavior in which the objects and agents of aggression are far out on the generalization continuum and are least like the Hero. In addition, the Hero in these folk tales is not likely to be triumphant in the outcomes.

3. In general, it is found that low punishment anxiety, when it is connected with the expression of aggression, leads to the kind of folk-tale behavior in which the objects and agents of aggression are chosen close to the Hero on the generalization continuum. In addition, the Hero is likely to be triumphant in the outcomes.

4. High punishment anxiety, when it is connected with the expression of aggression, leads to the display of a more intense kind of aggressive behavior in folk tales than is true for low punishment anxiety.

5. Finally, the study demonstrates that folk tales as fantasy material are fruitful for analysis. Enough consistency of trends has been found in the present study to suggest that the relationships of child-training practices and the expression of aggression in folk tales are real and not accidental or spurious. This consistency and its value are somewhat enhanced by the fact that the variables of child-training practices used in this analysis are data from an independent investigation which were collected and analysed by workers who were not directly involved in the scoring and analysis of the present folk-tale study.

References

1. DOLLARD, J., and MILLER, N. E., *Personality and Psychotherapy*, McGraw-Hill, 1950.
2. HOLLENBERG, E., and SPERRY, M., 'Some antecedents of aggression and effects of frustration in doll play', *Personality*, vol. 1 (1951), pp. 32–43.
3. SEARS, R. R., 'A theoretical framework for personality and social behavior', *American Psychologist*, vol. 6 (1951), pp. 476–83.
4. WHITING, J. W. M., and CHILD, I. L., *Child Training and Personality* Yale University Press, 1953.

Further Reading

The following is a list of selected references, many of which are quoted in the given selections and their introductions.

General surveys

DOOB, L., 'Psychology', in R. Lystad, ed., *The African World: A Survey of Social Research*, Praeger, 1965.

FRENCH, D., 'The relationship of anthropology to studies in perception and cognition', in S. Koch, ed., *Psychology: A Study of Science*, vol. 6, McGraw-Hill, 1963.

HALLOWELL, A. I., 'Cultural factors in the structuralization of perception', in J. H. Rohrer and M. Sherif, eds., *Social Psychology at the Cross-Roads* Harper, 1951. (See also this author's *Culture and Experience*, University of Pennsylvania Press, 1955.)

PRICE-WILLIAMS, D. R., 'Cross-cultural studies', in B. M. Foss, ed., *New Horizons in Psychology*, Penguin 1966.

TAJFEL, H., 'Social and cultural factors in perception', in G. Lindzey and E. Aronson, eds., *Handbook of Social Psychology*, 2nd edn, Addison-Wesley, 1968.

TRIANDIS, H., 'Cultural influence upon cognitive processes', in L. Berkowitz, ed., *Advances in Experimental Social Psychology*, Academic Press, 1964.

WHITING, J. W. M., 'The cross-cultural method', in G. Lindzey, ed., *Handbook of Social Psychology*, vol. 1, Addison–Wesley, 1954. pp. 523–31. (Reprinted as 'Methods and problems in cross-cultural research', in G. Lindzey and E. Aronson, eds., *Handbook of Social Psychology*, vol. 2, Addison–Wesley, 2nd edn, 1968, pp. 693–728.

On the scope, theory and general methodology of cross-cultural psychology

ANGELINI, A. L. L., 'Perspectives and problems in cross-cultural research', *Revista di Psicologia Normal e Patologica*, vol. II (1966), pp. 30–41.

BARKER, R. G., and BARKER, L. S., 'Behavior units for the comparative study of cultures', in Bert Kaplan, ed., *Studying Personality Cross-Culturally*, Row, Peterson, 1961.

BERRIEN, F. K., 'Methodological and related problems in cross-cultural research', *International Journal of Psychology*, vol. 2 (1967), pp. 37–43.

CAMPBELL, D. T., 'Distinguishing differences of perception from failures of communication in cross-cultural studies', in F. C. S. Northrop and H. H. Livingston, eds., *Cross-Cultural Understanding: Epistemology in Anthropology*, Harper and Row, 1964.

Further Reading

HOLTZMAN, W., 'Presidential address', *11th Inter-American Congress of Psychology Proceedings*, Mexico City, 1968.

PRICE-WILLIAMS, D. R., 'Towards a systematics of cross-cultural psychology', *11th Inter-American Congress of Psychology Proceedings* Mexico City, 1968.

On the problem of equivalence

ALMOND, G. A., and VERBA, S., *The Civic Culture*, Princeton University Press, 1963. (See chapter 2.)

ANDERSON, R. B., 'On the comparability of meaningful stimuli in cross-cultural research', *Sociometry*, vol. 30 (1967), pp. 124–36.

HUDSON, B. B., BARAKET, M., and LAFORGE, R., 'Problems and methods of cross-cultural research', *Journal of Social Issues*, vol. 15 (1959), pp. 5–19.

PRZEWORSKI, A., and TEUNE, H., 'Equivalence in cross-national research', *Public Opinion Quarterly*, vol. 30 (1966–7), pp. 551–68.

SEARS, R. R., 'Transcultural variables and conceptual equivalence', in B. Kaplan, ed., *Studying Personality Cross-Culturally*, Row, Peterson, 1961.

On the relation of the environment to tests

PORTEUS, S. D., *Intelligence and Environment*, Macmillan, 1937.

VERNON, P. E., 'Environmental handicaps and intellectual development', *British Journal of Educational Psychology*, vol. 35 (1965), part I, pp. 9–20, part II pp. 117–26.

VERNON, P. E., 'Ability factors and environmental influences', *American Psychologist*, vol. 20 (1965), pp. 723–33.

Tests in specific areas

BIESHEUVEL, S., *African Intelligence*, South African Institute of Race Relations, Johannesburg, 1943.

BIESHEUVEL, S., 'The study of African ability. Part I: The intellectual potentialities of Africans', *African Studies*, vol. II (1952), pp. 45–57.

BIESHEUVEL, S., 'Some African acculturation problems, with special reference to perceptual and motor skills', in Symposium on *The Inter-Relation of Biological and Cultural Adaptation*, Wenger-Gren Foundation, 1966.

CRYNS, A. G. J., 'African intelligence: a critical survey of cross-cultural research in Africa south of the Sahara', *Journal of Social Psychology*, vol. 57 (1962), pp. 283–301.

MACARTHUR, R. A., IRVINE, S. H., and BRIMBLE, A. R., *The Northern Rhodesia Mental Ability Survey*, Rhodes-Livingston Institute, Lusaka, 1963.

MCCONNELL, J., 'Abstract behavior among the Tepehuan', *Journal of Abnormal and Social Psychology*, vol. 49 (1954), pp. 109–10.

MAISTRAUX, R., 'La sous-évolution des Noirs-d'Afrique; sa nature, ses causes, ses remèdes', *Revue Psychologie des Peuples*, vol. 10 (1955), pp. 167–89, 397–456; vol. II (1956), pp. 80–90, 134–73.

MAISTRAUX, R., L'Intelligence noire et son destin', *Bruxelles Editions, Problémes d'Afrique Centrale*, 1956.

MANLEY, D. R., 'Mental ability in Jamaica', *Social and Economic Studies*, vol. 12 (1963), pp. 51–71. (University of West Indies, Institute of Social and Economic Research.)

OMBREDANE, A., ROBAYE, F., and PLUMAIL, H., 'Résultats d'une application répétée du matrix-coleur à une population de Noirs Congolais', *Bulletin C.E.R.P.*, vol. 6 (1956), pp. 129–47.

RICHELLE, M., 'Problem solving in African children: a genetic and cross-cultural study using Rey's performance tests', *International Journal of Psychology*, vol. 1 (1966), pp. 273–87.

VERNON, P. E., 'Educational and intellectual development among Canadian Indians and Eskimos', *Educational Review*, vol. 18 (1966), pp. 79–91, 185–95.

WINTRINGER, G., 'Considerations sur l'intelligence du Noir Africain' *Revue Psychologie des Peuples*, vol. 10 (1955), pp. 37–55.

On the problem of testing in non-Western societies

BIESHEUVEL, S., 'The study of African ability. Part II: A survey of some research problems', *African Studies*, vol. 2 (1952), pp. 105–17.

DOOB, L., 'The use of different test items in non-literate societies', *Public Opinion Quarterly*, vol. 21 (1957–8), pp. 499–504.

IRVINE, S. H., 'Towards a rationale for testing attainments and abilities in Africa', *British Journal of Educational Psychology*, vol. 36 (1966), pp 24–. 32.

JAHODA, G., 'Assessment of abstract behavior in a non-Western culture', *Journal of Abnormal and Social Psychology*, vol. 53 (1956), pp. 237–43.

SCHWARZ, P. A., 'Adapting tests to the cultural setting', *Educational and Psychological Measurement*, vol. 23 (1963), pp. 673–86.

On the geometric illusions

BONTE, M., 'The reaction of two African societies to the Müller–Lyer illusion', *Journal of Social Psychology*, vol. 58 (1962), pp. 265–8.

GREGOR, A. J., and MCPHERSON, D. A., 'A study of susceptibility to geometric illusion among cultural subgroups of Australian aborigines'. *Psychologia Africana*, vol. 11 (1965), pp. 1–13.

MERCADO, S. J., RUBES, J. E., and BARRERA, R. F., 'Depth cues effects on the perception of visual illusions', *Revista Interamericana di Psicologia*' (InterAmerican Journal of Psychology), vol. 1 (1967), pp. 137–42.

MORGAN, P., 'A study in perceptual differences among cultural groups in Southern Africa, using tests of geometric illusion', *Journal of National Personnel Research*, vol. 8 (1959), pp. 39–43.

RIVERS, W. H. R., 'Vision', in A. C. Haddon, ed., *Reports of the Cambridge Anthropological Expedition to the Torres Straits*, Part I. Cambridge University Press, 1901.

Further Reading

RIVERS, W. H. R., 'Observations on the senses of the Todas', *British Journal of Psychology*, vol. 1 (1905), pp. 321–96.

SEGALL, M. H., CAMPBELL, D. T., and HERSKOVITS, M. J., *The Influence of Culture on Visual Perception*, Bobbs-Merrill, 1966.

On illusion of movement

ALLPORT, G. W., and PETTIGREW, T. F., 'Cultural influence on the perception of movement: The trapezoidal illusion among Zulus', *Journal of Abnormal and Social Psychology*, vol. 55 (1957), pp. 104–13.

On pictorial representation

DEREGOWSKI, J. B., 'Difficulties in pictorial depth perception in Africa', *British Journal of Psychology*, vol. 59 (1968), pp. 195–204.

DEREGOWSKI, J. B., 'Pictorial recognition in subjects from a relatively pictureless environment', *African Social Research*, vol. 5 (1968), pp. 356–64.

DU TOIT, B. M., 'Pictorial depth perception and linguistic relativity' *Psychologia Africana*, vol. 11 (1966), pp. 51–63.

HUDSON, W., 'Pictorial depth perception in sub-cultural groups in Africa', *Journal of Social Psychology*, vol. 52 (1960), pp. 183–208.

HUDSON, W., 'Pictorial perception and educational adaptation in Africa', *Psychologia Africana*, vol. 9 (1962), pp. 226–39.

HUDSON, W., 'Cultural problems in pictorial perception', *South African Journal of Science*, vol. 58 (1962), pp. 189–95.

KILBRIDE, P. L., ROBBINS, M. C., and FREEMAN, R. B., 'Pictorial depth perception and education among Baganda school children', *Perceptual and Motor Skills*, vol. 26 (1968), pp. 1116–18.

SELLERS, W., 'The production of films for primitive peoples', *Overseas Education*, vol. 13 (1941), pp. 221.

WINTER, W., 'The perception of safety posters by Bantu industrial workers', *Psychologia Africana*, vol. 10 (1963), pp. 127–35.

On field dependence

BERRY, J. W., 'Temne and Eskimo perceptual skills', *International Journal of Psychology*, vol. 1 (1966), pp. 207–29.

WITKIN, H. A., 'Cultural influences in the development of cognitive style', *International Journal of Psychology*, vol. 2 (1967), (Although not directly on cultural aspects, for background material see: H. A. Witkin, H. B. Lewis, M. Hartman, K. Machover, P. B. Meissner and S. Wapner, *Personality through Perception*, Harper, 1954. Also H. A. Witkin, R. B. Dyk, H. F. Paterson, D. E. Goodenough and S. A. Karp, *Psychological Differentiation*, Wiley, 1962.)

WOBER, M., 'Sensotypes', *Journal of Social Psychology*, vol. 70 (1966), pp. 181–9.

On conservation

BRUNER, J. S., OLVER, R. R., and GREENFIELD, P. M., *Studies in Cognitive Growth*, Wiley, 1966. (Includes work other than on conservation alone.)

GOODNOW, J. J., 'A test of mileau differences with some of Piaget's tasks', *Psychological Monographs*, vol. 76 (1962), no. 36.

GOODNOW, J. J., and BETHON, G., 'Piaget's tasks – the effects of schooling and intelligence', *Child Development*, vol. 37 (1966). pp. 573–82.

GREENFIELD, P. M., and BRUNER, J. S., 'Culture and cognitive growth'. *International Journal of Psychology*, vol. 1 (1966), pp. 89–107.

HYDE, D. M., 'An Investigation of Piaget's theories and the development of the concept of number', *Ph.D. Thesis, University of London*, 1959.

PELUFFO, N., 'Les notions de conservation et de causalité chez les enfants prevénant de differents mileux physiques et socio-culturels', *Archives de Psychologie*, vol. 38 (1962), pp. 75–90.

PRICE-WILLIAMS, D. R., GORDON, W., and RAMIREZ, M., 'Manipulation and conservation: A study of children from pottery-making families in Mexico', *11th Inter-American Congress of Psychology Proceedings*, Mexico City, 1968.

On other aspects of perception

BAGBY, J. W., 'A cross-cultural study of perceptual dominance in binocular rivalry', *Journal of Abnormal and Social Psychology*, vol. 54 (1957), pp. 331–4.

BEVERIDGE, W. M., 'Some racial differences in perception', *British Journal of Psychology*, vol. 30 (1940), pp. 57–64.

DENNIS, W., 'The human figure drawings of Bedouins', *Journal of Social Psychology*, vol. 52 (1960), pp. 209–19.

MICHAEL, D., 'A cross-cultural investigation of closure', *Journal of Abnormal Psychology*, vol. 48 (1953), pp. 225–30.

NANDA, P. C., DAS, J. P., and MISHRA, H. K., 'Discrimination of geometrical patterns in tribal, rural and urban children', *Journal of Social Psychology*, vol. 67 (1965), pp. 197–200.

ROLLINGS, P. J., 'A note on the cultural direction of perceptual selectivity' *16th International Congress of Psychology Proceedings*, Bonn, 1960.

SCHWITZGEBEL, R., 'The performance of Dutch and Zulu adults on selected perceptual tasks', *Journal of Social Psychology*, vol. 57 (1962), pp. 73–7.

SHAPIRO, M. B., 'The rotation of drawings by illiterate Africans'. *Journal of Social Psychology*, vol. 52 (1960), p. 17.

SUCHMAN, R. G., 'Cultural differences in children's color and form preferences', *Journal of Social Psychology*, vol. 70 (1966), pp. 3–10.

THORNTON, P. K., Visual perception among the peoples of Malaya, *Ph.D. Thesis University of Reading*, 1956.

THOULESS, R. H., 'A racial difference in perception', *Journal of Social Psychology*, vol. 4 (1933), pp. 330–39.

Further Reading

On other aspects of cognition

COLE, M., GAY, J., and GLICK, J., 'Reversal and non-reversal shifts among a Liberian tribal people', *Journal of Experimental Psychology*, vol. 76 (1968), pp. 323–4.

COLE, M., KELLER, L., and KORZH, N. D., 'Some cross-cultural data on probability learning', *Psychonomic Science*, vol. 4 (1966), pp. 211–2.

DAVIS, R., 'The fitness of names to drawings: a cross-cultural study in Tanganyika', *British Journal of Psychology*, vol. 52 (1961), pp. 259–68.

DOOB, L., *Becoming More Civilized: A Psychological Exploration*, Yale University Press, 1960.

GAY, J., and COLE, M., *The New Mathematics and an Old Culture*, Holt, Rinehart and Winston, 1967.

GAY, J., and COLE, M., 'Some experimental studies of Kpelle quantitative behavior', *Psychonomic Monograph Supplement*, vol. 2 (1968), pp. 173–91.

GUERRERO, R. D., and PECK, R. T., 'Style of confrontation and approach: an investigation program', *Revista Interamericana di Psicologia*, vol. 1 (1967), pp. 127–36.

JAHODA, G., 'Child animism, I. A critical survey of cross-cultural research, II, A Study in West Africa', *Journal of Social Psychology*, vol. 47 (1958), pp. 197–213.

LEVY-BRUHL, L., *How Natives Think*, Allen and Unwin, 1926.

MACCOBY, M., MODIANO, N., and GALVAN, L., 'Culture and abstraction'. *7th Inter-American Congress of Psychology Proceedings*, Mexico City, 1963.

MERCADO, S. J., DIAZ-SVERRERO, R., and GARDNER, R., 'Cognitive control in children of Mexico and the United States', *Journal of Social Psychology*, vol. 59 (1963), pp. 199–208.

NADEL, S. F., 'Experiments on culture psychology', *Africa*, vol. 10 (1937), pp. 421–35.

NADEL, S. F., 'A field experiment in racial psychology', *British Journal of Psychology*, vol. 28 (1937), pp. 195–211.

PRICE-WILLIAMS, D. R., 'Abstract and concrete modes of classification in a primitive society', *British Journal of Educational Psychology*, vol. 32 (1962), pp. 50–61.

RUSSELL, R. W., and DENNIS, W., 'Studies in Animism, I. A standardized procedure for the investigation of animism, II. The development of Animism, *Journal of Genetic Psychology*, vol. 56 (1940), pp. 352–66.

On anthropological approaches to cognition via linguistic analysis

ROMNEY, A. K., and D'ANDRADE, R. G. (eds.), 'Transcultural studies in cognition', *American Anthropologist*, special publication, vol. 66 (1964), no. 3, part 2.

On achievement motivation

ATKINSON, J. W. (ed.), *Motives in Fantasy, Action and Society*, Van Nostrand, 1958.

ATKINSON, J. W., and FEATHER, N. T. (eds.), *A Theory of Achievement Motivation*, Wiley, 1966.

BRADBURN, N. M., 'Need achievement and father dominance', Journal of Abnormal and Social Psychology, vol. 67 (1963), pp. 464–8.

CAMERON, A., and STORM, T., 'Achievement motivation in Canadian, Indian, middle and working class children', Psychological Reports, vol. 16 (1963), pp. 459–63.

CAUDILL, W., and DE VOS, G., 'Achievement, culture and personality: the case of the Japanese Americans', American Anthropologist, vol. 58 (1956), pp. 1102–26.

CORTES, J. B., 'The achievement motive in the Spanish economy between the thirteenth and the eighteenth centuries', Economic Development and Cultural Change, vol. 9 (1960), pp. 144–63.

DE VOS, G., 'Achievement and innovation in culture and personality', in E. Norbeck, D. Price-Williams and W. McCord, eds., The Study of Personality: An Interdisciplinary Appraisal, Holt, Rinehart and Winston, 1968.

HECKHAUSEN, H., The Anatomy of Achievement Motivation, Academic Press, 1967.

LEVINE, R. A., Dreams and Deeds: Achievement Motivation in Nigeria, University of Chicago Press, 1966.

LLOYD, B., 'Education and family life in the development of class identification among the Yoruba', in P. C. Lloyd, ed., The New Elites of Tropical Africa, O.U.P. International African Institute, 1966, chapter 6.

MCCLELLAND, D. C., The Achieving Society, Van Nostrand, 1961.

MCCLELLAND, D. C., ATKINSON, J. W., CLARK, R. A., and LOWELL, E. L., The Achievement Motive, Appleton, 1953.

MCCLELLAND, D. C., and FRIEDMAN, G. A., 'A cross-cultural study of the relationship between child-training practices and achievement motivation appearing in folk tales', in G. E. Swanson, T. M. Newcomb and E. H. Hartley, eds., Readings in Social Psychology, Holt, 1952.

NUTTALL, R. L., 'Some correlates of high need for achievement among urban Northern Negroes', Journal of Abnormal and Social Psychology, vol. 68 (1964), pp. 593–600.

PAREEK, U., 'A motivational paradigm of development', Journal of Social Issues, vol. 24 (1968), pp. 115–22.

REBOUSSIN, R., and GOLDSTEIN, J. W., 'Achievement motivation in Navaho and White students', American Anthropologist, vol. 68 (1966), pp. 740–44.

ROGERS, G. M., and NEILL, R. E., Achievement Motivation among Columbian Peasants, Michigan State University, Department of Communications, 1966.

ROSEN, B. C., 'Race, ethnicity and the achievement syndrome', American Sociological Review, vol. 24 (1959), pp. 47–60.

ROSEN, B. C., 'Socialization and achievement motivation in Brazil', American Sociological Review, vol. 27 (1962), p. 623.

ROSEN, B. C., and D'ANDRADE, R. G., 'The psycho-social origins of achievement motivation', Sociometry, vol. 22 (1959), pp. 185–218.

TEDESCHI, J. T., and KIAN, M., 'Cross-cultural study of the TAT assessment for achievement motivation: Americans and

Persians', *Journal of Social Psychology*, vol. 58 (1962), pp. 227–34.
WILLIAMS, J. S., 'Maori achievement motivation', *University of Wellington Publications in Psychology*, no. 13, 1960.

On symbolism and dreams

BOURGUIGON, E. E., 'Dreams and dream interpretation in Haiti', *American Anthropologist*, vol. 52 (1954), pp. 262–8.

D'ANDRADE, R. G., 'Anthropological study of dreams', in F. L. K. Hsu, ed., *Psychological Anthropology*, Dorsey Press, 1961.

EGGAN, D., 'The significance of dreams for anthropological research', *American Anthropologist*, vol. 51 (1949), pp. 171–98.

EGGAN, D., 'Dream analysis', in Bert Kaplan, ed., *Studying Personality Cross-Culturally*, Harper and Row, 1961.

FIRTH, R., 'The meaning of dreams in Tikopia' in E. E. Evans-Pritchard *et al.*, eds., *Essays Presented to C. G. Seligman*, Kegan Paul, Trench, Trubner and Co., 1934.

HALLOWELL, A. I., 'Freudian symbolism in the dreams of a Salteaux Indian', *Man*, vol. 38 (1938), pp. 47–8.

HONIGMAN, J. J., 'The interpretation of dreams in anthropological field work: a case study', in Bert Kaplan, ed., *Studying Personality Cross-Culturally*, Harper and Row, 1961.

LINCOLN, J. S., *The Dream in Primitive Cultures*, Crescent Press, 1935.

ROHEIM, G., 'The psycho-analysis of primitive cultural types', *International Journal of Psychoanalysis*, vol. 13 (1932), pp. 1–224.

ROHEIM, G., *Psycho-Analysis and Anthropology: Culture, Personality and the Unconscious*, International Universities Press, 1950.

WILBUR, G. B., and MUENSTERBERGER, W., *Psychoanalysis and Culture: Essays in Honor of Geza Roheim*, Wiley, 1967.

On the Oedipus complex

BURTON, R. V., and WHITING, J. W. M., 'The absent father and cross-sex indentity', *Merill-Palmer Quarterly*, vol. 7 (1961), p. 20.

HERSKOVITS, M. J., 'Sibling rivalry, the Oedipus complex and myth', *Journal of American Folklore*, vol. 71 (1958), pp. 1–15.

LESSA, W. A., 'Oedipus-type tales in Oceania', *Journal of American Folklore*. vol. 69 (1956), pp. 63–73.

MALINOWSKI, B., *Sex and Repression in Savage Society*, Harcourt, Brace, 1937.

ORTEGES, M. C., and ORTIGUES, E., *Oedipe Africain*, Paris Plan, 1966.

PARSONS, A., 'Is the Oedipus complex universal? The Jones–Malinowski debate revisited and a south Italian "nuclear complex", in W. Muensterberger and S. Axelrod, eds., *The Psycho-Analytic Study of Society*, vol. 3. International Universities Press, 1964, pp. 278–301 310–26.

ROHEIM, G., 'The Oedipus complex, magic and culture', in G. Roheim, ed., *Psycho-Analysis and the Social Sciences*, vol. 2, International Universities Press, 1950.

STEPHENS, W. N., *The Oedipus Complex: Cross-cultural Evidence*, Free Press, 1962.

WHITING, J. M., KLUCKHORN, R., and ANTHONY, A. S., 'The function of male initiation ceremonies at puberty', in E. E. Maccoby, T. Newcomb and E. Hartley, eds., *Readings in Social Psychology*, Holt, 1958.

YOUNG, F. W., 'The function of male initiation ceremonies: a cross-cultural test of an alternative hypotheses', *American Journal of Sociology*, vol. 67 (1962), p. 380.

Child development: General surveys

ENDLER, N. S., BOULTER, L. R., and OSSER, H., *Contemporary Issues in Developmental Psychology*, Holt, Rinehart and Winston, 1968. Chapter 12, 'Socialization and cross-cultural studies'.

MEAD, M., 'Research on primitive children', in L. Carmichael, ed., *Manual of Child Psychology*, Wiley, 1946.

MEAD, M., and WOLFENSTEIN, M. (eds.), *Childhood in Contemporary Cultures*, Chicago University Press, 1955.

WHITING, J. W. M., and WHITING, B. B., 'Contributions of anthropology to the methods of studying child rearing', in P. H. Mussen, ed., *Handbook of Research Methods in Child Development*, Wiley, 1960.

Child development: General growth

EARLE, M. J., 'Rakau children: from six to thirteen years', *University of Wellington Publication in Psychology*, no. 11, 1958.

FALADE, S., *Le Developpement psycho-moteur du jeune Africain originaire du Senegal au cours de sa première Annee*, Foulon, 1955.

GERBER, M., 'The psycho-motor development of African children in the first year, and the influence of maternal behavior', *Journal of Social Psychology*, vol. 47 (1958), pp. 185–95.

MEAD, M., *Coming of Age in Samoa*, Morrow, 1928. [Penguin edition, 1944.]

MEAD, M., *Growing Up in New Guinea*, Morrow 1930. [Penguin edition, 1943.]

MEAD, M., and McGREGOR, F. M. C., *Growth and Culture: A Photographic Study of Balinese Childhood*, Putnam 1951.

RITCHIE, J., 'Childhood in Rakau: The first five years of life', *University College of Wellington Publications in Psychology*, no. 10, 1957.

On socialization issues[1]

BARRY, H., BACON, M. K., and CHILD, I. L., 'A cross-cultural survey of some sex differences in socialization', *Journal of Abnormal and Social Psychology*, vol. 55 (1957), pp. 327–32.

1. This subject is included under the general heading of Personality and Culture. For further references, the reader is directed to the list of books given below, under this title.

Further Reading

BARRY, H., CHILD, I. L., and BACON, M. K., 'Relations of child training to subsistence economy', *American Anthropologist*, vol. 61 (1959), pp. 51–63.

BENEDICT, R., 'Child rearing in certain European countries', *American Journal of Orthopsychiatry*, vol. 19 (1949), pp. 342–50.

LAMBERT, W. W., TRIANDIS, L. M., and WOLF, M., 'Some correlates of beliefs in the malevolence and benevolence of supernatural beings A: cross-societal study', *Journal of Abnormal and Social Psychology*, vol. 58 (1959), pp. 162–9.

MINTURN, L., and LAMBERT, W. W., *Mothers of Six Cultures*, Wiley 1964.

PROTHRO, E., 'Patterns of permissiveness among preliterate peoples', *Journal of Abnormal and Social Psychology*, vol. 61 (1960), pp. 151–4.

RAPP, D. W., 'Child-rearing attitudes of mothers in Germany and the U.S.', *Child Development*, vol. 32 (1961), pp. 669–78.

ROSENBLATT, P. C., 'A cross-cultural study of child-rearing and romantic love', *Journal Personality and Social Psychology*, vol. 4 (1966), pp. 336–8.

TRIANDIS, L. M., and LAMBERT, W. W., 'Pancultural factor analysis of reported socialization practices', *Journal of Abnormal and Social Psychology*, vol. 62 (1961), pp. 631–9.

WHITING, J. W. M., and CHILD, I. L., *Child Training and Personality*, Yale University Press, 1953.

On the growth of awareness of race and nationality

GOODMAN, M. E., *Race Awareness in Young Children*, Crowell-Collier, 1964.

JAHODA, G., 'Development of Scottish children's ideas and attitudes about other countries', *Journal of Social Psychology*, vol. 58 (1962), pp. 91–108.

JAHODA, G., 'The development of children's ideas about country and rationality. Part I: The conceptual framework', *British Journal of Educational Psychology*, vol. 23, (1963), pp. 47–60; 'Part II: National symbols and themes', loc. cit., pp. 143–53.

JAHODA, G., VENESS, T., and PUSKIN, I., 'Awareness of ethnic differences in young children: proposals for a British study', *Race*, vol. 8 (1966), pp. 63–74.

LAMBERT, W., and KLINEBERG, O., *Children's Views of Foreign Peoples: A Cross-National Study*, Appleton-Century-Crofts 1967.

LEVINE, R. A., 'Socialization, social structures and intersocial images' in H. Kelman, ed., *International Behavior*, Holt, Rinehart and Winston, 1965.

PROSHANSKY, H. R., 'The development of intergroup attitudes', in M. L. and L. W. Hoffman (eds.), *Review of Child Development Research*, vol. 2, Russell Sage Foundation, 1965.

TAJFEL, H., 'The formation of national attitudes: a social psychological perspective', in M. Sherif, ed., *Problems of Interdisciplinary Relationships in the Social Sciences*, Aldine, 1968.

TAJFEL, H., and JAHODA, G., 'Development in children of concepts and attitudes of their own and other nations: a cross-national study', *Symposium on Cross-Cultural Studies of Mental Development*, 18th International Congress of Psychology, Moscow, 1966, pp. 17–33.

VAUGHAN, G. M., 'Development of ethnic awareness in Maori and Pakeha school children', in J. E. Ritchie, ed., Race Relations: Six New Zealand Studies, *University of Wellington, Publication in Psychology*, 1964.

On behaviour mechanism[2]

EISENMAN, R., 'Scapegoating the deviant in two cultures', *International Journal of Psychology*, vol. 2 (1967), pp. 133–8.

PIERS, G., and SINGER, M. H., *Shame and Guilt*, Charles C. Thomas, 1953.

PRICE-WILLIAMS, D. R., 'Displacement and orality in Tiv witchcraft', *Journal of Social Psychology*, vol. 65 (1965), pp. 1–15.

SHAW, M. E., 'Some cultural differences in sanctioning behavior', *Psychonomic Science*, vol. 8 (1967), pp. 45–6.

SPIRO, M., and D'ANDRADE, R., 'A cross-cultural study of some supernatural beliefs', *American Anthropologist*, vol. 60 (1958), pp. 456–66.

TRIANDIS, L. M., and LAMBERT, W. W., 'Sources of frustration and targets of aggression', *Journal of Abnormal and Social Psychology*, vol. 62 (1961), pp. 640–48.

WHITING, B. B., Paiute Sorcery, *Viking Fund Publications in Anthropology*, no. 15, 1950.

WHITING, J. W. M., 'Sorcery, sin and the super-ego: a cross-cultural study of some mechanisms of social control', in M. R. Jones, ed., *Symposium on Motivation*, University of Nebraska Press, 1959.

Books and comprehensive articles on personality and culture

BARNOUW, V., *Culture and Personality*, Dorsey Press, 1963.

GOODMAN, M. E., *The Individual and Culture*, Dorsey Press, 1967.

HARING, D. G., *Personal Character and Cultural Mileau*, Syracuse, 1956.

HOLTZMAN, W. H., 'Cross-cultural research on personality development', *Human Development*, vol. 8 (1965), pp. 65–86.

HONIGMANN, J. J., *Personality in Culture*, Harper and Row, 1967.

HSU, F. L. K., *Aspects of Culture and Personality*, Abelard and Schuman, 1954.

HSU, F. L. K. (ed.), *Psychological Anthropology: Approaches to Culture and Personality*, Dorsey Press, 1961.

HUNT, R. (ed.), *Personalities and Cultures: Readings in Psychological Anthropology*, American Museum Natural History Press (New York), 1967.

INDELES, A., and LEVINSON, D. J., 'National character: the study of

2. This subject also comes under the general heading of 'Personality and culture'. For further bibliography, see under that heading.

modal personality and sociocultural systems', in G. Lindzey, ed., *Handbook of Social Psychology*, vol. 2, Addison-Wesley. 1954.

KAPLAN, B. (ed.), *Studying Personality Cross-Culturally*, Harper and Row, 1961.

KLUCKHOHN, C., MURRAY, H. A., and SCHNEIDER, D., *Personality in Nature, Society and culture*, A. Knopf, 2nd edn, 1953.

LINDZEY, G., *Projective Techniques and Cross-Cultural Research*, Appleton-Century-Crofts, 1961.

NORBECK, E., PRICE-WILLIAMS, D. R., and McCORD, W. M., *The Study of Personality: An Interdisciplinary Appraisal*, Holt, Rinehart and Winston, 1968.

SARGENT, S. S., and SMITH, M. W., *Culture and Personality*, Viking Press, 1949.

SPIER, L., HALLOWELL, I., and NEWMAN, S. S. (eds.), *Language, Culture and Personality*, Sapir Memorial Publications Fund, 1941.

WALLACE, A. F. C., *Culture and Personality*, Random House, 1961.

On the relationship between psychology and anthropology

CAMPBELL, D. T., 'On the mutual methodological relevance of anthropology and psychology', in F. L. K. Hsu (ed.), *Psychological Anthropology*, Dorsey Press, 1961.

FISCHER, J. L., 'Psychology and anthropology', in B. J. Siegel, ed., *Biennial Review of Anthropology*, Stanford University Press, 1965.

GOODENOUGH, F. L., and ANDERSON, J. L., 'Psychology and anthropology: some problems of import for the two fields', *Southwest Journal of Anthropology*, vol. 3 (1947), pp. 5–14.

KOHLER, W., 'Psychological remarks on some questions of anthropology', *American Journal of Psychology*, vol. 50 (1937), p. 274.

RIVERS, W. H. R., *Psychology and Ethnology*, Harcourt, Brace and World, 1926.

SEGALL, M. H., 'Anthropology and psychology', in O. Klineberg and R. Christie, eds., *Perspectives in Social Psychology*, Holt, Rinehart and Winston, 1965.

SELIGMAN, C. G., 'Anthropology and psychology: A study of some points of contact', *Journal of Royal Anthropological Institute*, vol. 54 (1924), pp 13–46.

SMITH, M. B., 'Anthropology and psychology', in J. Gillin, ed., *For a Science of Social Man*, Macmillan, 1954.

Journals that are largely concerned with cross-cultural research.

International Journal of Psychology

Inter-American Journal of Psychology (Revista Interamericana de Psicología)

Journal of Social Psychology

Psychologia Africana

Revue Psychologie des Peuples.

News letters

Cross-cultural social psychology news letter. First edited by Harry C. Triandis. Department of Psychology, University of Illinois, Urbana, Illinois 61801, U.S.A. Followed on by Yasumasa Tanaka, Department of Political Science, Gakashuin (Peers') University, Mejiro, Toshima-ku, Tokyo, Japan.

Culture and mental health in Asia and the Pacific news letter. Social Science Research Institute, 1914 University Avenue, Room 101, Honolulu, Hawaii 96822.

Transcultural psychiatric research review and news letter. Allen Memorial Institute, 1025 Pine Avenue, West, Montreal, Quebec, Canada.

Reference should also be made to an article by J. W. Berry entitled 'Directory of cross-cultural psychological research', published in the *International Journal of Psychology*, vol. 3 (1968), pp. 137–48, in which is listed scholars actively concerned with cross-cultural research.

Acknowledgements

Permission to reproduce the Readings in this volume is acknowledged from the following sources:

Reading 1 *American Anthropologist*
Reading 2 *International Journal of Psychology*
Reading 3 Evans Brothers Ltd and S. Biesheuvel
Reading 4 *Journal of Special Education* and P. E. Vernon
Reading 5 *Science* and M. H. Segall
Reading 6 The British Psychological Society and G. Jahoda
Reading 7 *International Journal of Psychology* and A. C. Mundy-Castle
Reading 8 *International Journal of Psychology*
Reading 9 *International Journal of Psychology*
Reading 10 The British Psychological Society and M. Wober
Reading 11 *International Journal of Psychology*
Reading 12 North-Holland Publishing Company
Reading 13 John Wiley & Sons, Inc.
Reading 14 Brunne/Mazel, Inc. and J. J.Goodnow
Reading 15 The Journal Press and A. L. Angelini
Reading 16 University of Chicago Press
Reading 17 *Ethnology* and L. Minturn
Reading 18 The Journal Press and S. G. Lee
Reading 19 *Anthropological Quarterly*
Reading 20 The Dorsey Press
Reading 21 The Macmillan Company
Reading 22 The British Psychological Society and R. C. Albino
Reading 23 American Psychological Association

Author Index

Author Index

Subject Index

Subject Index